HARVARD ORIENTAL SERIES

Edited by MICHAEL WITZEL

VOLUME NINETY-SEVEN

AN INDIAN THEORY OF DEFEASIBLE REASONING

The Doctrine of *upādhi* in the Upādhidarpaṇa

by

EBERHARD GUHE

PUBLISHED BY THE DEPARTMENT OF SOUTH ASIAN STUDIES
HARVARD UNIVERSITY
DISTRIBUTED BY HARVARD UNIVERSITY PRESS,
CAMBRIDGE, MASSACHUSETTS
AND LONDON, ENGLAND

2021

Printed in the United States of America

For information write to Editor, Harvard Oriental Series, Department of South Asian Studies, 1 Bow Street, Cambridge MA 02138, USA
617-495 3295; email: witzel@fas.harvard.edu

Library of Congress Cataloguing in Publication Data :
An Indian theory of defeasible reasoning. The Doctrine of *upādhi* in the Upādhidarpaṇa

Harvard Oriental Series; v. 97 ISBN 9780674273412

I. Guhe, Eberhard 1965-
II. Title
III. Series: Harvard Oriental Series; 97
CIP

In Loving Memory of My Parents
Edith and Wilfried Guhe

Contents

Preface

"Hier hackt nun der Gegner ein, ..."
(Erich Frauwallner, *Die Lehre von der zusätzlichen Bestimmung (upādhiḥ) in Gaṅgeśa's Tattvacintāmaṇiḥ*, p. 21)

The present volume is about an anonymous Sanskrit treatise entitled "Upādhidarpaṇa" (UD). The UD belongs to the tradition of the Navya-Nyāya school of Indian logic and deals exclusively with the epistemic usage of the term *upādhi*. As opposed to the ontological *upādhi*, i.e., the *upādhi* in the sense of a nominal or imposed property (cf. Halbfass 1992: 119 and Phillips 2002: 25), the epistemic *upādhi* is regarded as a vitiator of an assumed inference in Navya-Nyāya. By default, we will use the term *upādhi* with the tacit understanding that it refers to the epistemic variant, since the ontological usage plays only a minor role in the present context.

Stephen Phillips compares the *upādhi* to the undercutting defeater in John L. Pollock's theory of defeasible reasoning and he suggests "undercutting condition" as a translation of *upādhi* in epistemic contexts (cf. Phillips 2002: 27). According to Phillips Matilal's and Frauwallner's translations "associate condition" and "zusätzliche Bestimmung" (cf. Matilal 1998: 166 and Frauwallner 1970) are beside the point (cf. Phillips 2002: 27), because they suggest that an *upādhi* is also a corrector. In contrast to Naiyāyikas like Varadarāja and Śivādityamiśra, who regard every *upādhi* as a vitiator and as a corrector, Gaṅgeśa actually defines the concept of *upādhi* in such a way that it applies to vitiators, regardless of any potential utility as correctors. However, according to the UD the vitiating function and the corrector-function are interrelated, since an *upādhi* vitiates an invalid inference by demonstrating that the property functioning as a probandum can be inferred to be co-located with the property functioning as a probans only if the latter co-occurs with the *upādhi* as an "associate condition". Hence, Matilal's translation of *upādhi* is consistent with the UD's doctrine of *upādhi* and we will stick to it here. Alternatively, we will often leave *upādhi* untranslated.

There is still another reason why we have not adopted Phillips' translation of *upādhi*: Phillips is well aware that an *upādhi* is not exactly the same as an undercutting defeater in the technical sense of Pollock's theory. Properly speaking, Pollock's defeater is a mental state. In most cases it is a belief. If we identify a belief with its propositional content, the equivalents of a defeater in the Navya-Nyāya doctrine of *upādhi* can be said to be certain propositions, which are true of an *upādhi*, and not all of them are undercutters. Some of them are rebutters and some of them are rebutters and undercutters with respect to different prima facie reasons. These defeaters can be gleaned from specifications of an *upādhi*'s vitiating function and from the UD's so-called "specific defining characteristic" (*viśeṣalakṣaṇa*) of an *upādhi*, which serves to determine whether a certain property is an *upādhi* relative to a specific pair of probans and probandum.

The doctrine of *upādhi* plays already an important role in early Nyāya and in Mīmāṃsā. However, we find its most elaborate formulation in Navya-Nyāya. So far, the Navya-Nyāya doctrine of *upādhi* has mainly been studied with regard to the Upādhivāda-section in Gaṅgeśa's Tattvacintāmaṇi (cf. Frauwallner 1970, Phillips 2002 and Chakrabarti 2010). The UD is still longer than the latter and differs from Gaṅgeśa in important respects. The significance of the UD for a proper understanding of the early history of Navya-Nyāya was underscored by Erich Frauwallner (cf. Frauwallner 1970: 6).

My unpublished PhD-thesis submitted to the University of Vienna (cf. Guhe 1999) contains the first edition and an annotated German translation of the UD. In Guhe 1999 I also study the contents of the UD from the perspective of modern logical theories. For the present publication the edition and the translation in Guhe 1999 have been thoroughly revised. In the light of two more recent contributions to the study of the Navya-Nyāya doctrine of *upādhi*, viz. Phillips 2002 and Chakrabarti 2010, my interpretation of the contents of the UD had to be reconsidered as well. I am particularly indebted to Phillips' intriguing idea to study the doctrine of *upādhi* from the perspective of John L. Pollock's theory of defeasible reasoning. However, the relation between *upādhi*s and undercutting defeaters in the sense of Pollock's theory has only tentatively been explained in Phillips 2002. Phillips' formal explication of the concept of a so-called "dubious *upādhi*", e.g., is at best a "pedagogical prop" (Phillips 2002: 113), as he himself admits. I fully agree with Phillips that the theory of *upādhi* is essentially a theory of defeasible reasoning. However, I try to demonstrate here in greater detail in what way an *upādhi* is actually related to a defeater in the sense of Pollock's theory.

There is another completely different aspect of my formal reconstruction of the theory of *upādhi* in Guhe 1999, which I am holding onto in the present book. It concerns the so-called "general defining characteristic" (*sāmānya-lakṣaṇa*) of an *upādhi* in the UD, a property of all candidate *upādhi*s. It excludes everything which can never be used as an *upādhi* in any inference. In Guhe 1999 I analyzed certain puzzles related to this property by means of George Bealer's property theories. The utility of Bealer's calculus T1 for a formal reconstruction of the Navya-Nyāya theory of property and location in general has been demonstrated in several later publications. An important refinement of my 1999 approach consists in the different quasi set-theoretic extensions of T1 which I later designed to provide an axiomatic basis for proving many intuitions about properties in Navya-Nyāya. These hybrid systems (an ST_2-style and an Ackermann-style extension of T1 on the one hand, and an NFU-style extension of T1 on the other hand) serve to capture the well-founded property concept advocated by *prācīna* Naiyāyikas and by many Navya-Naiyāyikas on the one hand, and the non-well-founded property concept advocated by the UD on the other hand.

On a final note, I would like to add the following acknowledgements: First of all, I am indebted to Prof. Gerhard Oberhammer and Prof. Martin Goldstern, who directed my 1999 thesis. Prof. Oberhammer suggested the UD to me as a topic for my PhD-thesis and generously provided me with a microfilm copy of the manuscript of the UD and a handwritten transliteration, which he had accomplished together with the late Prof. Gopikamohan Bhattacharya many years ago. The financial support for my PhD-studies in Vienna is largely owing to a regular income from my jobs as an assistant in the former Institute for Indology and the former Institute for Tibetology and Buddhist Studies at the University of Vienna. Special thanks go to Prof. Oberhammer and Prof. Ernst Steinkellner for hiring me.

The completion of the present book would not have been possible without my wife's constant encouragement and the excellent working conditions at Fudan University/Shanghai, where I have been teaching Sanskrit, Indian philosophy and logic since 2009. Moreover, I am much obliged to Prof. Parimal Patil, who kindly invited me to spend a sabbatical (from August 2018 – April 2019) as a Harvard-Yenching research scholar at Harvard University. Parimal is an excellent partner in dialogue for my interdisciplinary research in the realm of Navya-Nyāya. The regular meetings with him have been an invaluable source of inspiration for my work on the UD. Moreover, I had the great privilege to discuss the logical content of the UD with eminent logicians at Harvard and at MIT. Thanks go especially to Prof. Mark Richard and Prof. Stephen Yablo. Last but not least, I would like to express my gratitude to Prof. Michael Witzel for including my book in the prestigious Harvard Oriental Series.

Shanghai, June 2021
Eberhard Guhe

Chapter 1

Introduction

1.1 Authorship and Date of the UD

The only extant manuscript of the UD contains no colophon or any other clue to the identity of the author. Although it starts with an auspicious verse, where the name of the author's teacher, Yajñeśvara, is mentioned, this does not help to identify the author of the UD. The Catalogus Catalogorum lists seven individuals named Yajñeśvara with vastly different biographical data (cf. Aufrecht 1962: 470). Some of them are only noted as relatives of authors of well-known works. Two of them are astronomers. Another one, a certain Yajñeśvara Dīkṣita, aka Yajñanārāyaṇa Dīkṣita, is the author of the extant Alaṃkārarāghava (cf. Satyanārāyaṇa 1980). However, since according to the New Catalogus Catalogorum Yajñeśvara Dīkṣita's father, Carakāri Koṇḍubhaṭṭa, flourished in the second half of the sixteenth century (cf. Raghavan 1969: 92), the assumption that Yajñeśvara Dīkṣita is the teacher of the author of the UD would entail a very late dating of the UD. References to famous late Navya-Naiyāyikas would have to be expected if the UD belonged to this very advanced stage of the development of the school. However, the only clearly identifiable authors which the UD refers to are pre-Gaṅgeśa (see below). A possible clue to the identity of Yajñeśvara is Potter's mentioning of a Vedāntin named Yajñeśvara, the author of the Vedāntasarvasaṃgraha (cf. Potter 1995: 889), a work which seems to be influenced by the tradition of Nyāya-Vaiśeṣika (cf. Hasurkar 1969). However, Potter is unable to date the work and he mentions none of Yajñeśvara's disciples.

Since no other evidence seems to be available, we will attempt a relative dating of the UD on the basis of other fairly well datable philosophers who are referenced in the UD, namely Udayana, Śrīdhara, Śivādityamiśra, Varadarāja and Vādīndra. As pointed out by R. M. Telang (cf. MV: xii), the youngest of these authors, viz. Vādīndra, flourished during the reign of the Yādava-king Singhana (1210 – 1247 AD). Hence, the middle of the thirteenth century AD might be an appropriate terminus a quo for the composition of the UD. According to D. C. Bhattacharya the UD was probably composed not long after 1325 AD (cf. Bhattacharya 1958: 167). He argues that this is the time when the influence of Gaṅgeśa starts being traceable in the works of Navya-Naiyāyikas (cf. Bhattacharya 1958: 101). However, the UD does not contain any reference to Gaṅgeśa. Hence, the UD is probably pre-Gaṅgeśa and the beginning of the fourteenth century seems to be a reasonable guess for the terminus ante quem.

1.2 Survey of the Contents of the UD and Our Exposition of the Doctrine of *upādhi*

The manuscript is divided into three parts (*paricchedas*). In the first part the author deals with the definition of an *upādhi* by means of a *sāmānyalakṣaṇa* ("general defining characteristic") and a *viśeṣalakṣaṇa* ("specific defining characteristic"). The former is a property shared by all *upādhis*. It is supposed to characterize candidate *upādhis*, i.e., individuals which may be used as *upādhis* in some inferential situation, and it excludes everything which can never be used as an *upādhi* in any inferential situation. Gaṅgeśa regards such a general defining characteristic as irrelevant to the theory of *upādhi* (cf. Chakrabarti 2010: 226) and he specifically rejects a certain general defining characteristic which according to the UD is actually a distinctive feature of all *upādhis*. Maybe, the UD is even one of the works which Gaṅgeśa is targeting when he denies the utility of a general defining characteristic, although he never explicitly mentions the UD.

The first part abounds in keen observations concerning the Navya-Nyāya logic of property and location. The author of the UD offers his own solution to a property version of the set-theoretical problem of foundation and endorses a non-well-founded characterization of *upādhis* by means of a general defining characteristic which is a property of itself. Although *ātmāśraya* ("self-dependence") is generally regarded as suspect in Nyāya, the author of the UD argues that at least in the case of the residence relation (i.e., the relation between a property and its locus) such a phenomenon need not be regarded as counterintuitive.

The purpose of a specific defining characteristic of an *upādhi* is to characterize the latter in relation to a specific pair of probans and probandum in an assumed inference. The UD's specific defining characteristic is the same as the one enunciated by Śivādityamiśra and several other early Naiyāyikas. Unlike Gaṅgeśa, the author of the UD requires the *upādhi* to pervade the probandum "coextensively" (*samavyāpaka*) and thereby ensures that the *upādhi* can function as both, a vitiator and a corrector of an assumed inference. The corrector-function consists in fortifying (*prayojaka*) a probans which is incapable of securing the probandum of its own accord. For Gaṅgeśa, who does not include the condition of a coextensive pervasion in his definition, the *upādhi* is rather a vitiator. Thus, some properties which function as vitiators, but fail to function as correctors, are regarded as genuine *upādhis* by Gaṅgeśa, whereas the UD classifies them as so-called "pseudo-*upādhis*" (*upādhyābhāsa*).

In the second part of the UD the author specifies the *upādhi*'s function of vitiating (*dūṣaṇa*) an inference. He agrees with Gaṅgeśa that the primary epistemological function of an *upādhi* as a vitiator of an assumed inference is to expose the probans as a so-called "conditional probans" (*vyāpyatvāsiddha*). This is a special type of "pseudo-probans" (*hetvābhāsa*) which only in combination with the *upādhi* allows us to infer the probandum. Since the probans's pervasion by the probandum is flawed by an associate condition, Gaṅgeśa also characterizes the *upādhi*'s function of vitiating as "indicating the absence of a pervasion" (*vyāptivirahonnāyaka*). Similarly, the author of the UD argues that the *upādhi* as a vitiator targets the absence of the probans's purported pervasion. It "is in effect the absence of a pervasion" (*vyāptivirahabhūta*). But, properly speaking, it is the absence of the *upādhi* which vitiates, and not the *upādhi* itself, because the absence of the *upādhi* in a locus of the probans entails the absence of the probandum. The proposition expressing the absence of the *upādhi* in a locus of the probans can be regarded as a defeater in the sense of Pollock's theory of defeasible reasoning (cf. Pollock 1987: 485).

In the third part the author of the UD deals with the so-called "dubious *upādhis*" (*saṃdigdhopādhi*) and with "pseudo-*upādhis*", i.e., apparent associate conditions (*upādhyābhāsa*). An associate condition is dubious if at least one of the criteria of the specific defining characteristic is dubious, whereas the remaining one(s) may be dubious or ascertained. An associate condition is apparent if one of the criteria of the specific defining characteristic is unfulfilled and at least one criterion is ascertained or dubious. Although the UD disagrees with Gaṅgeśa as regards the number of types of dubious and apparent associate conditions, both of them maintain that an associate condition can vitiate, even if it is dubious, in fact, even if all the defining criteria are dubious.

After this rough survey of the contents of the UD, we will now look at the UD's doctrine of *upādhi* in greater detail. Rather than following the three parts of the UD chronologically, we will, first of all, elucidate the defeasible character of the type of inference discussed in Navya-Nyāya, viz. the five-membered inference. After our exposition of the theory of inference in Navya-Nyāya we will proceed to the specification of the *upādhi*'s function of vitiating such inferences, which is the subject matter of the second part of the UD. It will then be easier to understand the subject matter of the first part of the UD, viz. the definition of the *upādhi* by means of a specific and a general defining characteristic. The final sections on dubious and apparent *upādhi*s, the subject matter of the third part of the UD, will provide important insights into affinities and differences between the UD's doctrine of *upādhi* and Pollock's theory of defeasible reasoning.

1.3 The Basics of the Nyāya Theory of Inference

According to the theory of inference in late Nyāya and in Navya-Nyāya the verbalized form of an inference (*anumāna*) consists of five members, a thesis, three members which are supposed to corroborate the claim formulated in the thesis, and a conclusion which restates the thesis as a result of the inference. We will study this type of inference with special regard to the third member, which seems to contain an inductive leap. Deductive components are involved in the five-membered inference as well, although from a Navya-Nyāya perspective the logical framework is essentially inductive.

In the case of a valid inference the content of each of the five members must be a veridical awareness (*pramā*).[1] Truth is here usually understood in the sense of correspondence to facts (which may be facts about a reasoner's epistemic state[2]). However, accepting the third member as true typically involves a pragmatic concept of truth as an evidentially constrained property.

Although Indian logicians did not symbolize the components of a correct five-membered inference, it is clear that they conceived of it as an instance of formally valid reasoning, since all the components are identified by certain technical terms and the way they are related to each other and the order in which they are supposed to appear is strictly determined. In Keśava Miśra's Tarkabhāṣā, a work which according to Dineśchandra Bhattacharya dates from the 12th century AD (cf. Bhattacharya 1958: 64), one can find the following stock example of a valid five-membered inference:

[1] *parvato 'yam agnimān*
[2] *dhūmavattvāt.*
[3] *yo dhūmavān so 'gnimān yathā mahānasaḥ.*[3]
[4] *tathā cāyam.*
[5] *tasmāt tathā.* (TBh: 40, 2f)

[1. Thesis (*pratijñā*)]	This mountain possesses fire.
[2. Reason (*hetu*)]	For, it possesses smoke.
[3. Example (*udāharaṇa*)]	Whatever possesses smoke, possesses fire, like the kitchen.
[4. Application (*upanaya*)]	This [mountain] is so (i.e., it possesses smoke as a token of fire).
[5. Conclusion (*nigamana*)]	Therefore, [it is] so (i.e., the mountain possesses fire).

In this example the mountain functions as the subject of the inference (*pakṣa*). Fire is the probandum (*sādhya*), a property which according to the first member can be proved to be present on the subject of the inference. Smoke is the probans or prover (*hetu* or *sādhana*), a property whose presence on the subject of the inference is an established fact according to the second member of the inference (which happens to be called *hetu* as well). The probans functions as an indicator of the probandum. According to the third member this is possible, because there is a universal relation called "pervasion" (*vyāpti*) between the probans and the probandum in the sense that every locus of the probans is a locus of the probandum. The reference to examples (*dṛṣṭānta*) in the third member indicates that the cognition of a pervasion involves an inductive generalization. The cognition is supported by wide experience of positive correlations such as smoke and fire on a kitchen hearth and negative correlations such as absence of smoke on a lake, where there is absence of fire. Thus, the cognition of a pervasion is the result of an extrapolation from certain known cases, i.e., it involves an inductive leap to all unobserved cases, past, present and future, including the case at issue in an inferential situation. Due to an epistemic process called *parāmarśa* ("reflective grasping"), which is indicated in the fourth member, the probans's presence on the subject of an inference is associated with the pervasion relation and it is this that finally gives rise to the "inferential awareness" (*anumiti*), the conclusion expressed in the fifth member, i.e., the cognition that the probandum is present on the subject of the inference.

1.3.1 Deductive Components in a Five-membered Inference

The third member of the five-membered inference, which accounts for its inductive character, is embedded in a deductive fabric. Thus, the five-membered inference can be turned into a purely deductive procedure if we regard only the result of the inductive process of determining the pervasion at issue as a part of the inference, not the process itself. Nevertheless, it should be understood that for the Navya-Naiyāyikas the inductive leap is an integral part of the five-membered inference, which transforms the latter into a defeasible type of inference.

The mere deductive content can be captured by means of the first-order formulas ...

(1) Fm
(2) Sm
(3) $\forall x(Sx \rightarrow Fx)$
(4) $Sm \wedge (Sm \rightarrow Fm)$
(5) Fm

..., where Sx, Fx and m translate into "x is a locus of smoke", "x is a locus of fire" and "the mountain", respectively.

Only (2) and (3) are premises. (1) (= (5)) is the conclusion. (4) is an intermediate step: It derives from (2) and (3) by means of universal instantiation and conjunction introduction. (5) is obtained from (4) by means of conjunction elimination (which yields: Sm, $Sm \rightarrow Fm$) and modus ponens. For the sake of perspicuity the argument is formulated in such a way that (4) and (5) follow from the immediately preceding step or from the two immediately preceding steps, respectively.

According to the present formalization either (1) or (5) is redundant.[4] In order to differentiate between the connotations of the first and the fifth member one might take into account that "the validity of the proposition to be proved, before the process of inference is complete, is doubtful, i.e., not yet established." (Matilal 1990: 49) Although the proposition expressed by the first member is identical to the one expressed by the fifth member, there is a difference between both members in terms of epistemic attitude.[5] In the case of the first member the proposition expressed by Fm is the object of a doubt. In the case of the fifth member the same proposition is the object of a confirmed belief. If we want to formalize semantic distinctions with respect to epistemic attitudes, we need methods of formalization which are beyond the scope of first-order logic.

The redundancy of the propositional content of the five-membered inference need not be dismissed as a lack of straightforwardness. If it serves the perspicuity of an argument, redundant formulations may come in handy. The design of the inference pattern consisting of steps (1) – (5) is, actually, quite similar to that of mathematical proofs. In mathematics it is common to formulate a proof by, first of all, stating the theorem and then giving a proof, where in the end the theorem reappears as a result of the proof. Sometimes mathematicians even start a proof by rewriting a theorem in an equivalent form if the equivalent formulation is easier to prove. However, nobody would think of complaining about redundancy in such cases.

H. N. Randle points out another redundancy concerning the second and the fourth member, since the occurrence of the probans on the inferential subject seems to be repeated in the fourth member (cf. Randle 1930: 163). Randle's impression is confirmed by my formalization. Stanislaw Schayer tries to exonerate the five-membered inference from the charge of redundancy in this respect by interpreting the fourth member merely as an implication, i.e., according to Schayer our formalization of the fourth member of the smoke/fire-inference should be reduced to $Sm \rightarrow Fm$ (cf. Schayer 2001: 94). In Oetke 1994 the author discusses also earlier versions of the five-membered inference in Nyāya, which do not seem to exhibit the same kind of redundancy concerning the second and the fourth member. However, in his formalization of the present version, which is presupposed in Navya-Nyāya sources, Oetke follows Schayer's understanding of the fourth member (cf. Oetke 1994: 18, 22f and 51).

Nevertheless, the recurrence of the second member in the fourth one is unmistakably stated in the following explication of the gist of the "reflective grasping" (*parāmarśa*) expressed in the fourth member of the smoke/fire-inference: *yathā vahnivyāpyadhūmavān ayaṃ parvata iti jñānaṃ parāmarśaḥ.* (TS: 34) – "Reflective grasping is a knowledge such as: 'This mountain possesses smoke pervaded by fire.'"[6] The pervasion which is mentioned here is probably not the same as the one in the third member, but rather a "particularized pervasion" (*viśeṣavyāpti*), i.e., a pervasion of the particular smoke on the mountain by fire (cf. Chakrabarti 2010: 111). $Sm \rightarrow Fm$ seems to be an appropriate formalization of this part of the fourth member.

The redundancy concerning Sm and $Sm \wedge (Sm \rightarrow Fm)$ need not be regarded as a defect. Although Sm is already mentioned in the second step, it is separated from $Sm \rightarrow Fm$ by the third step. For the sake of the perspicuity of the argument it makes good sense to repeat Sm in the fourth member, since both, Sm and $Sm \rightarrow Fm$, are needed as premises for the application of modus ponens in the transition from the fourth to the fifth member. Thus, the formulation which has been chosen by the Navya-Naiyāyikas ensures that the fifth member follows from the immediately preceding step.

1.3.2 The Third Member of Five-membered Inferences as a Rule of Enumerative Induction

An accurate formal explication of the third member should link the pervasion at issue to the examples. Nevertheless, if we confine ourselves to formalizing merely the pervasion of an arbitrary probans by an arbitrary probandum, the following seems to be a fairly close prima facie formal equivalent:

($\mathrm{V}_1^{\mathrm{pf}}$) $\forall x(Hx \rightarrow Sx)$ (where Hx translates into "x is a locus of the probans" and Sx translates into "x is a locus of the probandum")

Since Naiyāyikas conceive of pervasion as a relation (*saṃbandha*), one might object that the denotatum of ($\mathrm{V}_1^{\mathrm{pf}}$) is not a relation, but a proposition, which expresses a condition on the instantiating pairs. However, it is also customary in Nyāya to talk about pervasion in the sense of a proposition. Thus, Jinavardhana Sūri, a commentator on Śivādityamiśra's Saptapadārthī, defines pervasion as follows: *vyāptir yatra yatra sādhanaṃ tatra tatra sādhyam, yatra sādhyaṃ nāsti tatra sādhanam api nāstītilakṣaṇā.* (SP: 69, 24) – "Pervasion is defined as: 'Wherever there is the probans, there is the probandum. Wherever there is not the probandum, there is not the probans either'." Hereafter, we will use the term "pervasion" with reference to a relation and to propositions alike. If necessary, the context will help to disambiguate the intended meaning.[7]

With some reservations many interpreters accept (V_1^{pf}) as a formalization of the pervasion of "being an *H*" by "being an *S*" (cf. Phillips 2002: 11f) and they endorse a graphic representation by means of a Venn diagram such as Fig. A (cf. Phillips 2002: 23):

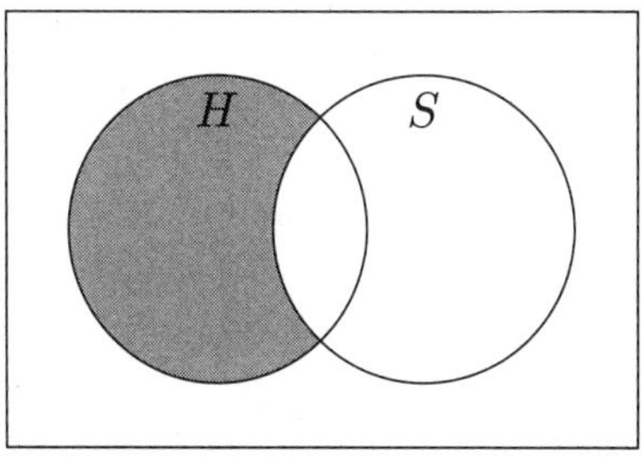

Fig. A[8]

The purpose of the examples mentioned in the third member does not seem to be confined to illustrating the pervasion at issue. They are rather indicative of the sense in which the content of the third member can be regarded as a veridical awareness. Since nobody can check whether all loci of smoke are loci of fire, it seems plausible to see the function of the examples in expressing epistemic humility in the sense that the pervasion at issue should be restricted to the available evidence of a concomitance.[9] Actually, Gaṅgeśa and the UD sometimes refer to a kind of "epistemic pervasion" (*jñānavyāpti*), which involves only loci where the probans and the probandum are known to be present. Chakrabarti quotes a passage from Mathurānātha's commentary Māthurī (cf. Chakrabarti 2010: 200), where this type of pervasion is apparently distinguished from a kind of "factual pervasion" (*vastuvyāpti*). The latter can be adequately formalized without taking into account a reasoner's epistemic ignorance with respect to the inferential subject. Thus, a wff like (V_1^{pf}), which contains an unrestricted quantification, seems to be a close formal equivalent to the concept of a factual pervasion.

By means of van Benthem's epistemic operators K_i and C_G for "i knows that" and "It is common knowledge in the group G that" (cf. van Benthem 2010: 135), the epistemic variant can be expressed as ...

(V_e) $\forall x \neq s(K_i Hx \rightarrow K_i Sx)$ or $\forall x \neq s(C_G Hx \rightarrow C_G Sx)$, where s denotes the inferential subject.[10]

Since s is an open issue with regard to the presence of the probandum, the wffs $K_i Hs \rightarrow K_i Ss$ and $C_G Hs \rightarrow C_G Ss$ are false. Hence, the range of quantification in the epistemic variant has to be restricted to loci $x \neq s$. However, bracketing the inferential subject deprives a pervasion of its function to ensure that the fifth member of an inference can be deductively inferred from the second and the third one. If there are other loci of the probans than s, (V_e)'s contribution to an enhancement of a cognitive agent's credence in the thesis is limited to that of the known positive examples, which provide inductive support for the thesis.

In order to include the inferential subject in an epistemic version of the pervasion relation, one might be inclined to explicate the latter in the sense that there are no known counter-examples to the concomitance, i.e., in the sense of ...

(V_e^*) $\neg\exists x(K_i Hx \wedge K_i \neg Sx)$ or $\neg\exists x(C_G Hx \wedge C_G \neg Sx)$

..., or equivalent universally quantified implications such as $\forall x(K_i Hx \rightarrow \neg K_i \neg Sx)$ and $\forall x(C_G Hx \rightarrow \neg C_G \neg Sx)$. However, these wffs in combination with $K_i Hs$ or $C_G Hs$ (as alternative interpretations of the second member: "The inferential subject s is known to be a locus of the probandum") only allow us to conclude that $\neg K_i \neg Ss$ or $\neg C_G \neg Ss$, respectively, which means that the inferential subject is still an open issue, since $\neg K_i \neg Ss$ and $\neg C_G \neg Ss$ are consistent with $\neg K_i Ss$ or $\neg C_G Ss$, respectively. (V_e^*) even exacerbates the problem of a cognitive agent's epistemic ignorance, because according to (V_e^*) every locus of the probans is an open issue. Hence, the epistemic version of the pervasion relation should rather be understood in the sense of (V_e), although (V_e^*) is surely a necessary condition for the identification of an instance of the pervasion relation: The pervasion relation is not instantiated by pairs which are known to fail the requirement of a universal concomitance.

Apparently, Navya-Naiyāyikas sometimes prefer to talk about pervasion in an epistemic rather than a factual sense in order to avoid any confrontation with a skeptic, who might argue that pervasion in a factual sense would be cognitively accessible only to an omniscient being. Moreover, a factual version of pervasion like ($\mathrm{V}_1^{\mathrm{pf}}$) can be regarded as a generalization of the conclusion of a five-membered inference. Thus, the argument might be said to involve a petitio principii. This is, however, not quite true, since the universality of a factual pervasion derives from an inductive generalization based on the available evidence. The reference to the factual variant in an inferential situation does not presuppose that all loci of the probans are known to be loci of the probandum. Nevertheless, as a concession to the skeptic, who does not accept a factual version like ($\mathrm{V}_1^{\mathrm{pf}}$) as an object of knowledge, the author of the UD sometimes confines himself to talking about the epistemic variant (V_e), since verifying (V_e) is just a matter of checking whether a cognitive agent's epistemic state warrants the claim that every known locus of the probans is known to be a locus of the probandum. Although epistemic modalities are not explicitly mentioned in references to (V_e) in the UD, the intended meaning is in this case indicated by means of the exclusion of the inferential subject from the range of loci involved in the pervasion at issue.

Despite these occasional references to the epistemic variant, Navya-Naiyāyikas commonly understand pervasion in a factual sense. In Navya-Nyāya definitions of pervasion we do not find any epistemic notions. Pervasion is defined as a property residing in a pervaded entity. The concepts involved in the formulation of the definiens are purely ontological and the inferential subject is not excluded from the range of loci involved in the pervasion at issue (cf. Wada 2007: 36f and Guhe 2017: 19f). By default, we will use the unspecified term "pervasion" with the tacit understanding that we are referring to the factual variant.

A factual concept of pervasion in the vein of ($\mathrm{V}_1^{\mathrm{pf}}$) presents us with the problem to explain how pervasion can become the object of a veridical awareness. Since a complete verification of ($\mathrm{V}_1^{\mathrm{pf}}$) might outrun an agent's cognitive abilities, a broader pragmatic concept of truth seems to be called for. Pragmatic theories focus on what people are doing when describing statements as true. They link truth to verifiability, assertibility, usefulness, or long-term durability. The author of the UD seems to refer to such a pragmatic theory of truth when he explains in what sense an inference can be accepted as valid, even though an acquaintance with all loci of the probans which are involved in the pervasion at issue is beyond the scope of a reasoner's limited cognitive abilities: *jīvanavilopaprasaṅgāt. pratidinam āhārārthina āhārasya hitasādhanatāṃ vijñāya samanantaraṃ bhāvino 'pi tad anumāyaiva pravartate. anyathā pravṛttivirodhaprasaṅgāt. yas tv anumānaṃ nāṅgīkaroti sa kathaṃ prativādībhavet.* (UD: 4b, 14f) – "[Proponent of the right view:] [Inferences which are not based on the knowledge of all substrates of a positive or negative correlation can also be valid], because [otherwise] there would be the undesirable consequence of a disturbance of everyday life. Observing day by day that for someone who seeks food eating brings about benefit, one acts [in accordance with that] immediately after having inferred that also for the future. Because, otherwise, there would be an obstacle to active life. Who, however, does not agree to [this] inference, how should he respond?"

According to William James' version of pragmatism the phrases "It is useful, because it is true" and "It is true, because it is useful" are interchangeable (cf. James 1907: 204). If we identify truth with mere utility, a generic generalization like "Birds fly" or the conclusion of a defeasible rule like "$WearsRing \Rightarrow Married$" in Modgil's and Prakken's system $ASPIC^+$ might be said to be true.[11] However, in contrast to generics and certain defeasible rules in $ASPIC^+$, pervasion is incompatible with the existence of exceptions. Pervasion is conceived of as an exceptionless universal generalization. The statement of a pervasion is surely fallible, because it is inductively inferred. However, a single exception suffices to falsify such a statement.

An adequate representation of the universality of a genuine pervasion is even beyond the scope of first-order formalizations like ($\mathrm{V}_1^{\mathrm{pf}}$). The universal quantifier in ($\mathrm{V}_1^{\mathrm{pf}}$) refers to a domain of existing objects. The pervasion at issue, however, should rather be understood in the sense that every possible H is an S. In the UD a "positive correlation" (*anvaya*), i.e., the co-presence of the relata of a pervasion, is defined as *yāvadbhūtabhaviṣyadvartamānaniṣṭhatva* (UD: 4b, 8) – "the residence (of the probans) [in a locus], insofar as it has a past, future or present [instance of the probandum]". Hence, pervasion is more like a physical law, which enables us to make predictions about future H's and S's.

An adequate interpretation of the third member needs to warrant the universality of a pervasion without compromising the requirement that in the case of a valid inference a reasoner needs to have cognitive access to the truth of the pervasion at issue in some sense. A possible solution to this problem is to interpret a pervasion as the conclusion of a rule, viz. the rule of enumerative induction.[12] (The precise definition will be given below.)

The conclusion of this type of induction is a so-called "nomic generalization". Pollock's concept of a nomic generalization (cf. section 1.3.3) seems to be a close approximation to what the UD understands by "pervasion". At this point a formal explication is still expendable. We will rather make do with informal renderings like "All H's are S" and tacitly assume that such formulations are meant in an even more general sense than ($\mathrm{V}_1^{\mathrm{pf}}$), since the range of quantification should also include future H's and S's.

Moreover, according to the rule of enumerative induction the evidential support provided by the examples is a reason for a cognitive agent $\mathcal{A}$ to believe that all H's are S, in fact that even future H's are S. This would be impossible if $\mathcal{A}$ knew about counterexamples, or if $\mathcal{A}$ had any strong reasons to believe that there will be counterexamples in the future. (The defeasible character of the rule admits only the logical possibility of there being counterexamples.) Since a genuine pervasion as the conclusion of an enumerative induction is supposed to hold up to ongoing examination, it can be said to be true in a pragmatic sense which is stricter than James' criterion of mere subjective satisfaction, viz. in the sense that sustained inquiry leads to a dependable final verdict. According to one version of pragmatism, which attempts to preserve truth's objectivity, truth is what will be accepted in the end of inquiry. This approach identifies "being true with being warrantedly assertible under epistemically ideal conditions" (Putnam 2013: 220). Such a pragmatic concept of truth, which Putnam had advocated at least for some time, seems to be close to what Pollock understands by "warrant": "In contrast to justification, *warrant* is what the system of reasoning is ultimately striving for. A proposition is warranted in a particular epistemic situation iff (if and only if), starting from that epistemic situation, an ideal reasoner unconstrained by time or resource limitations would ultimately be led to believe the proposition. Warranted propositions are those that would be justified 'in the long run' if the system were able to do all possible relevant reasoning. A proposition can be justified without being warranted, because although the system has done everything correctly up to the present time and that has led to the adoption of the belief, there may be further reasoning waiting to be done that will mandate the retraction of the belief. Similarly, a proposition can be warranted without being justified, because although reasoning up to the present time may have failed to reveal adequate reasons for adopting the proposition, further reasoning may provide such reasons. Analogously, reasoning up to the present may mandate the adoption of defeaters which, upon further reasoning, will be retracted. So justification and warrant are two importantly different notions, although they are closely related." (Pollock 1992: 5)

Enumerative induction is an inference relation between a so-called "prima facie reason" and a conclusion. In our formal reconstruction of the third member of a five-membered inference the claim of evidential support in the form of positive or negative examples functions as a prima facie reason and the pervasion at issue functions as the conclusion.

Prima facie reasons are defeasible: "There are two kinds of reasons – defeasible and nondefeasible. Nondefeasible reasons are those reasons that logically entail their conclusions. For instance, $(P \& Q)$ is a nondefeasible reason for P. Such reasons are conclusive reasons. Everyone has always recognized the existence of nondefeasible reasons, but defeasible reasons are a relatively new discovery in philosophy, as well as in allied disciplines like AI. Focusing first upon reasons that are beliefs, P is a defeasible reason for Q just in case P is a reason for Q, but adding additional information may destroy the reason connection. Such reasons are called 'prima facie reasons.'" (Pollock 1987: 484) More precisely, Pollock defines prima facie reasons in the following way:

(R) "P is a *prima facie reason* for S to believe Q if and only if P is a reason for S to believe Q and there is an R such that R is logically consistent with P but $(P \& R)$ is not a reason for S to believe Q." (Pollock 1987: 484)[13]

Enumerative induction has to be distinguished from statistical induction: "The simplest kind of induction is enumerative induction, which proceeds from the observation that all members of a sample X of A's are B's, and makes a defeasible inference to the conclusion that all A's are B's. This is what is known as the Nicod Principle. Goodman [1955] observed that the principle requires a projectibility constraint. With this constraint, it can be formulated as follows:

(7.1) If B is projectible with respect to A, then ⌜X is a sample of A's all of which are B's⌝ is a prima facie reason for ⌜All A's are B's⌝." (Pollock 1995: 77)

"Enumerative induction has been a favorite topic of philosophers, but statistical induction is much more important for the construction of a rational agent. It is rare that we are in a position to confirm exceptionless universal generalizations. Induction usually leads us to statistical generalizations that either estimate the probability of an A being a B, or the proportion of actual A's that are B's, or more simply, may lead us to the conclusion that most A's are B's. Such statistical generalizations are still very useful, because the statistical syllogism enables a cognizer to make defeasible inferences from them to nonprobabilistic conclusions." (Pollock 1995: 78)

Since, however, according to Pollock the conclusion of an enumerative induction is a nomic generalization, this type of induction is preferable to statistical induction for the purpose of a formal explication of the third member. Nevertheless, some refinement of the enumerative inductive inference pattern seems appropriate in order to assimilate it to the theory of inference in Navya-Nyāya. Since the Navya-Naiyāyikas also take into account negative examples of a co-absence of probans and probandum, one might want to include a second sample of negative examples in the prima facie reason. Thus, the prima facie reason would be the claim of evidential support in the form of a sample X exemplifying the co-presence of the properties "being an H" and "being an S" and of a sample Y exemplifying the co-absence of "being an H" and "being an S" (cf. the kitchen hearth as a locus of smoke and fire and the lake as a locus of the co-absence of smoke and fire in the above-mentioned smoke/fire-example).[14] However, such a set Y does not exist in cases in which the probandum is a property whose presence in all loci other than the inferential subject is warranted. Thus, the above-mentioned smoke/fire-example should not be taken to be representative of all kinds of five-membered inferences. Moreover, there are cases in which the occurrence of the probans is confined to the inferential subject, so that only the previously observed instances of a co-absence of "being an H" and "being an S" can serve as inductive support for the inferential subject's being H and S. Thus, from the perspective of Navya-Nyāya it seems desirable to have three enumerative induction principles, one for *anvayavyatirekyanumānas*, i.e., inferences with positive and negative inductive support (EI$^{\pm}$), one for *kevalānvayyanumānas*, i.e., inferences with only positive inductive support (EI^{+}), and one for *kevalavyatirekyanumānas*, i.e., inferences with only negative inductive support (EI^{-}).[15]

(EI$^{\pm}$) If S is projectible with respect to H, then ⌜There is a set X of H's, and all the members of X are S, and there is a set Y of things which are not S and they are all not H⌝ is a prima facie reason for ⌜All H's are S⌝.

(EI^{+}) If S is projectible with respect to H, then ⌜There is a set X of H's, and all the members of X are S⌝ is a prima facie reason for ⌜All H's are S⌝.

(EI^{-}) If S is projectible with respect to H, then ⌜There is a set Y of things which are not S and they are all not H⌝ is a prima facie reason for ⌜All H's are S⌝.

The projectibility constraint is actually well noted by Navya-Naiyāyikas. In Gaṅgeśa's Upādhivāda and in the UD there is a long discussion about the possibility of admitting "being different from the inferential subject" (*pakṣetaratva*) as an inductively inferable property of all things exhibiting the probandum. If this property were projectible with respect to the probandum, it would undermine all sound inferences based on (EI$^{\pm}$). Since the probandum of such inferences is supposed to occur in other loci than the inferential subject as well, there will always be a set X of examples which exhibit the probandum and the property "being different from the inferential subject". Hence, by (EI^{+}) every locus of the probandum would be different from the inferential subject, i.e., the inferential subject would not be an instance of the probandum.[16]

Naiyāyikas were apparently grappling with the defeasible character of an inference. Multiple observations (*bhūyodarśana*) of the concomitance of probans and probandum did not suffice to ease their concerns about the reliability of inference as a knowledge source. Hence, the cognition of a pervasion was not entrusted to an inductive generalization alone: Navya-Naiyāyikas hold that the perception of a member of a collection of F's involves an "extraordinary perception" (*alaukikapratyakṣa*), viz. "the perception that grasps the general character" (*sāmānyalakṣaṇapratyakṣa*). It consists in the collective perception of all past, present, future and distant F's, but it involves no acquaintance with the specific characteristics of each individual F apart from its F-ness and other characteristics which all F's have in common. Thus, Naiyāyikas claimed that the perception of all smoke individuals can be achieved by means of the perception of a particular smoke, because all smoke-individuals share the universal "smokeness". The perception that grasps the general character is also conceived of as a knowledge source for facts about common characteristics of all individuals of a certain kind, such as the co-occurrence of each smoke-individual with a fire-individual: "This [*sāmānyalakṣaṇāpratyāsatti* (author's note: This is the specific sense-object-contact in the case of the perception which grasps the general character.)] provides the notion of 'erverywhere' and enables one to grasp *vyāpti* in its universal form as '*wherever* there is smoke there is fire.'" (Iyer 1979: 66)

The property F-ness, which gives rise to the perception of all F's, can be a universal, but it can also be some other kind of common attribute: "*sāmānyalakṣaṇāpratyāsatti* – This relation is based on the knowledge of *sāmānya* which is used here in the sense of common attribute – *samānā-nāṃ dharmaḥ*. It may mean any common attribute such as *dhūmatva* which is an eternal generality or it may be any other thing such as a jar that is perceived as a common attribute in all places observed." (Iyer 1979: 53)

Since in the case of a genuine pervasion the presence of the probandum on the inferential subject was supposed to be a necessary precondition for the presence of the probans, one could rely on "hypothetical reasoning" (*tarka*), a kind of reductio ad absurdum, as a further epistemic backup (cf. Bhattacharyya/Potter 1993: 76f). In such a case the hypothetical assumption of the absence of the probandum on the subject of the inference entails the absence of the probans in the same place. One might, e.g., argue that smoke is caused by an aggregate including fire (cf. Chakrabarti 2010: 37, where this is proved deductively from plausible assumptions). Hence, if there were no fire on the mountain, there would be no smoke either. This is a counterfactual with a false consequent, which can be formalized as $\neg p \mathrel{\Box\!\!\rightarrow} \neg q$. Since modus tollens holds for counterfactuals (cf. Lewis 1973: 36), we can conclude that the antecedent is false:

$$\begin{array}{l} \neg p \mathrel{\Box\!\!\rightarrow} \neg q \\ \underline{q \qquad\qquad} \\ \therefore p \end{array}$$

1.3.3 Pervasion as a Nomic Generalization

In Navya-Nyāya pervasion is an ontological relation. There can be an ordinary causal connection between the relata, as in the case of the smoke/fire-example. Since the Navya-Naiyāyikas are realists, they also regard pervasions based on taxonomic classifications as ontological. Waterness, e.g., was assumed to be pervaded by substanceness: Whatever is a locus of waterness, i.e., whatever is water, is a locus of substanceness, i.e., it is a substance. In this case probans and probandum were conceived of as universals, the ontological correlates of the terms "water" and "substance".

"Realism is important along every dimension of Nyāya epistemology. A pervasion is held to obtain in nature, and for this reason, strictly speaking, one could be grasped from a single exhibited connection. For example, from a single instance of sight of smoke rising from fire, the pervasion, wherever smoke there fire, could be grasped, or from viewing a horse and a cow, one could know that a horse is not a cow and (to express the pervasion, here a negative one) whatever is a cow is not a horse and conversely. In other words, inductive generalization may proceed from a single instance, what we might call extrapolation (Fs as generally G from a single observation of an F as a G). However, repeated experience of the relation (along with no experience of an F as not a G) is said normally to be necessary for a firm impression to take hold in one's memory, an impression capable of informing or guiding an action including speech. In any case, recurrent experience normally means an increase in epistemic confidence." (Phillips 2002: 7f)

Since the relata of a genuine pervasion were always supposed to be grounded in the empirical world, all statements of a pervasion could be regarded as positive statements that can be tested, amended or rejected by referring to the available evidence. Thus, all five-membered inferences could be regarded as inductive, not only those based on causal pervasions. According to some interpreters Gaṅgeśa even seems to have construed pervasion in general as a causal relation, although in cases like, e.g., the pervasion of waterness by substanceness this seems possible only if we considerably extend our ordinary understanding of causality beyond the limits (cf. Phillips 2002: 11 and 99f and Chakrabarti 2010: 217).

Pervasion is a law-like relation in the sense that due to ontological regularities every locus of the probans is, has always been and forever will be a locus of the probandum. The presence of the probans necessarily entails the presence of the probandum. In order to formalize this kind of invariable concomitance, we can rely on the standard way of expressing metaphysical necessity, viz. by means of an S5 □-operator. By prefixing it to (V_1^{pf}) we obtain the following more accurate prima facie formalization:

(V_2^{pf}) $\Box\forall x(Hx \rightarrow Sx)$

Pollock's formalization of a nomic generalization is a bit more complex, because it is designed to be applicable to certain cases which are probably not relevant to an adequate formal explication of the concept of pervasion, viz. so-called "counterlegal nomic generalizations", i.e., nomic generalizations whose antecedents are counterlegal (cf. Pollock 1990: 43 and Garson 2013: 432f). Newton's First Law is an example:

(N) All objects unaffected by an outside force travel in a straight line at a constant velocity.

According to Newton's Law of Gravitation all objects exert a gravitational force on all other objects (albeit a small one for objects far from each other). Hence, there are no objects which are unaffected by an outside force. However, (N) is not vacuously true, because it is not equally true that an object which is unaffected by an outside force would not travel in a straight line at a constant velocity. Moreover, an adequate formalization of counterlegal nomic generalizations should be compatible with our intuition that "laws" like (N*) are false:

(N*) All objects unaffected by an outside force turn into a hippopotamus.

According to Pollock (N) and (N*) can be formalized as ...

(N_f) $\Diamond_p\exists xFx > \Box_p\forall x(Fx \rightarrow Gx)$ and

(N_f^*) $\Diamond_p\exists xFx > \Box_p\forall x(Fx \rightarrow Hx)$, where ...

... Fx, Gx and Hx translate into "x is unaffected by an outside force", "x travels in a straight line at a constant velocity" and "x turns into a hippopotamus", respectively, "$>$" is a counterfactual conditional, and "$\Diamond_p$" and "$\Box_p$" are S5 modalities translating into "It is physically possible that" and "It is physically necessary that", respectively (cf. Pollock 1990: 43).

Pollock regards nomic generalizations (including counterlegal ones) as counterfactuals, i.e., he reads (N) and (N*) as: "If objects unaffected by an outside force did possibly exist, it would necessarily be the case that they travel in a straight line at a constant velocity (or: that they turn into a hippopotamus)." According to this explication (N) can reasonably be regarded as true and (N*) as false.

The semantics of Pollock's counterfactual conditional ">" is similar to that of David Lewis' "$\Box\!\!\rightarrow$"-conditional: Pollock adopts Lewis' sphere conception in order to model the intuition that the accessible worlds are the most similar worlds at which the antecedent is true. However, according to Pollock similarity is cashed out in terms of consistency with the laws of nature, whereas for Lewis it is a comparative overall similarity which accounts for the fact that a world w' is regarded as more (or less) similar to a world w than a world w'' (cf. Pollock 1990: 41 and Lewis 1973: 91).

The idea of a counterlegal nomic generalization was by no means alien to the Naiyāyikas. Chakrabarti notes the following example: "An eternal entity that is independently productive is productive for ever." (Chakrabarti 2010: 40) However, the instances of pervasion which Navya-Naiyāyikas take into account are normally non-counterlegal nomic generalizations. Gaṅgeśa, e.g., explicitly excludes counterlegal pervasions by including the constraint of existential import in his definition of pervasion, i.e., the requirement that the probans should be instantiated at the actual world (cf. Goekoop 1967: 109). The author of the UD tacitly understands pervasion in the same way. As we will see later, the pervasion of the *upādhi* by the probandum as part of the UD's specific defining characteristic of the *upādhi* obviously presupposes that *upādhi* and probandum are co-locatable at the actual world. Hence, according to Gaṅgeśa and the UD pervasion should rather be formalized as ...

(V) $\Box\forall x(Hx \rightarrow Sx) \wedge \exists xHx$

..., where the quantifiers ought to be understood in an actualist sense (cf. Garson 2013: 249 and 252f). A possibilist reading of the existential quantifier in the second conjunct would strip the constraint of existential import of its ontological commitment, which is surely associated with it. If we replace the quantifiers in (V) by special present-tense quantifiers such as Garson's $\exists$p ("presently exists"), the modified version of (V) can be appropriately interpreted by means of a constant domain approach, which presupposes a single domain of all possible objects (cf. Garson 2013: 252f). Alternatively, one might hold onto the quantifiers in (V) and choose an interpretation by means of a varying domain model (cf. Garson 2013: 254f, Hughes/Cresswell 2005: 274f and Pollock 1984: 215f). According to the definition of truth in such a model $\exists xHx$ is true at a world w iff there is an object in the domain of w of which H is true at w.

A formalization of pervasion as a nomic generalization which is equivalent to (V) can be obtained from (V) by replacing the first conjunct by $\Diamond\exists xHx > \Box\forall x(Hx \rightarrow Sx)$, the corresponding formula for counterlegal and non-counterlegal nomic generalizations alike:

$$(\mathrm{V}')\ \underbrace{(\Diamond\exists xHx > \Box\forall x(Hx \rightarrow Sx))}_{\leftrightarrow:\,H\Rightarrow S} \wedge \exists xHx$$

Since the present modal framework is S5, $\exists xHx \rightarrow \Diamond\exists xHx$. Moreover, according to Pollock's Theorem (3.15) $\Diamond\exists xHx \rightarrow ((H \Rightarrow S) \leftrightarrow \Box\forall x(Hx \rightarrow Sx))$ (cf. Pollock 1990: 44), where $H \Rightarrow S$ is used as an abbreviation of $\Diamond\exists xHx > \Box\forall x(Hx \rightarrow Sx)$. The "$\Rightarrow$" between predicate symbols is Pollock's standard way of abbreviating nomic generalizations. It needs to be distinguished from the "$\Rightarrow$" as a means to represent defeasible rules in $ASPIC^+$. "$H \Rightarrow S$" in the sense in which we use such expressions here is not a rule, but the conclusion of a rule.

The utility of a (V)- or (V′)-like pervasion becomes obvious if we take into account that in S5 $\Box\forall x(Hx \rightarrow Sx) \rightarrow \forall x(Hx \rightarrow Sx)$, or that nomic generalizations entail material generalizations, i.e., $(H \Rightarrow S) \rightarrow \forall x(Hx \rightarrow Sx)$ (cf. Pollock 1990: 36). Thus, a (V)- or (V′)-like pervasion applies to all actually existing loci of the probans (including the inferential subject) in a particular inferential situation. Since the conclusion of a five-membered inference follows deductively from the second member and the material generalization involved in a pervasion, the following unmodalized variant of (V) has a special logical significance. It represents the gist of the pervasion at issue in a particular inferential situation:

$$(\mathrm{V}_{\mathrm{act}})\ \forall x(Hx \rightarrow Sx) \wedge \exists xHx$$

The quantifiers in ($\mathrm{V}_{\mathrm{act}}$) are to be understood in the same way as in (V) and (V′), i.e., in an actualist sense. Since ($\mathrm{V}_{\mathrm{act}}$) is a relativization of (V) and (V′) to a universal concomitance pertaining to all actually existing objects, we will refer to ($\mathrm{V}_{\mathrm{act}}$) as "the actualized version of the pervasion relation". Fig. B is its representation as a Venn diagram:

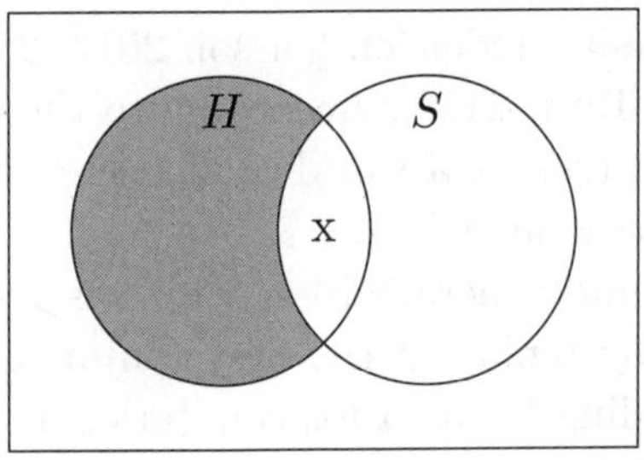

Fig. B

The condition of existential import ($\exists xHx$) in (V), (V′) and (V_{act}) is also crucial for a proper understanding of "positive" and "negative pervasion" (*anvayavyāpti* and *vyatirekavyāpti*) and of "deviation" (*vyabhicāra*), the antonym of "pervasion".

In the case of the smoke/fire-inference (cf. the beginning of section 1.3) the positive pervasion is expressed by means of the proposition "Wherever there is smoke, there is fire". Since there are loci of the absence of fire, the contraposed formulation "Wherever there is no fire, there is no smoke" fulfills the condition of existential import. Hence, the absence of fire can be said to be pervaded by the absence of smoke. This is the negative pervasion corresponding to the positive pervasion of smoke by fire. However, in the case of the positive pervasion of knowability by nameability, a corresponding negative pervasion does not even exist. The condition of existential import would be violated, because nameability is a universally positive property, i.e., $\neg\exists x$(x is a locus of the absence of nameability). Thus, a negative pervasion is not just an equivalent reformulation of its positive counterpart by means of the law of contraposition if an appropriate adaptation of the condition of existential import is taken to be part of the transformation of a positive pervasion into a negative one.

Since the pervasion of "being an H" by "being an S" is a conjunction with the condition of existential import as a conjunct, the non-pervasion of "being an H" by "being an S" might be said to apply to a case in which only the condition of existential import is unfulfilled. From the perspective of the actual world, the region with a cross in Fig. B would have to be shaded and H would be an empty term then:

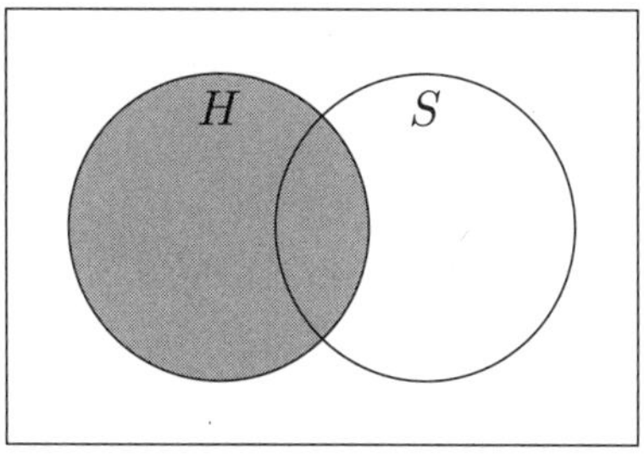

Fig. C

However, "deviation" (*vyabhicāra*), the antonym of "pervasion", is rather understood in the sense of an (actual) occurrence of the probans in a locus of the absence of the probandum: *sādhyābhāvavadvṛttitvaṃ vyabhicāraḥ.* (NKoś: 96, s.v. *avyabhicāraḥ*) "We can say that h deviates from s just in case the absence-range of the latter overlaps (intersects) the presence-range of the former." (Matilal 1990: 122) In a narrower sense, "deviation" applies only to cases of a co-occurrence of the probans with both, the presence and the absence of the probandum (cf. Iyer 1979: 105). This excludes the case of an "incoherence" (*viruddhatvam*), i.e., a pervasion of the probans by the absence of the probandum: *hetusādhyābhāvavyāptir viruddhatvam.* (NKoś: 775) Even in this case, the requirement of existential import, which is associated with a pervasion, ensures that the range of a joint occurrence of the probans and the absence of the probandum is non-empty. Thus, a deviation in a broader sense amounts to the failure of an assumed pervasion due to to the existence of a counter-example at the actual world, which can be expressed as the negation of ($\mathrm{V}_1^{\mathrm{pf}}$), i.e., as ...

($\mathrm{V}_{\mathrm{ant}}$) $\exists x(Hx \wedge \neg Sx)$

..., where the quantifier should be read in an actualist sense. Hence, the "x" in the corresponding Venn diagram Fig. D represents a member of the domain of actually existing objects:

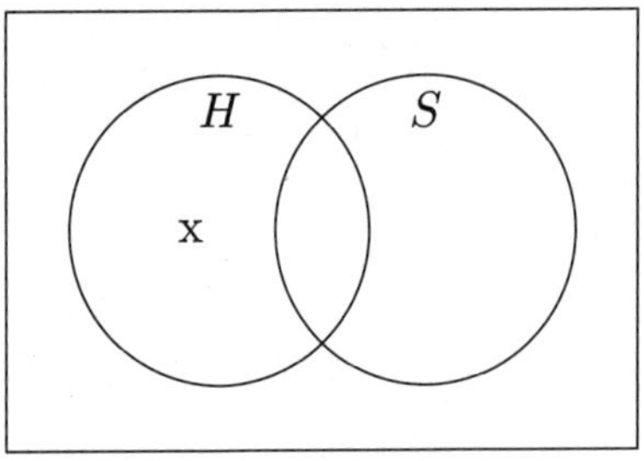

Fig. D

1.4 The *upādhi* and Its Function as a Vitiator

An *upādhi* is said to be a "vitiator"[17] of putative instances of pervasion and, hence, of pseudo-inferences. However the vitiating function is rather attributed to the *upādhi*'s absence in certain loci. According to the UD an *upādhi* vitiates putative instances of pervasion or pseudo-inferences by exposing the probans as a special type of "pseudo-probans" (*hetvābhāsa*), viz. the so-called "conditional probans" (*vyāpyatvāsiddha*). This is a type of pseudo-probans which only in combination with an *upādhi* allows us to infer the probandum.[18]

Here is a classical example: Although smoke is supposed to be pervaded by fire, the putative pervasion of fire by smoke is unwarranted. The sample from which this pseudo-pervasion might be extrapolated turns out to be not a fair one if we find out that in the case of all hitherto observed instances of fire the co-occurrence with smoke was owing to the presence of an *upādhi*, viz. wet fuel. Wherever there is fire without wet fuel, as in the case of molten metal, there is no smoke. Of course, the identification of a counter-example would suffice to refute the universality of a putative pervasion. The *upādhi* is supposed to account for the existence of counter-examples: The reason why there are loci of fire without smoke is that fire produces smoke only in the presence of wet fuel.

In this example the absence of the *upādhi* in a locus of the probans entails the absence of the probandum. However, an *upādhi* may also vitiate in the sense that its absence in a locus of the probans is a reason to doubt the presence of the probandum. Two basic senses of "vitiating" have to be distinguished:

1.) Vitiating in the sense of "overruling": We will see that in the case of the so-called ascertained *upādhi* (*niścitopādhi*) the claim of its absence in certain loci can be regarded as a defeater in the sense of Pollock's theory. A putative pervasion or inference are overruled by means of an ascertained *upādhi*.

2.) Vitiating in the more general sense of "blocking an inference": A dubious *upādhi* (*saṃdigdhopādhi*) or rather its absence in certain loci vitiates in the sense that it prevents us from drawing a conclusion if there are equally good reasons for and against denying the thesis of the inference or the universality of a putative pervasion. Thus, the Navya-Naiyāyika's way of resolving epistemic ties dovetails with the behaviour of a skeptical reasoner who acknowledges epistemic ignorance and withholds belief rather than choosing randomly like a credulous reasoner.

On the surface, an *upādhi* seems to be similar to a so-called "undercutting defeater" in the sense of Pollock's theory of defeasible reasoning. Pollock illustrates his concept of an undercutting defeater in the following way: "For example, something's looking red to me may justify me in believing that it is red, but if I subsequently learn that the object is illuminated by red lights and I know that that can make things look red when they are not, then I cease to be justified in believing that the object is red." (Pollock 1987: 481)

Stephen Phillips translates *upādhi* as "undercutting condition", although he is well aware that there are differences between an *upādhi* and an undercutting defeater in the sense of Pollock's theory (cf. Phillips 2002: 14f): An *upādhi* is an object of the domain such as, e.g., wet fuel, whereas a defeater is a mental state (cf. Pollock 1995: 55 and 86). A mental state can be a perceptual state or a belief. The mental states which constitute an argument are mostly beliefs. In Pollock's above-mentioned example the proposition "The object which looks red to me is illuminated by red lights" is just a "convenient shorthand" (Pollock 1995: 55) for the defeater, which should be more accurately rendered as "*believing* 'The object which looks red to me is illuminated by red lights'" (cf. Pollock 1995: 55). However, "when the constituents of arguments are belief states, we can just as well represent the beliefs in terms of the propositions believed, and doing so makes the arguments look more familiar." (Pollock 1995: 86) Hereafter, we will often talk about prima facie reasons and defeaters as if they were propositions. Thus, P, Q and R in the following definitions can conveniently be regarded as propositional variables, although – properly speaking – their referents should be taken to be beliefs:

(D) "R is a *defeater* for P as a prima facie reason for Q if and only if P is a reason for S to believe Q and R is logically consistent with P but $(P \,\&\, R)$ is not a reason for S to believe Q." (Pollock 1987: 484)

The defeater "rebuts" or "undercuts" a prima facie reason:

(D^R) "R is a *rebutting defeater* for P as a prima facie reason for Q if and only if R is a defeater and R is a reason for believing ~ Q." (Pollock 1987: 485)

(D^U) "R is an *undercutting defeater* for P as a prima facie reason for S to believe Q if and only if R is a defeater and R is a reason for denying that P wouldn't be true unless Q were true."[19] (Pollock 1987: 485)

In Pollock's example "X (= the object referred to) looks red" is a prima facie reason, "X is red" is the conclusion". "X is illuminated by red light" is a defeater. The defeater is here an undercutter: "This is a defeater, but it is not a reason for denying that X is red (red things look red in red light too). Instead, this is a reason for denying that X wouldn't look red to me unless it were red." (Pollock 1987: 485)

In the strict sense of Pollock's terminology it is inappropriate to say that in the case of the putative pervasion of fire by smoke smoke is a prima facie reason, which is defeated by wet fuel, or that "looking red to me" is a prima facie reason for "being red", which is defeated by the absence of red light.[20] If we want to assimilate the theory of the associate condition to his theory of defeasible reasoning, it cannot be done in quite the same way as Stephen Phillips suggests.

A prima facie reason in Pollock's sense cannot be the probans of an assumed pervasion relation. There are actually two other candidates for a prima facie reason which the UD seems to take into account and which can be said to be veritable prima facie reasons in Pollock's sense:

(R_1) There is evidential support for the pervasion at issue in the form of a sample $\{e_1, \ldots, e_n\}$ of positive or negative examples. (This claim of evidential support is part of the third member of a five-membered inference.)

$$(\mathrm{R}_2)\ \underbrace{\text{The inferential subject is a locus of the probans.}}_{\text{=the second member}} \wedge$$

$$\underbrace{(\mathrm{R}_1) \wedge ((\mathrm{R}_1) \text{ is a prima facie reason for ``All } H\text{'s are } S\text{''.)}}_{\text{=the third member}}$$

The pervasion at issue (All H's are S) can be regarded as the conclusion drawn from (R_1). The thesis of an inference (Ss) can be regarded as the conclusion drawn from (R_2).

In the Navya-Nyāya doctrine of *upādhi* we find also genuine equivalents of a defeater in the sense of Pollock's theory. Let us look again at Pollock's "red light"-example: Apart from the defeater-proposition (marked as $\sqrt[D]{\ldots}$ below) it contains a piece of background information (marked as $\sqrt[B]{\ldots}$ below), which warrants the latter's functionality as a defeater:

(E0) "For example, something's looking red to me may justify me in believing that it is red, but if I subsequently learn that $\sqrt[D]{\text{the object is illuminated by red lights}}$ and I know that $\sqrt[B]{\text{that can make things look red when they are not}}$, then I cease to be justified in believing that the object is red."

Similar propositions can be identified in Navya-Nyāya specifications of the vitiating function of an *upādhi*. Two propositions are involved in such specifications, viz. the statement of the *upādhi*'s absence in a locus of the probans, which in an inferential situation may be identical to the inferential subject (also marked as $\sqrt[D]{\ldots}$ below), and the statement that the absence of the *upādhi* in a locus of the probans entails the absence of the probandum (also marked as $\sqrt[B]{\ldots}$ below).

Gaṅgeśa defines an associate condition according to its essence (*svarūpa*) as follows:

(E1) *yad vā yaḥ sādhanavyabhicārī sādhyavyabhicāronnāyakaḥ, sa upādhiḥ.* (Frauwallner 1970: 13, 19f) – "$\sqrt[B]{\text{What indicates the deviation (of the probans) from the probandum}}$[21] if $\sqrt[D]{\text{it has the probans as something deviating from it}}$, that is an *upādhi*."

Gaṅgeśa cites also Maṇikaṇṭha, whose definition expresses basically the same: *anye tu yadvyāvṛttyā yasya sādhanasya sādhyaṃ nivartate, sa dharmas tatra hetāv upādhiḥ.* (Frauwallner 1970: 14, 30f) – "Others, however,

[say]: 'That property on account of whose absence the probans is lacking the probandum is an associate condition for that probans.'" We can paraphrase this as follows:

(E2) "If $\sqrt[\mathrm{D}]{}$the *upādhi* is absent from a locus of the probans, $\sqrt[\mathrm{B}]{}$its absence there entails the absence of the probandum."

The UD specifies the vitiating function of an *upādhi* with respect to an inferential context:

(E3) *asmin pakṣa upādhāv avidyamāne tanniṣṭhavyāpyatvahetor viruddhavyabhicārisādhāraṇabhūtasādhyābhāvasādhakatvaṃ tadvyatirekasya paryavasyatīti* (UD: 7b, 20f) – "If $\sqrt[\mathrm{D}]{}$an *upādhi* is not present on this inferential subject, then it (i.e., the property of being a vitiator) amounts to the fact that the absence of that (= the absence of the *upādhi* on the inferential subject) is like an incoherent or a deviating [pseudo-probans] and proves the absence of the probandum (from the inferential subject),[22] because of the pervadedness (by the absence of the probandum) resident in that (absence of the *upādhi*, i.e., because $\sqrt[\mathrm{B}]{}$the absence of the *upādhi* is pervaded by the absence of the probandum in the range of the probans)."

By means of first-order formalization techniques and the symbolization key . . .

Hx: "x is a locus of the probans"
Sx: "x is a locus of the probandum"
Ux: "x is a locus of the *upādhi*"
s: "the inferential subject"

. . . we can render the $\sqrt[\mathrm{B}]{\ldots}$-proposition in (E1) – (E3) as . . .

(B) $\forall x(Hx \land \neg Ux \rightarrow \neg Sx)$[23]

. . . and the $\sqrt[\mathrm{D}]{\ldots}$-proposition as . . .

(D_1) $\exists x(Hx \land \neg Ux)$

. . . in the case of (E1) and (E2) and as . . .

(D_2) $Hs \wedge \neg Us$

...in the case of (E3).

If (D_1) and (D_2) are conjoined with (B), they actually function as defeaters of the prima facie reasons (R_1) and (R_2). (D_1) and (D_2) rebut (R_1), because the conjunction of each of them with (B) entails $\exists x(Hx \wedge \neg Sx)$, which means that the conclusion drawn from (R_1), viz. the pervasion at issue, is false:

$$\vdash \exists x(Hx \wedge \neg Ux) \wedge \forall x(Hx \wedge \neg Ux \rightarrow \neg Sx) \rightarrow \exists x(Hx \wedge \neg Sx)$$

$$\vdash Hs \wedge \neg Us \wedge \forall x(Hx \wedge \neg Ux \rightarrow \neg Sx) \rightarrow \exists x(Hx \wedge \neg Sx)$$

The rebutting function of (D_1) and (D_2) with respect to (R_1) can be represented as follows:

$$\underbrace{\text{claim of evidential support}}_{\text{prima facie reason } (R_1)} \rightsquigarrow \underbrace{\text{pervasion}}_{\text{conclusion}}$$

↑ rebuts in combination with $\forall x(Hx \wedge \neg Ux \rightarrow \neg Sx)$

$\exists x(Hx \wedge \neg Ux) / Hs \wedge \neg Us$

(R_2) is rebutted by (D_2), because the conjunction with (B) entails $\neg Ss$, which means that the conclusion drawn from (R_2), viz. the thesis of the inference, is false:

$$\vdash Hs \wedge \neg Us \wedge \forall x(Hx \wedge \neg Ux \rightarrow \neg Sx) \rightarrow \neg Ss$$

(R_2) is undercut by (D_1), because the conjunction of (D_1) and (B) only implies that $\exists x(Hx \wedge \neg Sx)$. So, Ss may be true or false. (R_2) is just not a proper reason for Ss. The rebutting function of (D_1) and the undercutting function of (D_2) with respect to (R_2) can be represented as follows:

$$\underbrace{\text{second member} \wedge \text{third member}}_{\text{prima facie reason } (R_2)} \rightsquigarrow \underbrace{\text{thesis}}_{\text{conclusion}}$$

↑ rebuts in combination with $\forall x(Hx \wedge \neg Ux \rightarrow \neg Sx)$

$Hs \wedge \neg Us$

$$\underbrace{\text{second member} \wedge \text{third member}}_{\text{prima facie reason } (\mathrm{R}_2)} \rightsquigarrow \underbrace{\text{thesis}}_{\text{conclusion}}$$

$$\uparrow \text{undercuts in combination with } \forall x(Hx \wedge \neg Ux \rightarrow \neg Sx)$$

$$\exists x(Hx \wedge \neg Ux)$$

The following chart outlines the ways in which (D_1) and (D_2) are related to (R_1) and (R_2):

	rebuts	undercuts
(D_1)	(R_1)	(R_2)
(D_2)	(R_1), (R_2)	–

(D_2) can only be a rebutter, whereas (D_1) can be a rebutter and an undercutter, but with respect to different prima facie reasons. Since (D_2) implies (D_1), (D_2) rebuts everything that (D_1) rebuts. If we understand an undercutter as a proposition which can be true, while the conclusion may be true or false, only (D_1) can be an undercutter, because (D_1) does not give a clue to the locus of the deviation of the probans from the probandum. Hence, (D_1) is not a reason to deny the conclusion drawn from (R_2).

Let us look at an example: We assume that an agent $\mathcal{A}$ observes fire on a distant mountain in the dark and concludes that there is also smoke hidden in the dark. $\mathcal{A}$'s pseudo-inference involves the pseudo-pervasion of fire by smoke. In this situation $\mathcal{A}$ might get to know from a reliable source that there is no wet fuel on the mountain, and $\mathcal{A}$ knows that the absence of wet fuel entails the absence of smoke. The fire on the mountain actually emanates from a red-hot iron ball. Thus, the proposition that the mountain is a locus of fire without wet fuel is a (D_2)-like rebutter, because it is for $\mathcal{A}$ a reason to deny (i) the thesis of the inference as the conclusion drawn from an (R_2)-like prima facie reason and (ii) the universality of the putative pervasion of fire by smoke as the conclusion drawn from an (R_1)-like prima facie reason.

Now, let us assume that $\mathcal{A}$ gets to know from a reliable source that there are loci of fire without wet fuel, and $\mathcal{A}$ knows that the absence of wet fuel entails the absence of smoke. However, $\mathcal{A}$ does not know whether the mountain is a locus of the absence of wet fuel. In this situation the proposition that there is a locus of fire without wet fuel is a (D_1)-like rebutter, because it is for $\mathcal{A}$ a reason to deny (ii). Moreover, it is a (D_1)-like undercutter, because it is for $\mathcal{A}$ a reason to deny that (R_2) would not be true unless the thesis of the inference were true. The mountain may well be a locus of the probans and there may well be a sample of positive or negative examples providing evidential support for the pervasion at issue. Nevertheless, the thesis of the inference may be false, because the sample providing evidential support might not be a fair one.

It is important to note that a (D_1)-like undercutter attacks only the connection between (R_2) and the conclusion, viz. the thesis of the inference. The latter may be true or false. Thus, (D_1) can also function as an undercutter with respect to a pseudo-inference whose thesis is undeniably true. If, e.g., an agent $\mathcal{A}$ argues that a pot is produced, because it is nameable like a piece of cloth etc., one might refute the argument by defeating $\mathcal{A}$'s choice of a sample for drawing the conclusion that whatever is nameable is also produced. Although the thesis of the inference is uncontroversial, $\mathcal{A}$'s sample is apparently not a fair one, since only things which are nameable *and non-eternal* are produced. The proposition expressing the absence of the property "being non-eternal" in a locus of the property "nameability" functions here as a (D_1)-like undercutter.

The types of rebutting and undercutting defeaters which we are distinguishing here correspond to different characterizations of an *upādhi*'s vitiating functions which are discussed in the UD. The author of the UD prefers to characterize this vitiating function as "leading to the fallacy of the conditional probans" (*vyāpyatvāsiddhyāpādaka*). This might be understood as a portrayal of (D_1)'s and (D_2)'s function of rebutting (R_1) and of (D_1)'s function of undercutting (R_2). Alternatively, these rebutting and undercutting functions might be characterized as "indicating a deviation" (*vyabhicāronnāyaka*), i.e., showing that the purported universality of the pervasion at issue is unwarranted. Moreover, (D_2)'s function of rebutting (R_2) might be characterized as "amounting to [the affirmation of] the counter-thesis" (*pratipakṣaparyavasāna*).

It should be noted that the rebutting or undercutting function of (D_1) and (D_2) depends essentially on an appropriate background information. If (B) is true, (D_1) and (D_2) fulfill the criteria of a rebutting or undercutting defeater according to Pollock's definition. First of all, they are defeaters of (R_1) and (R_2), because ...

a) they are consistent with (R_1) and (R_2): Due to (B), the absence of the *upādhi* in a locus of the probans entails the absence of the probandum. But despite the absence of the probandum (from the inferential subject or from any other locus of the probans) there might be a sample of instances of a co-presence or co-absence of probans and probandum (in accordance with (R_1)). Moreover, despite the absence of the probandum (from the inferential subject or from any other locus of the probans) the inferential subject might be a locus of the probans and one might reasonably claim that a sample of instances of a co-presence or co-absence of probans and probandum provides inductive support for the pervasion at issue (in accordance with (R_2)).

b) (R_1) & (D_1) and (R_1) & (D_2) are no reasons to believe that all H's are S, and (R_2) & (D_1) and (R_2) & (D_2) are no reasons to believe that Ss, since due to (B), the absence of the *upādhi* in a locus of the probans entails the absence of the probandum.

Finally, (D_1) and (D_2) are rebutters for (R_1), because due to (B), they are a reason for believing that not all H's are S. (D_2) is a rebutter for (R_2), because due to (B), it is a reason for believing $\neg Ss$. (D_1) is an undercutter for (R_2), because due to (B), it is a reason to deny that (R_2) would not be true unless the conclusion Ss were true. (s might be a locus of the probans and there might be a sample X which provides positive inductive support for the pervasion at issue. Nevertheless, the sample might not be a fair one, since the H's in X are S, only because they are all U. However, s might be an H which is not U and in that case $\neg Ss$ due to (B).)

It is important to note that (B) is sufficient, but not necessary for (D_1)'s and (D_2)'s functionality as defeaters. (D_1), e.g., could also function as an undercutter for (R_2) if the absence of the *upādhi* in a locus of the probans co-occurs with both, the absence and the presence of the probandum, i.e., in the case of ...

(B′) $\exists x(Hx \wedge \neg Ux \wedge \neg Sx) \wedge \exists x(Hx \wedge \neg Ux \wedge Sx)$.

Due to (B′) (D_1) is also a reason to deny that (R_2) would not be true unless the conclusion Ss were true. However, if the *upādhi* is related to probans and probandum in the sense of (D_1) and (B′), it is only a so-called "apparent *upādhi*" (*upādhyābhāsa*) according to the author of the UD and also according to Gaṅgeśa, since both insist that the absence of the *upādhi* in a locus of the probans entails the absence of the probandum. Although the

Navya-Nyāya doctrine of an *upādhi* can be assimilated to Pollock's theory of defeasible reasoning in the manner outlined here, the latter is applicable to a far wider range of defeasible inferences. Thus, Pollock's example, the inference of "X is red" from "X looks red", is rather based on a defeasible rule of thumb than on an inductive generalization. Even if we regard "looking red" in this example as a probans and "being red" as a probandum, the object which comes closest to an *upādhi* here, viz. "the absence of red light", is only an apparent *upādhi*, since "looking red", "being red" and "the absence of red light" are related to each other in terms of (D_1) and (B′). (B) is not warranted in this case, because red light (= the absence of the apparent *upādhi*, i.e., the absence of the absence of red light) co-occurs with both, the absence of the probandum and the presence of the probandum: "Red objects look red in red light too." (Pollock 1987: 485)[24]

1.5 The Specific Defining Characteristic of an *upādhi*

Let us compare (D_1) to the following adaptation of Gaṅgeśa's definition of the *upādhi* to the canonical form of a specific defining characteristic, which defines an *upādhi*'s relation to probans and probandum in terms of pervasion and non-pervasion:

(G_1) The associate condition does not pervade the probans and

(G_2) it pervades the probandum in the range of the probans.[25]

If we take into account only the actualized version of the pervasion relation, i.e., the material generalization inherent in the pervasion at issue, (G_1) and (G_2) can be formalized as follows:

($G_1{}'$) $\exists x(Hx \wedge \neg Ux)$

($G_2{}'$) $\forall x(Hx \wedge Sx \rightarrow Ux) \wedge \exists x(Hx \wedge Sx \wedge Ux)$

($G_1{}'$) is identical to (D_1). In ($G_2{}'$) the first conjunct is equivalent to (B), i.e., $\forall x(Hx \wedge \neg Ux \rightarrow \neg Sx)$. From (B) and ($G_1{}'$) we can conclude that $\exists x(Hx \wedge \neg Sx)$. Hence, the first conjunct of ($G_2{}'$) warrants the rebutting or undercutting function of ($G_1{}'$). The second conjunct, which serves to warrant existential import for the universally quantified formula, is merely collateral to the formulation of the first conjunct of (G_2') in terms of the pervasion relation. Thus, Gaṅgeśa's specific defining characteristic of an associate condition implies that (G_1') is a (D_1)-like rebutting or undercutting defeater in the sense of Pollock's theory.

Fig. E below is a diagrammatic representation of this definition. The next diagram, Fig. F, represents the classical fire/smoke/wet fuel-example. It shows that in this case the associate condition fulfills the criteria (G_1) and (G_2).

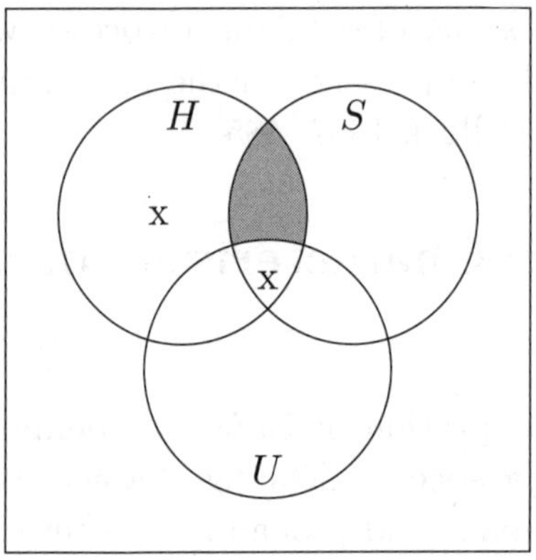

Fig. E

H = the class of loci of the probans
S = the class of loci of the probandum
U = the class of loci of the associate condition

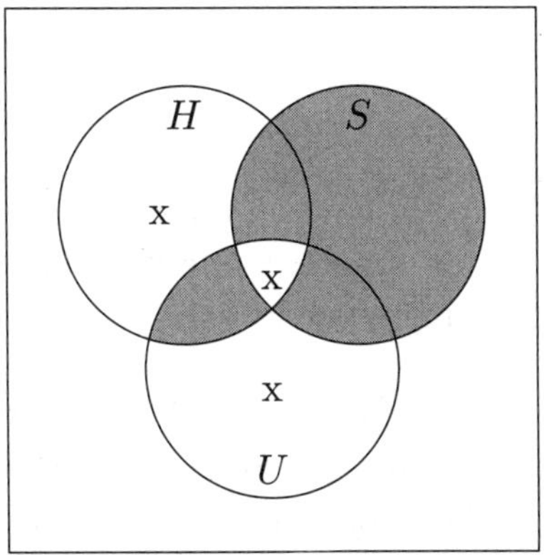

Fig. F

H = the class of loci of the probans "fire"
S = the class of loci of the probandum "smoke"
U = the class of loci of the associate condition "wet fuel"

molten metal $\in H \setminus (S \cup U)$; a locus of wet fuel which is not ignited $\in U \setminus (H \cup S)$; a locus of fire + smoke + wet fuel $\in H \cap S \cap U$

The fire/smoke/wet fuel-example matches also Udayana's specific defining characteristic of an *upādhi*:

(U_1) The associate condition does not pervade the probans and

(U_2) it pervades the probandum.

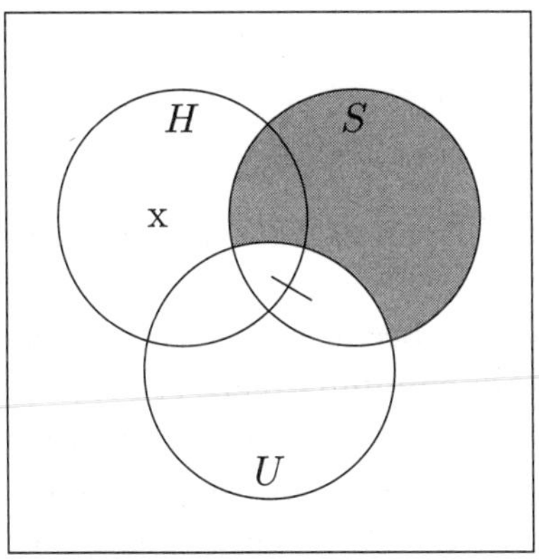

Fig. G[26]

In symbols:

(U_1') $\exists x(Hx \wedge \neg Ux)$ and

(U_2') $\forall x(Sx \rightarrow Ux) \wedge \exists x(Sx \wedge Ux)$

As indicated by the "x" $\in H \setminus (S \cup U)$ in Fig. G, (U_1) and (U_2) entail that $\exists x(Hx \wedge \neg Sx)$, and thus that an original apparent inference fails. In other words, the *upādhi* vitiates the apparent inference by showing that the required pervasion does not hold.

It is not difficult to see how Udayana might have derived his definition. In order to satisfy the condition of existential import, let us assume that the classes of the loci of the probans and the probandum, which we will symbolize as H and S, respectively, are non-empty. Then the material generalization involved in a pervasion can be expressed set-theoretically as:

$$H \subseteq S$$

Now, the equivalence ...

$$H \subseteq S \leftrightarrow \forall U(S \subseteq U \rightarrow H \subseteq U)$$

... is easily provable: The direction from left to right follows from the transitivity of the pervasion relation (cf. Matilal 1990: 125). The direction from right to left can be obtained by applying the rule of universal instantiation: If $S \subseteq U \rightarrow H \subseteq U$ is true of all U, it is especially true of S. Now, let us negate both sides of the equivalence:

$$\frac{H \subseteq S \leftrightarrow \forall U(S \subseteq U \rightarrow H \subseteq U)}{\therefore H \nsubseteq S \leftrightarrow \exists U(S \subseteq U \wedge H \nsubseteq U)}$$

Hence, there is no pervasion *iff* there is an *upādhi* in the sense of Udayana's definition.

For Gaṅgeśa this definition is too narrow, because it does not include cases where the *upādhi* does not pervade a probandum except in conjunction with a putative probans. Consider the following example of an assumed inference: The child to be born will be dark-complexioned, since it is Mitrā's child. ("Mitrā" is the name of a woman.) An appropriate *upādhi* would be "being prenatally nourished on vegetables". This is actually a dubious *upādhi*, since the non-pervasion-condition and the pervasion-condition are supposed to be uncertain. The example will be analyzed in greater detail in section 1.7.1. In order to simplify matters, we will treat both conditions here as if they were ascertained. Thus, we are to imagine that Mitrā has five sons who are all dark-complexioned, because Mitrā's diet during her previous pregnancies consisted of vegetables, which is a necessary and sufficient cause for a human baby's dark complexion. Only in the case of her sixth son Mitrā did not stick to her vegetable diet, so that he is not going to be dark-complexioned. It is then easy to see that the example matches Gaṅgeśa's definition, whereas it is beyond the scope of Udayana's definition, since in Fig. H an unbaked pot is $\in S \setminus (H \cup U)$, whereas in the Venn diagram for Udayana's definition the corresponding segment is shaded.

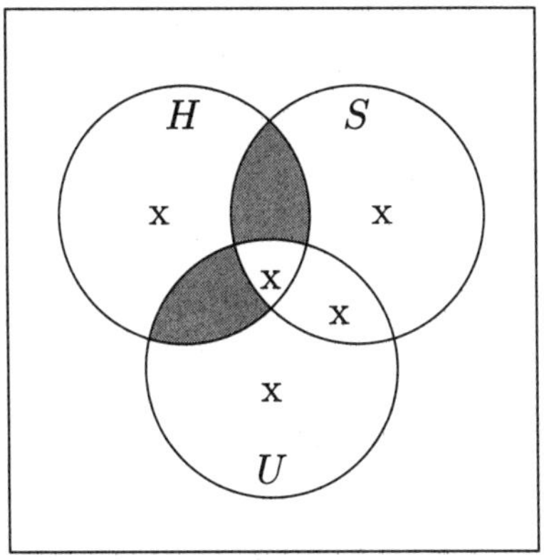

Fig. H

H = the class of loci of the probans *mitrātanayatva* ("being a son of Mitrā")

S = the class of loci of the probandum *śyāmatva* ("being dark-complexioned")

U = the class of loci of the associate condition *śākādyāhārapariṇatipūrvakatva* ("being prenatally nourished on vegetables etc.")

Mitrā's 6th son $\in H \setminus (S \cup U)$; Mitrā's first 5 sons $\in H \cap S \cap U$; an unbaked pot $\in S \setminus (H \cup U)$; someone else's dark-complexioned son nourished on vegetables $\in (S \cap U) \setminus H$; a white rabbit $\in U \setminus (H \cup S)$

In Fig. E and Fig. G the segment corresponding to $(H \cap U) \setminus S$ is not shaded. So, according to Gaṅgeśa's and Udayana's definitions the putative probans and the *upādhi* can occur in a locus where the probandum is absent. But this should not happen if the *upādhi* is supposed to be a corrector. In order to make sure that the *upādhi* functions as a corrector which secures the probandum in an assumed inference, the author of the UD adds a requirement to (G_2), the pervasion-condition of an *upādhi*: The *upādhi* should not only pervade the conjunction of probandum and putative probans (i.e., $\forall x(Hx \land Sx \rightarrow Ux)$, as in ($G_2$)). The conjunction of the *upādhi* and the putative probans should also be pervaded by the probandum (i.e., $\forall x(Hx \land Ux \rightarrow Sx)$). Thus, the pervasion relation between *upādhi* and probandum has to be symmetrical in the range of the putative probans. There should be a "coextensive pervasion" (*samavyāpti*) between both relata.

(UD_1) The associate condition does not pervade the probans and

(UD_2) it pervades the probandum coextensively in the range of the probans.[27]

In symbols:

(UD_1') $\exists x(Hx \land \neg Ux)$

(UD_2') $\underbrace{\forall x(Hx \land Sx \rightarrow Ux) \land \forall x(Hx \land Ux \rightarrow Sx)}_{\leftrightarrow \forall x(Hx \rightarrow (Sx \leftrightarrow Ux))} \land \exists x(Hx \land Sx \land Ux)$

In accordance with our understanding of Gaṅgeśa's specific defining characteristic the present one implies that (UD_1') is a (D_1)-like rebutting or undercutting defeater in the sense of Pollock's theory, while the presence of the *upādhi* functions as a corrector.

As shown in Fig. I below, the second conjunct in (UD_2'), i.e., ...

(Corr) $\forall x(Hx \land Ux \rightarrow Sx)$

... warrants the *upādhi*'s utility as a corrector: All loci where the *upādhi* co-occurs with the putative probans are loci of the probandum.

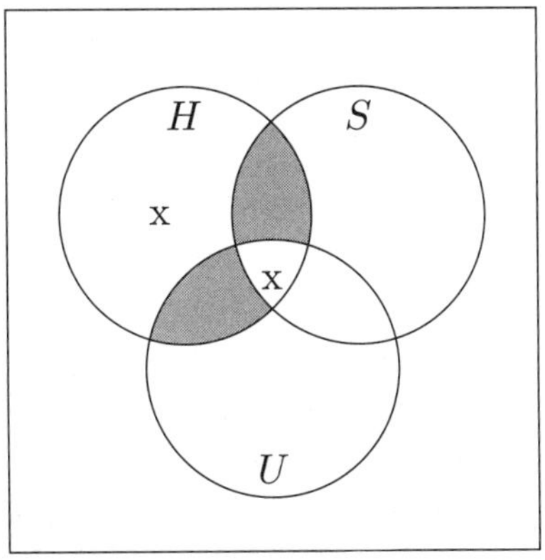

Fig. I

H = the class of loci of the probans
S = the class of loci of the probandum
U = the class of loci of the associate condition

The definition applies to the classical fire/smoke/wet fuel-example (cf. Fig. F), where the *upādhi* functions as both, a vitiator and a corrector. In this case the coextensive pervasion is restricted to the range of the probans. In the example represented in Fig. J the entire probans and the entire probandum are involved in the coextensive pervasion relation. This example is often cited as a paradigmatic example of an *upādhi* by advocates of a coextensive pervasion of the probandum by the *upādhi.*

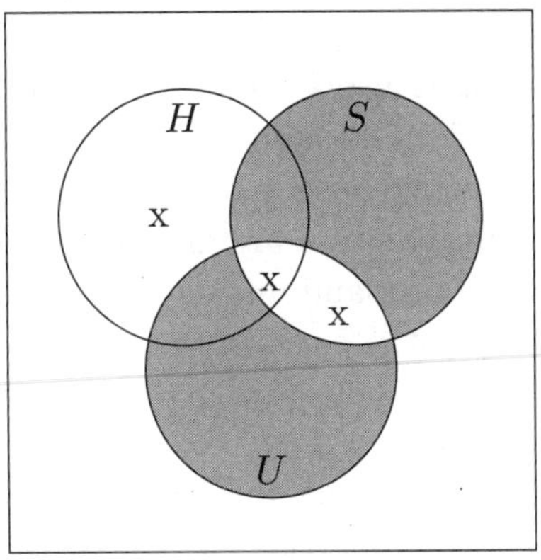

Fig. J

H = the class of loci of the probans *hiṃsātva* ("being an injury")

S = the class of loci of the probandum *adharmatva* ("being an offence")
U = the class of loci of the associate condition *niṣiddhatva* ("being forbidden")

an injury related to a sacrifice (*yāgīyahiṃsā*) $\in H \setminus (S \cup U)$; the murder of a brahmin (*brāhmaṇaghāta*) $\in H \cap S \cap U$; forbidden offences other than injuries (*hiṃsā*) $\in (S \cap U) \setminus H$

According to the UD the *upādhi*'s function as a vitiator is linked to its function as a corrector. The *upādhi* vitiates by exposing the probans as a special type of pseudo-probans, viz. the conditional probans (*vyāpyatvāsiddha*). The fallacy of the conditional probans is explained as the probans's incapacity to secure the probandum of its own accord. It needs to be fortified by means of an *upādhi* as a corrector.

However, the UD's purpose of incorporating (Corr) into the specific defining characteristic is not only to ensure that an *upādhi* can function as a corrector. By insisting on a coextensive pervasion of the probandum by the *upādhi* in the range of the probans the author of the UD tries to forestall that the specific defining characteristic pertains to the property of being different from the inferential subject (*pakṣetaratva*). If this property were ruled as an *upādhi*, it would undermine all positive and negative inferences, as we have seen above. The positive examples of a positive and negative inference can also be regarded as providing inductive support for the pervasion of the probandum by the *pakṣetaratva*. However, because of the negative examples the *pakṣetaratva* can occur in a locus of the absence of the probandum. Hence, it is not pervaded by the probandum.

Due to the equilocatability of *upādhi* and probandum (Corr) would even apply to the case of an "incoherent" (*viruddha*) pseudo-probans (*hetvābhāsa*) in inferences such as "It is a cow, because it is a horse", where the ranges of the putative probans and the probandum are disjoint. If there is a coextensive pervasion between *upādhi* and probandum, the ranges of the putative probans and the *upādhi* are also disjoint. Hence, in this case (Corr) is at least vacuously true. According to (Corr) an unlocatable property such as the ether could also be regarded as a corrector.

However, the UD seems to have misgivings about such a vacuous fulfillment of the corrector-function. Unlocatable properties like the ether are explicitly excluded by the UD's general defining characteristic of an *upādhi*, as we will see in section 1.6. According to the UD's general defining characteristic an *upādhi* has to be present somewhere. In order to restrict the scope of the specific defining characteristic to instances of an *upādhi* which actually co-occurs with the putative probans, it suffices to add the condition of existential import (cf. the third conjunct in (UD_2')). Although there is no definition of the pervasion relation in the UD, the UD's general defining characteristic seems to indicate that the condition of existential import is tacitly assumed in the UD's formulation of (UD_2).

Adding the condition of existential import affects also the *upādhi*'s applicability as a vitiator. Due to the "x" in the segment corresponding to $H \cap S \cap U$ in Fig. E and Fig. I an *upādhi* according to the definitions of Gaṅgeśa and the UD cannot vitiate an incoherent probans whose range is disjoint from the range of the probandum. In such a case the whole segment corresponding to $H \cap S$ would have to be shaded. It should be noted that an *upādhi* according to Udayana's definition is more versatile in this respect. Although the condition of pervading the entire probandum (cf. (U_2)) renders the definition inapplicable to many properties which can reasonably be regarded as *upādhis* (cf. Fig. H), it has the advantage that the condition of existential import does not have to be satisfied in the range of the putative probans. It can be satisfied in the segment corresponding to $(S \cap U) \setminus H$ instead, so that the class $H \cap S \cap U$ might be empty, as in the case of two disjoint properties chosen as probans and probandum. The UD has to resort to the fallacy of the incoherent probans in order to account for the failure of an inference such as "This is a cow, because it is a horse", since it cannot be vitiated by means of a UD-like *upādhi*.

1.6 The General Defining Characteristic of an *upādhi*

Defining an *upādhi* in relation to a putative probans and a probandum of an inference yields a so-called *viśeṣalakṣaṇa* ("specific defining characteristic"). The UD also gives us a general criterion for the kind of individuals which can be used as *upādhis*. This is the so-called *sāmānyalakṣaṇa* ("general defining characteristic").

Since an *upādhi* does not pervade the putative probans, it must be absent from some locus (cf. the "x" in the segment corresponding to $H \setminus (S \cup U)$ in Fig. I). Universally present properties (*kevalānvayidharma*) like nameability cannot function as an *upādhi*. The fact that an *upādhi* is absent somewhere can be rephrased in the technical language of Navya-Nyāya by saying that it is the counterpositive of an absolute absence (*atyantābhāvapratiyogin*). This might be a general defining characteristic of all *upādhi*s then. But it is still too general, because according to the UD the *upādhi* should pervade the probandum (coextensively). Since pervasion is a relation with existential import, the *upādhi* must also be present somewhere (cf. the "x" in the segment corresponding to $H \cap S \cap U$ in Fig. I). In the Navya-Naiyāyikas' ontology there are, however, entities like the ether and other eternal substances which do not reside in any locus. So, these must be excluded by the general defining characteristic of an *upādhi*, and for that reason an *upādhi* is also defined as a *dharma* ("property") in the UD, because: *dhriyate tiṣṭhati vartate yaḥ sa dharmaḥ. (...) yatra yo vartate sa tasya dharmaḥ.* (BN: 8, 9 – 11 = Guhe 2014: 60) – "What is fixed [somewhere], stands [somewhere or] is resident [somewhere] that is a property. (...) Whatever is resident somewhere that is a property of that [locus where it is resident]." So, the UD enunciates the following general defining characteristic of an *upādhi*: "being a property which is the counterpositive of an absolute absence" (*atyantābhāvapratiyogidharmatva*)

1.6.1 The Problem of Foundation Related to the UD's General Defining Characteristic

The *atyantābhāvapratiyogidharmatva* is itself present in some objects such as, e.g., wet fuel, which are present somewhere and absent somewhere, and it is absent from universally present properties like nameability and from unlocatable objects like the ether. Hence, it should be a property of itself. However, many Navya-Naiyāyikas regard the self-residence (*ātmāśraya*) of a property as a kind of absurdity. This might be the reason why Gaṅgeśa is reluctant to endorse the *atyantābhāvapratiyogidharmatva* as a general defining characteristic. Since, on the other hand, this property seems to be the most obvious candidate for a general defining characteristic, Gaṅgeśa rather chooses to avoid the logical pitfalls of taking a stance on this matter and simply denies the relevance of a general defining characteristic to the theory of *upādhi* (Chakrabarti 2010: 226). We will see that the Navya-Naiyāyika Maheśa Chandra explicitly rules out circular residence relations. If we want to model the intuitions of these mainstream Navya-Naiyāyikas about properties, we need a well-founded system as a framework for a formal reconstruction. By contrast, the author of the UD affirms the self-residence of the *atyantābhāvapratiyogidharmatva*. Hence, the UD's property concept is closely related to the idea of non-well-founded sets, which Peter Aczel regards as a plausible alternative to "the essentially naive but very intuitive image of a set being physically formed from its elements" (Aczel 1988: xviii).

In the following sub-sections we design three axiomatic systems which capture the different property concepts involved in logical inquiries concerning properties in Navya-Nyāya. All of them are hybrid systems based on George Bealer's property theory T1 plus property versions of the axioms of the set theory ST_2, the Ackermann set theory or NFU, excluding the axiom of extensionality in each of these systems.

T1-ST_2 and T1-A are both well-founded systems, in which we can prove many intuitions about properties advocated by Navya-Naiyāyikas who insist on a well-founded property concept, as I have shown elsewhere (cf. Guhe 2016, 2017, 2018 and 2019). T1-ST_2 and T1-A are equally well adapted to the purpose of modelling the intuitions of these Navya-Naiyāyikas. T1-A is more compact and notationally simpler than T1-ST_2. However, the abundance of axioms in T1-ST_2 turns out to be an advantage for proving certain theorems about properties. For these practical reasons we will introduce both well-founded systems here. As an aside, we will prove a T1-A-theorem concerning iterated absences which is relevant to an argument of the opponent in the *pūrvapakṣa* of the first *pariccheda* of the UD.

T1-ST_2 and T1-A are equipped with property versions of the axiom of regularity. We will show that the well-founded character of properties postulated by most Navya-Naiyāyikas can be proved from such an axiom. In contrast to T1-ST_2 and T1-A, T1-NFU is a non-well-founded system which captures the non-well-founded property concept of the UD. We will use it in particular to prove that the UD's general defining characteristic of *upādhis* is self-resident.

1.6.1.1 George Bealer's Property Theory T1 and His Quasi Set-Theoretic Extensions

T1 is equipped with a means to represent property abstraction: If $A(x)$ is a first-order formula in which x occurs free, we write $[A(x)]_x$ for "being an x such that x is A". We can also read this as "A-ness".[28] Relational abstraction can be expressed in a similar way. If R is a binary relation, we write $[xRy]_{xy}$ for "being an x and a y such that x is related to y by R".

We can also read this as "R-ness". The following axiomatization of T1 (cf. Bealer 1982: 58f) can be proved to be sound and complete:

A1: Truth-functional tautologies

A2: $\forall v_i A(v_i) \rightarrow A(t)$, where t is free for v_i in A, i.e., no free occurrence of v_i in A lies within the scope of a quantifier or a sequence of index variables in a term $[\ldots]_{v_1 \ldots v_m}$ which would bind a variable occurring in t.

A3: $\forall v_i(A \rightarrow B) \rightarrow (A \rightarrow \forall v_i B)$, where v_i is not free in A.

A4: $v_i = v_i$

A5: $v_i = v_j \rightarrow (A(v_i, v_i) \leftrightarrow A(v_i, v_j))$, where $A(v_i, v_j)$ is a formula that arises from $A(v_i, v_i)$ by replacing some (but not necessarily all) free occurrences of v_i by v_j, and v_j is free for the occurrences of v_i that it replaces.

A6: $[A]_{u_1 \ldots u_p} \neq [B]_{v_1 \ldots v_q}$, where $p \neq q$.

A7: $[A(u_1, \ldots, u_p)]_{u_1 \ldots u_p} = [A(v_1, \ldots, v_p)]_{v_1 \ldots v_p}$, where these two terms are alphabetic variants.

A8: $[A]_{u_1 \ldots u_p} = [B]_{u_1 \ldots u_p} \leftrightarrow \Box \forall u_1 \ldots \forall u_p (A \leftrightarrow B)$

A9: $\Box A \rightarrow A$

A10: $\Box(A \rightarrow B) \rightarrow (\Box A \rightarrow \Box B)$

A11: $\Diamond A \rightarrow \Box \Diamond A$

R1: If $\vdash A$ and $\vdash (A \rightarrow B)$, then $\vdash B$.

R2: If $\vdash A$, then $\vdash \forall v_i A$.

R3: If $\vdash A$, then $\vdash \Box A$.

A1 – A5 along with R1 and R2 constitute an axiomatization of first-order predicate logic including identity. A6 – A8 are specifically related to the intensional abstracts in T1. A9 – A11 and R3 are the modal part of the axiomatic system S5 of propositional modal logic.

A8 is a kind of counterpart of the axiom of extensionality in set theory. It captures the idea that for property terms identity is tantamount to necessary equivalence.[29] Navya-Naiyāyikas were well aware that the extensional equivalence of two predicates is not a sufficient condition for the identification of the property terms which are abstracted from these predicates. Thus, they did not equate properties like "being created" (*kṛtakatva*) and "being non-eternal" (*anityatva*), although the class of everything which is created and the class of all non-eternal entities were regarded as identical (cf. Matilal 1990: 131). Similarly, "knowability" (*jñeyatva*) and "nameability" (*abhidheyatva*) were conceived of as both universal, but nevertheless distinct properties (cf. Ingalls 1951: 61).

In order to adapt T1 to the purpose of providing an axiomatic basis for mathematics, Bealer adds property versions of the axioms of well-known set-theoretic systems, such as ZF, NBG or MK (aka "QM"), to the axioms of T1. Instead of a property version of the axiom of exensionality there is axiom A8 in these extensions of T1. The translation of the axioms of set theory into property-theoretic axioms is carried out in the following way: Class terms like $\{x \mid A(x)\}$ are replaced by $[A(x)]_x$. Moreover, Bealer introduces a predication relation Δ, which functions as a counterpart of the $\in$-relation in set theory (cf. Bealer 1982: 96). We read $a\Delta[A(x)]_x$ as "a possesses (or is a locus or an instance of) the property 'being an x such that A is true of x' ". By means of the Δ-relation an expression like $a \in \{x \mid A(x)\}$ can be translated into $a\Delta[A(x)]_x$.[30]

For the purpose of modelling logical inquiries concerning particulars like pots, mountains etc., urelements have to be taken into account in the targeted hybrid system. Moreover, since Navya-Naiyāyikas posit the existence of universal properties, such as, e.g., "nameability", the extension of T1 has to be patterned after a set-theoretic system which unlike ZF warrants the existence of proper classes. In an NBG- or MK-like system (with urelements) the property analogues of such proper classes, which we will call "properly class-like properties", can be proved to exist. However, since Navya-Naiyāyikas posit the existence of the universal property "nameability", nameabilityness should likewise exist.[31] It is a property which is unique to "nameability" and can be regarded as a property analogue of $\{V\}$, the singleton of the universal class, i.e., the class of all sets. We are then committed to accept "nameabilitynessness", an analogue of $\{\{V\}\}$, as a further existing property etc. One can show that the property "being a natural number" (*saṃkhyātva*) is also the analogue of a class of proper classes if we define natural numbers according to a Bealerian specification of the Navya-Nyāya concept of number (cf. Guhe 2019). However, the corresponding classes do not even exist in NBG or MK. Classes of proper classes, classes of classes of proper classes etc. will be called "hyper-classes" (Fraenkel/Bar-Hillel/Levy 1973: 142) hereafter.[32]

1.6.1.2 The System T1-ST_2

An appropriate set-theoretic system on which one can model a formal reconstruction of Navya-Nyāya logic should endorse the existence of hyper-classes. In Fraenkel/Bar-Hillel/Levy 1973 (cf. 142f) the authors design such a system by combining the set theories of MK and ZF. The resulting system ST_2 can serve as a set-theoretic prototype of the Navya-Nyāya logic of property and location if one additionally takes into account urelements.

We follow here a notational convention introduced by Mendelson for the purpose of incorporating urelements into the framework of NBG (cf. Mendelson [4]1997: 297f). He uses lower-case Latin letters (x, y, z) as restricted variables for sets, capital Latin letters (X, Y, Z) as restricted variables for classes (i.e., for sets and proper classes) and lower-case boldface Latin letters $(\mathbf{x}, \mathbf{y}, \mathbf{z})$ as variables for classes and urelements alike (cf. Mendelson [4]1997: 297). In the present property adaptation of set-theory the same kinds of variables are used for set-like properties, class-like properties (i.e., set-like, properly class-like and hyper-class-like properties) and for class-like properties and urelements, respectively.

In ST_2 with urelements $S\mathbf{x}$ (read: "$\mathbf{x}$ is a set") functions as a primitive monadic predicate. The system comprises the following axioms:

(a) A sethood axiom: Every member of a set is a set or urelement.

(b) All the axioms of MK with urelements (with due regard to the above-mentioned notational convention for variables).

(c) The axioms of ZF with all variables replaced by upper case variables.

This is a two-tier set theory with sets and urelements in the bottom tier and classes in the upper tier. (c) warrants the existence of hyper-classes in ST_2. Due to the ZF-axiom of pairing with upper-case variables one can, e.g., pair the universal class V with itself in order to obtain the hyper-class

$\{V\}$. Proper classes and hyper-classes can be elements in ST_2, but they should still be distinguishable from sets. This is achieved by adding (a), which ensures that proper classes and hyper-classes cannot be elements of sets.

A property-theoretic counterpart of ST_2 with urelements can be obtained by transforming (a), (b) and (c) into the corresponding property versions. Only the variants of the axiom of extensionality in (b) and (c) have to be exlcuded, because there is already a criterion for the identification of intensional abstracts in T1, namely A8. The extension of T1 which includes the above-mentioned axioms of a property adaptation of (a), (b) and (c) (exluding the variants of the axiom of extensionality in (b) and (c)) will be called "T1-ST_2" hereafter.

In T1-ST_2 the notion of a set-like property is taken as primitive. Unlike set-like properties and urelements properly class-like properties and hyper-class-like properties cannot be loci of set-like properties in the sense of the Δ-relation. So, if $\mathbf{x}\Delta y$, then for some set-like property x or urelement a, $x = \mathbf{x}$ or $a = \mathbf{x}$.

However, a properly class-like property or a hyper-class-like property can be a locus of a hyper-class-like property. If $X = [N(\mathbf{x})]_{\mathbf{x}}$ (where $[N(\mathbf{x})]_{\mathbf{x}}$ stands for "nameability"), then $X = [N(\mathbf{x})]_{\mathbf{x}} \vee X = [N(\mathbf{x})]_{\mathbf{x}}$. Hence, according to the property version of the axiom of pairing in (c), $[N(\mathbf{x})]_{\mathbf{x}}\Delta[X = [N(\mathbf{x})]_{\mathbf{x}}]_X$, i.e., nameability is a locus of nameabilityness.

1.6.1.3 The System T1-A

Instead of property versions of the axioms of ST_2 we might as well add property versions of the axioms of the Ackermann set theory including foundation and urelements to T1 (cf. Ackermann 1956: 344 and Fraenkel/Bar-Hillel/Levy 1973: 148f). We can prove the same theorems about sets in the Ackermann set theory as in ZF. Moreover, the Ackermann set theory also warrants the existence of proper classes and it even warrants the existence of $\wp^n V$ for any natural number n. However, proving the existence of such classes is more difficult in the Ackermann set theory than in ST_2, where this follows immediately from the axioms.[33]

On the other hand, in ST_2 we have to distinguish between two types of variables. If we take into account urelements (cf. above), we even end up with three types of variables. In the Ackermann set theory with urelements there is only one type of variables, typographically represented by means of lower-case Latin letters (x, y, z). Because of its notational simplicity and due to the fact that the Ackermann set theory consists of fewer axioms than ST_2 it seems convenient to pattern the targeted hybrid system after the Ackermann set theory. Only Ackermann's axiom of comprehension for classes, his axiom of comprehension for sets, his axiom of heredity and subsets and his axiom of regularity need to be transformed into property versions. Since there is A8 in T1 as a criterion for the identity between property terms, Ackermann's axiom of extensionality is of no purpose here.[34] Thus, an Ackermann-style extension of T1 (called "T1-A") can be obtained by adding the following axioms to T1:

(α^*) $\forall x(A(x) \rightarrow Ox) \rightarrow \forall x(x\Delta[A(y)]_y \leftrightarrow A(x))$, where x is free for y in A and vice versa.

(β^*) $Ox_1 \wedge \cdots \wedge Ox_n \rightarrow (\forall y(A_0(y) \rightarrow Oy) \rightarrow S[A_0(y)]_y \wedge \forall u(u\Delta[A_0(y)]_y \leftrightarrow A_0(u)))$

(γ^*) $Sx \wedge (y\Delta x \vee \forall z(z\Delta y \rightarrow z\Delta x)) \rightarrow Oy$

(δ^*) $Sx \wedge \exists y(y\Delta x) \rightarrow \exists y(y\Delta x \wedge \neg\exists z(z\Delta y \wedge z\Delta x))$

Ox (read: "x is an object") is defined by means of the primitive monadic predicates S and U: Ox *iff*$_{\text{df}}$ $Sx \vee Ux$. Sx and Ux translate into "x is set-like" and "x is an urelement", respectively. $A(y)$ denotes a wff in which y is free. $A_0(y)$ denotes a wff in which y is free and in which the predicate S does not occur. In (β^*) $x_1, \ldots, x_n$ are supposed to be the free variables in $A_0(y)$ apart from y. The antecedent $Ox_1 \wedge \cdots \wedge Ox_n$ is obsolete if there are no other free variables in $A_0(y)$ apart from y. Although our property-theoretic adaptation of the Ackermann set theory with urelements admits the existence of properties whose instances are properly class-like, a term of the form $[A(y)]_y$ will be understood here in the sense of "being an object y such that A is true of y" (cf. Fraenkel/Bar-Hillel/Levy 1973: 149, where class terms of the form $\{x \mid A(x)\}$ with the intended meaning "the class of all sets x such that $A(x)$" are introduced in the Ackermann set theory without urelements).

The utility of T1-A for proving intuitions about properties in Navya-Nyāya can be illustrated by means of the following example: In the *pūrvapakṣa* of the first *pariccheda* of the UD (cf. UD: 3b, 15) the opponent suggests a purportedly equivalent reformulation of the expression "any one of the triad" (*tattrayānyatama*) in terms of the elementary ontological categories of Navya-Nyāya ontology. The three items in the triad he is referring to are three types of *upādhis* as loci of three tentative specific defining characteristics $[C_1x]_x$, $[C_2x]_x$ and $[C_3x]_x$. Since each $[C_ix]_x$ has been proved to be too narrow by the respondent, the opponent suggests that an *upādhi* might be adequately defined by the "disjunction" of the three (i.e., by the property which is abstracted from $C_1x \vee C_2x \vee C_3x$), so that they complement each other. Hence, an *upādhi* can be said to be an instance of $[C_1x \vee C_2x \vee C_3x]_x$.

The expression "any one of many" (*anyatama*) has no obvious ontological correlate according to the Navya-Nyāya system of ontological categories. In order to ensure that it nevertheless denotes an entity, the opponent paraphrases it by means of the two types of "absence" in Navya-Nyāya, viz. 1) "mutual absence" (*anyonyābhāva*), aka "difference" (*bheda*), and 2) "relational absence" (*saṃsargābhāva*), aka "absolute absence" (*atyantābhāva*).[35]

Following Bealer, who names property operators after their corresponding first-order operators, both types of absence can be regarded as the result of "negating" a property term: "..., what is the most obvious relation between $[Fx]_x$ and $[\neg Fx]_x$? As before, the second is the negation of the first." (Bealer 1982: 47)

The term $[\neg Fx]_x$ may serve as a formal representation of the "mutual absence" *of*, i.e., of the "difference" *from* an F (more accurately: from anything which is an F). The indefinite article has been added here in front of F in order to facilitate a smooth English translation. In Sanskrit there is no article. A phrase like "the mutual absence of a piece of cloth" is commonly expressed by means of a compound (*paṭānyonyābhāva*) and the literal meaning would be "cloth-mutual-absence". Similarly, "the relational absence of a pot" would be rendered as a compound which literally translates into "pot-relational-absence" (*ghaṭasaṃsargābhāva*). When asked to specify the absentees, the so-called "counterpositives" (*pratiyogin*) of these absences, a Navya-Naiyāyika might say "cloth" (*paṭa*) and "pot" (*ghaṭa*), where "cloth" and "pot" are usually meant in the sense of expressions which refer to any piece of cloth or any pot, respectively. In order to emphasize that no reference to one particular pot or piece of cloth is intended here, a Navya-Naiyāyika might say that in these cases the counterpositiveness is "limited" (*avacchinna*) by clothness or potness, respectively. On the other hand, by adding a demonstrative like "this" (*etad*) in front of "cloth" or "pot" he might indicate that these expressions are meant in the sense of singular terms.

One can regard $[\neg Fx]_x$ as a shorthand version of the following formalization, which duly mirrors the fact that Navya-Naiyāyikas conceive of a mutual absence, i.e., of a difference, as a denial of an identity between the absentee and the locus of the absence:

(†) $[\neg\exists y(Fy \wedge x = y)]_x$

The "relational absence" of an F (more accurately: of anything which is an F) can be construed as a property which characterizes something as being devoid of (or: no locus of) anything which is an F. Sometimes it is called "absolute absence" (*atyantābhāva*) or simply "absence" (*abhāva*). This property will be formalized here by means of the dyadic predicate L with the intended meaning "... is a locus of ...". L is supposed to be a more general occurrence relation than the Δ-relation in the sense that xLy might also be true if y is an urelement. Thus, one can infer xLy from $x\Delta y$, but not vice versa.

Using the L-relation for the purpose of formalizing a relational absence is appropriate in cases where there is no specification of the occurrence relation which fails to subsist between the absentee and the locus of the absence. Thus, an unspecified relational absence can be formalized in the following way:

(‡) $[\neg\exists y(Fy \wedge xLy)]_x$

If the relational absence is more specifically meant in the sense of a relational absence via contact or inherence etc., one can replace L by the corresponding symbols for these relations (such as, e.g., C or I).

Since the present formalization of relational absences has basically the same syntactic structure as a mutual absence, namely $[\neg\phi(x)]_x$, where $\phi(x) :\leftrightarrow \exists y(Fy \wedge xLy)$, one can also regard a relational absence as a negation, i.e., as the negation of the property "being a locus of an F" ($[\exists y(Fy \wedge xLy)]_x$). Possessing a relational absence of an F means to be different from a locus of an F. So, a relational absence turns out to be a special case of a mutual absence. Both can be regarded as negations.

Navya-Naiyāyikas see the essential difference between the two types of absence in the relation by which the absentee fails to reside in the locus of the absence. In the case of mutual absence this relation is identity. In the case of relational absence it is some kind of occurrence relation. This distinctive feature is duly mirrored in the present formalizations (†) and (‡), because they differ only with respect to the relations (L and $=$).

An absence can also be the absentee of another absence. Navya-Naiyāyikas study such iterated absences with respect to the question whether they are reducible to some simpler properties. The Navya-Naiyāyika Mathurānātha, e.g., equates the relational absence of the difference from a pot with the property "potness" (cf. Guhe 2016 and 2017). The same kind of iterated absence is involved in the above-mentioned passage of the UD concerning the disjunction of three defining characteristics of an *upādhi*, which an opponent in a *pūrvapakṣa* suggests as a new defining characteristic. He explicates the expression "one of the triad" (i.e., "an x such that $C_1x \vee C_2x \vee C_3x$ is true of x") by means of the expression "the absolute absence of the mutual absence of this triad": *etattrayānyonyābhāvātyantābhāva eva tattrayānyatamam asti.* (UD: 3b, 15)

There is, however, a blunder here: Being an instance of $[C_1x]_x$, $[C_2x]_x$ or $[C_3x]_x$ can reasonably be understood in the sense of *possessing* the absolute absence of the mutual absence of the triad. Anything which is an instance of one of the three should be a locus of the absence of the difference from anything which is not an instance of either of the three. However, since the compound *etattrayānyonyābhāvātyantābhāva* is masculine here, it cannot be a Bahuvrīhi referring to the neuter *tattrayānyatamam.* The author might have forgotten to equip the compound *etattrayānyonyābhāvātyantābhāva* with a neuter ending.

Another way to fix the opponent's claim is to add an abstract suffix to *tattrayānyatamam.* The resulting statement ...

(∗) "The property of being one of the triad (*tattrayānyatamatvam*) is the absolute absence of the mutual absence of this triad."

... has the same structure as the above-mentioned identity between potness and the absence of the difference from a pot, which we proved in Guhe 2016 and 2017 by means of the axioms of T1-ST_2. In the present section we will provide a proof of (∗) in the notationally simpler system T1-A. For that purpose we formalize the property of being a C_1-like, a C_2-like or a C_3-like *upādhi* as $[C_1x \vee C_2x \vee C_3x]_x$. Hereafter, we will abbreviate this term as $[A(x)]_x$, where $A(x) :\leftrightarrow C_1x \vee C_2x \vee C_3x$. The mutual absence of the triad can be understood in the sense of the difference from anything which is C_1, C_2 or C_3, i.e., in the sense of $[\neg A(x)]_x$. The formalization of the absolute absence of the mutual absence of the triad ensues from substituting Fy in (‡) by $y = [\neg A(x)]_x$. Thus, (∗) can be formalized as follows:

THEOREM (in T1-A):
$[\neg\exists y(y = [\neg A(x)]_x \wedge x\Delta y)]_x = [A(x)]_x$

PROOF:

A1, R2	$\forall x(\neg A(x) \wedge Ox \rightarrow Ox)$
(α^*)	$\forall x(\neg A(x) \wedge Ox \rightarrow Ox) \rightarrow \forall x(x\Delta[\neg A(x) \wedge Ox]_x \leftrightarrow \neg A(x) \wedge Ox)$
R1	$\forall x(x\Delta[\neg A(x) \wedge Ox]_x \leftrightarrow \neg A(x) \wedge Ox)$
A2, R1	$x\Delta[\neg A(x) \wedge Ox]_x \leftrightarrow \neg A(x) \wedge Ox$
A1, R1	$x \not\Delta [\neg A(x) \wedge Ox]_x \leftrightarrow A(x) \vee \neg Ox$
A1, R1	$Ox \wedge x \not\Delta [\neg A(x) \wedge Ox]_x \leftrightarrow Ox \wedge (A(x) \vee \neg Ox)$
A1, R1	$Ox \wedge x \not\Delta [\neg A(x) \wedge Ox]_x \leftrightarrow Ox \wedge A(x)$
A1 – A5, R1, R2	$Ox \wedge \neg\exists y(y = [\neg A(x) \wedge Ox]_x \wedge x\Delta y) \leftrightarrow Ox \wedge A(x)$[36]
R2, R3	$\Box\forall x(Ox \wedge \neg\exists y(y = [\neg A(x) \wedge Ox]_x \wedge x\Delta y) \leftrightarrow Ox \wedge A(x))$
A8, R1	$[Ox \wedge \neg\exists y(y = [\neg A(x) \wedge Ox]_x \wedge x\Delta y)]_x = [Ox \wedge A(x)]_x$
	$[\neg\exists y(y = [\neg A(x)]_x \wedge x\Delta y)]_x = [A(x)]_x$[37] ■

1.6.1.4 The System T1-NFU

The property logic T1-NFU, which we use to model the UD's non-well-founded property concept, is patterned after NFU (Quine's New Foundation with urelements). NFU has only two axioms (comprehension and extensionality) and one type of variables. The NFU axiom of extensionality is obsolete in the present context. So, one might just reformulate the NFU comprehension axiom:

(C_{NFU}) $\exists y\forall x(x \in y \leftrightarrow A(x))$, where y is not free in A and A is stratified, i.e., it is possible to index the variables in A such that $\in$ occurs only between variables with consecutive indices (cf. Fraenkel/Bar-Hillel/Levy 1973: 161f and Quine 1973: 210f).

Since $x = x$ is stratified, one can prove in NFU that $V \in V$. Similarly, one can prove the self-residence of a universal property by means of the following property adaptation of the NFU comprehension axiom:

($\mathrm{C}_{\mathrm{T1\text{-}NFU}}$) $\forall x(x\Delta[A(y)]_y \leftrightarrow A(x))$, where $A(x)$ is "stratified" with respect to the Δ-relation and x is free for y in A and vice versa.

1.6.1.5 Advocates of a Well-Founded Property Concept

In standard systems of set theory the axiom of regularity (or "foundation") excludes the existence of sets which are elements of themselves or – generally speaking – the existence of (potentially looping) infinite sequences $(a_n)_{n\in\mathbb{N}}$ such that $a_{i+1} \in a_i$ for all $i \in \mathbb{N}$:

(R_{ZF}) $\forall x(\exists y(y \in x) \rightarrow \exists y(y \in x \wedge \neg\exists z(z \in x \wedge z \in y)))$ ("Every non-empty set x contains an element y which is disjoint from x.")

THEOREM (in ZF):
$\neg\exists(a_n)_{n\in\mathbb{N}}\forall i \in \mathbb{N}(a_{i+1} \in a_i)$

PROOF:
If an infinite series $(a_n)_{n\in\mathbb{N}}$ such that $a_{i+1} \in a_i$ for all $i \in \mathbb{N}$ did exist, then there would be a set $x = \{a_1, a_2, a_3, \dots\}$ and $\forall a_i(a_i \in x \rightarrow a_{i+1} \in a_i \cap x)$, i.e., no element of x would be disjoint from x. But according to (R_{ZF}) there is no such set x. ■

The majority of Naiyāyikas would endorse a property analogue of the axiom of foundation, which excludes looping or infinitely descending chains of properties, where each property depends on the successor as its locus. Looping chains of dependence relations involving one member (*ātmāśraya* – "self-dependence"), two members (*anyonyasaṃśraya* – "mutual dependence") or more than two members (*cakrakāśraya* – "circularity"), and the regressus ad infinitum (*anavasthā* – literally: "ungroundedness") have no ontological footing in early Nyāya.[38] Any kind of epistemic ungroundedness resulting from the admission of such dependence relations between cognitions should likewise be ruled out. The early Naiyāyika Varadarāja associates these phenomena with the fallacy of the "essentially unestablished" (*svarūpāsiddha*) probans:

ātmāśrayas tathānyonyasaṃśrayaś cakrakāśrayaḥ/
anavasthety amī tarkāḥ svarūpāsiddhihetavaḥ// (TR: 234f)

"Self-dependence and also mutual dependence, circularity,
the regressus ad infinitum – these instances of hypothetical reasoning are the causes of the [probans's] being essentially unestablished."

The terms *ātmāśraya*, *anyonyasaṃśraya*, *cakrakāśraya* and *anavasthā* are not only used with reference to dependence relations, but also with reference to instances of "hypothetical reasoning" (*tarka*). In contrast to the afore-mentioned instances of hypothetical reasoning (cf. section 1.3.1.2), which are "favorable *tarkas*" (*anukūlatarka*), the cases of hypothetical reasoning which Varadarāja is referring to here are "unfavorable *tarka*s" (*pratikūlatarka*). "Counterfactual reasoning against an apparent (false but credible) inference, i.e., *pratikūla-tarka*, "unfavorable *tarka*", is an inferential blocker, showing that the target is wrong." (Phillips 2002: 94) "Self-dependence" (*ātmāśraya*), e.g., is a *tarka* because of the undesirable consequence that a property would be split up into two entities if it were a locus of itself (cf. Solomon 1976: 485). The above-mentioned *tarka*s can function as inferential blockers in cases in which we would encounter an instance of ungroundedness if the probans's presence on the inferential subject were deemed possible. The probans would then turn out to be "essentially unestablished" (*svarūpāsiddha*), i.e., it would qualify as a type of pseudo-probans whose presence on the inferential subject "is in doubt" (cf. Matilal 1990: 51).[39]

A respondent in the *pūrvapakṣa* of the UD cites Varadarāja's verse (cf. UD: 2a, 10) to support his view that the property of being an *upādhi* cannot be inferred from a general defining characteristic *u* whose cognition depends on the cognition of the property of being an *upādhi*, so that the definition of the *upādhi* by means of *u* proves to be circular. *u* would have to be regarded as "essentially unestablished" if it is used as a probans in an inference such as: "This is an *upādhi*, because it possesses *u*." According to the respondent a self-resident property is another type of nominal property, which cannot function as a genuine probans in an inference. Thus, he regards both, epistemic and ontological ungroundedness, as potential sources of the fallacy of the "essentially unestablished" probans.

Similarly, Maheśa Chandra insists on the well-foundedness of the residence relation, which he characterizes as irreflexive and asymmetric. So, there can be no loops involving one or two members: *saṃbandho yadyapy ubhayaniṣṭho yathā kuṇḍabadarayoḥ saṃbandhaḥ kuṇḍe badare cāsti tathāpi kenacit saṃbandhena kaścid eva kutracid eva tiṣṭhati. yathā saṃyogena saṃbandhena kuṇḍa eva badaraṃ tiṣṭhati na tu badare kuṇḍam. evaṃ bhūtala eva ghaṭo vartate na tu ghaṭe bhūtalam iti. atra kāraṇam etat. saṃbandhasyaikaṃ pratiyogi. aparaṃ cānuyogi bhavati. yasya saṃbandhasya yat pratiyogi bhavati tena saṃbandhena tad eva tiṣṭhati. yac ca yasya saṃbandhasyānuyogi bhavati tena saṃbandhena tatra pratiyogi tiṣṭhati. yathā kuṇḍabadarayoḥ saṃyoge badaraṃ pratiyogi kuṇḍaṃ cānuyogīti kuṇḍe badaraṃ vartate. dharmadharmiṇoḥ saṃbandhasya dharmaḥ pratiyogī dharmi cānuyogi bhavati. ata eva dharma eva dharmiṇi vartate na tu dharmi dharme.* (BN: 12, 19f = Guhe 2014: 72) – "Although a relation is situated in both [things], such as the relation between pot and dried ginger in a pot and in dried ginger, something nevertheless depends on something via a certain relation. Dried ginger, e.g., is in the pot on account of the relation contact, but the pot is not in dried ginger. In the same way the pot occurs on the ground, but not the ground on the pot. Here is this the reason: One is the adjunct of the relation and the other is the subjunct. That is the adjunct of that relation which depends [on something] via that relation. And that is the subjunct of that relation on which the adjunct depends via that relation. In the case of the contact of the pot and the dried ginger, e.g., the dried ginger is in the pot, because the dried ginger is the adjunct and the pot is the subjunct. In the case of property and property bearer the property is the adjunct of the relation and the property bearer is the subjunct. Therefore, the property occurs on the property bearer, but not the property bearer on the property."

The existence of self-resident properties is explicitly denied in the following passage: *ata eva pratiyogyanuyoginor abhede 'pi ghaṭe ghaṭo nāstīti saṃsargābhāvapratītiḥ.* (BN: 17, 16f = Guhe 2014: 86) – "Therefore, when there is no difference between adjunct and subjunct, there is the cognition of the relational absence 'A pot is not in a (i.e., in the same) pot'." This statement should be understood in a more general sense, since the word "pot" (*ghaṭa*) is used in Navya-Nyāya as a kind of dummy singular term and in some contexts it can have the function of a variable (cf. Matilal 1968: 23).

In order to exclude the existence of infinitely descending or looping chains of dependence relations for properties (in accordance with Maheśa Chandra's misgivings about such phenomena) one can postulate the following property-theoretic version of the MK-axiom of regularity (cf. Mendelson 1997: 302), which is part of T1-ST$_2$:

$$(\mathrm{R}_{\text{T1-ST}_2})\ \forall X(\exists \mathbf{y}(\mathbf{y}\Delta X) \rightarrow \exists \mathbf{y}(\mathbf{y}\Delta X \wedge \forall \mathbf{z}(\mathbf{z}\Delta X \rightarrow \neg \mathbf{z}\Delta \mathbf{y})))$$

THEOREM (in T1-ST$_2$):
$\neg\exists(a_n)_{n\in\mathbb{N}}\forall i \in \mathbb{N}(a_{i+1}\Delta a_i)$

PROOF:
Assume indirectly: There is a sequence $(a_n)_{n\in\mathbb{N}}$ such that $\forall i \in \mathbb{N}(a_{i+1}\Delta a_i)$. Let X be a property whose loci are the members of $(a_n)_{n\in\mathbb{N}}$, i.e., $X = [\exists n \in \mathbb{N}(x = a_n)]_x$.[40] $\Rightarrow \forall a_i(a_i\Delta X \rightarrow a_{i+1}\Delta a_i \wedge a_{i+1}\Delta X)$. $\Rightarrow \forall a_i(a_i\Delta X \rightarrow \exists \mathbf{z}(\mathbf{z}\Delta X \wedge \mathbf{z}\Delta a_i))$, which contradicts $(\mathrm{R}_{\text{T1-ST}_2})$. ■

1.6.1.6 The UD's Non-Well-Founded Property Concept and the Self-Residence of the UD's General Defining Characteristic

The author of the UD does not approve of any such restriction (cf. Guhe 2015). He affirms the existence of non-well-founded properties *svasmin svavṛttitvābhyupagamena* (UD: 4a, 4f), i.e., "by assenting to the occurrence of something in itself".

The axiom of regularity, which captures the idea of well-foundedness in standard systems of set theory, is relatively independent, i.e., it is possible to construct models for the other axioms of these systems in which it fails. So, the assumption of such an axiom is optional from a logical point of view. Some set theorists just leave it out: "It therefore seems prudent (...), not to assume the axiom of foundation. In practice that is no great concession, however, since we shall focus exclusively on grounded collections (i.e. sets) in everything that we do from now on. Readers who believe there are ungrounded collections as well will thus find nothing here with which they can reasonably disagree: the most they are entitled to is a mounting sense of frustration that I am silent about them." (Potter 2004: 53)

By contrast, set theorists like Peter Aczel replace the axiom of regularity by an anti-foundation axiom, which "expresses, in a particular way, that every possible non-well-founded set exists." (Aczel 1988: xviii) It is especially designed to provide solutions to certain equations which cannot be solved in standard systems of set theory. Thus, in Aczel's non-well-founded set theory the reflexive set Ω is the solution of the equation $x = \{x\}$.

It would surely be hazardous to incorporate a similar anti-foundation axiom referring to properties into a formal reconstruction of the logical framework of the UD. In Navya-Nyāya there is no solution to the equation $x = x$-*tva*. However, in order to model non-well-founded intuitions about properties, such as in the UD, one might want to adopt the idea of a stratified comprehension embodied in the NFU comprehension axiom. Stratified comprehension can be used to prove the self-residence of the UD's general defining characteristic of an *upādhi*.

This defining characteristic ("being present somewhere and absent somewhere") applies to urelements and properties alike. However, if an urelement x (such as wet fuel) functions as an associate condition with respect to an assumed inference, we can always replace x by the equilocatable property x-*vattva* (such as the property "being a locus of wet fuel"), which may equally well serve as an associate condition with respect to the same inference. So, it would be sufficient to take into account only class-like properties as associate conditions and then one can use the Δ-relation in order to state the defining characteristic of an associate condition as a property ...

$$u =_{\mathrm{df}} [\exists y(y\Delta x) \wedge \exists y(y\not\Delta x)]_x.$$

THEOREM (in T1-NFU):
$\exists y(y\Delta u) \wedge \exists y(y\not\Delta u) \vdash u\Delta u$ ("If u is supposed to be present somewhere and absent somewhere, then u is self-resident.")

PROOF:
The formula $\exists y(y\Delta z) \wedge \exists y(y\not\Delta z)$ is stratified with respect to the Δ-relation. $\Rightarrow \forall z(z\Delta u \leftrightarrow \exists y(y\Delta z) \wedge \exists y(y\not\Delta z))$ by ($\mathrm{C}_{\mathrm{T1\text{-}NFU}}$). $\Rightarrow u\Delta u \leftrightarrow \exists y(y\Delta u) \wedge \exists y(y\not\Delta u)$ $(*)$ by A2. Now, u is supposed to reside in locatable properties which are not universal and to be absent from non-locatable properties and universal properties. $\Rightarrow \exists y(y\Delta u) \wedge \exists y(y\not\Delta u)$. $\Rightarrow u\Delta u$ by $(*)$. ∎

1.7 Dubious and Apparent *upādhis*

An associate condition is dubious due to epistemic ignorance with respect to at least one of the criteria of the specific defining characteristic, whereas the remaining one(s) may be dubious or ascertained. Apparent *upādhis* are properties which only appear to be *upādhis*. Thus, they fulfill or may well fulfill at least one of the criteria of the specific defining characteristic and fail to fulfill another one, whereas the remaining one may be unfulfilled, dubious or ascertained. Since the UD's specific defining characteristic comprises three criteria (non-pervasion of the probans, pervasion *of* the probandum in the range of the probans and pervasion *by* the probandum in the range of the probans), there are according to the UD $2^3 - 1 = 7$ types of dubious *upādhis* and the author might have taken into account $2^3 - 2 = 6$ types of apparent *upādhis*. However, one of the combinatorial possibilities to construct an apparent *upādhi* has been ignored by him. There might be a reason behind it, as we will see below.

By contrast, Gaṅgeśa's specific defining characteristic comprises two criteria. Hence, he distinguishes $2^2 - 1 = 3$ types of dubious *upādhis*. According to the UD's classification schema Gaṅgeśa would be committed to assume two types of apparent *upādhis*. However, Gaṅgeśa's taxonomy of apparent *upādhis* comprises ten types and it is based on the different ways in which a putative *upādhi* might fail to function as a vitiator (cf. section 1.7.3). The UD agrees with Gaṅgeśa that an associate condition can vitiate, even if it is dubious, in fact, even if all the defining criteria are dubious. Thus, the UD's and Gaṅgeśa's intuitions coincide with the position of a skeptical reasoner (cf. section 1.7.2).

1.7.1 Ascertained vs. Dubious *upādhis* – Some Examples

According to the UD an attack on (R_1) or (R_2) by means of the corresponding UD-like defeater is successful if it is based on an ascertained *upādhi*, i.e., if the *upādhi* at issue is known to fulfill the criteria of the specific defining characteristic. The proposition "There are loci of fire without wet fuel", e.g., actually rebuts the claim of evidential support consisting in a sample of co-occurring instances of fire and smoke as a prima facie reason for the putative pervasion of fire by smoke as the conclusion, because a locus like molten metal provides evidence for the existence of a locus of fire without wet fuel. So, the probans "fire" is actually not pervaded by the *upādhi* "wet fuel". Moreover, the probandum "smoke" is actually pervaded by the *upādhi* in the range of the probans, i.e., wherever there is both, fire and smoke, there is wet fuel, which is equivalent to: Wherever there is fire devoid of wet fuel, there is no smoke. This is the background information which in combination with the defeater "There are loci of fire without wet fuel" rebuts the prima facie reason for the pseudo-pervasion of fire by smoke.

A doubt may arise if the required *upādhi*'s absence in a locus of the probans is an open issue. Another occasion for doubt is the *upādhi*'s pervasion of the probandum. Even if the *upādhi* is known to be absent from a locus of the probans (cf. the Dṛṣadvatī-example below), its absence may or may not be a token of the absence of the probandum. Thus, an *upādhi*'s reliability as a vitiator could be challenged. A doubtful pervasion of the *upādhi* by the probandum affects only a subject's confidence in the *upādhi*'s function as a corrector.

In the case of the Dṛṣadvatī-example the pervasion of the associate condition by the probandum in the range of the probans and the non-pervasion of the probans by the associate condition are both warranted. Only the pervasion of the probandum by the associate condition in the range of the probans is dubious. We are to imagine that Dṛṣadvatī has five sons who are near at hand and they are all dark-complexioned. Her sixth son "has gone to another region" (*deśāntaragata*), and it is assumed that his complexion is unknown to us. Hence, if someone is a son of Dṛṣadvatī who is near at hand, then he is dark-complexioned, i.e., $(H \cap U) \setminus S = \emptyset$ in both diagrams in Fig. K. However, if someone is a son of Dṛṣadvatī who is not near at hand, then he may or may not be dark-complexioned. Both alternatives of the doubt involved in this example are represented by means of two Venn diagrams below. Following a convention introduced by Shin, we connect both of them by means of a straight line, which encodes disjunctive information. It is reminiscent of the bar across the boundary of two adjacent regions as a means to express that at least one of them is non-empty (cf. Shin/Lemmon/Mumma 2018).

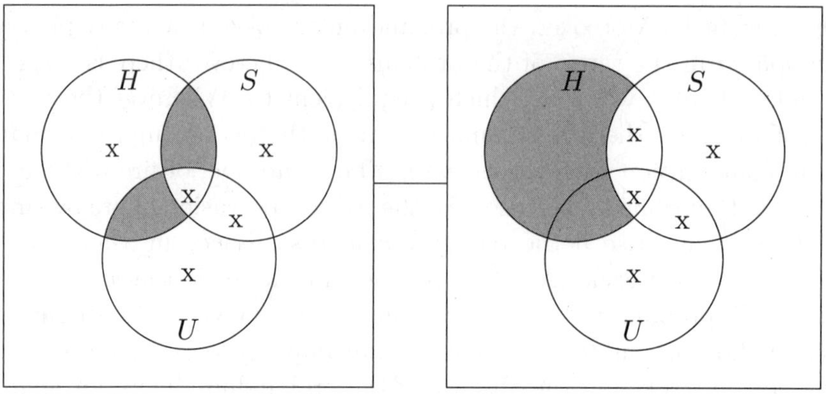

Fig. K

H = the class of loci of the probans *dṛṣadvatītanayatva* ("being a son of Dṛṣadvatī")

S = the class of loci of the probandum *śyāmatva* ("being dark-complexioned")

U = the class of loci of the associate condition *saṃnihitatva* ("being near at hand")

Dṛṣadvatī's 6th son is fair-complexioned and $\in H \setminus (S \cup U)$, or he is dark-complexioned and $\in (H \cap S) \setminus U$; Dṛṣadvatī's other 5 sons $\in H \cap S \cap U$; an unbaked pot $\in S \setminus (H \cup U)$; someone else's dark-complexioned son being near at hand $\in (S \cap U) \setminus H$; a nearby white rabbit $\in U \setminus (H \cup S)$

The Mitrā-example is understood by Gaṅgeśa in such a way that both, the non-pervasion of the probans by the probandum and the pervasion of the conjunction of probans and probandum by the associate condition, are dubious (cf. Frauwallner 1970: 59 and Phillips 2002: 19f and 111f). It is assumed that eating vegetables during pregnancy is a sufficient cause for the baby's dark complexion. Hence, $(H \cap U) \setminus S = \emptyset$ in both diagrams in Fig. L, i.e., the pervasion of the associate condition by the probandum in the range of the probans is warranted. However, the vegetable diet is not a necessary condition for the baby's dark complexion. The dark complexion may as well be genetically determined by the father's dark complexion. Moreover, Mitrā may or may not have eaten vegetables while she was pregnant with her first five sons. Therefore, her first five sons, who are dark-complexioned, are $\in (H \cap S) \setminus U$ or $\in H \cap S \cap U$ (cf. the bar across the boundary between the corresponding areas in Fig. L, which indicates an alternative). We are also not sure about Mitrā's diet during her current pregnancy. Mitrā might not have eaten vegetables during her current pregnancy, or she has so far eaten vegetables, but will not stick to her diet, until she gives birth to her sixth son. Thus, the unborn sixth son may turn out to be fair-complexioned (cf. the leftmost diagram in Fig. L). If he turns out to be dark-complexioned (cf. the rightmost diagram in Fig. L), he is like the other sons $\in H \cap S$.

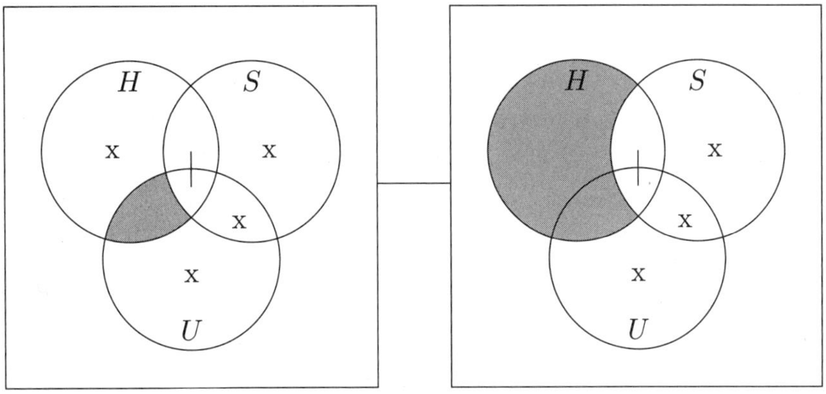

Fig. L

H = the class of loci of the probans *mitrātanayatva* ("being Mitrā's son")
S = the class of loci of the probandum *śyāmatva* ("being dark-complexioned")
U = the class of loci of the associate condition *śākādyāhārapariṇatipūrvakatva* ("being prenatally nourished on vegetables etc.")

Mitrā's 6th son is fair-complexioned and $\in H \setminus (S \cup U)$, or he is dark-complexioned and $\in H \cap S$; Mitrā's first 5 sons $\in H \cap S$; an unbaked pot $\in S \setminus (H \cup U)$; someone else's dark-complexioned son nourished on vegetables $\in (S \cap U) \setminus H$; a white rabbit $\in U \setminus (H \cup S)$

1.7.2 Credulous vs. Skeptical Reasoning

The UD agrees with Gaṅgeśa that if there is a tie between the alternatives involved in the doubt concerning the criteria of the defining characteristic of an *upādhi*, the latter can still vitiate. Thus, being faced with the alternatives between drawing the conclusion that Mitrā's unborn sixth son is dark-complexioned or not doing so, Gaṅgeśa and the UD hold that a rational agent would not choose randomly, i.e., they would distance themselves from what a credulous reasoner would do. Their position clearly coincides with that of a skeptical reasoner, i.e., they argue that the *upādhi* prevents us from drawing any conclusion. This is a situation which Pollock describes as "collective defeat" (Pollock 1995: 62). A typical example is the Nixon diamond, with two arguments "Nixon is a pacifist, because he is a Quaker" and "Nixon is not a pacifist, because he is a Republican". If there are no grounds for preferring one argument over the other, they intuitively defeat each other (cf. Fig. M).

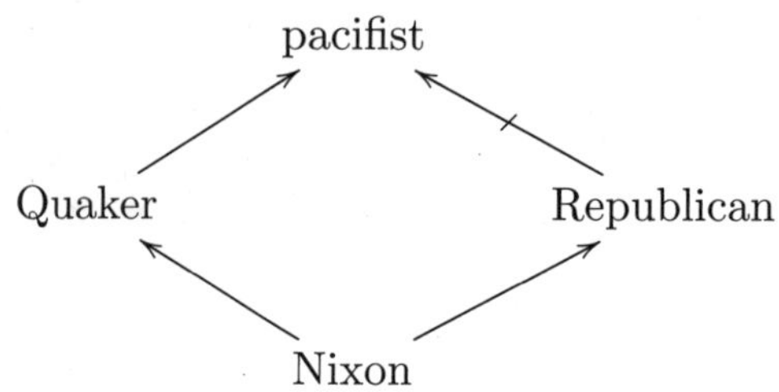

Fig. M

The Mitrā-example can also be understood along the lines of the situation of collective defeat. We will assume that Mitrā may well refrain from eating the vegetables during her current pregnancy and that not eating them may well have the effect that the baby turns out to be fair-complexioned. In this case the following diamond can be said to represent a collective defeat:

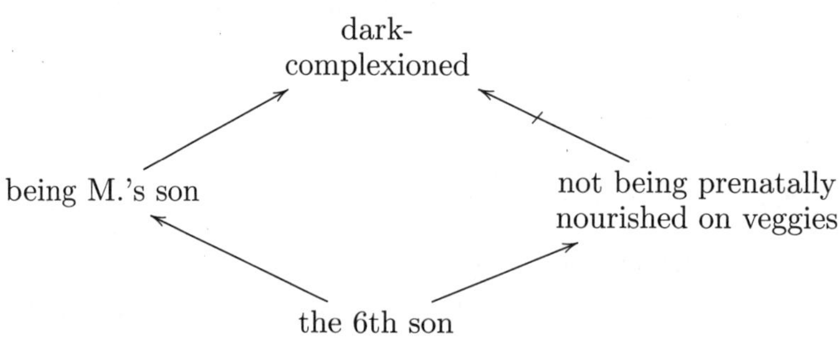

Fig. N

According to Gaṅgeśa and the UD, choosing randomly does not seem to be an option for responding to epistemic ignorance. Similarly, Pollock argues that a rational agent would rather resolve epistemic ties skeptically and withhold belief when there are equally good reasons for and against a conclusion: "The preceding considerations suggest that the controversy over skeptical and credulous reasoning stems from a confusion of epistemic reasoning with practical reasoning. In practical reasoning, if one has no basis for choosing between two alternative plans, one should choose at random. The classical illustration is the medieval tale of Buridan's ass who starved to death standing midway between two equally succulent bales of hay because he could not decide from which to eat. This marks an important difference between practical reasoning and epistemic reasoning. An agent making practical decisions must first decide what to believe and then use those beliefs in deciding what to do, but these are two different matters. If the evidence favoring two alternative hypotheses is equally good, the agent should record that fact and withhold belief. Subsequent practical reasoning can then decide what to do given that epistemic conclusion. In some cases it may be reasonable to choose one of the hypotheses at random and act as if it is known to be true, and in other cases more caution will be prescribed. But what must be recognized is that the design of the system of practical reasoning is a separate matter from the design of the system of epistemic reasoning that feeds information to the practical reasoner. Epistemic reasoning should acknowledge ignorance when it is encountered rather than drawing conclusions at random. This is what the principle of collective defeat mandates." (Pollock 1995: 64)

From the point of view of a skeptical reasoner an *upādhi* which is dubious in the sense that the *upādhi*'s non-pervasion of the probans or its pervasion of the probandum is dubious can still vitiate, insofar as it blocks an inference. However, $\exists x(Hx \wedge \neg Ux)$ and $Hs \wedge \neg Ss$ might not rebut if they are dubious. The rebutter should be a reason to believe the negation of the conclusion drawn from the rebutted prima facie reason. For a skeptical reasoner a doubt attached to these propositions incapacitates their rebutting force if there are equally good reasons for the conclusion that the probans is pervaded by the probandum or that the inferential subject is a locus of the probandum. Moreover, if $\exists x(Hx \wedge \neg Ux)$ is dubious and there are equally good reasons for the conclusion that the inferential subject is a locus of the probandum, a skeptical reasoner would not rely on $\exists x(Hx \wedge \neg Ux)$ as a reason to deny that (R_2) would not be true unless the thesis of the inference were true. So, for a skeptical reasoner $\exists x(Hx \wedge \neg Ux)$ is not an undercutter in this case.

Even if they are ascertained, the propositions $\exists x(Hx \wedge \neg Ux)$ and $Hs \wedge \neg Ss$ might not be able to function as defeaters, because their role as a rebutter or undercutter depends on the background information $\forall x(Hx \wedge \neg Ux \rightarrow \neg Sx)$, which follows from the second criterion of the defining characteristic. If the latter is dubious, there might again be equally good reasons for the conclusion that the probans is pervaded by the probandum or that the inferential subject is a locus of the probandum.

Thus, due to the dubiety of either of two criteria of an *upādhi*'s defining characteristic, viz. its non-pervasion of the probans or its pervasion of the probandum, $\exists x(Hx \wedge \neg Ux)$ and $Hs \wedge \neg Ss$ may lose their rebutting or undercutting force. Nevertheless, the *upādhi* can still vitiate in a situation of collective defeat. Instead of overruling an inference, it blocks an inference, i.e., it prevents a skeptical reasoner from drawing any conclusion.

1.7.3 Apparent *upādhi*s

The UD's taxonomy of apparent *upādhi*s seems to be incomplete. According to the UD a putative *upādhi* is apparent if it only appears to be an *upādhi*, i.e., it exhibits or may well exhibit at least one of the three features of the UD's specific defining characteristic, while it fails to exhibit at least one of the other two features. Thus, the author might have distinguished $2^3 - 2 = 6$ types of apparent *upādhi*s. However, he mentions only five of them. For the type which he ignores, viz. the combinatorial possibility which only fails to be not pervading the probans, we have concocted an example below:

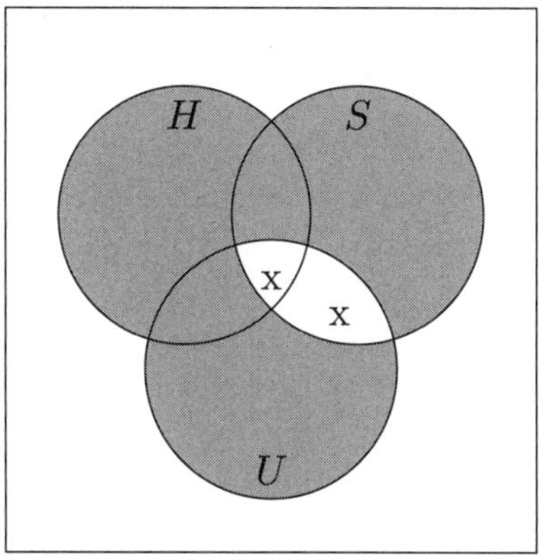

Fig. O

H = the class of loci of the probans *ghaṭatva* ("potness")
S = the class of loci of the probandum *kṛtakatva* ("being produced")
U = the class of loci of the associate condition *anityatva* ("being non-eternal")

a pot $\in H \cap S \cap U$, a piece of cloth $\in (S \cap U) \setminus H$

The reason why the author of the UD does not classify such a property as an apparent *upādhi* might be that he does not regard it as an *upādhi* at all, because its characterization ensures that the probans is genuinely pervaded by the probandum in this case: If the probans is pervaded by such a property and the latter is also pervaded by the probandum in the range of the probans, then $H \setminus S = \emptyset$, i.e., $H \subseteq S$. As the characterization of this kind of property excludes the possibility of there being an *upādhi*, it does not even appear to be an *upādhi*. This might be the reason why the author of the UD does not include it in his taxonomy of apparent *upādhi*s.

Since the UD's specific defining characteristic comprises one more criterion than the one enunciated by Gaṅgeśa, there are properties which the UD regards as apparent *upādhi*s, whereas for Gaṅgeśa they would be genuine *upādhi*s. Here is an example: *caturthodāharaṇaṃ tu kṛtakatvānumāna 'śrāvaṇatvādayaḥ.* (UD: 9a, 15) – "An example for the fourth [type] is inaudibility etc. in the case of the inference with the [property of] being produced (as a probans)." The probandum is not mentioned here, but *ghaṭatva* would be an appropriate choice, because it is pervaded by *aśrāvaṇatva*. As shown in Fig. P below, *aśrāvaṇatva* matches Gaṅgeśa's definition. However, since *aśrāvaṇatva* is not pervaded by *ghaṭatva* in the range of the probans, it is not an *upādhi* in the sense of the UD.

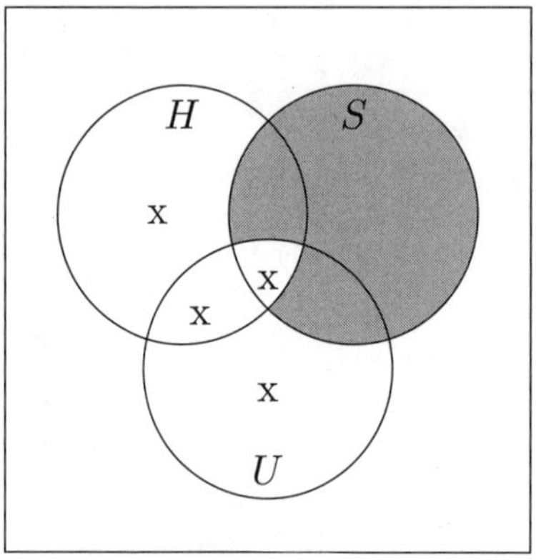

Fig. P

H = the class of loci of the probans *kṛtakatva* ("being produced")
S = the class of loci of the probandum *ghaṭatva* ("potness")
U = the class of loci of the associate condition *aśrāvaṇatva* ("inaudibility")

sound (*śabda*) $\in H \setminus (S \cup U)$; a piece of cloth $\in (H \cap U) \setminus S$; a pot $\in H \cap S \cap U$; the soul (*ātman*) $\in U \setminus (H \cup S)$

In section 1.4 we already pointed out that Pollock's "red light"-example is actually beyond the scope of the Navya-Nyāya theory of *upādhi*, because it is based on a defeasible rule of thumb (like "$WearsRing \Rightarrow Married$"), which is weaker than induction. Nevertheless, suppose for the sake of argument that the pervasion of "looking red to me" by "being red" can be inductively inferred. Moreover, let us assume that if an object which looks red to me without being illuminated by red light, is actually red. In this case "X looks red to me and X is not a locus of the absence of red light" functions as a (D_2)-like undercutter. However, the absence of red light, is only an apparent *upādhi* with respect to the probans "looking red to me" and the probandum "being red" (cf. Fig. Q, where the segment corresponding to $(H \cap S) \setminus U$ is not shaded).

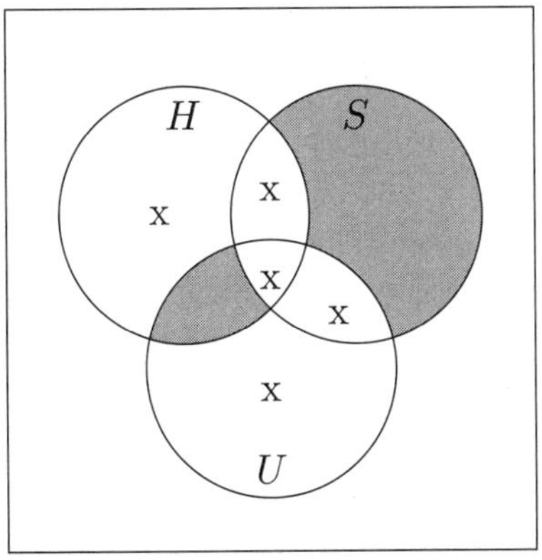

Fig. Q

H = the class of loci of the probans "looking red to me"
S = the class of loci of the probandum "being red"
U = the class of loci of the associate condition "absence of red light"

an object under red light which is not red $\in H \setminus (S \cup U)$; a red object under red light $\in (H \cap S) \setminus U$; a red object which looks red to me without being illuminated by red light $\in H \cap S \cap U$; a red object in the dark $\in (S \cap U) \setminus H$; a blue object in the dark $\in U \setminus (H \cup S)$

The object which is illuminated by red light may or may not be red. Red objects under red light look red too. An undercutter for (R_2) does not give a clue to the truth value of the conclusion drawn from (R_2). It attacks only the connection between (R_2) and the conclusion. This connection is assailable in the present example, because $\exists x(Hx \wedge \neg Ux \wedge \neg Sx) \wedge \exists x(Hx \wedge \neg Ux \wedge Sx)$ (cf. Fig. Q and the two "x's" in the segments for $H \setminus (S \cup U)$ and $(H \cap S) \setminus U$, respectively). In order to ensure that (D_2) functions as an undercutter here, it would even be off the mark to require the *upādhi* to be vitiating as an ascertained *upādhi*: The vitiating function of such an *upādhi* mandates that $\forall x(Hx \wedge \neg Ux \rightarrow \neg Sx)$, which tells us immediately that the conclusion drawn from (R_2) is false. Therefore, (D_2) can never be an undercutter if the *upādhi* is ascertained. It is only a rebutter in this case.

Pollock gives a genuine example of an undercutter of a defeasible inductive inference which is beyond the scope of the Navya-Nyāya doctrine of *upādhi*: "An important variety of undercutting defeater charges that X is not a 'fair sample'. This is easy to illustrate but hard to characterize in a general fashion. For example, suppose there is a random telephone poll of Tucson voters, and we discover to our amazement that everyone polled intends to vote for the Democratic candidate for mayor. By (7.1) (author's note: Pollock refers here to his formulation of enumerative induction.), this poll gives us a reason for believing that all Tucson voters will vote for the Democratic candidate. Now suppose it is subsequently ascertained that, purely by chance, everyone who was called in the survey was a registered Democrat, whereas only about half of the Tucson voters are Democrats. On this basis, we would reject the inductive inference, charging that the sample was not a fair one. There is no inclination to protest that the process of sampling was done incorrectly. It was, after all, a random telephone poll, and we would expect a random poll to choose an approximately equal number of Democrats and Republicans. However, upon discovering that this did not happen, it is no longer reasonable to accept the conclusion of the inductive inference. In other words, the discovery has given us a defeater for the inference. On the other hand, the discovery has not given us any reason (that we did not already have) for thinking that the conclusion is false. After all, it could happen that all of the Republicans are going to vote for the Democratic candidate. The defeater must be an undercutting defeater rather than a rebutting defeater." (Pollock 1995: 77f) The conclusion of this example of an enumerative induction is that every inhabitant of Tucson will vote for the Democratic candidate. However, if "being an inhabitant of Tucson" and "voting for the Democratic candidate" are construed here as probans and probandum, "being a registered Democrat" is only an apparent *upādhi*, because its absence in an inhabitant of Tucson may co-occur with both, the absence and the presence of the probandum. Some inhabitants of Tucson who are not registered Democrats may vote for the Republican candidate, some may vote for the Democratic candidate, even though they are Republicans. The undercutting function of the (D_1)-like proposition "Some inhabitants of Tucson (in fact, at least half of the inhabitants of Tucson) are not registered Democrats" does not depend on the background information that every inhabitant of Tucson who is not a registered Democrat will not vote for the Democratic candidate. Moreover, this is a (D_1)-like undercutter for an (R_1)-like prima facie reason, whereas the Navya-Nyāya doctrine of *upādhi* admits only (D_1)-like undercutters for (R_2)-like prima facie reasons.

Gaṅgeśa's taxonomy of apparent *upādhis*, of which we will only give a glimpse here, is based on a classification schema with ten partially overlapping types. Despite its seemingly less systematic character it offers some insightful ideas concerning the classification of the property of being different from the inferential subject by harking back to an *upādhi*'s role as a constituent of a rebutting or undercutting defeater. "Although an adjunct (author's note: This is Chakrabarti's translation of *upādhi.*) is a fault, it successfully blocks the inference of the probandum by way of showing absence of the probandum on the ground of absence of the adjunct itself." (Chakrabarti 2010: 246) Thus, a putative *upādhi* should be regarded as apparent in relation to a particular inference or pervasion *iff* the corresponding substitution instance of (D_1) or (D_2) is not a defeater, although at least one of the features of Gaṅgeśa's defining characteristic is certainly or dubiously fulfilled. This criterion can help to rule out that the property of being different from the inferential subject (*pakṣetaratva*) qualifies as a dubious *upādhi* in relation to valid inferences. It does not pervade the probans of an inference and might be said to pervade the probandum dubiously if the latter is not omnilocated. Thus, it is liable to be classified as a dubious *upādhi.* However, in Gaṅgeśa's taxonomy it is the first type of apparent *upādhis* in relation to valid inferences. In the case of the valid inference of fire from a smoke on a mountain, e.g., this property is an apparent *upādhi*, because the absence of the property of being different from the inferential subject is the property of being the inferential subject (*pakṣatva*). Thus, the corresponding substitution instance of (D_2) would be a rebutter for (R_2) if the property of being the inferential subject were a clue to the absence of the probandum. However, the mountain is an open issue with regard to the presence or absence of fire on it. Therefore, the corresponding substitution instance of (D_2) is not a reason for denying the thesis in the face of the second and the third member of the inference and it is therefore not a rebutter. Similarly, the corresponding substitution instances of (D_1) and (D_2) are no reasons for denying that smoke is pervaded by fire in the face of the evidential support. Moreover, the corresponding substitution instance of (D_1) is not a reason for denying that the conjunction of the second and the third member of the inference would not be true, unless the thesis were true, i.e., it is not a reason to believe that the conjunction of the second and the third member of the inference may well be true, even though the thesis is false, and it is therefore not an undercutter.

There are, however, cases in which the property of being different from the inferential subject proves to be useful as a vitiator. According to Gaṅgeśa "being different from the inferential subject which is induced by a patent falsehood" (*bādhonnītapakṣetaratva*) should be regarded as a genuine *upādhi* (cf. Phillips 2002: 117). It can be used to vitiate pseudo-inferences that are instances of the fallacy "patent falsehood" (*bādha*). If the thesis of an inference is "countermanded" (*bādhita*), the property of being different from the inferential subject can be a constituent of a (D_2)-like rebutter. The inference "Fire is not hot, because it is an object of knowledge (*padārtha*)", e.g., can be rebutted by means of the defeater "Fire is an object of knowledge and it is different from what is different from fire", because fire is the only object of knowledge which is hot, i.e., whatever is different from fire, is not hot. In this case, the (D_2)-like rebutter (fire is an object of knowledege $\wedge$ $\neg$(fire $\neq$ fire)) is logically equivalent to a (D_1)-like rebutter ($\exists x$(x is an object of knowledege $\wedge$ $\neg$(x $\neq$ fire))). Both are equivalent to "Fire is an object of knowledge", which rebuts (R_1) and (R_2). In this way, the above-mentioned criterion for apparent *upādhis* helps to ensure that the property of being different from the inferential subject can still be regarded as a genuine *upādhi* in the case of a countermanded thesis.

According to the UD, however, there is no need to resort to an *upādhi* in order to vitiate patent falsehoods. The defect of this type of inferences can also be traced to a violation of the inferential-subject-proviso (*pakṣatā*), which mandates that a valid inference starts with a "doubt or uncertainty which should be expressed in the form 'perhaps the subject possesses the probandum, perhaps it does not'." (Matilal 1990: 139f) Such a doubt can never arise in the case of a patent falsehood. As an aside, it is worth mentioning that, nevertheless, the property of being different from the inferential subject which is induced by a patent falsehood fulfills the criteria of the UD's specific defining characteristic, since it does not pervade the probans, while being coextensively pervaded by the probandum.

1.8 Taking Stock

According to the UD an *upādhi* functions as a vitiator and as a corrector of pseudo-inferences and of pseudo-pervasions. The defeasible character of a five-membered inference and its liability to be vitiated by an *upādhi* are owing to an inductive leap, i.e., an application of the rule of enumerative induction in the third member. It gives rise to the cognition that the probans is pervaded by the probandum. Pervasion is a nomic generalization, viz. the exceptionless universal co-occurrence of the probans with the probandum. It admits the inference of the probandum from the probans in any past, present or future inferential situation. This nomic generalization entails the material generalization which involves only the instances of probans and probandum at issue in a particular inferential situation. Existential import is tacitly presupposed. Deriving the inferential cognition, the fifth member, from the pervasion at issue and the second member is a purely deductive procedure, in which the fourth member functions as an intermediate step.

The so-called dubious *upādhi* being bracketed, an *upādhi* typically vitiates a pseudo-inference or pseudo-pervasion in the sense that its absence in a locus of the probans entails the absence of the probandum. If the locus of the absence of the probans is identical to the subject of an inference, the *upādhi* serves to demonstrate that the thesis of the inference is false. If no reference to any particular inference is intended, the *upādhi* serves to demonstrate that the purported universality of a pervasion does not hold.

If we identify a belief with its propositional content, the propositions expressing the *upādhi*'s absence (i) from the inferential subject or (ii) from some locus of the probans can be regarded as defeaters in the sense of John L. Pollock's theory of defeasible reasoning. As a rebutter for the prima facie reason which consists in the conjunction of the second and the third member of an inference (i) is a reason to deny the thesis of the inference. As rebutters for the prima facie reason which consists in the claim of evidential support (i) and (ii) are reasons to deny the purported universality of the pervasion. As an undercutter (ii) attacks the connection between the conjunction of the second and the third member of an inference as a prima facie reason and the thesis as the conclusion, i.e., it is a reason to deny that the second and the third member of an inference would not be true, unless the thesis of the inference were true.

In order to be able to function as a rebutter or as an undercutter, Naiyāyikas require (i) and (ii) to entail the proposition expressing the probandum's absence from the inferential subject or from a locus of the probans in general. This is achieved by requiring the *upādhi* to pervade the probandum in the range of the probans. Thus, Gaṅgeśa's specific defining characteristic of an *upādhi* comprises both, the *upādhi*'s non-pervasion of the probans (i.e., its absence in a locus of the probans) and its pervasion of the probandum in the range of the probans. In accordance with Pollock's theory of defeasible reasoning we can also read this specific defining characteristic as: "The proposition expressing the *upādhi*'s absence in a locus of the probans is a rebutter of the claim of evidential support and an undercutter of the conjunction of the second and the third member of an inference".

According to the UD the *upādhi*'s function as a vitiator is linked to its function as a corrector. The *upādhi* vitiates by exposing the probans as a special type of pseudo-probans, viz. the so-called "conditional probans" (*vyāpyatvāsiddha*). The fallacy of the conditional probans is explained as the probans's incapacity to secure the probandum of its own accord. It needs to be fortified by means of an *upādhi* as a corrector. In order to ensure that the *upādhi* can function as a corrector, the author of the UD requires the *upādhi* to pervade the probandum coextensively, i.e., his specific defining characteristic is the one advocated by Gaṅgeśa plus the additional requirement of the pervasion of the *upādhi* by the probandum.

The UD's specific defining characteristic pertains to the property of being different from the inferential subject (*pakṣetaratva*) in cases in which the thesis of an inference is countermanded. However, the author of the UD does not regard the property of being different from the inferential subject which is induced by a patent falsehood (*bādhonnītapakṣetaratva*) as a genuine *upādhi*. Since the defect of a patent falsehood can also be said to be owing to a violation of the inferential-subject-proviso (*pakṣatā*), an *upādhi* is not needed as a vitiator in this case. The UD's insistence on a pervasion of the *upādhi* by the probandum prevents the property of being different from the inferential subject from turning into a universal *upādhi* as a vitiator of all positive and negative inferences.

According to the UD there is also a general defining characteristic of all *upādhi*s, viz. the property of being present somewhere and of being absent somewhere else (*atyantābhāvapratiyogidharmatva*). It pertains to everything which is a candidate for being used as an *upādhi* in some inference: Since an *upādhi* does not pervade the probans, it has to be absent somewhere. Since its (coextensive) pervasion of the probandum is associated with existential import, it also needs to be present somewhere.

The property of being present somewhere and of being absent somewhere else resides in all locatable properties which are (unlike nameability etc.) not omnilocatable and it is absent from all unlocatable properties (such as, e.g., the ether). Hence, this property seems to be a locus of itself. Although self-dependence (*ātmāśraya*) is normally regarded as an absurdity in Nyāya, the author of the UD regards it as unobjectionable wherever it manifests itself in the form of self-residence. Only self-dependence in the form of self-causation or epistemic ungroundedness should be regarded as inadmissible. The author of the UD advocates a non-well-founded property concept. In a property calculus such as T1-NFU the self-residence of his general defining characteristic turns out to be a theorem.

An *upādhi* is dubious if one of the three criteria of the specific defining characteristic is dubious in the sense that the alternatives of its fulfillment and its non-fulfillment are equally matched. A doubt concerning (i) the *upādhi*'s non-pervasion of the probans or (ii) its pervasion *of* the probandum affects its utility as a vitiator. A doubt concerning (iii) its pervasion *by* the probandum affects only a subject's confidence in the *upādhi*'s utility as a corrector.

The UD's intuitions about doubt due to epistemic ignorance coincide with that of a skeptical reasoner. If there are equally good reasons for and against drawing a conclusion (i.e., in a situation of collective defeat) the UD holds that a rational agent does not behave like a credulous reasoner and choose randomly, but rather like a skeptical reasoner, who resolves epistemic ties by withholding belief. In the case of a doubt concerning (i) or (ii) skeptical reasoning mandates not to draw any conclusion from the conjunction of the second and the third member of an inference or from the claim of evidential support as prima facie reasons. Thus, a dubious *upādhi* can still be said to be a vitiator in the sense that it blocks an inference, although from the point of view of a skeptical reasoner the proposition expressing an *upādhi*'s absence from a locus of the probans is not a rebutter or undercutter in this case.

An apparent *upādhi* is a property which resembles a genuine *upādhi*. It normally exhibits or may well exhibit at least one of the three features of the UD's specific defining characteristic, while it fails to exhibit at least one of the other two features. However, since a property's pervasion of the probans and its coextensive pervasion of the probandum (in the range of the probans) warrant the pervasion of the probans by the probandum, the author of the UD seems to regard something which only fails to be not pervading the probans as not even remotely similar to a genuine *upādhi*. Hence, he is reluctant to classify such a property as an apparent *upādhi*.

An apparent *upādhi* can be a vitiator and the proposition expressing its absence in a locus of the probans can be a defeater if it only fails to be pervaded by the probandum, and thus, fails to be a corrector. The fact that according to the UD such properties are only apparent *upādhi*s is a token of the great importance which the author attaches to the corrector-function of an *upādhi*.

1.9 Notes: Chapter 1

1. "It is important to appreciate that deductively valid arguments are viewed as fallacies in Nyāya if in fact there is no pervasion or *a* is not H (this is called *asiddhi*, failure to know the prover as a property of the inferential subject or failure to know the *vyāpti*), even though it is recognized that if (counterfactually) *a were* H and all Hs *were* Ss, then *a would be* S. The premises have to be known by the inferring subject in a good inference, and only those inferences that produce knowledge (implying truth of belief) are good or genuine as opposed to *anumāna-ābhāsa*, pseudo-inferences, close imitators of the real McCoys, imitators that however slight the deviation from the genuine do not produce new knowledge." (Phillips 2017a: 88f)

2. According to Gärdenfors an epistemic state can be modeled as "a representation of a person's knowledge and belief at a certain point in time, as, for example, Oscar's state of belief at the moment he discovered that his ring was stained." (Gärdenfors 1988: 7) In section 1.3.2 we will see that the third member of a five-membered inference is sometimes understood in the sense that it expresses a fact about a reasoner's epistemic state.

3. A few lines later Keśava Miśra adds the following to the third member: *evaṃ yatrāgnir nāsti tatra dhūmo 'pi nāsti yathā mahāhrada iti vyatirekeṇa vyāptiḥ.* (TBh 40, 8f) – "Similarly, 'Wherever there is no fire, there is also no smoke, such as in a big lake.' [This] is pervasion in terms of the negative correlation."

4. "Hinsichtlich des Verhältnisses von *pratijñā* und *nigamana* geht aus mehreren Texten eindeutig hervor, daß eine Identität des propositionalen Gehalts beider Glieder zugrundezulegen ist." (Oetke 1994: 46)

5. Gärdenfors introduces the concept of epistemic attitude in order to distinguish between different kinds of belief: "In the models of epistemic states different 'kinds' of belief are expressible. For example, in a model based on a set of propositions, one can distinguish three different kinds: (1) a proposition A may be *accepted*, which simply means that A belongs to the set representing the epistemic state; (2) A may be *rejected*, which is to say that the negation of A is accepted in the state; and (3) A may be *kept in suspense* or *indetermined*, which means that neither A nor its negation is an element of the relevant set of propositions." (Gärdenfors 1988: 12)

6. Ingalls explicates the knowledge which results from the operation of reflective grasping in the same way: *vahnivyāpyadhūmavān parvataḥ.* (Ingalls 1951: 31) – "The mountain possesses a smoke which is pervaded by fire."

7. As a condition on the instantiating pairs of the pervasion relation (V_1^{pf}) seems to suggest that pervasion should be construed as a second-order relation between predicates such as S ("...is a locus of smoke") and F ("...is a locus of fire"). However, it is also common in Nyāya to regard the relata as objects of the domain, which includes properties. Thus, the property "being a locus of smoke" (*dhūmavattva*) is said to be pervaded by the property "being a locus of fire" (*vahnimavattva*). In section 1.6.1.1 we will introduce George Bealer's property calculus T1, in which properties are expressed by means of special terms. Instead of the predicates S and F the T1-terms $[Sx]_x$ ("being an x such that x is a locus of smoke") and $[Fx]_x$ ("being an x such that x is a locus of fire") can be regarded as denotations of relata of the pervasion relation. However, instead of construing pervasion as a first-order relation, Navya-Naiyāyikas rather conceive of it as a "relation-in-intension" (cf. Matilal 1990: 170f). Hence, a semi-formal representation by means of Bealer's formalization methods, such as $[x \text{ is pervaded by } y]_{xy}$ ("being an x and a y such that x is pervaded by y"), comes closer to the Navya-Nyāya understanding of pervasion as a relation.

8. In a Venn diagram the shading of a region indicates emptiness. Non-emptiness of a region is indicated by means of a cross ("x"). The whiteness of a region means lack of information (cf. Quine 1966: 69f).

9. The pattern of inference which we are dealing with here represents an advanced stage of the development of the Nyāya theory of inference. In formulations of five-membered inferences in early Nyāya-sources such as the Nyāyasūtra there is no reference to a pervasion. The third member consists only of the examples and their function does not seem to be to provide inductive support. Ganeri convincingly argues that this early Nyāya model of inference can be understood as a type of case-based reasoning (cf. Ganeri 2004: 327f).

10. To be more precise, (V_e) should be read with the tacit understanding that $\exists x \neq sK_iHx$ or $\exists x \neq sC_GHx$, since the quantification in (V_e) is surely meant to be non-vacuous.

The alternative formalizations by means of the operators K_i and C_G, respectively, are owing to the fact that a pervasion can be part of (i) an autoepistemic "inference for oneself" (*svārthānumāna*) or (ii) an "inference for others" (*parārthānumāna*), i.e., an argument to convince others, viz. the opponent and the audience in a debate. (ii) is identified with a five-membered inference, while (i) consists merely of the last three steps (cf. Iyer 1979: 70f). In the context of (i) a pervasion can be regarded as a claim about a reasoner's private knowledge, whereas in the context of (ii) a pervasion is rather a claim about the knowledge which a debater shares with other members in a group G consisting of the debater, her opponent and the audience. $C_G\varphi$ means that every member of G knows that φ and the debater knows that everybody else in G knows that φ etc. "This knowledge up to every finite depth of iteration is called *common knowledge*. It mixes 'factual' information with 'social' information about the information of others." (van Benthem 2010: 135)

11. Modgil and Prakken designed a framework for structured argumentation called "$ASPIC^{+}$", which allows to compose arguments from wffs interconnected by means of strict or defeasible rules. The precise internal structure of the wffs and a specification of the inference rules beyond their characterization as strict or defeasible are irrelevant to their system. They use the symbol "$\Rightarrow$" to render defeasible rules, such as "$WearsRing \Rightarrow Married$", and the symbol "$\rightarrow$" to render strict rules, such as "$Married \rightarrow \neg Bachelor$" (cf. Modgil and Prakken 2018: 18).

12. Although Navya-Naiyāyikas clearly refer to induction as a method of grasping the pervasion relation (*vyāptigrahaṇa*), it should not be overlooked that induction is not accepted as a knowledge source (*pramāṇa*) sui generis in Navya-Nyāya. From a Navya-Nyāya point of view it is perception (*pratyakṣa*) in combination with multiple observation (*bhūyodarśana*) and the resulting mental impressions (*saṃskāra*) which functions as a knowledge source for the cognition of the pervasion relation: *nanu dhūmāder anvayavyatirekayor grahaṇaṃ yujyate. tathā hi. yatra dhūmas tatrāgnir iti bhūyodarśanaṃ jāyate. yatra vahnivyatirekas tatra dhūmavyatireka iti ca taj jāyate. tac ca bhūyodarśanaṃ tādṛśaṃ saṃskāram ādadhāti. tādṛśasaṃskāralakṣaṇasāmarthyavaśāt tatsahakṛtaṃ cakṣur yāvadvahnimadvṛttim anvayaṃ gṛhṇāti.* (UD: 4b, 4f) – "[Counterobjection of the proponent of the right view:] Grasping a positive and negative correlation for smoke etc. is possible. After all, frequent observation arises [in the case of the positive correlation:] 'Wherever there is smoke there is fire.' And it (i.e., frequent observation) arises [in the case of the negative correlation:] 'Wherever there is the absence of fire, there is the absence of smoke.' This frequent observation imparts a corresponding mental impression. Due to a causal efficacy which is characterized by such a mental impression the faculty of sight aided by that [mental impression] grasps the positive correlation, [i.e.] the occurrence on something, insofar as it possesses fire."

13. The purpose of the consistency condition is to ensure that the existence of such an R would not be trivially fulfilled. If R would not have to be consistent with P, one might, e.g., choose $R :\leftrightarrow \neg P$. In this case $P \,\&\, R$ is false and then it is

trivially not a reason for S to believe Q. Hence, without the consistency condition every reason would be a prima facie reason.

14. As noted by Matilal (cf. Matilal 1998: 17f), the reference to positive and negative examples in a five-membered inference is reminiscent of Mill's "Joint Method of Agreement and Difference" (cf. Mill 1851: 402f).

15. Here are two examples which Navya-Naiyāyikas regard as shortcuts of valid inferences with only positive inductive support (1) and only negative inductive support (2):

(1) *ghaṭo 'bhidheyaḥ prameyatvāt.* (TS: 40) – "The pot is nameable, because it is knowable."

(2) *pṛthivītarebhyo bhidyate gandhavattvāt.* (ibid.) – "Earth is different from other things (than earth), because it possesses smell."

Interpreting (1) and (2) as examples of inductive inferences seems rather odd at first sight. However, in section 1.3.3 we will see that such an interpretation stands to reason if we take into account the strong realist footing of Navya-Nyāya epistemology.

16. As pointed out by Chakrabarti, "different from the inferential subject" (*pakṣetara*) is a "grue"-like predicate (cf. Chakrabarti 2010: 80). Goodman defined "grue" relative to an arbitrary but fixed time t: An object is "grue" if and only if it is observed before t and is green, or else is not so observed and is blue (cf. Goodman 1983: 73f). The assumption that "grue" is projectible with respect to "being an emerald" leads to the following paradox: (i) All emeralds observed before t are green. Hence, they provide inductive support for the thesis that emeralds observed from t onwards are green. (ii) All emeralds observed before t are also grue. Hence, they provide inductive support for the thesis that emeralds observed from t onwards are grue (i.e., blue).

Chakrabarti also discusses the projectibility problem with respect to another predicate which was concocted by Gaṅgeśa, viz. "other than either the inferential subject or a disagreeing instance" (*pakṣavipakṣānyatarānya*). This is a kind of extended version of the predicate "different from the inferential subject". Due to the additional disjunctive component it is formally closer to Goodman's concoction (cf. Chakrabarti 2010: 72).

17. I am adopting here Stephen Phillips' translation of *dūṣaṇa* (cf. Phillips 2002: 52f).

18. The type of pseudo-probans which is called *vyāpyatvāsiddha* (literally: "unestablished with respect to pervadedness") is twofold (cf. Iyer 1979: 97). One of the

two varieties is characterized by the absence of a knowledge source as a means to ascertain the pervasion of such a probans by the probandum. The other one is the "conditional probans" (*sopādhikahetu*). This is the variety which the author of the UD is referring to whenever he addresses the *vyāpyatvāsiddha*-fallacy. Hence, in the UD the term *vyāpyatvāsiddhi* is used in the sense of "the fallacy of the conditional probans".

19. Denying that P wouldn't be true unless Q were true means to claim that P can be true, even though Q is false.

20. The counterpart of wet fuel in the smoke/fire-example is the absence of red light in Pollock's example, since the absence of the absence of red light, i.e., the presence of red light, is a vitiator in his example, in the same way as the absence of wet fuel functions as a vitiator in the smoke/fire-example.

21. According to the "If"-clause, i.e., the $\sqrt[D]{\ }$-part, this can be explicated as: "What indicates the absence of the probandum due to its own absence in a locus of the probans, ..."

22. The "incoherent" (*viruddha*) probans is a special type of "pseudo-probans" (*hetvābhāsa*). According to the Nyāyasūtra a probans is called "incoherent" if "it is contrary to some doctrine which the propounder has already accepted." (Solomon 1976: 274) In later Nyāya a probans is called "incoherent" if it is "constantly accomapanied (sic!) by the absence of the *sādhya*" (Pandeya 1984: 115), as in the inference "Sound is eternal, because it is produced". The absence of the associate condition can be related to the probandum in the same way as an incoherent probans is related to the probandum in an invalid inference. If the associate condition pervades the entire probandum, every locus of the absence of the associate condition is a locus of the absence of the probandum. According to the UD's specific defining characteristic of the *upādhi* (cf. section 1.5), the latter needs to pervade the probandum only in the range of the probans. If the associate condition pervades the probandum only partially, the absence of the former co-occurs with the presence as well as the absence of the latter. In this case the absence of the *upādhi* is related to the probandum in the same way as a "deviating" (*savyabhicāra*) pseudo-probans is related to the probandum in an invalid inference (cf. section 1.3.3).

23. (D_1) and (D_2) (cf. below) ensure that the quantification in (B) is not vacuous. Hence, (B) is an adequate rendering of the actualized concept of pervasion expressed in the $\sqrt[B]{\ldots}$-proposition in (E3).

24. The concept of an apparent *upādhi* and its relation to Pollock's example will be studied in greater detail in section 1.7.3.

25. In the UD and in Gaṅgeśa's Upādhivāda there is a close Sanskrit equivalent of this defining characteristic: *sādhanāvacchinnasādhyavyāpakatve sati sādhanāvyāpaka upādhiḥ.* – "The associate condition does not pervade the probans, while it pervades the probandum limited by the probans." This defining characteristic is a kind of proto-version of Prabhākara Upādhyāya's defining characteristic (cf. section 4.3).

Gaṅgeśa advocates a different defining characteristic, viz.: *yadvyabhicāritvena sādhanasya sādhyavyabhicāritvaṃ sa upādhiḥ.* (Frauwallner 1970: 12 [§6], 36 = Phillips 2002: 80) – "That is an *upādhi* due to whose deviation (from the probans) the probans deviates from the probandum." The difference between Gaṅgeśa's defining characteristic and the above-mentioned proto-version of Prabhākara Upādhyāya's defining characteristic is, however, rather a matter of form than of content. Gaṅgeśa expresses (G_1) in terms of a "deviation" (*vyabhicāra*). As indicated by the instrumental *yadvyabhicāritvena*, this deviation entails the deviation of the probans from the probandum. Phillips understands Gaṅgeśa's formulation in the sense of $\forall x(Hx \wedge \neg Ux \rightarrow Hx \wedge \neg Sx)$, which is equivalent to (*) $\forall x(Hx \wedge Sx \rightarrow Ux)$ (cf. ibid. 80f). One might object that there is still a difference in meaning between (*) and (G_2), since (*) does not express the requirement of existential import which is associated with the pervasion at issue. However, in the Upādhivāda-section where Gaṅgeśa distinguishes between ascertained and dubious *upādhis* he explicitly attaches the credibility criterion involved in this distinction to the non-pervasion condition and the pervasion condition in a defining characteristic of the *upādhi* (cf. Frauwallner 1970: 15 [§8], 7f). Hence, it seem plausible that he understands the entailment between the two deviations in his own defining characteristic in the sense of (G_2).

26. The bar indicates non-emptiness of a compound region (cf. Quine 1966: 79f).

27. Prima facie, the UD seems to call for a coextensive pervasion of the entire probandum by the *upādhi*: *tasmāt samavyāptikasyopādhitvam.* (UD: 5b, 4) – "Therefore, something which has a coextensive pervasion is an associate condition." However, the author explicitly states that properties which fit the profile of a kind of nutshell version of Prabhākara Upādhyāya's defining characteristic (cf. section 4.3) are included in his concept of *upādhi*: *na sādhyasādhanasaṃbandhavyāpakopādhyasaṃgrahaḥ.* (UD: 6b, 2f) – "It is not the case that the defining characteristic which pervades the relation between probans and probandum is not comprehended (by our defining characteristic)." In the nutshell version of Prabhākara Upādhyāya's defining characteristic the expression "the relation between probans and probandum" refers to the probandum limited by the probans.

28. Bealer's square bracket notation with subscripted binding variables is a variant of the notation for λ-terms in λ-calculus. However, his property terms should not be regarded as extensional or intensional descriptions of functions. They rather denote properties as intensional metaphysical objects (cf. Alama 2018). Therefore, his approach has much in common with the reification of properties in Navya-Nyāya.

Although Bealer does not identify properties with functions, functions do play a role in the construction of his semantic framework. However, "these metatheoretic constructions may be viewed as only a convenient shorthand for a metatheoretic construction within a property-theoretic framework." (Bealer 1982: 116) In T1 property terms are interpreted in general via functions which assign to each property in the domain of an algebraic model structure an actual extension as well as alternative possible extensions. Thus, it is possible for a property's contingent instances to be different from what they actually are.

29. It should be noted that the semantic model structure of T1 is very different from that of ordinary modal systems. Bealer treats modalities as predicates applied to propositions, which he formalizes by means of his square bracket notation for properties. In contrast to property terms, terms for propositions have no index variables. Thus, $[A]$ is a proposition expressing "that A". An expression of the form $\Box A$ is adopted as a convenient abbreviation of expressions such as $N[A]$, where N is a one-place predicate expressing "... is necessary".

We will use T1 solely for the purpose of modeling logical inquiries concerning properties. A formal reconstruction of the concept of pervasion as a nomic generalization can be conveniently handled by means of standard modal systems, as we have seen (cf. section 1.3.3).

30. Property terms and the Δ-relation can be used to formalize a Navya-Nyāya counterpart of the naive class abstraction in set theory, viz. *tattvavat tad eva* (cf. Ingalls 1951: 36). – "Anything which possesses the property 'being that' is that."

An unproblematic substitution instance of this principle derives from replacing the pronoun *tat* ("that"), which has the same function as a schematic variable here, by the noun *ghaṭa* ("pot"). *ghaṭatvavān ghaṭa eva* means: "Anything which possesses the property 'potness' is a pot."

If we understand the *tattvavat tad eva*-principle in the sense of "a possesses (or is a locus of) the property 'being an x such that A is true of x' *iff* A is true of a", we can formalize it in the following way:

(C*) $a\,\Delta\,[A(x)]_x \leftrightarrow A(a)$, where a is free for x in A and vice versa.

Our interpretation of the *tattvavat tad eva*-principle as an equivalence is confirmed by Matilal, who characterizes the specific style of Navya-Nyāya texts in the following way: "Simple predicate formulations, such as 'x is F' are noted, but only to be rephrased as 'x has *F-ness*' (where '*F-ness*' stands for the property derived from 'F')." (Matilal 1990: 115)

A problematic substitution instance of the *tattvavat tad eva*-principle derives from replacing the pronoun *tat* by *asvavṛttitva* ("being not resident in itself"). With $x \Delta x$ as a formal equivalent of "x resides in itself", "being not resident in itself" can be expressed as ...

$$r =_{\text{df}} [\neg x \Delta x]_x.$$

There is apparently no textual evidence that Navya-Nyāya logicians were aware that r can be used to derive a variant of Zermelo-Russell's antinomy from the *tattvavat tad eva*-principle (cf. Guhe 1999: 22 and Guhe 2018: 14):

(a) If r is resident in itself (i.e., if it is *svavṛtti*), then the property "being not resident in itself" (*asvavṛttitva*) resides in r. Therefore, (according to the *tattvavat tad eva*-principle) r is not resident in itself, i.e., it is *asvavṛtti.* (Contradiction!)

This is the formal counterpart of the argument:

$$r \Delta r \Rightarrow \underbrace{r \Delta [\neg x \Delta x]_x}_{\text{can be substituted for } a \Delta [A(x)]_x \text{ in (C*)}} \Rightarrow \neg r \Delta r$$

(b) If r is not resident in itself (i.e., if it is *asvavṛtti*), then (according to the *tattvavat tad eva*-principle) the property "being not resident in itself" (*asvavṛttitva*) resides in r. Therefore, r is resident in itself, i.e., it is *svavṛtti.* (Contradiction!)

This is the formal counterpart of the argument:

$$\underbrace{\neg r \Delta r}_{\text{can be substituted for } A(a) \text{ in (C*)}} \Rightarrow r \Delta [\neg x \Delta x]_x \Rightarrow r \Delta r$$

(a) and (b) together yield the following variant of Zermelo-Russell's antinomy:

$$r \Delta r \leftrightarrow \neg r \Delta r$$

Since T1-ST$_2$, T1-A and T1-NFU contain reformulations of safe comprehension principles in the corresponding set theories, the antinomy is blocked in these systems.

31. Navya-Naiyāyikas regard some abstract nouns as denotations of universals (*sāmānya* or *jāti*), which are part of their system of ontological categories. Of course, not every abstract noun can be said to name some kind of real entity. Matilal refers to discussions in Navya-Nyāya concerning unlocatable pseudo-properties such as "being the son of a barren woman", "being a golden mountain" etc.: "An unlocatable property is a suspect in Navya-nyāya. It is regarded as a fictitious property which cannot be located in our universe of loci." (Matilal 1998: 147)

Nameability, nameabilityness etc. are neither regarded as universals nor as fictitious properties in Navya-Nyāya. They belong to a category of properties which happens to be called *upādhi* as well. So, we have to distinguish between the epistemic *upādhi* (which is the topic of the UD) and an ontological *upādhi*, the so-called "imposed property": "The meanings of a large number of general terms in our language are construed as *upādhis*, i.e., 'nominal' properties, not objective universals. Kaṇāda and Praśastapāda did not really address this issue. It was, above all, Udayana who tried to provide a set of criteria for the exclusion of invalid or counterfeit universals, such as 'cookness' (*pācakatva*) or 'being an inhabitant of Ayodhyā' (*ayodhyāvāsitva*); ..." (Halbfass 1992: 119) Some nominal properties are like the latter example compound, whereas universals should be elementary. Udayana notes six other invalidating factors (*jātibādhaka*). (Cf. Halbfass 1992: 132)

Although such imposed properties do not belong to the elementary constituents of the empirical world, it would be a mistake to regard them as mere fabrications of the mind: "A failed universal as an *upādhi* would be a cognized property that like universals is 'repeatable,' i.e., can occur in more than one instance, but that falls to one or another of six 'blockers of natural-kind status', *jāti-bādhaka*. Such would be then a 'surplus property,' a property surplus to the system of ontological analysis. In other words, this would be a 'condition' in a very abstract and non-concomittal sense, a 'something extra' that is not just mind generated, that is a real property of something, but a property whose taxonomical character we have not determined. Some 'surplus properties' do seem to be mainly due to verbal excess, to saying things non-perspicaciously. But others do not seem so, and all *upādhi*-s are grounded in some fashion or other in the way the world is. Otherwise, they would not become objects, cognitive objects, that is, indicated by our perceptions and conversations about the world." (Phillips 2002: 25)

32. The concept of a hyper-class should, however, not be confounded with the concept of a hyperset (i.e., a non-well-founded set) in non-well-founded systems of set theory (cf. Barwise and Moss 1996: 6).

33. For proving the existence of $\{V\}$ and of $\wp^n V$ for any natural number n in the Ackermann set theory we need the axiom of foundation for sets (cf. Levy/Vaught 1961, Fraenkel/Bar-Hillel/Levy 1973: 153 and Kanamori 2006: 237 and (δ^*) below).

34. Ackermann integrates an axiom of extensionality labelled (β') into his set theory with urelements, viz. $x \subseteq y \wedge y \subseteq x \rightarrow x = y$ (cf. Ackermann 1956: 344). However, if we take into account urelements, (β') should rather be formulated as follows: $\neg Ux \wedge \neg Uy \rightarrow (x \subseteq y \wedge y \subseteq x \rightarrow x = y)$. Otherwise, (β') could be used to prove that all urelements are identical, because urelements have no elements. Hence, $x \subseteq y \wedge y \subseteq x$ for all urelements x and y.

35. *abhāvaś ca punar dvividho 'nyonyābhavaḥ saṃsargābhāvaś ca.* (BN: 17, 1 = Guhe 2014: 84) – "And absence is, again, twofold, [namely] mutual absence and relational absence." Commonly, Naiyāyikas subdivide "relational absence" into 3 varieties by taking into account 3 possibilities of an absence's temporal expansion, viz. a) "prior absence" (*prāgabhāva*), i.e., the beginningless absence of a thing somewhere, before it is created, b) "posterior absence" (*dhvaṃsābhāva*), i.e., the ever-lasting absence of a thing somewhere, after it has been destroyed, and c) "absolute absence" (*atyantābhāva*). As suggested by its name, type c) refers to cases of an absence whose absentee never occurs in a particular locus, such as the absence of colour in the air, but it includes also impermanent absences, such as the temporary absence of a pot on the ground (cf. Iyer 1979: 32 and 216). Viśvanātha Nyāyapañcānana Bhaṭṭācārya apparently justifies the classification of such absences as absolute absences by pointing out that "absolute absence" can be taken to refer to the absence of an object o during a certain time interval $[t_1, t_2]$. If o is present in a locus l during $[t_1, t_2]$, there is no $[t_1, t_2]$-related absolute absence of o residing in l. However, if o is absent from l during $[t_1, t_2]$, the $[t_1, t_2]$-related absolute absence of o resides in l not only during $[t_1, t_2]$, but also at any moment $t \notin [t_1, t_2]$, even if o is present in l at t: *niytasaṃsargābhāvatvam atyantābhāvatvam. yatra tu bhūtalādau ghaṭādikam apasāritaṃ punar ānītaṃ ca tatra ghaṭakālasya saṃbandhāghaṭakatvād atyantābhāvasya nityatve 'pi ghaṭakāle na ghaṭātyantābhāvabuddhiḥ. tatrotpādavināśaśālī caturtho 'yam abhāva iti kecit.* (SM: 92, 3f) – "The [property of] being an absolute absence is the [property of] being an eternal relational absence. But when a pot etc. on the ground etc. are removed and brought back, then, since the time of (the presence of) the pot does not form a constituent part (author's note: I am following here Mādhavānanda's understanding of *ghaṭaka* as a "factor" which anchors the relation between an absence and its locus to a certain time interval. Cf. Mādhavānanda 1954: 17) of the relation, there is not the cognition of the absolute absence of the pot at the time of (the presence of) the pot, even though the absolute absence is eternal. (author's note: However, even in the presence of the pot there can be a cognition of the absolute absence of the pot with respect to the time interval when it was absent.) Some [say] with regard to that that this is a fourth absence which is endowed with origin and destruction." The "fourth absence" which Viśvanātha Nyāyapañcānana Bhaṭṭācārya is referring to here seems to be the so-called "temporary absence" (*sāmayikābhāva*), a new category introduced by Vaiśeṣikas as an umbrella term for impermanent absences such as the absence of a pot during its temporary removal from the ground. Annambhaṭṭa treats "temporary absence" as a sub-category of "absolute absence" (cf. TS: 367). Whenever Navya-Naiyāyikas talk about the absolute absence of x in y, this can apparently be understood in the sense of "x is not in y" (Matilal 1968: 136), so that "absolute absence" comes close to an alias of

"relational absence" in the general sense of a "simple absence" (Ganeri 2004: 379), i.e., a temporally indefinite non-occurrence.

36. This line can be obtained by proving both directions of the equivalence:

$$x \not\Delta [\neg A(x) \wedge Ox]_x \leftrightarrow \neg\exists y(y = [\neg A(x) \wedge Ox]_x \wedge x\Delta y)$$

($\rightarrow$):

A1, A2, A5, R1, R2	$y = [\neg A(x) \wedge Ox]_x \rightarrow (x \not\Delta [\neg A(x) \wedge Ox]_x \rightarrow x \not\Delta y)$
A1, R1	$x \not\Delta [\neg A(x) \wedge Ox]_x \rightarrow (y = [\neg A(x) \wedge Ox]_x \rightarrow x \not\Delta y)$
R2	$\forall y(x \not\Delta [\neg A(x) \wedge Ox]_x \rightarrow (y = [\neg A(x) \wedge Ox]_x \rightarrow x \not\Delta y))$
A3, R1	$x \not\Delta [\neg A(x) \wedge Ox]_x \rightarrow \forall y(y = [\neg A(x) \wedge Ox]_x \rightarrow x \not\Delta y)$
Def. $\exists$	$x \not\Delta [\neg A(x) \wedge Ox]_x \rightarrow \neg\exists y(y = [\neg A(x) \wedge Ox]_x \wedge x\Delta y)$ ■

($\leftarrow$):

A2	$\forall y(y = [\neg A(x) \wedge Ox]_x \rightarrow x \not\Delta y) \rightarrow ([\neg A(x) \wedge Ox]_x = [\neg A(x) \wedge Ox]_x \rightarrow x \not\Delta [\neg A(x) \wedge Ox]_x)$
A1, A2, A4, R1, R2	$\forall y(y = [\neg A(x) \wedge Ox]_x \rightarrow x \not\Delta y) \rightarrow x \not\Delta [\neg A(x) \wedge Ox]_x$
Def. $\exists$	$\neg\exists y(y = [\neg A(x) \wedge Ox]_x \wedge x\Delta y) \rightarrow x \not\Delta [\neg A(x) \wedge Ox]_x$ ■

37. This line is owing to the above-mentioned convention that property terms like $[A(x)]_x$ are to be understood in the sense of "being an object x such that ...". Hence, the Ox in the preceding line is redundant.

38. Naiyāyikas usually refer to an *anavasthā* in the sense of a vicious regressus ad infinitum. Innocuous variants such as the case of seed and sprout are duly noted as an exception (cf. Solomon 1976: 488).

39. To be more precise, a pseudo-probans is called "essentially unestablished" (*svarūpāsiddha*) if (1) its absence is located (1a) on the inferential subject as a whole or (1b) only on a part of the inferential subject, or if (2) it is a complex property such that (2a) only one of its components can be said to be located on the inferential subject, or (2b) one of its components is irrelevant to the purpose of securing the probandum (cf. Iyer 1979: 98 and 234f).

40. Natural numbers can be defined as properties (cf. Bealer 1982: 120f and Guhe 2019).

Chapter 2

Detailed Synopsis of the Contents of the UD

(**1**) A benediction in the form of a *maṅgala*-verse contains a statement of the topic of the UD, viz. the definition of the *upādhi* by means of a specific and a general defining characteristic.

(**1.1**) A long *pūrvapakṣa* starts with the opponent's question whether there is a general or a specific defining characteristic.

(**1.1.1**) The respondent argues that "being the counterpositive of an absolute absence" cannot be such a general defining characteristic because of over-pervasion with regard to the eternal substances.

(**1.1.2**) The opponent suggests another general defining characteristic, viz. "being a property which is the counterpositive of an absolute absence".

(**1.1.2.1**) However, according to the respondent, the present putative defining characteristic is not an associate condition (1) or it is an associate condition (2).

In case (1) it is afflicted with the defect of over-pervasion, because – being itself a counterpositive of an absolute absence – it should be self-resident and would then occur in something which is not an associate condition.

In case (2) the present defining characteristic does not reside in itself (2a) or it does reside in itself (2b). In case (2a) there is the defect of non-pervasion. In case (2b) the present defining characteristic *proper* resides in itself ($2b_1$) or an equilocatable variant resides in the present defining characteristic ($2b_2$). Case ($2b_1$) incurs the defect of self-dependence. In case ($2b_2$) the equilocatable variant would also be an associate condition, since it is supposed to be equilocatable with an associate condition, and in order to prevent it from being self-resident, one would have to assume another equilocatable property etc. The result would be a regressus ad infinitum.

(**1.1.2.2**) An alternative attempt to derive a fallacy from the assumption of the present defining characteristic involves properties which are unique to it. These properties are associate conditions (1) or not (2).

In case (1) the present defining characteristic itself occurs there (1a) or another equilocatable defining characteristic occurs there (1b). Case (1a) would incur a mutual dependence between the present defining characteristic and its peculiar properties. Case (1b) would incur the non-pervasion of the present defining characteristic, since the latter would not reside in its peculiar properties, although they are associate conditions. If an equilocatable defining characteristic fills in for the present defining characteristic and characterizes its peculiar properties as associate conditions, this equilocatable defining characteristic would be afflicted with the same problems as the present defining characteristic and we would need another equilocatable defining characteristic which fills in for the latter etc. The result would be a regressus ad infinitum.

Case (2) would incur the defect of over-pervasion, since properties which reside *only* in the present defining characteristic are not omnipresent. Hence, the present defining characteristic should reside in them. If they were not associate conditions (as presupposed in the present case), the defining characteristic would reside in something which is not an associate condition.

(**1.1.2.3**) A further alternative attempt to derive a fallacy from the assumption of the present defining characteristic does not presuppose that this property is a specific defining characteristic. So, we will just refer to it as the *atyantābhāvapratiyogidharmatva*. The respondent does presuppose that there is some specific defining characteristic u. Either the *atyantābhāvapratiyogidharmatva* is different from u (1) or not (2).

In case (1) it is a defining characteristic of an associate condition (1a) or not (1b). In case (1b) u needs to be specified in such a way that it does not reside in itself. Since the *atyantābhāvapratiyogidharmatva* is apparently afflicted with the problem of self-residence, the same might be true of u. In case (1a) u is an associate condition, since the *atyantābhāvapratiyogidharmatva* resides in it. But then u would reside in itself.

Case (2) would incur the defect of self-dependence.

(**1.1.2.4**) The opponent agrees to the inadmissibility of causal loops and epistemic ungroundedness. However, he denies that self-dependence is a fault in the case of the residence relation. Such a phenomenon cannot be ruled out, because otherwise one would have to challenge the existence of universally positive properties and the validity of all only positive inferences.

(**1.1.2.5**) According to the respondent the assumption that self-dependence is not a fault would jeopardize valid positive and negative inferences. In his opinion forfeiting the only positive inferences is the lesser evil.

(**1.1.2.6**) The respondent summarizes the defects (self-dependence, non-pervasion and a regressus ad infinitum) which are in his opinion inevitably connected with assumption 1.1.2. He concludes that any attempt to define the concept of an associate condition is doomed to fail.

(**1.1.3**) The opponent points out that *upādhi* is an expression of ordinary language, whose application must be motivated somehow, and it cannot be traced to a universal *upādhitva*, because such a putative universal would be afflicted with the defect of "overlap" (*jātisaṃkara*). Moreover, *upādhitva* cannot be a universal, because it resides also in universals.

The respondent argues that the root *upādhā*, from which *upādhi* derives, can account for the fact that the expression *upādhi* refers to something which transmits a property residing in itself to something else, in the same way as the China rose transmits its red colour to the crystal in its vicinity. The opponent objects that according to this derivation the China rose would have to be an *upādhi*, which the respondent does not deny, because in some inferential contexts the China rose might function as an *upādhi*.

The opponent suggests an alternative defining characteristic as a potential warrant of the applicability of the expression *upādhi*, viz. "the bringing to light of its own pervadedness". However, the respondent objects that in this case the applicability of the expression *upādhi* would be unduly restricted to *upādhi*s with coextensive pervasion.

(**1.1.4**) The respondent attacks again the claim that "being a property which is the counterpositive of an absolute absence" is an appropriate general defining characteristic (cf. 1.1.2). He tries to prove that this general defining characteristic would also apply to knowability, an omnipresent property. The opponent's modification "being a property which is the counterpositive of an absolute absence which has a substrate" might be a way to avoid the charge of over-pervasion, but it is rejected by the respondent, who tacitly assumes that the respondent conceives of this property as a universal and fails to realize that it violates the "overlap"-restriction for universals. The respondent concludes that the opponent has not succeeded in determining a general defining characteristic. Hence, there is also no basis for determining a specific defining characteristic.

(**1.1.5**) The opponent denies that the specific defining characteristic needs to be grounded in the general one. According to the respondent, however, the general defining characteristic is prerequisite for the identification of something as an associate condition and for designating it accordingly. The specific defining characteristic rather focuses a particular instance of an associate condition.

(**1.1.6**) The opponent suggests Udayana's defining characteristic (non-pervasion of the probans cum pervasion of the probandum) as a general defining characteristic. The specific defining characteristic derives from it by substituting appropriate properties for the expressions "probans" and "probandum", which are taken to be functioning as variables in Udayana's defining characteristic.

(**1.1.6.1**) The respondent's rejection of the present defining characteristic trades on the assumption that pervasion is a relation without *upādhi* (*anaupādhikasaṃbandha*). The cognition of this defining characteristic depends on itself (i), since the pervasion relation is a part of it and the cognition of the latter depends on the cognition of the general defining characteristic of an *upādhi*. One can also argue that (ii) a mutual dependence between the cognition of an *upādhi* and the cognition of the general defining characteristic of an *upādhi* is at stake here or (iii) a circular chain of epistemically grounding factors consisting of the cognition of the defining characteristic, the cognition of the state of being devoid of an associate condition and the cognition of an *upādhi*. Following Varadarāja, the respondent regards any kind of epistemic ungroundedness as an inferential blocker, since it can account for the probans's being "essentially unestablished" (*svarūpāsiddha*). A probans whose cognition results in a non-terminating epistemic procedure cannot be located on the inferential subject. Similarly, the ontological ungroundedness associated with self-resident properties disqualifies them from being used as genuine probantia in an inference.

(**1.1.6.2**) The respondent reads an undue narrowness into Udayana's defining characteristic and claims that it is also afflicted with the defect of non-pervasion.

(**1.1.6.3**) Moreover, he deems Udayana's defining characteristic afflicted with the defect of over-pervasion with regard to the property of being different from the inferential subject (*pakṣetaratva*). This property should not be regarded as an *upādhi*, because it would also vitiate valid inferences. The opponent argues that the pervasion of the probandum as part of the defining characteristic is meant in the sense of a positive and negative pervasion. However, there is no negative inductive support for the pervasion of the probandum by the *pakṣetaratva*.

The respondent rejects the opponent's apparently factitious explication. Moreover, he points out that the *pakṣetaratva* is needed to vitiate pseudo-inferences that are instances of the fallacy "patent falsehood" (*bādha*). The opponent insists that without his explication the *pakṣetaratva* would have to be regarded as a universal vitiator in the sense of Udayana's defining characteristic. According to the respondent we may then simply deny that an *upādhi* can vitiate. This is no solution for the opponent, since an *upādhi* does actually vitiate. He tentatively observes that at least in the case of a patent falsehood the inference itself can be taken to be a clue to the failure of an assumed pervasion.

The opponent then reaffirms Udayana's defining characteristic and his understanding of the required pervasion of the probandum by the *upādhi*. He modifies Udayana's defining characteristic by only adding the *pakṣetaratva* which is induced by a patent falsehood (*bādhonnītapakṣetaratva*) as an exceptional case. The respondent argues that associate conditions and deviations can be detected without a defining characteristic, so that the effort to rule out the *pakṣetaratva* in general as a potential locus of such a defining characteristic is in vain.

Moreover, the *pakṣetaratva* cannot be excluded by the opponent's requirement that the *upādhi* should pervade the probandum positively and negatively, because the *pakṣetaratva* is a locus of its own absence. Hence, it can still function as an *upādhi* vitiating a valid inference like the inference of a fire from the smoke on a mountain. Since the *pakṣetaratva* is a locus of the co-absence of fire and the *pakṣetaratva*, there is negative inductive support for the pervasion of the probandum by the *pakṣetaratva*.

Moreover, the property of being an agreeing instance (*sapakṣatva*) would be another undesirable instance of the opponent's defining characteristic, since in the case of a positive and negative inference it is absent from the inferential subject and co-occurs with the absence of the probandum in the realm of disagreeing instances (*vipakṣa*). Thus, it pervades the probandum positively and negatively. As a vitiator it would then also serve to debunk valid inferences.

The opponent tries to fix his defining characteristic by adding that the *pakṣetaratva* which is not induced by a patent falsehood (*bādhonnīta*) is not an *upādhi.* He seems to have realized that his insistence on a positive and negative pervasion in the pervasion condition of Udayana's defining characteristic is not sufficient to exclude the *pakṣetaratva.*

However, the respondent is still not satisfied, because the opponent has not done anything to clear his defining characteristic of the defect of over-pervasion with regard to the property of being an agreeing instance. Actually, a general recipe for concocting a universal *upādhi* would be to choose any property which is absent from the inferential subject and otherwise resides in all and only loci where the probandum is present. A case in point is the property of being produced by a body as an *upādhi* with respect to the design inference in Nyāya: "The earth etc. have a creator, because they are products."

The opponent argues that the property of being an agreeing instance does not pervade the probandum, because "being an agreeing instance" has to be understood in the sense of "being ascertained as a locus of the probandum" and there may be unascertained cases of the occurrence of the probandum.

The respondent takes issue with the opponent's understanding of the pervasion of the probandum in the sense of the occurrence of the *upādhi* in every potential (though as yet unascertained) locus of the probandum. In this case the *bādhonnītapakṣetaratva* could not be said to pervade the probandum "being not hot", since it is definitely not present on the inferential subject "fire". Thus, the opponent's defining characteristic would exclude the *bādhonnītapakṣetaratva.* The respondent disregards the opponent's previous suggestion to include the *bādhonnītapakṣetaratva* in the defining characteristic as a separate case.

The opponent insists that the inferential subject should not be excluded from the realm of loci involved in the pervasion of the inference at issue. Prior to any inquiry the occurrence of the probandum on the inferential subject needs to be an open issue. "Patent falsehood" should rather be regarded as a fallacy which derives from a violation of the inferential-subject-proviso (*pakṣatā*).

The respondent disagrees with the opponent's characterization of the inferential subject as an open issue with respect to the presence or absence of the probandum on it. His counter-example is Śaṅkara's inference of the illusionary nature of the phenomenal world. From an Advaita perspective the thesis of this inference is an absolute truth. The respondent attributes doubt concerning the thesis of an inference solely to the cognitive agent, whereas from an objective point of view the probandum is either definitely present *on* or absent *from* the inferential subject. Hence, an instance of the fallacy "patent falsehood" cannot be vitiated by simply referring to a violation of basic requirements of a sound inference. The *bādhonnītapakṣetaratva* is needed as an *upādhi* to vitiate it.

(**1.1.7**) The respondent also disagrees with a modified version of Udayana's defining characteristic which posits a coextensive pervasion of the probandum by the *upādhi* instead of a pervasion simpliciter.

(**1.1.7.1**) According to the respondent this defining characteristic is afflicted with the same defects as the previous one, viz. self-dependence, non-pervasion and over-pervasion with respect to the *pakṣetaratva* as a vitiator of valid inferences. He disagrees with the opponent's claim that the new defining characteristic does not pertain to the *pakṣetaratva* as a vitiator of valid inferences. He refers to variants of the *pakṣetaratva* which reside only in loci of the probandum. Thus, the possession of fire in other loci than the mountain might be said to be an *upādhi* with coextensive pervasion, which vitiates the valid inference of fire from smoke on a mountain.

(**1.1.7.2**) Moreover, the present defining characteristic fails to pertain to *upādhi*s which pervade the probandum non-coextensively. Such *upādhi*s also serve as vitiators which indicate a deviation (*vyabhicāronnāyaka*).

According to the opponent, however, an *upādhi* should function as a corrector which superimposes its own pervadedness by the probandum on the putative probans in an inference (*svagatavyāpyatvāropaka*). Therefore, the required pervasion of the probandum by the *upādhi* has to be coextensive. The opponent attributes the function of a vitiator to an inference, viz. "This probans deviates from this probandum, because it deviates from something which pervades this probandum, such as in the case of (the given) object of cognition." An *upādhi* would be obsolete if its function were confined to vitiating.

The respondent insists that vitiating by indicating a deviation is the primary function of an *upādhi*. Moreover, even *upādhi*s with a non-coextensive pervasion can function as correctors. All that is needed is a pervasion of the *upādhi* by the probandum in the range of the probans.

(**1.1.8**) The respondent also criticizes that the opponent's insistence on a coextensive pervasion excludes properties which qualifiy as *upādhi*s due to a proto-version of Prabhākara Upādhyāya's defining characteristic: "The associate condition does not pervade the probans, while it pervades the probandum limited by the probans." *upādhi*s according to this defining characteristic can also serve as correctors. If there is no coextensive pervasion of the *upādhi* by the probandum in the range of the probans, an *upādhi* which matches the proto-version of Prabhākara Upādhyāya's defining characteristic is at least an effective vitiator. Moreover, the coextensive pervasion is a useless restriction, since a variant of the *pakṣetaratva* which resides only in loci of the probandum is not excluded by it.

(**1.1.9**) The opponent's defining characteristic also fails to pertain to *upādhi*s according to a nutshell version of Prabhākara Upādhyāya's defining characteristic: "The *upādhi* does not pervade the probans, while it pervades the relation between probans and probandum." An *upādhi* according to this defining characteristic vitiates, insofar as its absence entails the absence of "the relation between probans and probandum" (i.e., of the property of being a locus of the co-occurrence of probans and probandum), which is tantamount to a deviation.

(**1.1.10**) The opponent agrees to the nutshell version of Prabhākara Upādhyāya's defining characteristic, which he identifies as the one advocated by Śivādityamiśra. He revokes his former insistence on a coextensive pervasion and credits the present defining characteristic with the advantage that it pertains also to the *pakṣetaratva* in the case of a pseudo-inference that is an instance of the fallacy "patent falsehood".

One might object that an inference with a probans and a probandum whose ranges are disjoint cannot be vitiated by means of an *upādhi* according to this defining characteristic. However, an *upādhi* is not needed to vitiate such an inference, since it suffices to point out that in this case the probans is a special type of pseudo-probans, viz. the "incoherent" (*viruddha*) probans.

(**1.1.10.1**) The respondent regards the present defining characteristic as over-pervaded by the property of being an *upādhi*, which also pertains to *upādhi*s as vitiators of pseudo-inferences with an incoherent probans.

Since pervasion is a relation without an *upādhi*, the failure of an assumed pervasion must be traceable to an *upādhi*.

(**1.1.10.2**) The opponent denies that the present defining characteristic is too narrow, because regarding pervasion as a relation without an *upādhi* does not entail that every failure of an assumed pervasion should be traceable to an *upādhi*. It rather means that if a relation is pervasion, then there is no *upādhi*, i.e., if there is an *upādhi*, there is a deviation. In this sense the explication of pervasion as a relation without an *upādhi* entails a positive correlation with a deviation. However, the present defining characteristic does not warrant the reverse, viz. that there should be an *upādhi* in every case of a deviation.

(**1.1.10.3**) The respondent points out that a total disparity of probans and probandum (a "mere deviation") cannot be perceived. Therefore, the *upādhi* is needed as a knowledge source which indicates a deviation in this case.

(**1.1.10.4**) Moreover, the co-occurrence of probans and probandum does not always involve a contact or an inherence between the two. Hence, the defining characteristic would be too narrow if "relation" (*saṃbandha*) is understood in the sense of "contact" or "inherence".

(**1.1.10.5**) If the word "relation" in the present defining characteristic is understood in the sense of "pervasion", then there should be no vitiator, because probans and probandum would be related to each other as in a valid inference and an *upādhi* as a vitiator would be useless.

(**1.1.10.6**) If the word "relation" in the present defining characteristic is understood in the sense of "co-occurrence", the absence of the *upādhi* would only entail the absence of the joint occurrence of probans and probandum. Nevertheless, the probandum could still occur in a locus of the absence of the *upādhi*. However, the opponent points out that the absence of such an *upādhi* indirectly entails the absence of the probandum, because it entails the absence of the probans or the absence of the probandum. Thus, wherever the absence of such an *upādhi* co-occurs with the probans, there is the absence of the probandum.

(**1.1.11**) The respondent suggests to replace the nutshell version of Prabhākara Upādhyāya's defining characteristic with the less ambiguous proto-version of Prabhākara Upādhyāya's defining characteristic, because the absence of an *upādhi* according to the former defining characteristic can be said to be equilocatable with the absence of an *upādhi* according to the latter defining characteristic. Thus, both absences entail a deviation in the same loci of the probans. The opponent agrees to the reinstatement of the proto-version of Prabhākara Upādhyāya's defining characteristic. However, the respondent revokes his consent to it because of over-pervasion with regard to the property of "being such a locus which is different from the inferential subject" (*tādṛśapakṣetaratva*). This property is the ordinary *pakṣetaratva* restricted to loci of the co-occurrence of probans and probandum.

(**1.1.12**) The respondent further charges the proto-version of Prabhākara Upādhyāya's defining characteristic with the defect of non-pervasion, because it fails to pertain to genuine *upādhis* according to a defining characteristic which is mentioned by Jānakīnātha in a *pūrvapakṣa*: "The *upādhi* does not pervade the probans, while it pervades the probandum limited by a certain qualifier." (Gaṅgeśa refers to a similar defining characteristic which differs from the latter, only insofar as the qualifier limiting the probandum is specified as the alternative consisting of the probans and a property of the inferential subject.)

The opponent suggests to endorse this new defining characteristic, since it has a wider range of applications than the nutshell version of Prabhākara Upādhyāya's defining characteristic and the proto-version of Prabhākara Upādhyāya's defining characteristic, which he regards as mere specifications of the former. However, the respondent objects that the difference between the new defining characteristic and the other two is not just a matter of scope, but it concerns also the mode of presentation (*udbhāvanaprakāra*) of the *upādhi* as the definiendum.

Moreover, the respondent charges the new defining characteristic with the defect of characterizing the *upādhi* in such a way that it is easy to concoct *upādhis* which can be turned as universal vitiators against all valid inferences. He claims that every property F-ness which is absent from the inferential subject p, but pertains to an example in a valid inference, matches the present defining characteristic, because it does not pervade the probans, while it pervades the probandum limited by the property "being F or p" if p is excluded from the loci involved in the pervasion relation. The opponent observes that the examples of a valid only positive inference are all agreeing instances (*sapakṣa*). Hence, such an inference cannot be vitiated by a property F-ness pertaining to a disagreeing instance (*vipakṣa*). However, according to the respondent the *upādhi* u-ness as a vitiator of an only positive inference $\mathcal{I}$ due to the present defining characteristic can be regarded as a property which is indirectly established as a property of a disagreeing instance. We can first vitiate an only positive inference $\mathcal{I}'$ in which u functions as the inferential subject and the probandum is the same as in $\mathcal{I}$. Since u is proved to be a locus of the absence of this probandum, u-ness can be regarded as a property of a disagreeing instance in $\mathcal{I}$.

Finally, the respondent takes issue with the incorporation of "a certain qualifier" as a limitor of the probandum in the defining characteristic, which he regards as an undue restriction.

(**1.1.13**) The opponent reaffirms Udayana's defining characteristic. It is, however, rejected by the respondent because of the previously mentioned mistakes, and because *upādhi*s according to both, Udayana's defining characteristic and the preceding one, are characterized by the latter in a way which is not expressed by the former.

(**1.1.14**) The opponent suggests to endorse the disjunction of both defining characteristics as a defining characteristic of *upādhi*s.

(**1.1.15**) Since the respondent is not satisfied with this solution either, the opponent suggests to include the nutshell version of Prabhākara Upādhyāya's defining characteristic as a further alternative in the disjunction.

(**1.1.15.1**) The respondent disagrees with this suggestion, because any attempt to specify disjunctive properties with arbitrary disjuncts results in a regressus ad infinitum.

(**1.1.15.2**) Moreover, each disjunct would be encumbered with the aforementioned mistakes. Finally, a proper defining characteristic should rather be a uniform property.

(**1.1.16**) The opponent suggests a new defining characteristic: "The *upādhi* does not pervade the probans, while it pervades only the examples." This defining characteristic is purportedly not afflicted with the mistakes which result from restricting the pervasion of the probandum in the same way as in the preceding defining characteristics. However, the respondent disagrees with the opponent's suggestion, because something which functions as an example in one inference might function as the inferential subject in another. Moreover, the present defining characteristic would be afflicted with the defect of non-pervasion if "pervading only the examples" were meant here in the sense of "only some examples". Finally, there is the defect of over-pervasion with respect to the property of being different from the inferential subject limited by the probandum.

(**1.1.17**) The opponent suggests another defining characteristic: "That is an associate condition with respect to that probans without which there is no concomitance between the two and there is a deviation of that probans with respect to that probandum." The respondent rejects it too, because the pronouns contained in it have no fixed referent. Moreover, since the expressions "probans" and "probandum" can only be explicated by means of the concept of *upādhi*, the present defining characteristic proves to be circular.

(**1.1.18**) The respondent concludes that all the afore-mentioned defining characteristics which contain the expressions "probans" and "probandum" fail as general defining characteristics if "probans" and "probandum" are treated here as variables. Therefore, specifying these expressions by means of appropriate substitutions does not yield specific defining characteristics, because there can be no specific defining characteristic without a general one.

(**1.2**) The author announces the beginning of the *siddhānta*.

(**1.2.1**) The proponent of the right view (*siddhāntin*) enunciates the property of being a property which is a counterpositive of an absolute absence (*atyantābhāvapratiyogidharmatva*) as a general defining characteristic of all *upādhis*. This defining characteristic is also an *upādhi*. Therefore, it resides in itself. Self-dependence in the sense of self-residence should not be regarded as a defect. A general defining characteristic is needed to identify something as an *upādhi*. The self-residence of the *atyantābhāvapratiyogidharmatva* is not an obstacle to its identification as a counterpositive of an absolute absence. The awareness that the *atyantābhāvapratiyogidharmatva* resides in itself is only a spin-off of the correct identification of the *atyantābhāvapratiyogidharmatva* as a counterpositive of an absolute absence.

(**1.2.1.1**) The general defining characteristic is also needed to motivate the application of the expression "*upādhi*". The root "*upadhā*", from which "*upādhi*" derives, does not serve this purpose. It refers to the action of transmitting, not to an *upādhi*'s function of vitiating.

(**1.2.1.2**) Moreover, the *atyantābhāvapratiyogidharmatva* is not afflicted with the defect of over-pervasion with regard to universally positive properties. The *siddhāntin* refutes various attempts to prove that knowability is a counterpositive of an absolute absence.

(**1.2.1.3**) A counterpositive of an absolute absence can be cognized despite the fact that the counterpositive is not present to the cognizing subject. It is also possible to have cognitive access to something in the future. A counterpositive is the object of an awareness (*anubhava*) which highlights its role as a correlate of an absolute absence. It might be tempting to classify a counterpositive as an indicative mark (*upalakṣaṇa*) signifying an absence. However, as an object of an awareness a counterpositive differs from an indicative mark which is an object of a recollection.

(**1.2.2**) The proponent of the right view endorses a defining characteristic of the *upādhi* which requires the pervasion of the probandum by the *upādhi* to be coextensive, because he wants to ensure that an *upādhi* functions as both, a vitiator and a corrector.

(**1.2.2.1**) Moreover, by requiring the pervasion of the probandum by the *upādhi* to be coextensive, the *siddhāntin* tries to forestall that the defining characteristic pertains to the property of being different from the inferential subject. He does not pursue the opponent's alternative strategy to insist on a positive and negative pervasion of the probandum by the *upādhi*, although he acknowledges that it would have the same effect. However, he favors a defining characteristic which can account for the *upādhi*'s function as a corrector.

(**1.2.2.2**) The opponent objects that the *siddhāntin*'s defining characteristic fails to exclude the *pakṣetaratva* limited by the probandum. However, according to the *siddhāntin* this property cannot be pervaded by the probandum, because there are epistemic restrictions for the relata of a pervasion. The cognition of the pervasion of F by G means to conceive of F as something which is specified by the pervasion relation. Hence, G cannot be less specific than F, i.e., fire occurring in other loci than the mountain, e.g., cannot be pervaded by fire.

The opponent tries to concoct an *upādhi* according to the *siddhāntin*'s defining characteristic which vitiates the design inference in Nyāya. However, the *siddhāntin* shows that the purported pervasion of the opponent's *upādhi* by the probandum can be vitiated by means of another *upādhi*.

The *siddhāntin* refutes the opponent's attempt to demonstrate that an only positive inference can be vitiated by means of the *pakṣetaratva* if the latter is conceived of as an *upādhi* according to the *siddhāntin*'s defining characteristic. If the probandum is an omnipresent property, the *pakṣetaratva* surely cannot pervade it.

Moreover, the *pakṣetaratva* or the *pakṣetaratva* limited by the probandum are bogus qualifiers. They do not serve an *upādhi*'s purpose of restricting the range of the probans to loci of the probandum.

The *siddhāntin* further explains that the specification of the pervasion of the probandum by the *upādhi* as coextensive is by no means useless. The cognition of a pervasion depends on the frequent observation of the concomitance of the relata by the faculty of sight. The faculty of sight cannot distinguish between a pervasion which is characterized as coextensive and a pervasion which is characterized as non-coextensive, i.e., if the faculty of sight grasps a pervasion, it might be non-coextensive. Hence, in order to exclude the possibility that an associate condition pervades an assumed probandum non-coextensively, this needs to be further investigated. The condition of a coextensive pervasion has to be included in the defining characteristic in order to account for the fact that the epistemic procedure of identifying a property as an *upādhi* is incomplete, as long as its coextensive pervasion of the assumed probandum is still an open issue.

(**1.2.2.3**) The opponent objects that the concept of an *upādhi* should not be confined to properties which pervade the probandum coextensively, because there are also *upādhi*s which pervade only the "relation" between probans and probandum, i.e., the range of loci of their co-occurrence. In order to tailor the defining characteristic to such *upādhi*s he suggests to drop the constraint of a coextensive pervasion and to specify the concept of a probandum in an appropriate way.

If "probandum" is meant in the sense of "pervader", i.e., in the sense of the instance of the probandum whose presence on the inferential subject is supposed to be inferred, then mountainness might be regarded as an associate condition which vitiates the valid inference of fire from smoke on a mountain. Hence, the opponent suggests to understand "probandum" in the sense of "pervaderness", a property which pertains only to loci of the joint occurrence of probans and probandum.

(**1.2.2.3.1**) The *siddhāntin* disagrees with the opponent, because he still insists that the defining characteristic should express the corrector function of an *upādhi*.

Moreover, the absence of a non-coextensively pervading associate condition would not be an indicator of the truth of the counter-thesis in the sense of a necessary antecedent of the absence of the probandum: The absence of a non-coextensively pervading associate condition from the inferential subject warrants the truth of the counter-thesis, i.e., the absence of the probandum from the inferential subject. However, in the case of the presence of a non-coextensively pervading associate condition on the inferential subject the counter-thesis may or may not be true. The constraint of a coextensive pervasion yields a one-to-one correspondence between the absence of the associate condition and the absence of the probandum.

The *siddhāntin* emphasizes that a non-coextensively pervading property cannot be admitted as another variety of *upādhi*. *upādhis* have to be coextensively pervading, because all genuine *upādhis* are correctors.

(**1.2.2.3.2**) The *siddhāntin* argues that a property need not be an *upādhi* if it only pervades "the relation between probans and probandum", i.e., the range of loci of their co-occurrence, without being pervaded by the probandum in the range of the probans. However, such a property can be a genuine *upādhi* if it functions as a corrector (i.e., if it is pervaded by the probandum in the range of the probans). The *siddhāntin* also accepts *upādhis* which pervade the probandum limited by a certain property, as long as they pervade the probandum coextensively in the range of the probans.

(**1.2.2.4**) The *siddhāntin* defends his defining characteristic against the charge of over-pervasion with regard to the probans. Since it is impossible that the probans does not pervade itself, it does not fulfill one of the criteria of an *upādhi*.

The *siddhāntin* further defends his defining characteristic against the charge of non-pervasion with regard to a mode of presentation which is expressed by another defining characteristic, viz. "having a coextensive pervasion and being different from the subject of the inference". In contrast to properly formulated specific defining characteristics the present one contains no explicit specification of the *upādhi*'s relation to probans and probandum in an invalid inference.

The *siddhāntin* also issues a caveat against the proto-version of Prabhākara Upādhyāya's defining characteristic, since in the case of a defeasible coextensive pervasion of the putative probans by the putative probandum the associate condition pervades the probandum coextensively, so that it makes no sense to limit the pervasion of the probandum by the associate condition to the range of the probans.

The opponent concocts two properties which match the defining characteristics according to which the *upādhi* pervades the probandum limited by a property of the subject of the inference or by a property of an agreeing instance. Since the pervasion is apparently coextensive in both cases, the *siddhāntin* should be committed to accept them as genuine *upādhis*. However, the inferences which are supposed to be vitiated by these properties are valid. The *siddhāntin* traces the defect of each of these pseudo-*upādhis* to the fact that they are less specific than the probanda which they putatively pervade.

The *siddhāntin* concludes that his general and specific defining characteristics have been proved to be unobjectionable.

(**2**) The *siddhāntin* announces the topic of the second *pariccheda*, viz. the functional specification of the *upādhi*, which accounts for the adequacy of his general and his specific defining characteristic.

(**2.1**) He renders four different views concerning an *upādhi*'s function as a vitiator, viz. the views that it indicates a deviation (i), that it validates the counter-thesis (ii), that it exposes the probans as a conditional probans (*vyāpyatvāsiddha*), a special type of pseudo-probans (*hetvābhāsa*) (iii), and, finally, the view that the *upādhi* does not vitiate at all (iv).

(**2.1.1**) The *siddhāntin* explains how an *upādhi*'s non-pervasion of the probans and its pervasion of the probandum are conducive to its function as a vitiator in the sense of (i). However, the adherents of (i) regard the co-extensive pervasion of the probandum by the *upādhi* as a merely accidental phenomenon.

The opponent argues that an *upādhi*'s function of vitiating or correcting cannot be explained reductively by means of the concept of pervasion. However, according to the *siddhāntin* the attribution of these functional features needs to be demonstrated.

(**2.1.2**) The opponent argues that (ii) is inadmissible, because an *upādhi* can only yield a negative result. However, according to the *siddhāntin* this is not true, because an *upādhi* functions also as a corrector. The opponent defends (ii) against (i) by pointing out that (i) refers only to a secondary function of the *upādhi*. Moreover, he argues that the functions of a vitiator and a corrector are incompatible.

(**2.1.3**) The *siddhāntin* approves of (iii).

(**2.1.3.1**) The opponent tries to unmask the *upādhi* as a sophistry. He argues that the absence of an *upādhi* cannot be a criterion for the validity of an inference. If an inference is valid, there is no *upādhi* and an absence cannot be the absence of something non-existent. The *siddhāntin* responds that as long as an inference's validity is an open issue, one can reasonably suspect that it is liable to be vitiated by an *upādhi.* The validity of an inference can be determined by eliminating candidate *upādhi*s and by applying a favorable reductio ad absurdum (*anukūlatarka*) as a means to resolve the doubt concerning the pervasion at issue.

A favorable reductio ad absurdum is based on an absurd conclusion which follows from denying what is to be proven. The absurdity of such a conclusion is self-evident, i.e., there is no epistemic ungroundedness involved in the method of reductio ad absurdum.

(**2.1.3.2**) The *siddhāntin* explains the fallacy of the conditional probans (*vyāpyatvāsiddhi*) as the probans's incapacity to secure the probandum of its own accord. It needs to be fortified by means of an *upādhi.* In this way the *upādhi*'s function as a vitiator is linked to its function as a corrector. In addition to the property of leading to the fallacy of the conditional probans (*vyāpyatvāsiddhyāpādakatva*) the *siddhāntin* endorses the property of being in effect the absence of a pervasion (*vyāptivirahabhūtatva*) as a proper characterization of the associate conditions's function of vitiating.

(**2.1.4**) The *siddhāntin* argues that an assumed pervasion cannot be directly vitiated by an unfavorable reductio ad absurdum, which might render the *upādhi* superfluous. He agrees only to the utility of a) a favorable reductio ad absurdum (*anukūlatarka*) for the purpose of securing the pervasion of the probandum by the *upādhi* and b) an unfavorable reductio ad absurdum (*pratikūlatarka*) for the purpose of refuting the denial of an *upādhi*'s pervadedness by the probandum.

(**2.1.5**) The opponent objects that an invalid only negative inference cannot be corrected by means of an *upādhi* according to the *siddhāntin*'s defining characteristic. The co-occurrence of *upādhi,* probans and probandum outside the inferential subject would contradict the only negative character of the inference.

The *siddhāntin* argues that in the case of an invalid only negativ inference an *upādhi* according to his defining characteristic is a vitiator and a corrector of the corresponding negative pervasion, i.e., such an *upādhi* does not pervade the absence of the probandum, while it pervades the absence of the probans coextensively.

The *siddhāntin* rules out (iv) by concluding that an *upādhi* according to his specific defining characteristic can function as a vitiator of any kind of pseudo-inference (including only negative ones).

(**3**) The *siddhāntin* announces the topic of the third *pariccheda*, viz. the typology of the *upādhi*.

(**3.1**) He divides (genuine) *upādhi*s into ascertained and dubious ones, where the ascertained ones are subdivided into those which pervade the entire probandum and those which pervade only the probandum in the range of a qualifier such as, e.g., the probans.

(**3.1.1**) He subdivides the dubious *upādhi*s into two basic types, viz. those whose non-pervasion of the probans is ascertained (i) and those whose non-pervasion of the probans is dubious (ii). Although he does not do it, (i) can again be subdivided into three dubious subtypes and (ii) can be subdivided into four dubious subtypes (according to the ascertained or dubious fulfillment of the other criteria of an *upādhi*). He illustrates (i) by means of the Dṛṣadvatī-example and (ii) by means of the Mitrā-example.

Moreover, by interchanging the roles of probandum and *upādhi* in the Mitrā-example the *siddhāntin* derives an example of a dubious *upādhi* where all three criteria of an *upādhi* are dubious. The opponent refers to a putatively analogous case. However, his example involves an ascertained *upādhi*, which he replaces with a coextensive property. The *siddhāntin* points out that the thesis of an inference based on the same probans and probandum as in the opponent's example might even be verified by means of a reductio ad absurdum, whereas no such reductio ad absurdum is available for the purpose of verifying the thesis in the Mitrā-example.

(**3.1.2**) The *siddhāntin* suggests an alternative taxonomy of dubious *upādhi*s which is based on the different ways in which the *upādhi* pervades the probandum. He distinguishes between pervasions of (i) the entire probandum, (ii) the probandum limited by a certain qualifier and (iii) the absence of the probans as the pervader in a negative pervasion related to an only negative inference. Oddly enough, the manuscript also refers to a type of *upādhi*s which pervade the absence of the probandum. However, none of the *siddhāntin*'s examples matches this specification. Due to a lacuna and an unconjecturable corrupt reading in the manuscript the nature of the remaining two types of *upādhi*s is inscrutable.

(**3.2**) The opponent points out the problem of a mutual dependence between the concept of pervasion (as a relation without *upādhi*) and the *siddhāntin*'s defining characteristic of an *upādhi*, which involves the concept of pervasion. In order to avoid the apparent circularity he suggests to conceive of *upādhi*s as (indefinable) atomic individuals. However, according to the *siddhāntin* the defining characteristic is needed to distinguish between valid probantia and pseudo-probantia.

The *siddhāntin* holds that the second member of an inference is a statement of the *upādhi*-independent character of the probans. The opponent, however, regards it as a mere statement of the probans's occurrence on the inferential subject. He holds that the *siddhāntin*'s explication would render the third member of an inference redundant, since the latter refers to a pervasion as an *upādhi*-independent relation. According to the *siddhāntin* redundance is a common feature of a five-membered inference anyway, because the probans's occurrence on the inferential subject is also mentioned twice, viz. in the second and in the fourth member. The second member is only enunciated after careful consideration of the probans's unimpeded conclusiveness.

The opponent objects that one can never be sure about the probans's unimpeded conclusiveness, because the inferential subject might be an exception to the loci of the probans's co-occurrence with the probandum, so that the property of being different from the inferential subject has to be taken into account as a universal vitiator. However, the *siddhāntin* does not accept this property as an *upādhi.*

(**3.3**) A putative *upādhi* is "apparent" if it exhibits or may well exhibit at least one of the three features of the *siddhāntin*'s specific defining characteristic, while it fails to exhibit at least one of the other two features. The *siddhāntin*'s taxonomy of apparent *upādhi*s comprises (i) those properties which only pervade the probandum, (ii) those which are only pervaded by the probandum, (iii) those which only do not pervade the probans, (iv) those which do not pervade the probans, but pervade the probandum without being pervaded by the probandum, and (v) those which do not pervade the probans, but are pervaded by the probandum without pervading the probandum.

The *siddhāntin* ignores the combinatorial possibility which only fails to be not pervading the probans. If this is not just an oversight, the *siddhāntin*'s reluctance to classify such a property as an apparent *upādhi* might be owing to the fact that its characterization warrants the genuine pervasion of the probans by the probandum.

(**3.3.1**) The *siddhāntin* illustrates each type of apparent *upādhi*s by means of an example.

(**3.3.2**) The property of being different from the inferential subject is not needed as an *upādhi* in order to vitiate a countermanded thesis. For that purpose one might as well take into account the inferential subject's failure to function as a proper abode of the probandum, i.e., as a locus which fulfills the inferential-subject-proviso (*pakṣatā*).

(**3.4**) The *siddhāntin* takes stock: Genuine and apparent *upādhi*s can be systematized according to his classification schemas. His general and specific defining characteristics serve to identify *upādhi*s. The *upādhi* is a vitiator in its own right and a corrector.

Chapter 3

Manuscript and Edition of the UD

3.1 Description of the Manuscript of the UD

acquirer	Bhandarkar Oriental Research Institute
date of acquisition	1898 – 1899
inventory number in the manuscript catalogue of the Bhandarkar Oriental Research Institute	No. 6
apograph	undated
script	Devanāgarī and Jainanāgarī
language	Sanskrit
title	Upādhidarpaṇa[1]
author	unknown
size	9 folios (folio 9b left blank)
writing material	ink on paper
lines per folio	∅ ≈ 21
akṣaras per line	∅ ≈ 60
readability	very good
state of preservation	excellent

[1]There is no front page. However, the title is mentioned several times in the text (cf., e.g., UD: 9a, 18).

3.2 Editorial Policy

The present edition is semi-diplomatic. Obvious and suspected scribal errors are corrected and the original readings of the manuscript are reported in footnotes (in the form: "Ms. ..."). Exceptions (such as tacit editorial corrections of orthographic abnormalities etc.) are noted in the next section. Scribal deletions and interlinear or marginal corrections are always reported (revealing the readings *ante* and *post correctionem* in the form "Ms. ... corrected to ..."), but they are not always adopted, so that the reading of the constituted text may be different. In this case the scribal correction is also reported in a footnote, but marked with an asterisk (in the form "Ms. ... corrected to ... *").

3.2.1 Conventions in the Text

1. The beginning of a new front page or back page of a folio is indicated in square brackets in the text (such as, e.g., "[M1a]").

2. Division into paragraphs is editorial.

3. The full stop indicates a *daṇḍa* or semi-*daṇḍa* in the manuscript, but occasionally the punctuation marks used in the manuscript are ignored or a full stop is added in the present edition where the manuscript has no punctuation. "/" marks the end of a hemistich. "//" marks the end of a verse.

4. Orthography and *saṃdhi*

   (a) *ba* and *va*, being indistinguishable from each other, have been read according to expectation.

   (b) The following orthographic variants are not reported:

      i. gemination of consonants after a semi-vowel
      ii. use of *anusvāra* for homorganic nasal or the reverse
      iii. use of class sibilant for *visarga* before a sibilant
      iv. non-application of *saṃdhi*
      v. non-occurrence of *avagraha*

   (c) The classical rules of *saṃdhi* have been consistently applied.

3.2.2 Editorial Signs and Abbreviations

<. . . > (in combination with a footnote)	indicates that the accompanying footnote refers to the whole text enclosed in angular brackets, which may be either (i) an emendation of a manuscript reading or (ii) an adopted scribal correction of an error or (iii) the literal rendering of an unconjecturable corrupt passage
Ms. . . . corrected to . . .	indicates an adopted scribal correction
Ms. . . . corrected to . . . *	indicates a dismissed scribal correction
. . . (≈ *n* *akṣara*s missing)	indicates a lacuna represented by means of *n* horizontal strokes (for the missing *akṣara*s) in the manuscript[2]
(. . . ?)	indicates barely legible *akṣara*s or parts of such *akṣara*s
(?)	indicates illegible *akṣara*s or parts of such *akṣara*s
+	indicates decoration
om.	omisit

3.3 The UD (Text)

(**1**) [M1a]+ *oṃ namaḥ.*

> *śrīrāmacandraṃ śirasā praṇamya guruṃ ca yajñeśvaram asmadīyam/*
> *upādhisāmānyaviśeṣalakṣyavinirṇayo 'yaṃ kriyate gabhīraḥ//1*

(**1.1**) *nanūpādheḥ kiṃ sāmānyalakṣaṇaṃ viśeṣalakṣaṇaṃ vā.*

(**1.1.1**) *tatra na tāvat sāmānyalakṣaṇaṃ saṃgacchate. tathā hi. atyantābhāvapratiyogitvaṃ hi sāmānyalakṣaṇam ity uktam. tan na. nityadravyeṣv*

[2] However, the number of *akṣara*s which fill the lacuna in the constituted text may be different.

ativyāpteḥ. tathā hi. gaganādayaḥ[3] *svaniṣṭhātyantābhāvenātyantābhāvapratiyogina eva na ca te tatra vartante. ātmāśrayatāprasaṅgāt. na ca teṣām upādhitvaṃ. sarvānumānabhaṅgaprasaṅgāt.*

(**1.1.2**) *nanv atyantābhāvapratiyogidharmatvaṃ. teṣām anāśritatvena dharmatvābhāvān nopādhitvam iti cet.*

(**1.1.2.1**) *tan na. atyantābhāvapratiyogidharmatvaṃ svayam anupādhir upādhir vā. ādye lakṣaṇasya tatraivātivyāptiḥ. svaniṣṭhātyantābhāvapratiyogitvāt. anupādhidharmatvāc ca. dvitīye pakṣe tatra cedaṃ na vartate vartate vā. no ced avyāptiḥ*[4]*. dvitīye svayaṃ vartate. anyad vā. ādya ātmāśrayatvam. dvitīye sāmānyatvalakṣaṇavyāghātaḥ. anavasthāprasaṅgāc ca.*

(**1.1.2.2**) *kiṃca. etallakṣaṇamātraniṣṭhadharmā upādhir anupādhir vā. ādye tatra tad eva lakṣaṇaṃ vartate 'nyad vā. nādyaḥ parasparāśrayatvaprasaṅgāt. svaniṣṭhadharme hi svasya vṛttiḥ. svasmiṃs tasya <dharmasya vṛttir>*[5] *iti. anyac cet pūrvoktadoṣaḥ. dvitīye lakṣaṇasyātivyāptiḥ. tanmātraniṣṭhadharmasya <taditaraniṣṭhātyantābhāvapratiyogitvān nityadravyaprameyatvādīnāṃ>*[6] *dharmātyantābhāvapadābhyāṃ vyāvṛttatvena tallakṣaṇaṃ tatra na vartata iti na vaktavyam. tathā ca tadubhayaniṣṭhātyantābhāvapratiyogitvāl*[7] *lakṣaṇadharmatvāc ca lakṣaṇaṃ tatrāvaśyaṃ vartata iti vaktavyam. anyathā nityadravyaprameyatvādīnāṃ tatra prasaṅgāt.*

(**1.1.2.3**) *tathā lakṣaṇe vartamānam atyantābhāvapratiyogidharmatvam asmāl lakṣaṇād bhinnam abhinnaṃ vā. ādya idam apy upādhilakṣaṇaṃ no vā. no cel lakṣaṇaniṣṭhatvarahitam ity upādhilakṣaṇaṃ viśeṣaṇīyam. anyathā lakṣaṇasaṃdehāpatteḥ. lakṣaṇaṃ ced vyāhatam upādhilakṣaṇaniṣṭhasyopādhivyāvartakatva*[8]*virodhāt. abhinnapakṣa ātmāśrayatvam.*

(**1.1.2.4**) *nanu sthitāv ātmāśrayatvam adūṣaṇam utpattijñaptipratibandhakatvāt tasya. anyathā kevalānvayitvabhaṅgaprasaṅgaḥ. tathā hi. vivādādhyāsitaṃ kasyacit pratyakṣaṃ prameyatvāt karatalāmalakavad ityādikaṃ*[9] *kevalānvayyudāharaṇam. atra sādhye sādhyaṃ vartate na vā. no cet sādhyābhāvavati sādhye hetuvṛttāv anaikāntikam āpadyeta. ādye pakṣe 'nyasya <vṛttāv anavasthā>*[10] *svavṛttāv ātmāśrayatvaṃ ca bhavet. tathā ca dūṣaṇaṃ yadi ced bhavet kevalānvayitvaṃ bhajyata*[11] *iti cet.*

[3]Ms. *gaganādayo* corrected to *gaganādayaḥ* [4]Ms. *ativyāptiḥ* [5]Ms. *dharmasya dharmavṛttir* [6]Ms. *taditaraniṣṭhātyantābhāvapratiyogitvānityadravyaprameyatvādīnāṃ* [7]Ms. *tadubhayaniṣṭhātyatāvapratiyogitvāl* [8]Ms. *-vyārtakatva-* corrected to *-vyāvartakatva-* [9]Ms. *ityādikeṃ* corrected to *ityādikaṃ* [10]Ms. *vṛtto 'navasthā* [11]Ms. *bha(j-y?)ata*

(**1.1.2.5**) *tan na. ātmāśrayadūṣaṇatvānabhyupagame*[12] *'nvayavyatirekyādyanumānam api bhajyate. tathā hi. parvato 'gnimān. dhūmavattvād ity anumāne*[13] *dhūmavattvādeḥ svavṛttātmāśrayatvasya bādhakatvābhāve sādhyābhāvavati*[14] *svasmin*[15] *vṛttisaṃbhavād anaikāntikam āpadyeta. tathā ca sthitāv ātmāśrayatvaṃ dūṣaṇam evety anvayavyatirekiprāmāṇyaṃ*[16] *samarthanīyam.*

nanu dūṣaṇatvābhyupagame kevalānvayyanumānaṃ bhajyata iti cet.

bhajyatām anvaya[17]*vyatirekadvayavatas*[18] *tasya*[19] *prāmāṇyābhyupagamasyāvaśyakatvāt. tasmād ātmā*[M1b]*śrayatvaṃ sthitāv api dūṣaṇam eveti sthitam.*

(**1.1.2.6**) *kiṃca*[20].

vyāvṛtter apy upādhitve pakṣadoṣopaveśane/
vyāvṛttyantarasadbhāvān nānavasthā kathaṃ bhavet//1[21]
tasyā eva prasādhyatva ekadeśavihīnatā/
vyāvṛttyantarapakṣe tu pūrvadoṣaprasañjanam//2[22]

tasmād upādhilakṣaṇasya prayojanābhāvād anārambhanīyam eveti siddham.

(**1.1.3**) *nanu loke tāvad upādhiśabdo vyavahriyate. so 'pi vyavahāro vyutpattisāpekṣaḥ. vyutpattir api vyaktiṣu na saṃgacchate. vyaktīnām ānantyāt. atas tāvad anugataṃ pravṛttinimittaṃ vaktavyam.*

tallakṣaṇānām[23] *eva jāter api bhāvāt tadaṅgīkāre jātisaṃkaradoṣa āpadyeta. tathā hi. sattopādhitvasāmānyaṃ parityajya nityadravyeṣu vartate. sattāṃ*[24] *parityajyopādhitvasāmānyaṃ*[25] *sāmānyādau vartate. tadubhayor api guṇādau saṃkaraḥ sāmānyādau vidyamānatvāc ca na sāmānyarūpateti cet.*

tan na. lokaprasiddhaprayogabalenaiva[26] *tatpravṛtteḥ. upa samīpe svaniṣṭhaṃ dharmam*[27] *anyatrādadhāti. na kriyāṅgavattvād*[28] *upādhiśabdo vṛddhavyavahārasiddhaḥ. ato bhavaduktam anapekṣya copādhiśabdaḥ pravartata iti siddham.*

---

[12]Ms. *ātmāśrayadoṣesyaṇatvānabhyupagame* corrected to *ātmāśrayadūṣaṇatvānabhyupagame* [13]Ms. *anumāneṣu* corrected to *anumāne* [14]Ms. *sādhyo bhāvavati* corrected to *sādhyābhāvavati* [15]Ms. *svasmin svasmi* corrected to *svasmin* [16]Ms. *anvayavyatirekaprāmāṇyaṃ* corrected to *anvayavyatirekiprāmāṇyaṃ* [17]Ms. *anvayi-* corrected to *anvaya-* [18]Ms. *-dvayavata(s?)* [19]Ms. *tesya* corrected to *tasya* [20]Ms. *kiṃci* corrected to *kiṃca* [21]Ms. / corrected to *//1* [22]Ms. / corrected to *//2* [23]Ms. *tallakṣasām* [24]Ms. *satyāttāṃ* corrected to *sattāṃ* [25]Ms. *parityajyopādhitvasanyaṃ* [26]Ms. *lokaprasiddhayogabalenaiva* corrected to *lokaprasiddhaprayogabalenaiva* [27]Ms. *dh* corrected to *dharmam* [28]Ms. *kiyāṅgavatvād*

nanu saṃyogas tāvaj japākusumādisādhāraṇatvenātiprasaṅgīti cet.

tan na. atyantābhāvapratiyogidharmatvam upādhilakṣaṇam iti vadato japākusumāder api kutracid upādhitvābhyupagamāt.

nanv evaṃ cet svagatavyāpyatvāvabhāsakatvam evopādhilakṣaṇaṃ bhavet. nāsmākaṃ tasyeti cet.

maivam. viṣamavyāptikopādheḥ svagatavyāpyatvāvabhāsakatvaṃ nāstīty anaupādhikatvaprasaṅgāt. tasmād vyāvṛttivyavahārānupayuktatvāt[29] *siddhaṃ niṣprayojanatvam upādhilakṣaṇasyeti*[30].

(**1.1.4**) *kiṃca na. prameyatvam atyantābhāvapratiyogi dharmatvād ityādinā prameyatvāder atyantābhāvapratiyogitvasādhanād upādhitvenāsaṃpratipanne*[31] *meyatvādau lakṣaṇasya vṛtter ativyāptiḥ.*

nanu <prameyatvādyatyantābhāvāśrayaḥ pramito>[32] *na vā. na ced āśrayābhāvāt tadatyantābhāvo na saṃgacchate. āśrayapratinirūpyatvād <abhāvasya pratītiś>*[33] *cet tasyāpi prameyatvena tadatyantābhāvāśrayatvaṃ vyāhatam. tathā ca vyāghātaparāhatatvān*[34] *nedam anumānam iti cet.*

na. anāśritāśrayatātyantābhāvapratiyogitvasamarthanenāpi[35] *paryavasānāt.*

nanv atyantābhāvaḥ kvacid āśrito 'bhāvatvād ity āśrayasamarthanena pūrvadoṣāpattir iti cet.

na. tasmād atyantābhāvasya pramityapramitibhyāṃ virodhāt. tathā hi. apramitaś ced āśrayāsiddhiḥ. pramitaś cet kutracit pramitaḥ.

tatpramityapramitibhyāṃ pūrvadoṣāpādatvāt pramāṇābhāvāc <cāsmadādeḥ pūrvānumānāt>[36] *saṃpratipannam iti cet.*

na.[37] *upajīvyavirodhena bhavadanumānasyāsattvāpatteḥ. asmadanumānasyānāśritātyantābhāvaviṣayatvena vyāghātatarkāpratihatatvāt siddhir*[38] *upādhilakṣaṇasyātivyāpteḥ*[39].

nanu tarhy āśritātyantābhāvapratiyogidharmatvam upādhilakṣaṇaṃ syāt[40] *prameyatvāder anāśritātyantābhāvapratiyogitvena tathātvābhāvād iti cet.*

---

[29] Ms. *vyāvṛttivyavahānupayuktatvāt* corrected to *vyāvṛttivyavahārānupayuktatvāt*
[30] Ms. *upādhilakṣṇasyeti* [31] Ms. *upādhitvenāsaṃtipanne* corrected to *upādhitvenāsaṃpratipanne* [32] Ms. *prameyatvādyatyantābhāvāśrayāpramito* [33] Ms. *abhāvasyāpratītiś*
[34] Ms. *vyāghātaparāha(ta?)parāhatatvāt* [35] Ms. *anāśrātāśrayatātyantābhāva-* [36] Ms. *cāsmadāde pūrvānumānāt* corrected to *cāsmadādeḥ pūrvānumānāt* [37] Ms. om. *na*
[38] Ms. *siddham* [39] Ms. *upādhilakṣaṇasyātivyāpteḥ* corrected to *upādhilakṣaṇasyātivyāptaḥ** [40] Ms. *syāt bhavet*

na.[41] *pūrvoktasaṃkaratvadoṣānativṛtteḥ. tasmān nopādhisāmānyalakṣaṇaṃ siddhaṃ viśeṣalakṣaṇaṃ vā*[42]. *sāmānyalakṣaṇābhāvād eva vi*[M2a]*śeṣalakṣaṇābhāvāt.*

(**1.1.5**) *nanu saptapadārthasāmānyalakṣaṇābhāve dravyādravyādiviśeṣaṇānāṃ yathā pravṛttis tathātrāpi vinā sāmānyalakṣaṇam*[43] *viśeṣaṇaṃ bhaved iti. atrotpattau <jñaptāv avasthitau>*[44] *sāmānyalakṣaṇaṃ viśeṣalakṣaṇāni nāpekṣante. ata upapannāny eva*[45] *sāmānyalakṣaṇaṃ vinā viśeṣalakṣaṇāni.*

atra tu jñaptau tāvad apekṣā vidyate. tathā hi. sāmānyalakṣaṇābhāva upādhiśabdasya bhavanmate <pravṛtter evābhāvāt. abodhakatvāpattau tadanumānopādhijñānārthaviśeṣalakṣaṇābhijñānābhāvena teṣām eva pratīter abhāvāt>[46].

na ca padārthasthale 'pi samāno 'yaṃ doṣaḥ. lakṣaṇaṃ śabdādivat saptabhir dravyādilakṣaṇair eva <tatra tatra>[47] *vyutpattisaṃbhavāt.*

kiṃca. laukikaḥ padārtha iti pakṣe padalakṣaṇaniruktau satyām eva tatsaṃbandhini vācye padārthavyutpattiḥ.

prakṛte tūpādhilakṣaṇaviśeṣaṇānām[48] *anantatvenākṣaśabdavan na nānārthavattvalābhaḥ. upādhivyaktīnām <ānantyena tu>*[49] *vyutpatter evāśakyatvāt.*

yogapakṣas tv asaṃbhāvita[50] *evopa samīpe svaniṣṭhadharmam ādadhātīti tasya dharmasya bhavadvivakṣitopādhyavyāpanāt.*

tasmād bhavadvivakṣitopādhiṣv eva śabdapratītyartham[51] *sāmānyalakṣaṇaṃ nibudhyaiva viśeṣalakṣaṇaṃ vaktavyam iti prakṛte sāmānyalakṣaṇābhāve viśeṣalakṣaṇaṃ nāstīti siddhiḥ.*

(**1.1.6**) *nanu sādhanāvyāpakatve sati sādhyavyāpakatvaṃ sāmānyalakṣaṇam. idam eva prakṛtatvādiviśeṣaṇena viśeṣalakṣaṇaṃ ceti.*

(**1.1.6.1**) *na. sādhyavyāpakatvaṃ na sādhyena <saṃpanno nopādhikaḥ>*[52] *saṃbandhaḥ. <sa upādhijñānādhīnaḥ>*[53] *so 'pi lakṣaṇajñānādhīna evety ātmāśrayetaretarāśrayacakrakatrayāpatteḥ*[54]. *tathā hi. upādhilakṣaṇenaivopādhijñānam. tenaivānaupādhikatvajñānapūrvakaṃ lakṣaṇam iti*

---

[41]Ms. om. *na* [42]Ms. om. *vā* [43]*sānyalakṣaṇaṃ* corrected to *sāmānyalakṣaṇaṃ* [44]Ms. *jñaptāvasthitau* [45]Ms. interpolates *vinā* after *eva* [46]Ms. *pravṛtter abhāvāt* corrected to *pravṛtter evābhāvāt. abodhakatvāpattau tadanumānopādhijñānārthaviśeṣalakṣaṇābhijñānābhāvena teṣām eva pratīter abhāvāt* [47]Ms. *tatra 2* [48]Ms. *-viśeṣeṇānām* corrected to *-viśeṣaṇānām* [49]Ms. *ānantye. nanu* [50]Ms. *asaṃbhāvitā* [51]Ms. *śabdapratyartham* [52]Ms. *sampannopādhikaḥ* [53]Ms. *sa copādhijñānādhīnaḥ* [54]Ms. *-cakrakayāpatteḥ* corrected to *-cakrakatrayāpatteḥ*

svamūlatvamātravivakṣāyām ātmāśrayatvaṃ[55] *vartate*[56] *dvayavivakṣāyāṃ parasparāśrayatvaṃ trayavivakṣāyāṃ tu cakraketi.*

tasmāl lakṣaṇam asaṃbhāvi. ātmāśrayāder virodhagarbhasya[57] *svarūpāsiddhyāpādakatvāt*[58] *tathā ca varadarājaḥ.*

> *ātmāśrayas tathānyonyasaṃśrayaś <cakrakāśrayaḥ/*
> *anavasthety>*[59] *amī tarkāḥ svarūpāsiddhihetavaḥ*[60]*//+*

(**1.1.6.2**) *asya tu lakṣaṇasya sāmānyalakṣaṇatvād*[61] *eva sādhyapadena sakalasādhyābhidhāne sati sādhanasyāpi kvacit sādhyatvāpattau tadvyāpakatvābhāvena lakṣaṇasya tādṛśopādhāv avyāptiḥ.*

(**1.1.6.3**) *<pakṣetare lakṣaṇam>*[62] *ativyāptaṃ parvatetaratvasya vahnimattvarūpasādhyavyāpakatvāt pakṣe sādhanavati vyāvṛttatvena sādhanāvyāpakatvāc ceti. tasyāpy upādhitve sarvānumānocchedaprasaṅgaḥ.*

nanu sādhyavyāpakatvaṃ[63] *nāma sādhyena sahānvayavyatirekavyāptimattvam*[64]. *tac ca pakṣetaratvasya nāsti. pakṣe sādhyābhāvaniścayābhāvād iti cet.*

na. anumānamātreṇa vyāpyavyāpakatvopapattau tadvyāvṛttau vyāpyavyāvṛtter āvaśyakatvena[65] *vyabhicāronnāyakatvopapattau vyatirekavyāpter āvaśyakatvābhāvena tadaṃśe lakṣaṇasya vaiyarthyāpatteḥ*[66].

parvatānumāpakaṃ na bhañjakapakṣe pakṣetaravyāvṛttyartham[67] *iti cet.*

upādhidūṣaṇadvāre samāne sati vyabhicāronnāyakatvāvaśyaṃbhāvāt[68] *tasya vyāvartanam asaṃgatam eva.*

nanv anyathā sarvānumānabhañjakaḥ syād iti cet.

evaṃ ced upādher dūṣaṇatvaṃ māstu. tāvatā hetāv upādhibhītipraśāntir na bhaviṣyatīti.

nanu vyabhicāronnāyakasya katham adūṣaṇatvaṃ vadāmaḥ.

<nanv anumānasyonnītavyabhicāre>[69] *dūṣaṇatvād iti cet.*

nanu[70] *tarhi pakṣetare 'pi dṛṣṭis te tathaiva*[71] *dīyatām. tasyāpy asmaduktaprakāreṇa vyabhicāronnāyakatvāt. tatrānvayo 'pi nāstīti cet.*

---

[55]Ms. *āśrayatvaṃ* [56]Ms. *vartava* [57]Ms. *-garttasya* [58]Ms. *svarūpasidhyāpādatvāt* corrected to *svarūpasi(ddhyā?)pādatvāt** [59]Ms. misquotes TR (cf. 234f) as follows: *cakrakānava. ... sthety* (≈ 3 *akṣaras* missing) [60]Ms. *svarūpāsiddhahetavaḥ* [61]Ms. *sāmānyālakṣaṇatvād* [62]Ms. *pakṣetaralakṣaṇam* [63]Ms. *sādhanāvyāpakatvaṃ* [64]Ms. *sahānvayavyatirekivyāptimattvaṃ* [65]Ms. *āvaśyakatvana* [66]Ms. *vaiyārthyāpatteḥ* [67]Ms. *-vyāvṛtyartham* [68]Ms. *-bhāvet* [69]Ms. *nanu mānasyonnītivyabhicāre* [70]Ms. *na. nanu* [71]Ms. *tathaiva dṛṣṭir*

na. upādhivyabhicārayor anudbhāvanena samayamātratvāt. tasmāt pakṣetaratvam asyopādhitvavādibhir vyāvartayitum[72] *aśakyatvāl lakṣaṇasya vyarthaviśeṣaṇatvam āpadyeta.*

kiṃca pakṣetaratvasyātmāśrayatayā svasmin svavṛttyasaṃbhavena tasyaiva vyatirekasyāpi saṃbhavāt tādṛśavyāpakatvavivakṣāyām[73] *api lakṣaṇasyātivyāptir*[74] *durṇivārā.*

kiṃca. sapakṣatvātivyāpteś ca tatra vipakṣa eva vyatirekasadbhāvāt.

nanu pakṣetaratvānyatve satīti viśeṣaṇena pakṣetare 'py ativyāptir vyāvartyata iti cet.

astu. tathāpi sapakṣatve 'tivyāptis tadavasthaiveti tasyāpi pakṣamātravyāvartakaviśeṣaṇatvena[75] *śarīrajanyatvā*[M2b]*divat pakṣetaratva*[76] *evāntarbhāvāt.*

sapakṣatvaṃ niścitasādhyavattvam. niścipadakaṃ[77] *tu pakṣamātrasyaiva vyāvartakaṃ <sādhyapadenaiva vipakṣavyāvṛtteḥ>*[78]*. tathāpi nātivyāptir lakṣaṇasyeti cet.*

tan na. bādhonnītapakṣetaravyāpteḥ[79]*. tathā hi. agnir anuṣṇaḥ. padārthatvād ghaṭādivad ityādiṣu pratyakṣādibādhitānumāneṣu vyāptibhāvo vaktavyaḥ. anyathāvyāptatve sati pakṣadharmatvena sāmānyopapatteḥ.*

nanu saṃdigdhasādhyavān <pakṣaḥ. tatra>[80] *sādhyābhāvanirṇayāt sādhyasaṃdehābhāvena tādṛśapakṣadharmatvam eva nāstīti na*[81] *pakṣadharmatvalakṣaṇānumānam. vaikalyād evābhāsatvaparyavasānān na vyāptibhāvena. tathā ca nopādhyudbhāvanaṃ tatrāvaśyakam iti cet.*

na. prapañcamithyātvādau tārkikādeḥ satyatvādipramāṇadārḍhyābhimānavataḥ saṃdehābhāvāt prapañcādipakṣo na syāt. tathā ca parānabhyāsagatadharmavān pakṣa iti lakṣaṇaṃ vaktavyam. tathā ca sati vahnir anuṣṇaḥ <padārthatvād ityādāv>[82] *anabhyupagamasaṃbhavena pakṣatvopapattau padārthatvahetoḥ*[83] *pakṣadharmatvam api saṃbhāvitam eveti siddhau paryavasānābhāvād vyāptibhāvodbhāvane 'vaśyabhāve nirupādhikasaṃbandharūpavyāptivirodhyupādhyudbhāvanāpattāv upādhyantarabhāvāt pakṣetaratvam eva vyabhicāronnāyakatvenopādhir bhaviṣyatīty avyāptir durṇivāraiva.*

(1.1.7) *ata eva na sādhanāvyāpakatve sati sādhyasamavyāpakatvam*[84] *ity udayanoktam apy upādhilakṣaṇam.*

---

[72]Ms. *vyāvarttayatum* [73]Ms. *-vivakṣām* [74]Ms. *lakṣa ... syātivyāptir* (≈ 1 *akṣara* missing) [75]Ms. *pakṣamātravyāvarttake viśeṣaṇatvena* [76]Ms. *pakṣetaravattva* [77]Ms. *-padakiṃ* [78]Ms. *sādhyapadenaiva ... pakṣavyāvṛtteḥ* (≈ 1 *akṣara* missing) [79]Ms. *-vyāptiḥ* [80]Ms. *pakṣa. statra* [81]Ms. om. *na* [82]Ms. *padārthatvādāv* [83]Ms. *padārthatvahenutoḥ* corrected to *padārthatvahetoḥ* [84]Ms. *-vyāpikatvam* corrected to *-vyāpakatvam*

(**1.1.7.1**) *viṣamavyāptikabādhonnītapakṣetaratva evāvyāpteḥ. pūrvoktakatipayadoṣāviṣṭatvāc*[85] *ca. tathā hi. sādhyavyāpakaprayuktātmāśrayatvādikaṃ sādhyapadena sakalasādhyābhidhānāyattam avyāptidūṣaṇaṃ pakṣetaratvādāv ativyāptiś cāsaṃbhavaś*[86] *caiva*[87].

nanu samavyāptyasaṃbhavāt[88] *pakṣetarasya tatrāpi vyāptiḥ kathaṃ bhaved iti cet.*

na. samavyāptikapakṣetarasyāsaṃbhavāt. tathā hi. śabdo 'bhidheya ityādāv aśabdatvādeḥ parvatetaravahnimattvādeś ca samavyāptisaṃbhavāt.

(**1.1.7.2**) *viṣamavyāptikopādhyavyāpanāc*[89] *ca nedaṃ lakṣaṇam.*

tathā hi. pārthivaparamāṇurūpādayo nityāḥ paramāṇuviśeṣaguṇatvāt. āpyaparamāṇurūpādivad iti. tatra pārthivaparamāṇuviśeṣaguṇatvābhāva upādhiḥ. sa tu viṣamavyāptika eva. tasyāpy upādhitvaṃ samavyāptikānagnitvādivaj jñeyam.

vyabhicāronnāyakatvena tadupādhitvam[90] *abhihitam. pakṣe sādhyavyāpakopādhinivṛttau sādhyavyāvṛtter āvaśyakatvena sādhyābhāvavati hetor vartamānatvāt tadunnāyakatvam upapadyate*[91]. *prayogas tv etatsādhanam etatsādhyavyabhicāry etatsādhyavyāpakavyabhicāritvāt prameyavad iti tad etad viṣamavyāptikasyāpi samānam iti tatrāvyāptiḥ siddhā.*

nanu svagatavyāpyatvāropakatvenopādhitvaṃ tac ca viṣamavyāptikopādhau nāsty eva. tathā hi. yāgīyahiṃsā pāpasādhanaṃ <*hiṃsātvād arthahiṃsāvad*>[92] *ity atra niṣiddhatvaṃ hi samavyāptikopādhiḥ. tasya sādhyavyāpakatvam etadvyāpyatvaṃ*[93] *cāsti niṣiddhatvahiṃsātvayor adharmasādhanatvena saha dṛṣṭāntena sahabhāvaś cāsti. tathā ca sāhacaryavaśān niṣiddhatvaṃ svagatavyāpyatvaṃ hi sādhyahetāv avabhāsayaty eva saṃnidhānāj japākusumam iva*[94] *sphaṭike lauhityam. viṣamavyāptikasya tathā svagatavyāpyatvāvabhāsakatvābhāvād*[95] *upādhiśabdapravṛttiḥ svaniṣṭhadharmābhāsakatvāl* <*lokaprasiddhasamavyāptikopādhāv eva yuktā*>[96] *bhavet.*

vyabhicāronnāyakatvena tu prameyatvādivyabhicārāvabhāsakapramāṇavaśād upādher dūṣaṇatvenodbhāvyatvaṃ na syāt. anyathā vyabhicāronnāyakatve 'sya pramāṇasyāpi dūṣaṇāntaratvenodbhāvyatvaṃ[97] *syāt. tasmād viṣamavyāptikasyānupādhitvān nāvyāptis tatreti cet.*

---

[85]Ms. *pūrvoktakatipayadoṣā āviṣṭa(tv?)āc* corrected to *pūrvoktakatipayadoṣāviṣṭa(tv?)āc* [86]Ms. *ca saṃbhava(ś?)* [87]Ms. *(cai?)va* [88]Ms. *samavyāsaṃbhavāt* corrected to *samavyāptisaṃbhavāt** [89]Ms. *-vyāptikopādhyāvyāpanāc* [90]Ms. *tātadupādhitvam* seems to be corrected to *tadupādhitvam* [91]Ms. *upapadyete* seems to be corrected to *upapadyate* [92]Ms. *hiṃsātvāt rthahiṃsāvad* [93]Ms. *itadvyāpyatvaṃ* [94]Ms. *iva yathā* corrected to *iva* [95]Ms. *svagatavyāpyatvābhāvāt* [96]Ms. *lokaprasiddhasamavyāptikopādhau ... yuktā* (≈ 4 *akṣaras* missing) [97]Ms. *dūṣaṇāntaratvenodbhāvyakaṃ ... na* (≈ 1 *akṣara* missing)

maivam. vyabhicāronnāyakapramāṇānām[98] *ekopasaṃgrāhakalakṣaṇābhāvāt. vyabhicārasya puraḥsphūrtikatve na*[99] *tasyaivodbhāvanārthatvāt. prakṛte tūktaprakāreṇopasaṃgrāhakāsaṃbhavāc ca. vyabhicāronnāyakopādher udbhāvanaṃ yuktam eveti tadunnāyakasyāpi prayo*[M3a]*jakatvam*[100] *ity atrāpi siddham evopādher dūṣaṇatvam. kiṃca viṣamavyāptikasyāpi svagatavyāpyatvāvabhāsakatvenopādhitvopapattau vyāpyatvāvabhāsakatvasyāprayojakatvāt.*

(**1.1.8**) *kiṃca. yatra sādhyasādhanayoḥ samavyāptis tatra sādhanāvacchinnaviṣamavyāptikasyopādhitvaṃ na*[101] *yujyate.*

tac ca kevale sādhane 'vabhāsanāt svavyāpyatvāvabhāsakatvam asyaiveti kathaṃ viṣamavyāptikasyānupādhitvam[102]*. tasmād viṣamavyāptikopādhāv avyāptiḥ siddhā.*

kiṃcāsmil̃ lakṣaṇe samapadaṃ vyartham. vyāvartyābhāvāt. viṣamavyāptikasyāpy upādhitvāt. samavyāptikaparvatetaravahnimattve[103] *loke 'pi vidyamānatvān na pakṣetaram api vyāvartyam.*

(**1.1.9**) *kiṃca sādhyasādhanasaṃbandhavyāpakopādhyavyāpanāc ca nedaṃ lakṣaṇam.*

tathā hi samavāyaḥ sammataḥ saṃbandhatvāt saṃyogavad ity atra saṃyogatvakāryatvasattādayaḥ[104] *saṃyoganiṣṭhā dharmāḥ sādhyasādhanasaṃbandhavyāpakā*[105] *upādhayaḥ. na ca teṣāṃ <sādhyavyāpakatvābhāvenānupādhitvaṃ vyabhicāronnāyakatvenopādhyantaravad>*[106] *atrāpy upādhitvasaṃbhavāt. tathā hi. sādhyasādhanasaṃbandhavyāpakopādhiḥ pakṣād vyāvartamānaḥ svavyāpyaṃ sādhanasaṃbandham api vyāvartayati. sādhyasādhanasaṃbandhavyāvṛttiś*[107] *ca tredhā saṃbhavati. sādhanavyāvṛttyā sādhyavyāvṛttyobhayathāvyāvṛttyā*[108] *ceti tatrādyacaramau <sādhanasyobhayavādisiddhatve 'nupapannāv>*[109] *iti. dvitīye sādhyābhāvavati pakṣe sādhyasya vṛtter hetor vyabhicāronnāyakatvam api siddham eva. tasmāt tasyāpy upādhitvena tatrāvartamānasya lakṣaṇasyāvyāptiḥ*[110] *siddhā.*

(**1.1.10**) *tarhi sādhyasādhanasaṃbandhavyāpakatve sati sādhanāvyāpakatvam*[111] *iti śivādityamiśroktam evopādhilakṣaṇaṃ bhavatu saṃbandhavyā-*

---

[98]Ms. *-pramāṇonam* corrected to *-pramāṇānam** [99]Ms. om. *na* [100]Ms. *prayojakam* [101]Ms. om. *na* [102]Ms. *viṣamavyāptikasyānupādhikatvam* [103]Ms. *-vahnimatve* [104]Ms. *saṃyogatvakāryatve sattādayaḥ* [105]Ms. *sādhyasādhanathasaṃbandhavyāpakā* corrected to *sādhyasādhanasaṃbandhavyāpakā* [106]Ms. *sādhyavyāpakatvābhāvenānupādhitvavyabhicāronnāyakatvenopādhyantaravad* [107]Ms. om. *-saṃbandha-* [108]Ms. *sādhyavyāvṛ ubhayathāvṛttyā* corrected to *sādhyavyāvṛttyā ubhayathāvṛttyā* [109]Ms. *-siddhatvānupapannāv* [110]Ms. *lakṣpa ... syātivyāptiḥ* (≈1 *akṣara* missing) [111]Ms. *sādhanavyāpakatvam*

pakopādhivyāpanāt. viṣamavyāptikopādher api saṃbandhavyāpakatvasyāpi vidyamānatvena tatrāpi vartanāt[112]*. ata eva bādhonnītapakṣetare 'pi nopādhāv*[113] *avyāpteḥ.*

tathā hi. nityaḥ. kṛtakatvād iti[114]*. tatra sādhyasādhanasaṃbandha eva nāsti. kutas tadvyāpakatvam upādheḥ. maivam. tatra viruddhatvād*[115] *eva hetor duṣṭatvāt. katham upādhyudbhāvanam iti cet.*

(**1.1.10.1**) *maivam. anumānasya dve 'ṅge vyāptiḥ pakṣadharmatā ca. tatra sarvābhāse hy anyatarāṅgavaikalyam avaśyaṃbhāvi. anyathā pramāpakatvāpatteḥ. tatha ca viruddhasthale pakṣadharmatvasya sadbhāvād vyāptyabhāva eva vaktavyaḥ. vyāptiś ca nirupādhisaṃbandhaḥ*[116]*. tathā ca tadvirodhyupādhyudbhāvanam. viruddhatvadoṣodbhāvanena prativādinā pariṣatprativādijijñāsāyām avaśyaṃbhāvitanmātratvātivyāptaṃ lakṣaṇam.*

(**1.1.10.2**) *nanu yasya mate 'vyabhicārasaṃbandho vyāptir iti vyāptilakṣaṇaṃ tasya mate vyabhicāra evānvayaḥ*[117]*. tatropādhitvasya*[118] *tadviparītarūpatvābhāvāt. tathā ca nāpy avyāptir iti cet.*

(**1.1.10.3**) *na. tasyāpi mate kevalavyabhicārasya pratyakṣādyabhāvenodbhāvayitum*[119] *<aśakyaḥ. tadunnāyakopādhir>*[120] *avaśyaṃ vaktavyaḥ. anyathā vyabhicārasyāprāmāṇikatvaprasaṅgāt. tathā ca vyabhicārāvinābhūtopādhyudbhāvanena tatra lakṣaṇasyāvyāptir durvāreti siddham.*

(**1.1.10.4**) *kiṃca saṃbandhapadena saṃyogasamavāyādivivakṣāyām avyāptiḥ sarvatra sādhyasādhanayos tatprayogābhāvāt.*

(**1.1.10.5**) *nirupādhikasaṃbandhavyāptivivakṣāyām upādhyudbhāvanam eva vṛthā bhaved <anumānasya nirupādhikasaṃbandhavaśena>*[121]*nirduṣṭatvāt.*

(**1.1.10.6**) *sādhyasādhanasāmānādhikaraṇyavivakṣāyāṃ tūpādhivyāvṛttau sāmānādhikaraṇyamātraṃ vyāvṛttaṃ bhavet. na ca sādhyavyāvṛttir upādheḥ sādhyaṃ prati vyāpakatvābhāvāt*[122]*.*

nanu sāmānādhikaraṇyavyāvṛttiś ca saṃbandhadvayānyataravyāvṛttivyāpyatve saty anyataravyāvṛttiṃ gamayaty eveti. paraṃparayā sādhyābhāvo[123] *vartata iti cet.*

---

[112]Ms. *varttamānāt* corrected to *varttanāt* [113]Ms. *dhopādhāv* [114]Ms. interpolates *hetuḥ* after *iti* [115]Ms. *viddhatvād* corrected to *viruddhatvād* [116]Ms. *nirupādhikasaṃbandhaḥ* corrected to *nirupādhisaṃbandhaḥ* [117]Ms. *evānvaya* corrected to *evānvayaḥ* [118]Ms. *tatropādhitasya* [119]Ms. *-bhāvitum* corrected to *-bhāvayitum* [120]Ms. interpolates *na*: *aśakya na tadunnāyakopādhir* [121]Ms. *anumānasyānirupādhikasaṃbandhaviśena* corrected to *anumānasyānirupādhikasaṃbandhavaśena** [122]Ms. *vyāpakatvābhāvā* ... (≈ 1 *akṣara* missing) [123]Ms. *sādhyabhāvo*

(**1.1.11**) *maivam. kim āyāsena sādhanāvacchinnasādhyavyāpakatvavivakṣāyāṃ*[124] *tūpādhivyāvṛttau tāvad aviśiṣṭavyāvṛtteḥ. viśeṣyarūpasādhyavyāvṛttigatāyāḥ siddhatvena vyabhicāronnāyakasya siddhatvāt. tasmān naitad api sāmānyalakṣaṇam.*

nanu sādhanāvacchinnasādhyavyāpakatve sati sādhanāvyāpakatvam evopādhilakṣaṇam astu. tathā ca pūrvoktavistāri syād iti cet.

maivam. tādṛśapakṣetaratvādāv ativyāpter durṇivāratvāt.

(**1.1.12**) *yatkiṃcidviśeṣaṇāvacchinnasādhyavyāpakopādhāv avyāpteś ca. tathā ca śrīdharācāryaḥ. vāyuḥ sparśanapratyakṣaḥ. upalabhyamāna*[M3b]-*sparśādhiṣṭhānatvāt. ghaṭavad ity atra dravyasya sparśanatvaṃ*[125] *cākṣuṣatvena vyāptam. tataś cākṣuṣatvaṃ vyāvartamānaṃ sparśanatvam api vyāvartayatīti.*

nanv evaṃ ced <*yatkiṃcidviśeṣaṇāvacchinnasādhyavyāpakatve*>[126] *sati sādhanāvyāpakatvam evopādhilakṣaṇaṃ bhavatu. pūrvoktopādhisaṃgrahād iti cet.*

na. sādhyasādhanasaṃbandhavyāpakopādhyudbhāvanaprakārāvyāpteḥ[127].

nanu tatrāpi <*yatkiṃcidviśeṣaṇāvacchinnasādhyavyāpakatvam asty*>[128] *eva. katham avyāptir iti cet.*

maivam. na vayaṃ vastuvyāvṛttyāvyāptiṃ[129] *brūmaḥ kiṃtūdbhāvanaprakārāvyāptim. tathā hi. yad udbhāvanaṃ vā lakṣaṇaṃ tathodbhāvanaprakāro 'vaśyaṃbhāvi. na caital lakṣaṇaṃ sādhyasādhanasaṃbandhavyāpakopādhyudbhāvanaprakāreṇa*[130] *vartate kiṃtu yatkiṃcidavacchinnasādhyavyāpakatvād*[131] *iti.* <*lakṣaṇam upādhyudbhāvanaprakāreṇa*>[132] *vartate. tathā codbhāvanaprakāravisaṃvādenodbhāvanaprakārāvyāptir ukteti mantavyam.*

kiṃca sarvānumānabhaṅgaprasaṅgaś ca. yatkiṃcidavacchinnasādhyavyāpakopādheḥ[133] *sarvatrodbhāvayituṃ*[134] *śakyatvāt*[135]. *tathā hi. śabdo 'nityaḥ*[136] *kṛtakatvād ghaṭavad ity atra ghaṭaśabdānyataratvena*[137] *viśeṣite sādhye ghaṭatvam*[138] *upādhiḥ. evaṃ pakṣasapakṣānyataratvena*[139] *viśeṣite*

---

[124]Ms. *sādhanāvavadāchinnasādhyavyāpakatvavivakṣāyāṃ* corrected to *sādhanāvachinnasādhyavyāpakatvavivakṣāyāṃ* [125]Ms. *sparśana(vattvaṃ?)* [126]Ms. *kiṃcidvennaśeṣaṇāvachinnasādhyavyāpakatve* corrected to *kiṃcidveśeṣaṇāvachinnasādhyavyāpakatve** [127]Ms. *-udbhavanaprakāśavyāpteḥ* corrected to *-udbhāvanaprakāśavyāpteḥ** [128]Ms. *-vyāpakatvasty* corrected to *-vyāpakatvam asty* [129]Ms. *vastuvṛttyāvyāptaṃ* [130]Ms. *-udbhāvanāprakāreṇa* [131]Ms. *yatkiṃcidachinna-* [132]Ms. *lakṣaṇopādhyudbhāvanaprakāreṇa* [133]Ms. *-vyāpakatvopādheḥ* [134]Ms. *sarvatrodbhāvayidhitum* corrected to *sarvatrodbhāvayitum* [135]Ms. *aśakyatvāt* [136]Ms. *nityaḥ* [137]Ms. *ghaṭaśabdānyataratve* [138]Ms. *paṭalam* [139]Ms. *sapakṣānyataratvena*

<sādhye tattaddṛṣṭāntaniṣṭhadharma>[140] *upādhir abhidheyaḥ. evaṃ kvacid vipakṣaniṣṭhadharmasyāpy*[141] *upādhitvam āpadyeta.*

atrāsminn eva ghaṭadṛṣṭānte prameyatvābhāva upādhiḥ. vivādādhyāsito ghaṭaḥ[142] *prameyaḥ. abhidheyatvāt. gaganavad ity atra ghaṭasyāpi prameyatvasādhanena bhavaduktopādhir asaṃbhāvīti*[143] *cet.*

na ca atrānumāne ghaṭagaganānyataratvena viśeṣite sādhye gaganatvam[144] *upādhiḥ. tac ca ghaṭād vyāvartamānaṃ ghaṭagaganānyataratve sati prameyatvaṃ vyāvartayati. tathānyatarasyobhayavādisiddhatvāt prameyatvaṃ vyāvartayati. tathā ca prameyatvābhāvo*[145] *vaḥ sādhyaty eveti paraṃparayā vipakṣaniṣṭhadharmasyopādhitvaṃ bhavet.*

evaṃ śabdasyāpi yathā viyadādidṛṣṭāntatvaṃ tadā pakṣaniṣṭhadharmasyāpy upādhitvaṃ bhavet. śabdo[146] *hi ghaṭād vyāvartamāno*[147] *viśeṣitaṃ prameyatvaṃ vyāvartayati tatra viśeṣaṇasyobhayavādisiddhatvāt. prameyatvam eva vyāvartayatīti prameyatvābhāvalakṣaṇopādhyupāyatvena paraṃparayā <pakṣadharmatve 'py>*[148] *upādhitvaṃ vijñeyam. tasmāt sarvānumānabhaṅgaprasaṅgaḥ.*

viśeṣaṇapadavaiyarthyaṃ ca. yatkiṃcidavacchinnasādhyavyāvartakatvavyāpakatvamātravivakṣāyām[149] *ubhayavādyudbhāvitopādhisaṃgrahāt*[150].

(**1.1.13**) *nanu tathaiva lakṣaṇam astv iti cet.*

na.[151] *tathāpi pūrvadoṣānistārāt. kevalasādhyāvyāpake 'vyāpteś ca.*

(**1.1.14**) *<tarhi sādhyayatkiṃcidavacchinnasādhyānyataratve>*[152] *vyāpakatve sati sādhanāvyāpakatvam upādhilakṣaṇam astv iti cet.*

na.

(**1.1.15**) *saṃbandhavyāpakopādhāv <avyāptes tatrānyatamaṃ vyāpakaṃ>*[153] *lakṣaṇam astv iti cet.*

(**1.1.15.1**) *na. anyatamatvāniruktеḥ.*

etattrayānyonyābhāvātyantābhāva[154] *eva tattrayānyatamam*[155] *astīti*[156] *cet.*

---

[140]Ms. *sādhyatattaddṛṣṭāntenihyadharma* corrected to *sādhyatattaddṛṣṭāntaniṣṭhadharma** [141]Ms. *vipakṣani iti dharmasyāpy* [142]Ms. *ghaṭa* corrected to *ghaṭaḥ* [143]Ms. *asaṃbhavatīti* [144]Ms. *gaganavattvam* [145]Ms. *prameyatvābhāso* [146]Ms. *śabdatvam* [147]Ms. *vyāvartamānaṃ* [148]Ms. *pakṣadharmatvopy* corrected to *pakṣadharmatve 'py* [149]Ms. *-vyāvarttakatvam avyāpakatvamātravivakṣāyām* [150]Ms. *uyavādy-* corrected to *ubhayavādy-* [151]Ms. om. *na.* [152]Ms. *tarhi yatkiṃcidavachinnavachinnasādhyānyataratve* corrected to *tarhi yatkiṃcidavachinnasādhyānyataratve** [153]Ms. *avyāpte. starayānyataram avyāpakaṃ* [154]Ms. *etattrayānyobhāvātyantābhāva* corrected to *etattrayānyonyābhāvātyantābhāva* [155]Ms. *tattrayānyamam* [156]Ms. *astiti* corrected to *astīti*

na. etattrayapratiyogikānyonyābhāvānām[157] *etattrayavyatiriktasakalavastuniṣṭhānāṃ bahutvena pratiyogikātyantābhāvānām api bahutvād ekaikātyantābhāvasyaikaikatra vṛttir na tv itarayor ity arthāptiḥ. tatrānyatamavivakṣāyām anavasthāpattiḥ*[158].

nanv[159] *atyantābhāvatvam ekaṃ vivakṣitam iti cet.*

na. ekaikātyantābhāvavaty evāvyāpteḥ. ekatra medakābhāvāt.

(**1.1.15.2**) *kiṃca. sādhyavyāpakatvādipakṣadūṣaṇam*[160] *asaṃbhavāc ca.*

(**1.1.16**) *nanu dṛṣṭāntamātravyāpaka upādhilakṣaṇaṃ bhavatu. mātrapadena sākalyāvadhāraṇam. rūpadvayavivakṣāyāṃ sādhyasamavyāptisādhanāvyāpakatvayor lābhaḥ sādhyavyāpakādipadaprakṣepaṇena tatprayuktaṃ dūṣaṇam iti cet.*

na. dṛṣṭāntaśabdena parvatādidṛṣṭāntavivakṣāyām[161] *asaṃbhavitvaṃ kasyāpy upādheḥ sarvānumānadṛṣṭāntavyāpakatvābhāvāt*[162]. *yatkiṃciddṛṣṭāntamātravivakṣāyām <avyāptir yatkiṃcitpakṣetaratvādāv>*[163] *ativyāptiś*[164] *ca. tasmān nedaṃ lakṣaṇam.*

(**1.1.17**) *nanu yena vinā na*[165] *yayoḥ sahabhāvadarśanaṃ tatra yasya ca vyabhicāraḥ sa tasminn upādhir iti sāmānyalakṣaṇam astu. evaṃ ca pūrvadoṣo nāstīti cet.*

<na. yattacchabdārthānanugamāt>[166]. *na hi yattvaṃ tattvaṃ sāmānyalakṣaṇam*[167] *asti ca yattattvayor*[168] *eva yattacchabdānyavyavahārābhāvaprasaṅgāt*[169]. *tatrāpi <vṛddhānām ātmāśrayatvam>*[170] *āpadyeta. tasmān naitāni sarvāṇy upādhisāmānyalakṣaṇāni*[171].

(**1.1.18**) *vināpi prakṛtatvādiviśeṣaṇaṃ*[172] *naitāny eva* [M4a] *viśeṣalakṣaṇāni. sāmānyalakṣaṇābhāve viśeṣalakṣaṇābhāvasyoktatvāt tattadudbhāvitopādhiprakārabhedena pūrvoktasāmānyalakṣaṇasya*[173] *tattadviśeṣaparyavasānāc ca. tasmān naitāny upādhisāmānyalakṣaṇāni. nāpi viśeṣalakṣaṇāni. siddham upādhilakṣaṇasyānirvacanam iti pūrvapakṣaḥ.+*

(**1.2**) *abhivandya padāṃbhojayugalaṃ jagadīśituḥ/*
yathāmati yathāśāstraṃ siddhāntaḥ samyag ucyate//1

[157]Ms. *etattrayāpratiyogi-* [158]Ms. *anavasthāpatteḥ* [159]Ms. *na tv* [160]Ms. *sādhyāvyāpakatvādi-* [161]Ms. *parvatādṛṣṭāntavivakṣāyām* corrected to *parvatādidṛṣṭāntavivakṣāyām* [162]Ms. *sarvānumānadṛṣṭāntavyāpyatvābhāvāt* [163]Ms. *avyāptiḥ kiṃcitpakṣetaratvādāv* [164]Ms. *ativyāpteś* [165]Ms. om. *na* [166]Ms. *na ... tachabdārthānanugamāt* (≈ 1 *akṣara* missing) [167]Ms. *sāmānyalakṣam* [168]Ms. *hatatvayor* [169]Ms. *yattachabdānyānavyavahārābhāvaprasaṅgāt* [170]Ms. *vṛddhattāmātmāśrayatvam* [171]Ms. *upāsāmānyalakṣaṇe* corrected to *upādhisāmānyalakṣaṇe** [172]Ms. *-viśeṣaṇe* [173]Ms. *pūrvoktasakalalakṣaṇasya*

(**1.2.1**) *tatra tāvad upādheḥ sāmānyalakṣaṇam atyantābhāvapratiyogidharmatvam abhāvapratiyogimātrasya prameyatvādisādhāraṇyāt. atyantābhāvapratiyogitvanityadravyasādhāraṇyāt.*

na cedaṃ lakṣaṇam upādhir anupādhir veti pūrvoktadoṣaḥ svasmin svavṛttitvābhyupagamena tasyāpy upādhitvāt. na svabhāvātmāśrayatvaṃ dūṣaṇaṃ pramādilakṣaṇavirodhaprasaṅgāt.

tathā hi. pramāṇādilakṣaṇaṃ <lakṣaṇatvāt siddham. kasmiṃścit siddhe>[174] *vā lakṣaṇadūṣaṇaṃ vyāhataṃ duṣṭena lakṣaṇena <tatpramiter abhāvāt>*[175]*. pratītasya pramāṇānaṅgatve*[176] *hetutadābhāsaviplavatvaprasaṅgaḥ.*

anupādhikoṭipratiyogitvavyāvṛtteś[177] *ca. pratiyogikoṭipraveśavyāhatatvena tatrāpratiṣṭhā. kutracit svāntarbhāvam upekṣate.*

upādhilakṣaṇapravṛttitve velāyāṃ sā tu svayaṃ saṃdihyamānā. dharmikoṭim api tadānīṃ na praviśaty eva. paścāl lakṣaṇena siddhā satī. lakṣaṇāśrayatvenopādhikoṭiṃ praviśaty eva. lakṣaṇasaṃdehāvasthāyāṃ tu praveśābhāvān nāśrayaikadeśāsiddhir iti rahasyam.

<atha vā>[178] *parānabhyupagatadharmavān pakṣa iti lakṣaṇapakṣe 'vyāvṛtter*[179] *api vyāvṛttyanabhyupagamāt pakṣatvam upapadyate vipratipannaṃ prati prasādhayitum abhipretatvena*[180] *sādhyatvaṃ copapadyata ubhayalakṣaṇopapannatvenobhayavyavahārāt. tulāpramāṇaprameye*[181] *vyavahāravat. tasmāl lakṣaṇasyāvyāvṛttau nāvyāptir*[182] *nānavastheti <siddham.*

(**1.2.1.1**) *nāpi>*[183] *<niṣprayojanatvam iti>*[184] *siddham. vyavahāro 'py atra lakṣaṇārthaḥ*[185]*. upādhiśabdapravṛttinimittaṃ tu lakṣaṇam eva jātyabhāvasya pūrvoktatvāt.*

na ca svaniṣṭhadharmādhānakriyāyogabalād vyutpattiḥ. upādhiśabdasyānumānadūṣaṇārthaprayuktatvāt. svaniṣṭhadharmādhānamātrān nānumānadūṣaṇasphūrtiḥ. kiṃtu vyāpyatvāvabhāsanāt. etādṛśakriyāyoge tu na laukikavyutpattiḥ. japākusumādau tathābhāvaprasaṅgāt.

tasmāl lokavyavahāravisaṃvādād anumānadūṣaṇārthavattvam upādhiśabdasya viśeṣaṇalakṣaṇagarbhasāmānye lakṣaṇapravṛttinimittatvenaiva yujyata iti siddham eva lakṣaṇasya vyavahārārthavattvam[186]*.*

(**1.2.1.2**) *na ca prameyatvādāv*[187] *ativyāptir iti saṃbhavati. prameyatvādīnām atyantābhāvapratiyogitve kevalānvayibhaṅgaprasaṅgāt.*

---

[174]Ms. *lakṣaṇatvāt . . . siddhe* (≈ 7 *akṣaras* missing) [175]*tatpramiteparabhāvāt* corrected to *tatpramiter abhāvāt* [176]Ms. *pramāṇāṅgatve* [177]Ms. *-pratiyogikavyāvṛtteś* [178]Ms. *athayavā* corrected to *atha vā* [179]Ms. *vyāvṛtter* [180]Ms. *pretatvena* corrected to *abhipretatvena* [181]Ms. *tulāṃ pramāṇa-* [182]Ms. *nāvyāpter* [183]Ms. *siddhāṃ nāpi* [184]Ms. *niṣprayojanatvapi* [185]Ms. *lakṣaṇ(ā?)kṣerthaḥ* [186]Ms. *vyavahārārthatvaṃ* [187]Ms. *prameyatvāv* corrected to *prameyatvādāv*

nanu sakalavastuniṣṭhatvaṃ kevalānvayitvam. kena[188] *tatra pramāṇam eva. nāsti prameyatvādeḥ sakalaniṣṭhatvaṃ*[189] *grāhakapratyakṣābhāvāt. nāpy anumānaṃ sakalavastūni prameyatvādeḥ*[190] *sadṛṣṭāntābhāvagrastatvāt. na sakalavastuniṣṭhatvaṃ prameyatvādiniṣṭham*[191] *ityāder āśrayāsiddhatvāt. prameyatvaṃ sakalavastuniṣṭham*[192] *ityāder aprasiddhaviśeṣaṇatvāt. āgamādis tv asaṃbhāvita eva. tasmāt prameyatvādeḥ kevalānvayitve mānābhāvāt kevalānvayyanumānabhaṅgaduṣṭa eveti cet.*

tadā[193] *kevalānvayitvābhāvasya sakalavastuniṣṭhatve*[194] *sa eva dharmaḥ kevalānvayī bhaved iti sakalavastuniṣṭhatvābhāve tu yatra svayaṃ nāsti tatraiva kevalānvayī bhaved iti.*

tasmāt ke bādhakatarkāṇāṃ viparyayāparyavasānenābhāsatvopapattau. avaśyaṃbhāvinī[195] *kevalānvayidharmasadbhāvāpattir iti pramāṇābhāvād iṣṭāpattir*[196] *ity asiddham. kiṃca. dharmatvahetos tvadabhimatasakalavastuniṣṭhakevalānvayidharmabhāve*[197] *'nyataratvānaikāntikatvaṃ ca dhūmavattvāder anvayavyatirekayoḥ pramāṇābhāvena kevalānvayyanumānavat prāmāṇyaṃ na syāt.*

[M4b] *dhūmavattvasyānvayo*[198] *nāma svasāmānādhikaraṇyaṃ*[199] *yāvatsādhyavadvṛttitvam.*

tatra na tāvat pratyakṣaṃ pramāṇam. bhūtabhaviṣyadvartamānasvasamānādhikaraṇayāvatsādhyavatpadārthavṛttitvagrahaṇasāmarthyābhāvāt[200] *pratyakṣasya.*

nāpy anumānaṃ tatra pramāṇaṃ dhūmavattvasya yāvatsādhyavadvṛttitvasādhakāṅgābhāvāt[201]. *bhāve cānavasthāpattiḥ. tasyāpy aṅgasya yāvatsādhyavadvṛttitvagrāhakāṅgāntarāpattau*[202] *tasyāpy evam iti pravāhāvaśyaṃbhāvāt. evam eva yāvadvipakṣavṛttitvābhāvalakṣaṇavyatireke 'pi mānābhāvo vaktavyaḥ. āgamādis tv asaṃbhāvita eva.*

---

[188]Ms. *ke* [189]Ms. *sakalaniṣṭhātvaṃ* [190]Ms. *prameyatvādeḥ* corrected to *prameyatvadhārā(ṇī?)deḥ** [191]Ms. *prameyatvādiniṣṭhām* corrected to *prameyatvādiniṣṭham* [192]Ms. *sakavalastuniṣṭhatvam* corrected to *sakalavastuniṣṭhatvam** [193]Ms. *sadā* corrected to *tadā* [194]Ms. *-niṣṭatve* [195]Ms. *avaśyaṃbhāvini* corrected to *avaśyaṃbhāvinī* [196]Ms. *tiṣṭāpattir* corrected to *iṣṭāpattir* [197]Ms. *tvadabhimatasakalavastuniṣṭhakevalānvayidharmabhāve* corrected to *tvadabhimatasakalavastuniṣṭhakevalānvayibhāve** [198]Ms. *dhūmavattvāsyānvayo* [199]Ms. *svasamānādhikaraṇaṃ* [200]Ms. *bhūtabhaviṣyadvarttamānasthasamānādhikaraṇaṃ yāvatsādhyavatpramāṇapadārthavṛttitvagrahaṇasāmarthyābhāvāt* corrected to *bhūtabhaviṣyadvarttamānasthasamānādhikaraṇaṃ yāvatsādhyavatpadārthavṛttitvagrahaṇasāmarthyābhāvāt** [201]Ms. *yāvatsādhyavadvṛttitvasādhakābhāvāt* corrected to *yāvatsādhyavadvṛttitvasādhakāṅgābhāvāt* [202]Ms. *yāvatsāvadvṛttitvagrahakāṅgāntarāpattau*

nanu dhūmāder anvayavyatirekayor grahaṇaṃ yujyate. tathā hi. yatra dhūmas tatrāgnir iti bhūyodarśanaṃ jāyate. yatra vahnivyatirekas tatra dhūmavyatireka iti ca taj jāyate. tac ca bhūyodarśanaṃ tādṛśaṃ saṃskāram ādadhāti. tādṛśasaṃskāralakṣaṇasāmarthyavaśāt tatsahakṛtaṃ cakṣur yāvadvahnimadvṛttim anvayaṃ gṛhṇāti. tathaiva vahnimattvam. cakṣuṣā[203] *sahakārivaśāt tādṛśaṃ sāmarthyam upalabhyata eva. tathā hi. yogadharmasahakṛtaṃ cakṣur bhūtabhāve sakalavastujātaṃ gṛhṇāti*[204]. *tathāñjanādisahakṛtaṃ cakṣur bhūtatvāntam api nidhyādikam api jñāpayati. tathā ca*[205] *ratnagāndhārvādiśāstrābhyāsasaṃskārasaṃskṛtacakṣurādi*[206] *ratnajātyādibhedavat svarādīn paripaśyati tathā ca kālakāmalādisahakṛtaṃ deśāntarastharajatatvādisaṃsargam avagāhate. tasmāt sahakārisampannaṃ cakṣur eva yāvadbhūtabhaviṣyadvartamānaniṣṭhatvalakṣaṇānvayaṃ*[207] *tathaiva vyatirekaṃ cakṣur gṛhṇātīti.*

athānvayavyatirekyanumānabhaṅga iti cet.

tarhy <evaṃ prameyatvāder>[208] *api yāvatsādhyavadvṛttilakṣaṇānvaye 'pi gṛhyatām. tatrāpi bhūyodarśanajanitasaṃskārasahakāriṇaś*[209] *ca vidyamānatvāt.*

prameyatvādyanvayaṃ gṛhṇataḥ sārvajñyaṃ[210] *bhavatīti cet.*

maivam. dhūmavattvāder anvayavyatirekau gṛhṇataḥ kim iti tan na syāt.

tādṛśaṃ sārvajñaṃ tatra niṣṭham iti cet.

kiṃ prakṛtapradveṣeṇa.

nanu prameyatvāder anvayagrahaṇaṃ vinā na saṃgacchate. <dharmagrahaṇe dharmigrahaṇaṃ>[211] *vinā sambandhagrahaṇābhāvāt.*

tac cāṅgīkurmaḥ[212]. *yadi na kathayiṣyati mama manasi na*[213] *vartata iti.*

na hy evaṃ tathā ca yāvatprameyagrahaṇābhāvāt. yāvatprameyatvayutalakṣabhāve[214] *na prameyatvādes tadgrahaṇaṃ*[215] *yuktam iti cet.*

na dhūmādyanvayavyatirekayor api grahaṇe yāvadanvayavyatirekāśrayagrahaṇam avaśyaṃbhāvīti. katham <ivāsāveṣaṃ saṃbhavet>[216].

nanu māstu sarvānumānaprāmāṇyam[217] *iti cet.*

---

[203]Ms. *cakṣusu* [204]Ms. *gṛhṇāṇati* corrected to *gṛhṇāti* [205]Ms. *cā* corrected to *ca* [206]Ms. *ratnagāndhārvādiśāstrābhyāsaṃ saṃskārasaṃskṛtacakṣurādi* [207]Ms. *yāvadbhūtabhavi ... niṣṭhalakṣaṇānvayaṃ* (≈ 1 *akṣara* missing) [208]Ms. *evam evaṃ prameyatvāder* [209]Ms. *-sahakāraṇaś* [210]Ms. *sāvarjñyaṃ* [211]Ms. *dharme grahanadharmigrahaṇaṃ* [212]Ms. *ca tadaṃkākurmaḥ* [213]Ms. om. *na* [214]Ms. *yāvatprameyatvanidyūtvalakṣajña ca bhāve* [215]Ms. interpolates *na* after *tadgrahaṇaṃ* [216]Ms. *ivāveṣamyaṃ bhavet* [217]Ms. *sarvānumānāprāmāṇyam*

jīvanavilopaprasaṅgāt[218]. *pratidinam āhārārthina āhārasya hitasādhanatāṃ vijñāya samanantaraṃ bhāvino 'pi tad anumāyaiva pravartate. anyathā pravṛttivirodhaprasaṅgāt. yas tv anumānaṃ nāṅgīkaroti sa kathaṃ prativādībhavet.*

<kevalavākyaparaṃparā nānunirṇāyakā>[219] *bhavet. na ca vijayam āpādayati na ca paraprasiddhyāparo bodhanīya*[220] *iti pakṣo 'nyataraḥ siddhavilopaprasaṅgāt. kiṃca prasiddhaviśeṣaṇaṃ nodbhāvyaṃ bhavet. svāsiddhiḥ pramāṇavirodhitvābhāvāt. paraprasiddher eva pramāṇāṅgatvāt. kiṃca svarādipravṛttau*[221] *parapravṛttiṃ*[222] *kathaṃ pādayiṣyati. svārthānumānaparasyaivābhāvāt tatrāvyāptiḥ. vyāptiḥ*[223] *pakṣadharmatā cāṅgīkṛteti cet.*

tarhy upagatam anumānasya prāmāṇyam. tasmāt kevalānvayyanvayavyatirekino vaiṣamyaṃ nāstīty aṅgīkartavyam. tathā ca prameyatvādeḥ kevalānvayitvaṃ[224] *siddham iti neṣṭāpattiḥ. ataḥ kevalānvayyanumānābhaṅga*[225] *iti siddham.*

nanu prameyatvāder anāśritātyantābhāvapratiyogitvaṃ sādhyate. naitāvatā kevalānvayibhaṅgaprasaṅgaś ca. prameyatvādeḥ sakalavastuniṣṭhatve 'py atyantābhāvavirodhābhāvāt[226]. *evaṃ copādhilakṣaṇasyāpy*[227] *ativyāptir*[228] *durṇivāreti cet.*

na. vināpi bhavatsādhyaṃ dharmatvahetor upapattyabhāvāt. dharmatvaṃ[229] *<nāmāśritatvaṃ cāśrayaṃ>*[230] *vinā nopapadyate. na tv atyantābhāvapratiyogitvam. kiṃca dharmatvahetur āśritātyantābhāvapratiyogitvenaiva* [M5a] *sahacaritaḥ. sa na tādṛśābhāvapratiyogitvaṃ sādhayann eva paryavasyati. na tv anāśritātyantābhāvapratiyogitvam.*

nanu pakṣadharmatābalāt siddhiḥ. tathā hi. kāryatvaṃ[231] *sarvajñakartṛpūrvakatvādisahacaritaiḥ*[232] *saty*[233] *api pakṣadharmatābalād aśarīriṇaṃ sarvajñam eva kartāraṃ sādhayati. tathā dharmatvam api sadbhāvamātravyāpakatvaprameyatvalakṣaṇapakṣagataṃ sāmarthyādināśritātyantābhāvapratiyogitvam eva sādhayatīti cet.*

maivam. siddhe vipakṣe bādhake sādhakatvāvaśyaṃbhāvāt. dṛṣṭaviruddhe 'pi paryavasyati. na cātra pakṣe bādhakam upalabhyate.

---

[218]Ms. *jīvanalopaprasaṅgāt* corrected to *jīvanavilopaprasaṅgāt* [219]Ms. *kevalavākyaparaṃparānunanirṇāyakā* [220]Ms. *bodhanīyata* [221]Ms. *svārādi-* [222]Ms. *parapravṛtti* [223]Ms. om. *vyāptiḥ* [224]Ms. *kevalānvayitva* [225]Ms. *kevalānvayyanumānabhaṅga* [226]Ms. *-virodhābhāvān na* [227]Ms. *-lakṣasyāpi* [228]Ms. *t(i?)vyāptir* [229]Ms. *dharmitvaṃ* [230]Ms. *nāmāśritatvaṃ āśritatvaṃ cāyaṃ* corrected to *nāmāśritatvaṃ āśritatvaṃ cāśrayaṃ** [231]Ms. *kāryatvara* [232]Ms. *-pūrvakatvena sahacaritaiḥ* [233]Ms. *sann*

kiṃca. yady atyantābhāvasyānāśritatvaṃ[234] *syāt. tarhy apratiyogini rūpasvabhāvaḥ kathaṃ vyāhanyeta. vyāhataṃ vā mātṛvaṃdhyatvānumānavat*[235] *kathaṃ nābhāsībhavet. tasmād anāśritātyantābhāvapratiyogitvasādhanaṃ na yujyata iti na prameyatvāder ativyāptir upādhilakṣaṇasyeti*[236] *siddham.*

(**1.2.1.3**) *nanūpādhilakṣaṇam asaṃbhavi niṣpratiyogitvātyantābhāvasya. tathā hi. na tāvad yadādi prati śūnyavādāpatteḥ. nāpi saṃsargaḥ*[237]*. tasya sattve 'tyantābhāvapratiyogitvavyāghātāt. asattve tu pramitir eva na syāt.*

abādhitānubhāvāt pramiteḥ.

nanv iyaṃ pramitir abhāvamātraṃ gṛhṇāti. na pratiyogitvam[238]*.*

tarhi katham iva seṣṭapravṛttir[239] *iti bhāvyaneyaneye*[240] *viṣṭapratipattiḥ.*

kiṃtūpalakṣaṇapratipattiḥ. upalakṣaṇatvaṃ tv avidyamānasyāpi bhavati. kurubhir ākrāntaṃ kurukṣetram ityādau tathādarśanāt. tathā ca pratiyogino 'pramitir iti vyāhatam iti cet.

maivam. upalakṣaṇatve 'pi kadācit pramiter āvaśyakatvāt. kurvādikam api pratyakṣenāgamādinā vā pramitam. paścāt smaryamāṇam upalakṣaṇīyaṃ bhavati. tathā ca kadācit pramiter āvaśyakatvāt. pramitasya sarvatvaniyamāt.

sataś ca tatpratiyogitvaṃ vyāhatam iti siddham. viyogitvātyantābhāvasyeti[241] *lakṣaṇaṃ tad asaṃbhāvīti*[242] *cet.*

na. upapadyate saṃsṛjyamānapratiyogitvād atyantābhāvasya. tathā hi. iha bhūtale ghaṭo nāstīty atyantābhāvo 'nubhūyate yathānubhavaṃ hi yathā[243]*padārthakalpanam. tathā cāhodayanaḥ. saṃvid eva hi bhagavatīti viṣayasattvopagame*[244] *śaraṇyam iti. atrānubhava āśrayāsiddhatvābhāvasaṃsargī*[245] *ghaṭaḥ pratiyogitvena sphurati. na ghaṭamātraṃ nāpi saṃsargamātraṃ yady api kevalaghaṭāder atyantābhāvatvena*[246] *yujyate tathāpi saṃsṛjyamānatvākāreṇa*[247] *yujyata eva. saṃprayujyamānākāras*[248] *tv avidyamāna eveti.*

---

[234]Ms. interpolates *na* after *atyantābhāvasyānāśritatvaṃ* [235]Ms. *-vaṃdhyātvānumāvat* [236]Ms. *upādhilakṣaṇesyeti* corrected to *upādhilakṣaṇasyeti* [237]Ms. *saṃsar(gja?)ḥ* [238]Ms. *pramitiyoginam* [239]Ms. *śeṣṭa-* [240]Ms. *-neyaneyaṃ* [241]Ms. *niyogitvātyantābhāvasyeti* [242]Ms. *asaṃbhavatīti* [243]Ms. om. *yathā* [244]Ms. *viṣasattvopagame* corrected to *viṣayasattvopagame* [245]Ms. *āyāsiddhatvābhāvasaṃsargī* corrected to *āśrayāsiddhatvābhāvasaṃsargī* [246]Ms. *atyantābhāvatvaṃ na* [247]Ms. *saṃsṛjyamātvākāreṇa* corrected to *saṃsṛjyamānatvākāreṇa* [248]Ms. *saṃprayumānākāras* corrected to *saṃprayujyamānākāras*

tasyātyantābhāvapratiyogitvaṃ yujyata eveti. na[249] *tūpalakṣaṇam eva. tasya kadācitpramitatvaniyamaḥ*[250] *pramāṇabhāvāt. upalakṣyapramitis tūpalakṣaṇajñānam apekṣate. tac ca jñānaṃ prakṛte smṛtir eva. sāpi pūrvānubhavamātram ākṣipati. na pramāṃ pramitivyāptyabhāvāt. tatrāntaraprakṛtādismṛter*[251] *api vidyamānatvāt. so 'py anubhava*[252] *ābhāsādhībhyo*[253] *bhavati. pramāṇena pratipannasyātyantābhāvavirodhāprakṛte*[254] *smṛtibījodbodhakaṃ cintādi. tathā rūpasaṃsṛjyamānapratiyogitvāpattāv atyantābhāvasya niṣpratiyogitvābhāvād upādher lakṣaṇaṃ nāsaṃbhāvīti*[255] *siddham. tasmād iṣṭopādheḥ sāmānyalakṣaṇaṃ siddham eveti siddham.+ śrī.*

(**1.2.2**) *nanv astu sāmānyalakṣaṇam. viśeṣalakṣaṇaṃ tu pūrvoktanyāyena nirvaktum aśakyam. tadabhāve*[256] *bhavatopādhidūṣaṇaṃ na nirvāhyam. sāmānyalakṣaṇalakṣitadharmamātrasyopādhitvopanyāse sarvatra sarvathāpy*[257] *upādhitvaṃ bhaved iti. sarvānumānabhaṅga āpadyeta. sādhyavyāpakasādhanāvyāpakatvalakṣaṇalakṣitadharmopanyāsam*[258] *upakṣipan*[259] *sādhyadharmasya vyāvṛttiṃ jñāpayan sādhyābhāvavati tatraiva sādhanavṛttitvam api jñāpayatīti vyabhicāronnayanaṃ sukaram eveti yuktam upādher dūṣaṇam. bhavatāṃ*[260] *tādṛśalakṣaṇaṃ nirvaktum aśakyam iti cet.*

atrocyate. sādhyasamavyāptikatve sati sādhanāvyāptikatve sati sādhanāvyāpakatvaṃ bhaved iti. tathāhur bhaṭṭācāryāḥ.

> *samāsamāvinābhāvāv ekatra sto yadā tadā/*
> *samena yadi no vyāptas tayor hīno 'prayojakaḥ//+*

ity udayanācāryā api samavyāptikasyopādhitvam āhuḥ.

> *ekasādhyāvinābhāve mithaḥ saṃbandhaśūnyayoḥ/*
> *sādhyābhāvāvinābhāvī sa <upādhir yadatyayaḥ>*[261]*//*

ity atraikasādhyāvinābhāva iti padena vyāpakatvam uktam. yadatyayaḥ sādhyābhāvāvinābhāvīty[262] *anena vyāpakatvam uktam iti.*

---

[249] Ms. *sa* [250] Ms. *kadācitpramitatvatvaniyamaḥ* corrected to *kadācitpramitatvaniyamaḥ* [251] Ms. *tatrāntarakṛtādi-* [252] Ms. *anubhavam* [253] Ms. *ābhāsādhibhyo* [254] Ms. *-virodhā-(nu?)prakṛte* [255] Ms. *nāsaṃbhavīti* [256] Ms. *tadābhāve* [257] Ms. *sarvathām apy* [258] Ms. *-dharmepinyāsam* corrected to *-dharmopanyāsam* [259] Ms. *upakṣi* corrected to *upakṣipan* [260] Ms. *bhavetāṃ* corrected to *bhavatāṃ* [261] Ms. misquotes TR (cf. 67, 9f) as follows: *upādhiyadatyaya* [262] Ms. *sādhyābhāvavinābhāvīty*

samavyāptir vivakṣiteti mantavyam. [M5b] *jaropādhivyāpyatvābhyupagamo*[263] *vṛtheti vaktavyam. prayojako dharma upādhir bhavatīty upādhidūṣaṇodbhāvakasya tathaiva vivakṣodayāt. tathā hi. bhavatāprayujyamānaṃ hiṃsātvam adharmasādhakaṃ na bhavati. kiṃtu vyāpakatvavyāpyatvābhyām avyabhicaritaniṣiddhatvam eva sādhakaṃ*[264] *bhavatīty upādhivādino vivakṣā. anyathāyam*[265] *atropādhir iti nodbhāvyetodbhāvakasya taddharmagatavyāpyatvamātrāvabhāsāt. tava bhrāntyānanusādhanagataṃ pāramārthikavyāpyatvam astīty abhimānād upādhyudbhāvanam. na tu virodhonnāyakatvābhimānāt. anyathāyam atropādhir iti nodbhāvyeta. kiṃtv idam atra*[266] *vyabhicāronnāyakam iti vadet. tasmāt samavyāptikasyopādhitvam.*

(**1.2.2.1**) *nanu samapadasya kiṃ vyāvartyam iti* <*cet.*

viṣamavyāptikapakṣetaratvam.

nanu pakṣetarasya sādhyavyāpakatvam eva nāsti. kathaṃ samapade vyāvṛtyam iti cet.

na>[267]. *yatra sādhyaṃ tatra pakṣetaratvam iti vyāptau satyām upādhivyabhicārād bhāvyavyāptyabhāvasya vaktum aśakyatvāt.*

nanu pakṣetaratvasyopādhitve[268] *sarvānumānabhaṅgaprasaṅgād iti bādhakavaśāt sādhyavyāpakatvam*[269] *eva*[270] <*bhajyata iti*>[271] *cet.*

na. <*vyādāma maivam*>[272]. *pakṣetaratvopādhisarvānumānabhaṅgayor*[273] *vyāptiḥ kutrāpi na dṛṣṭeti katham ayaṃ tarko bhavet. vyāpyatvasyopādhitvayojakatvābhyupagamas*[274] *taṃ nirāsaḥ. kim anena bādhakatarkodbhāvanatvaprayāsena.*

nanu kathaṃ tasya vyatirekavyāptyabhāvād vyāpakatvam[275] *iti cet.*

maivam. vyāpakatvaṃ hi vyāptikartṛtvam. anvayavyāptir api vyāptir eva na vyatirekamātram. anyathānvayavyatirekikevalānvayivirodhāpattiḥ. tathā ca pakṣetaratvasyāpy anvayavyāptyā vyāpyatvaṃ siddham.

<*na tv anvayamātrād*>[276] *vyāpakatvam. upādhilakṣaṇe tathā vyāpakapadenānvayavyatirekavyāptidvayam*[277] *vivakṣitaṃ pakṣetaratvopādhitānirāsāyeti*[278] *cet.*

---

[263]Ms. *jaropādhi ... vyāpyatvābhyupagamo* (≈ 1 *akṣara* missing) [264]Ms. interpolates *na* after *sādhakaṃ* [265]Ms. *ayathāyam* corrected to *anyathāyam* [266]Ms. *atro* corrected to *atra* [267]Ms. *cet. na* corrected to *cet. viṣamavyāptikapakṣetaratve nanu pakṣetarasya sādhyavyāpakatvam eva nāsti. kathaṃ samapade vyāvṛtyam iti cet. na** [268]Ms. *pakṣetarasyopādhitve* corrected to *pakṣetaratvasyopādhitve* [269]Ms. *sādhyavyāpakam* corrected to *sādhyavyāpakatvam* [270]Ms. *eve* corrected to *eva* [271]Ms. *bhajyateti* [272]Ms. *vyādamaivam* [273]Ms. *-bhayor* corrected to *-bhaṅgayor* [274]Ms. *-yojakatvābhyupagamana* [275]Ms. *vyāpyakatvam* [276]Ms. *na svanvamamātrād* corrected to *na tv anvayamātrād* [277]Ms. *paka-* corrected to *vyāpaka-* [278]Ms. *-nirāyeti* corrected to *-nirāsāyeti*

kim anayā vivakṣayā. prasiddhyānukūlam evopādhivyāpyatvaṃ kiṃ na vivakṣyate. tāvatāpi pakṣetaratvanirāso bhavaty eva.

(**1.2.2.2**) *nanv evam api samavyāptikapakṣetarasyānirāsa iti cet.*

na. tatra vyāpyatvasyābhāvāt. vyāpyatvaṃ hi mānādhīnam. na hi yatra parvatetaravahnimattvaṃ <tatra vahnimattvam>[279] *iti tad eva saviśeṣaṇaṃ nirviśeṣaṇaṃ caikajñānena*[280] *grahaṇayogyaṃ*[281] *na bhavati virodhāt. tathā hi. na hy ekajñānam eva nailyāvacchinnam anavacchinnaṃ*[282] *ca gṛhṇāti. avacchinnagrāhakasyānavacchinnagrāhakavirodhāt*[283]. *tathaivāvacchinnagrāhakasyānavacchinnagrāhakatvaṃ*[284] *vyāhatam iti. tasmād idam anena vyāptam ity ekakāryalīnobhayaviṣayavilakṣaṇavyāptigrahaṇābhāvāt*[285] *parvatetaravahnimattvavahnimattvayor*[286] *vyāptir eva nāstīti. ataḥ samavyāvartyaṃ siddham.*

nanu kṣityādikasakartṛkatvānumāne sāvayavatvādau samavyāptikaśarīrijanyatvādeḥ[287] *pūrvanyāyena nirāsābhāvāt katham iva teṣāṃ samapadaprakṣepanirāsa iti cet.*

na. tatrāpi sopādhikatvena vyāptyabhāvāt. vyabhicāro vācakaviśeṣaṇavata[288] *upādheḥ samavyāptikaviśeṣasopādhikatvaniyamāt*[289]. *tathā ca yatra śarīrijanyatvaṃ*[290] *tatra sakartṛkatvam ity atra viśeṣyabhūtajanyatvam evopādhir bhavet. na ca sādhanavyāpakatvenānupādhitvaṃ*[291] *sādhanopādhisaṃbandhe sādhyasyaivopādhitvāt. tathā ca sopādhikatve sādhanāvyāpakatvabhāvāj*[292] *janyatvaviśiṣṭopādhisādhyasaṃbandha*[293] *upādhir bhaved*[294] *iti śarīrajanyatvopādhivyāpyatvābhāvāt*[295] *samapadena nirāso bhaved iti siddham.*

nanu śabdo 'bhidheyaḥ prameyatvād ityādāv aśabdatvādeḥ pūrvoktaprakāreṇa vyāptigrahaṇābhāvavyāptyabhāvayor[296] *vaktum aśakyatvāt samavyāptivādinaḥ kathaṃ samavyāptikasyānupādhitvam iti cet.*

maivam. arthāśabdatvaṃ nāma śabdānyonyābhāvavattvam. tathā ca viśeṣopādher viśeṣyasyaivopādhitvaṃ tasya ca sādhanasya ca saṃbandhe 'bhidheye yasyopādhitvam ity ajanyatvādinirāsaprakāraṃ ko vā nivārayeṣyatīti

---

[279]Ms. *tatra vahnimattvaṃ tatra vahnimattvam* [280]Ms. *-jñānyanena* corrected to *-jñānena* [281]Ms. *-yog(y?)aṃ* [282]Ms. *avacchinnaṃ* [283]Ms. *-grāhakasyāvachinna-* [284]Ms. *-grāhakasyānavachinnavachigrāhakatvaṃ* [285]Ms. *-viṣa-* corrected to *-viṣaya-* [286]Ms. *parvatetaravahnimattvayor* [287]Ms. *samavyāptikaśarīriajanytvādeḥ* [288]Ms. *-viśeṇavata* [289]Ms. *-viśeṣacaupādhikatva-* [290]Ms. *śarīajanyatvaṃ* corrected to *śarīriajanyatvaṃ** [291]Ms. *sādhanāvyāpakatvenānupādhitvaṃ* [292]Ms. *sādhanāvyāpakatvābhāvāt* [293]Ms. *-sādhyāsaṃbandhe* [294]Ms. *bhaveāt* corrected to *bhavet* [295]Ms. *śarīraajatvopādhi-* corrected to *śarīraajanyatvopādhi-** [296]Ms. *-vyāptābhavayor*

tasyāpi samapadenaiva[297] *nirāsaḥ. kiṃca vyarthaviśeṣaṇatvāc*[298] *ca na teṣāṃ vyāpyatvam.*

nanu vyarthatvaṃ nāsty eva. viśeṣaṇaṃ tasya sādhanavyāptiparihārārthatvād iti cet.

na. viśeṣaṇatvaṃ hi vyabhicārāvārakatvenaiva saprayojanam. anyathā viśeṣalakṣaṇavyāghātāt. avacchedakaṃ hi viśeṣaṇaṃ bhavaty upalakṣaṇaṃ vā. na hi yatkiṃcitprayojanavad viśeṣaṇam upalakṣaṇaṃ vā kasyacit saṃmatam. tathā ca yatkiṃcitprayojanatvena[299] *viśeṣaṇaṃ na bhavatīti vyabhicāravārakatvāvaśyaṃbhāve* [M6a] *prakṛte tu tadabhāvād*[300] *vyarthaviśeṣaṇatvam eveti.*

na vyāpyatvaṃ yuktaṃ pakṣetaratvopādhīnāṃ samavyāvṛttikopādhivādināṃ samavyāpyatāsvīkārād. upādher vyabhicārāvāraviśeṣaṇatvaṃ na doṣa iti cet.

na. tathātve samavyāpter evābhāvāt. tathā hi. vyāptigrahaṇaṃ bhūyodarśanabalād bhavati. tatkāleṣu vyaktīnām[301] *ajanyatvāc copādhiviśeṣaṇaṃ.*

sakartṛtvādinā saha vyabhicārāt katham avyabhicāri. na hi bhūyodarśanasaṃskārasahakṛtaṃ <cakṣus tadullaṅghyaviśiṣṭagataṃ>[302] *vyāpyatvaṃ gṛhṇāti. anyathā dhūmavattvādikam apy ullaṅghyaviśiṣṭagatam*[303] *eva vyāpyatvaṃ gṛhṇīyād iti. tasyāpi vyāpyatvaṃ syāt. tathā ca vyabhicārasāhacaryād bhūyodarśanaṃ yatra yatra tatra tatraiva saṃskārasahakṛtaṃ*[304] *cakṣur vyāpitvaṃ gṛhṇātīti viśiṣṭagatavyāpyatvasyaiva grahaṇābhāvāt. vyarthaviśeṣaṇavato vyāpyatvam eva nāstīti. tādṛśapakṣetarasya*[305] *samapadenaiva nirāsa iti siddham.*

(**1.2.2.3**) *nanu kathaṃ viṣamavyāptikasya nirāsaḥ. tasyāpi vyabhicāronnāyakatvena svagatavyāptyavabhāsakatvena vā samavyāptisādhakopādhisāmyāt.*

saṃbandhavyāpakopādheś ca kathaṃ vānena saṃgrahaḥ. tasya sādhyasamavyāpyatvābhāvāt. kvacit saṃbandhasamavyāpakatve 'pi sādhyasamavyāpyatvābhāvāt.

nanu sādhyapadena vyāpakaṃ vivakṣitaṃ na tu sādhyamātram.

---

[297] Ms. *samadenaiva* corrected to *samapadenaiva* [298] Ms. *-viśeṣatvāc* corrected to *-viśeṣaṇatvāc* [299] Ms. *-prayojanetvena* corrected to *-prayojanatvena* [300] Ms. *dabhāvod* corrected to *tadabhāvād* [301] Ms. *(vya?)ktīnām* corrected to *vyaktīnām* [302] Ms. *cakṣustatvadullaṅghya-* corrected to *cakṣus tadullaṅghya-* [303] Ms. *-viśiṣṭanatam* [304] Ms. *satsaṃskāra-* [305] Ms. *tādṛśapakṣetasya* corrected to *tādṛśapakṣetarasya*

anye <ca dhūmānumāne>[306] *parvatatvāder upādhitvaprasaṅgāt sādhyalakṣaṇaṃ hi vipratipannam. pratipakṣe sādhayitum abhipretatvaṃ tādṛśasādhyavyāpakatvasya*[307] *parvatatvavyāpakatvāder*[308] *apy astīti.*

sādhanāvyāpakatvaṃ ca sapakṣa eva hy[309] *arūpalakṣaṇam aṃśābhāvād vyabhicārāc ceti. tathā ca vyāpakatvam eva sādhyapadena <vivakṣitam iti>*[310] *vaktavyam. tac ca vyāpakatvaṃ sādhyasādhanasaṃbaddhasyāpy avaśiṣṭam eva. śiṣṭam evam evācchinnasādhyavyāpakasthale 'pi yojyam. tathā ca lakṣaṇaparyavasānaṃ*[311] *vyāpakatvavyāpakatve*[312] *sati vyāpyāvyāpakatvam ity āptitaḥ*[313]. *tasmāt saṃbandhavyāpakasya saṃyogatvāder apy anenaiva lakṣaṇena saṃgraho bhaviṣyatīti cet.*

(**1.2.2.3.1**) *maivam.*

astu vyāpakatvam eva vivakṣitam. tathāpi samavyāptikasādhanasyāpy etallakṣaṇārthatvenopādhim āpadyeta. tathā hi. sādhyāsamavyāpakatvādihetor[314] *anityatvādis tv avyāpakavyāpakatvāt svavyāpakatvābhāvena vyāpyavyāpakatvāc*[315] *ceti. tasmāt saṃbandhādivyāpakasya bhavaduktasādhyasamavyāpakatvādilakṣaṇena*[316] *saṃgrahābhāvād bhavadvivakṣitopādhisāmyena viṣamavyāptikasya nirāsāyogāc ca katham ivaital lakṣaṇaṃ bhaved iti cet.*

atrocyate. viṣamavyāptikasya prayojakatvābhāvād[317] *anupādhitvam. prayojakatvaṃ tu vyāpyatvādhīnam. anyathā sādhanatvābhāvena prayojakatvavyāghātāt. upādhidūṣaṇatvam api svagatavyāpyatvāvabhāsakatvenaiva yuktaṃ na tu vyāpakatvāṃśaprādhānyena vyabhicāronnāyakatvāt. svagatavyāptyavabhāsakatvād*[318] *vā tadvyatirekasya. pratipakṣabhāve 'pi na vyāpakatvadvāradūṣaṇamātraparyavasānāt. svagatavyāptyavabhāsakadvāraṃ*[319] *tu dūṣaṇatvam anvayavyatirekābhyām api <pratipakṣadūṣaṇam aparyavasitam>*[320] *eveti vyāpyatvāsiddhau paryavasyati. na hi niṣiddhatvādyupādhir anvayavyāptyā sādhanasya pratipakṣībhavati. nāpi vyatirekavyāptyā. vyāpyatvadvāravyatirekasya pratiyogivyāpakatvam. anujīvyasādhyābhāvavyāpyatvābhāvena pratipakṣadūṣaṇam ayuktam eva. vyāpyavyatirekasyāpi vyāpyatve <dhūmābhāvasya vahnyabhāvavyāpyatvam>*[321] *āpad-*

---

[306] Ms. *cānumāne* corrected to *ca dhūmānumāne* [307] Ms. *-vyāpakatvaṃ* [308] Ms. *parvatavyāpakatvāder* [309] Ms. *(hy?)* [310] Ms. *vivakṣitami ... ti* (probably mistaken notification of a lacuna up to the extent of ≈ 1 *akṣara*) [311] Ms. *-paryavasādhanam* [312] Ms. *vyāpakavyāpakatve* [313] Ms. *āpattitaḥ* [314] Ms. *sādhyasama-* [315] Ms. *vyāp(ya?)vyāpakatvāc* [316] Ms. *bhavaduktatvasādhya-* [317] Ms. *prayojakatvabhāvād* [318] Ms. *svagatavyāptyavabhā(sa?)katvād* [319] Ms. *svagatavyāptyavasabhākadvāraṃ* corrected to *svagatavyāptyavabhāsakadvāraṃ* [320] Ms. *pratipakṣadūṣaṇaṃ maparyavasitam* corrected to *pratipakṣadūṣaṇam aparyavasitam* [321] Ms. *dhūmābhāvasyāvahnivyāpakatvam* corrected to *dhūmābhāvasya vahnivyāpakatvam**

yeta. vyāpakatvād vā[322] *vyatirekasya yadyapi*[323] *vyāpakatvaṃ yujyate tathāpi vyāpyatvābhyupagamena pratipakṣaparyavasānābhāve 'pi prayojakī. bhūtasyopādheḥ prayojakatvāvirodhenaiva svagatavyāpyatvāvabhāsakatvena sādhanāvyāpakatvāsiddhim āpādayato vyāpyatvāsiddhyāpādakatvaṃ yuktam eveti viṣamavyāptikopādhes tathābhāvenopādhitvaṃ nāstīti yuktam eva viṣamavyāptikopādher lakṣaṇenāsaṃgrahaṇam. kiṃca vyāpakatvaṃ tu viṣamavyāptikopādheḥ sādhyābhāvasādhakaṃ pratipakṣarūpavyāpyavyatirekāyattam iti nopādher dūṣaṇadvāram.*

nanv evaṃ ced vyāpyatvamātrasyaivopādhidūṣaṇopayogitatvena vyāpakasya prayojanābhāvāt. kim iti samavyāptikopādhes tadaṅgīkriyata iti cet.

maivam. samāvinābhūtāsamāvinābhūtadharmasamavāye samāvinābhūtadharmā[M6b]*pekṣayā sāhacaryavyabhicārābhāvasyobhayathāpi* <*siddhatvaṃ prayojakatvaprātalyāt*>[324]. *prayojakatvatulāvadhāraṇayeti*[325] *mantavyam. tasmāt prayojakatvābhāvena svagatavyāptyavabhāsakatve voktanyāyena*[326] *vyabhicāronnayakatvena vā paryavasānābhāvād viṣamavyāptikasyopādhitvābhāvāl* <*lakṣaṇe na*>[327] <*saṃgrahaḥ. aṅgam*>[328] *avaśyaṃbhāvīti*[329] *sthitam*[330].

(**1.2.2.3.2**) *na sādhyasādhanasaṃbandhavyāpakopādhyasaṃgrahaḥ. tatrāpi viṣamavyāptikakāryatvādisādhyasādhanasaṃbandhavyāpakopādhīnāṃ pūrvoktanyāyenopādhitvābhāvād asaṃgraho yukta eva. samavyāptikasaṃyogādes tu vyāpakasamavyāpakasādhanasaṃbandhasamavyāpakatvasya vidyamānatvena saṃgraho yukta*[331] *eva. lakṣaṇam apy asyāvyāpakasamavyāpakatve sati vyāpyavyāpakatvam ity evaṃ vivakṣitam. yatkiṃcidavacchinnasādhyavyāpakasyāpy etallakṣaṇasaṃgraho yujyata eva. dravyatvāvacchinnasādhyavyāptikasya sādhanaṃ prati vyāpakatvasya vidyamānatvena cākṣuṣatvāder api vyāpakavyāpakatvāt.*

(**1.2.2.4**) *vyāpyāvyāpakatvam. na sādhanena lakṣaṇasyātivyāptiḥ. doṣo 'pīti tatra vyāpyāvyāpakatvarūpalakṣaṇāṃśābhāvāt. tasyāpi svavyāpyavyāpakatvāt. tathā hi. sādhanāvyāpakatvaṃ nāma sādhanavanniṣṭhātyantābhāvapratiyogitvam*[332]. *na hi tad eva sādhanaṃ svasamānādhikaraṇātyantābhāvapratiyogi bhavati vyāghātāt. tasmāt tadvyāpakatvena tadvyāpakatvābhāvāl lakṣaṇasya sādhane nātivyāptiḥ. sādhyavyāpakatvaṃ hi sādhanavanniṣṭhātyantābhāvapratiyogivivakṣitam.*

---

[322] Ms. *vā* corrected to *vā(?)** [323] Ms. *ya(dya?)pi* [324] Ms. *siddham aprayojakatva-* [325] Ms. *prayojatūlavadhāraṇayeti* [326] Ms. *-nyāyeāna* corrected to *-nyāyena* [327] Ms. *lakṣa ... na* (≈ 1 *akṣara* missing) [328] Ms. *saṃgraho(ṃ?)ṃgaṃ* [329] Ms. *avaśyabhāvīti* [330] Ms. *sthiddhatam* corrected to *sthitam* [331] Ms. *yuktam* [332] Ms. *-pratiyogitvaṃ ca*

tan na.

tathā sati coktātmāśrayatvādidoṣaleśo[333] *'pi prakṛtatvaviśeṣaṇāc ca sādhanasyāpi kvacit sādhyatvenetyādidūṣaṇam api nirastam.*

na cāvyāptidoṣaḥ[334]. *viśeṣalakṣaṇatvād asya samavyāptikapakṣetaratvādau lakṣaṇād bhedena prakārāvyāptis tu nirastaiva.*

viṣamavyāptikopādhyavyāptis tu na bādhakety uktam eva. yatra sādhyasādhanayoḥ samavyāptiḥ. tatra sādhanāvacchinnaviṣamavyāptikasyopādher vyāpakatvaṃ na[335] *yujyata iti yuktam uktam. vyarthaviśeṣaṇaṃ śarīrijanyatvādyupādher iva. vyarthaviśeṣyakṛtakatvāvacchinnāśrāvaṇatvādyupādher*[336] *api vyāptigrahaṇābhāvena vyāpyatvābhāvāt.*

nanu bhavaduktalakṣaṇapakṣe 'pi ghaṭaśabdānyataratvādiviśeṣaṇānityatvādisamavyāpakaghaṭatvādeḥ sarvānumāneṣu pravartamānatvena sarvānumānabhañjakasyopādhitvāpattiḥ. tasyānupādhilakṣaṇasyātivyāptiḥ syād iti cet.

na. viśeṣitānityatvādeḥ[337] *kṛtakatvasādhanaṃ prati vyāpakatvapratīter*[338] *evābhāvāt. vyāpyavyāpakatvarūpalakṣaṇāṃśābhāvena tasyānupādhitvalakṣaṇasyāpi nātivyāptir iti siddham. tasmād upādhilakṣaṇam apy uktaprakāreṇa nirvaktuṃ śakyam*[339] *iti siddham eva. upādheḥ*[340] *sāmānyalakṣaṇaṃ viśeṣalakṣaṇaṃ veti susthitam.*

> *yathā <śrīrāmabāṇasya pratipakṣo>*[341] *na vidyate/*
> *tathā cāsya vicārasya na virodhī*[342] *kadācana//+*

ity <upādhidarpaṇe lakṣaṇanirūpaṇaṃ>[343] *nāma prathamaḥ paricchedaḥ.+*

(**2**) *athopādhivicāraḥ kriyate.*

(**2.1**) *tatra vādino vivadante. kecid upādher vyabhicāronnāyakatvena dūṣaṇatvaṃ vadanti. pare tu pratipakṣaparyavasāneneti saṃgirante. anye tu vyāpyatvāsiddhyāpādanamūleneti*[344] *bruvate*[345]. *vādīndrās tv upādher*[346] *dūṣaṇam eva na bhavatīti bhaṇanti.*

(**2.1.1**) *atra vyabhicāronnāyakatvenopādher dūṣaṇatvaprakāraḥ pradarśyate. tathā hi. sādhyavyāpakatvaṃ sādhanāvyāpakatvaṃ cety aṃśad-*

---

[333]Ms. *va ... ktātmāśrayatvādi-* (≈ 1 *akṣara* missing) [334]Ms. *ca vyāpti-* [335]Ms. *ca* [336]Ms. *-kṛtakatvāvachinnaśrāvaṇa(tv?)ā(ju?)dyupādher* corrected to *-kṛtakatvāvachinnaśrāvaṇa(tv?)ādyupādher** [337]Ms. *viśeṣitā. nityatvādeḥ* [338]Ms. *-pratītir* [339]Ms. *aśakyam* [340]Ms. *evopādheḥ* [341]Ms. *śrīrāmabāṇasyāpratipakṣo* [342]Ms. *virodhi* [343]Ms. *upādhidarpaṇalakṣaṇanirūpaṇaṃ* [344]Ms. *vyāpakatvāsidhyāpādhanūleneti* corrected to *vyāpakatvāsiddhyāpādhanūleneti** [345]Ms. *bravate* [346]Ms. *uthādir*

vayaṃ vidyate. upādhir api pakṣe 'vidyamāna eva bhavati. anyathā sādhanāvyāpakatvopapattāv avyāpakatvāṃśavirodhāt. sādhanavyāpakasya[347] *tūpādhitve sāmānyavattve saty asmadādibāhyendriyagrāhyatvenānityatvasādhye kṛtakatvam upādhiḥ syāt.*

sādhanāvyāpakatvam upādheḥ. kvacit sādhanasyopādhitvaṃ vyabhicārāt. bhavati so 'pi vyabhicāraḥ sapakṣe <yadi tat sādhyavyāpakatvam>[348] *evopādher vyāhanyeta. tathā ca sapakṣa eveti vaktavyam.*

sādhyam api pakṣe na[349] *vartata ity evaṃ vaktavyam. anyathā sādhyavyāpakatvabhaṅgaprasaṅgāt. na hi sādhyaṃ vihāya vyāvartamānaṃ*[350] *sādhyavyāpakaṃ bhavati virodhāt.*

na[351] *ca sādhyavyāpakopādhivyāvartamānaṃ*[352] *sādhanaṃ <sādhyābhāvavati pakṣe>*[353] *vartamānatvena vyabhicāri bhavati. so* [M7a] *<'pi vyabhicāraḥ sādhyavyāpakabhūtasyopādheḥ>*[354] *pakṣe 'vidyamānatvād bhaved ity <upādhir vyabhicāronnāyaka>*[355] *ity abhidhīyate.*

prayogas tu vivādādhyāsitaṃ[356] *hiṃsātvādisādhanam adharmasādhanatvādisādhyavyabhicāri tadvyāpakavyabhicāritvāt. yāgīyahiṃsātvādivad*[357] *iti. tad eva tat sarvam upādheḥ pakṣe 'vidyamānasya vyāpakatvāyattam ity upādher vyāpakatvam*[358] *<āvaśyakaṃ vyabhicāronnāyakatvapakṣe>*[359] *tu vyāpyatvam anupayogīti <vyāpyatvamataṃ nāṅgīkurvanti>*[360]*. kvacid avarjanīyatayā kvacid vidyamānam api vyāpyatvam āste.*

nanūpādher dūṣaṇatvaṃ sādhyaprayojakatvaṃ[361] *ca vyāpyatvavyāpakatvābhyāṃ*[362] *nirvahatīti kim ity ubhayaṃ nāṅgīkṛtam iti cet.*

na. vādyuktānumānasya prativādinā dūṣaṇodbhedasyaivārhatvāt[363]*. tasyāpi tadupayogam evāṅgīkārārham iti teṣāṃ matam iti.*

(2.1.2) *pratipakṣaparyavasānaprakāro 'pi varṇyate. tathā hi. upādhiḥ sādhyavyāpako bhavati. vyāpakodbhedanaṃ ca tadvyāvṛttyā sādhyavyāvṛttijñāpanāya*[364] *bhavati. pratipakṣaparyavasānaṃ <tv ittham>*[365]*. vipratipannaṃ pāpasādhanaṃ na bhavati. aniṣiddhatvād iti.*

---

[347]Ms. *sādhanasya vyāpakasya* corrected to *sādhanavyāpakasya* [348]Ms. *yadi tatsopādhyavyāpakatvam* [349]Ms. om. *na* [350]Ms. *vartamānaṃ* [351]Ms. *nā* corrected to *na* [352]Ms. *-vyāpakopādhivivarttamānaṃ* [353]Ms. *sādhyābhāvapratipakṣe* [354]Ms. *vyabhicārasādhyavyāpabhūtasyopādheḥ* [355]Ms. *upādhivyabhicāronnāyaka* [356]Ms. *āvivādādhyāsitaṃ* corrected to *vivādādhyāsitaṃ* [357]Ms. *prameyatvādivad* [358]Ms. *vyāvarttakatvam* [359]Ms. *āvaśakavyabhicāronnāyakatvapakṣe* [360]Ms. *vyāpyatvamataṃ kurvanti* [361]Ms. *sādhyapratiyojakatvaṃ* [362]Ms. *vyāpyatvābhyāṃ* [363]Ms. *dūṣaṇodbhedesyaivārhatvāt* corrected to *dūṣaṇodbhedasyaivārhatvāt* [364]Ms. *sādhyajñāpanāya* [365]Ms. *tu śatthaṃ*

nanu vyabhicāronnāyakatvapakṣe prajā[366] *katham asya pakṣasyotthānam iti cet.*

maivam. asmin pakṣe vidyamānasyeti samānam.

kiṃca vyabhicāronnāyakatvapakṣo jaghanyo vyāpakībhūtopādhivyāvṛttim upajīvya sādhyābhāvavati pakṣe sādhanavṛttilakṣaṇaṃ vyabhicāraṃ[367] *yāvat*[368] *sādhayati tāvad evopādhivyāvṛttiḥ*[369] *pratipakṣībhūya hetudūṣaṇāya vyabhicāraṃ*[370] *paryavasyatīti. katham iva paścādbhāvi vyabhicāraparyavasānam ākāṅkṣitaṃ bhavet.*

kiṃca prayojakatvanivāraṇaṃ vinā bhavanmate vyāpakavyāvṛttimātreṇa sādhyābhāvaniścayābhāvāt sādhyābhāvavadvṛttitvalakṣaṇavyabhicāraparyavasānam upādheḥ kathaṃ bhavet. tasmāt pratipakṣaparyavasānapakṣa eva jyāyān iti tanmatam iti.

(**2.1.3**) *vyāpyatvāsiddhiparyavasānapakṣo 'pi tadāsmatsaṃmato yathāvat pratipādyate.*

(**2.1.3.1**) *nanūpādhidūṣaṇapakṣo*[371] *jātiḥ. katham ayaṃ pakṣo bhavatsaṃmataḥ. tathā hi. prakṛtasādhyavyāpakaḥ prakṛtasādhanāvyāpakaḥ prakṛtopādhir iti vaktavyam. yadi tādṛśo dharmaḥ sadanumāneṣu na*[372] *pramitas tathā katham iva tadabhāva upamīyate. aprasaktasya pratiṣedhābhāvāt. yadi pramitas tadā*[373] *pratiṣedha eva na saṃgacchate. na hi bhūtale ghaṭapramitau tadabhāvaḥ pratyetuṃ śakyo bhavati. paramārthataḥ*[374] *pratiyogini vidyamāne 'pi nāyam upapadyate. tasmād upādhyabhāvasya sadanumāne 'pi niścetum aśakyatvāt sadanumānapradhvaṃsena*[375] *tasya dūṣaṇam eva nāstīty abhyupagantavyam iti cet.*

aho bhavatāṃ prajñātiśayo yenātmānam api na jānate. tathā hi. yathā śaṅkā tathā parihāro bhaviṣyati. tathā hi. <śaṅkitā api>[376]. *sādhyavyāpakadharmāṇāṃ*[377] *tatra prakṛtopādhitvaṃ yadi śaṅkyate tadā sādhanāvyāpakatvābhāvāt teṣām upādhitvaṃ niṣidhyate. atha sādhanāvyāpakatvāṃśānām upādhitvaṃ śaṅkyate. tarhi sādhyavyāpakatvābhāvāt teṣām upādhitvaṃ niṣidhyate. tadatiriktadharmāṇāṃ*[378] *tūpādhitvaprasakter evābhāvāc chaṅkaiva nāsti. yadi kaścil loke siddhāntaśaṅkāmaryādām atikramya hetoḥ sopādhikatvaṃ vyabhicāraṃ vā śaṅketa sa tv anukūlatarkān nirasanīyaḥ.*

[366]Ms. *jāpra* [367]Ms. *vyabhicārakaṃ* [368]Ms. *yat* [369]Ms. *evopādhivṛttiḥ* [370]Ms. om. *vyabhicāraṃ* or *vyabhicāre* (cf. the next sentence where *vyabhicāra* is compounded with *paryavasāna*) [371]Ms. *nanūpādhidūṣaṇe pakṣo* [372]Ms. om. *na* [373]Ms. *tathā* corrected to *tadā* [374]Ms. *pratiparamārthataḥ* [375]Ms. *madanumānapradhvaṃ(sa?)nena* [376]Ms. *śaṅkitāpi* [377]Ms. om. *-vyāpaka-* [378]Ms. *tedatiriktadharmāṇāṃ* corrected to *tadatiriktadharmāṇāṃ*

<tarko vyāptāv atipattitvaṃ>[379] *vartamānā*[380] *śaṃkyapiśācāvyājena*[381] *dūrīkṛtā satī svata eva vartate. tathāsya na vyāptisāpekṣateti. nānavasthā. tasya virodhapramiter eva mūlatvāt.*

udāharaṇaṃ tu mama mātā vandhyā vināpi vahnyādikāraṇaṃ[382] *dhūmādikāryaṃ bhaved ityādisthalam. upādhivyabhicāraśaṅkāvicchedo hi vyāghātasya phalam.*

tasya tu vahnyudbhāvito[383] *'pi yaḥ kaścit prekṣāvān. puraḥsphūrtikaṃ virodham*[384] *apy ullaṅghya vyāghātam apy ābhāsīkartuṃ mātur vandhyātvaṃ*[385] *vināpi kāraṇaṃ kāryotpattim api*[386] *nābhyupagacchet*[387]. *abhyupagame ca tasya kaḥ pakṣas tarhi na bhavet. bhaved vā vināpi vādyuktasādhanaṃ*[388] *sādhyasiddhiḥ kathaṃ na saṃbhāvyeta. vahnyanuṣṇatvādisādhanam*[389] *api ka*[M7b]*tham iva na pramāpakam. tasya so 'pi na virodhaḥ.*

sarveṣāṃ laukikānāṃ prāmāṇikānāṃ ca tattadbādhakaśaṅkānirāsakaḥ sann api katham ivātikrāntamaryādo na syāt. tatphalam anaṅgīkurvata unmattādisadṛkṣatāṃ kathaṃ nāpādayet.

nanu so 'pi virodho <mātṛvandhyatvābhāvāt kāryakāraṇādeś>[390] *ca vyāptim upajīvyaiva pravartata iti. tathāpi vyabhicāraśaṅkā prasakteti cet.*

na. virodhe tu na vyāptir mūlam. kiṃtu tathātvānabhyupagama eva. na kaścin mātur <vandhyatvaṃ kāryasya>[391] *kāraṇavyatiriktatvaṃ*[392] *siddhāntādāv abhyupagacchati*[393]. *yadi kadācit kaścid abhyupagacchaty*[394] *abhyupagamānabhyupagamayor virodho bhavet. tādṛśavirodha eva vyāghātamūlam iti śāstravidāṃ rahasyam.*

nanv astv evam. akāraṇakāryotpattyupagame[395] *tu na*[396] *virodhaḥ kāraṇāntarād utpattiśaṅkāyāṃ virodhasyaivābhāvāt*[397]. *dhūmavattvāder niyataṃ vahnyādikāraṇaṃ na syād iti cet.*

na. yadi tatkāraṇāntaraṃ kadācid dṛṣṭaṃ vā śrutaṃ vā bhavet tadāśaṅkyeta[398]. *yadi sarvathā*[399] *na dṛṣṭaṃ na śrutaṃ ca tarhi <tena na śaṅkitvā svatvam asvasyāgnikakāśādinā>*[400] *kaṃ kim iti nāśaṅkyeta. dhūmāder*

---

[379]Ms. *tarkavyāptāvatipitvaṃ* [380]Ms. *vamānā* [381]Ms. *śaṃkyapiśācāvyātena* [382]Ms. *vahnyāhnyādikāraṇaṃ* corrected to *vahnyādikāraṇaṃ* [383]Ms. *vahnyudbhāvite* [384]Ms. *virodhem* corrected to *virodham* [385]Ms. *vindhyātvaṃ* [386]Ms. *apyu* corrected to *apy** [387]Ms. *abhyupagacheta* [388]Ms. *vāhyuktasādhanaṃ* corrected to *vādyuktasādhanaṃ* [389]Ms. interpolates *sādhanamad vā vināpi vādyuktasādhanaṃ sādhyasiddhiḥ. kathaṃ bhāvasaṃbhāvyeta vahnyanuṣṇatvādi* between *vahnyanuṣṇatvādi* and *sādhanam* [390]Ms. *mātravaṃdhyātvābhāvakāryakāraṇādeś* [391]Ms. *vadhyātvāryasye* [392]Ms. *kāravyatiriktaṃ* [393]Ms. *abhyupagachati* [394]Ms. *abhyupagachati* [395]Ms. *akāraṇakāryotpadyupagame* corrected to *akāraṇakāryotpattyupagame* [396]Ms. om. *na* [397]Ms. *virodhasyeva bhāvāt* [398]Ms. *tadāśaṅketa* corrected to *tadāśaṅk(y?)eta* [399]Ms. *sarvapyā* corrected to *sarvathā* [400]Ms. *tena śaṅkitvā svatvāsvasyākāśagikanādinā*

vahnisadṛśakṣamasādhāraṇakāraṇāntaram añjanādinā sahakārakeṇāpi cakṣurādi darśayatīti siddham.

(**2.1.3.2**) *tasmād uktaprakāreṇopādher dūṣaṇatvopapattau svagatavyāpyatvābhāsakatvenopādher vyāpyatvāvabhāsakatvam*[401] *asmatsaṃmatam. tat pratipādyate. tathā hi. vyāptikatvam*[402] *iti <nirupādhikaḥ saṃbandhaḥ>*[403]*. tasya saṃbandhasya saṃbandhinau dvau*[404] *vyāpyavyāpakau*[405] *<vyāpyasya vyāpakatvaṃ>*[406] *ceti vyāpakatvaṃ nāma vyāptikartṛtvaṃ vyāpyatvaṃ tu tatkarmatvam. tathā*[407] *tadvyāpyatvaṃ yatra mukhyaṃ sphurati tat pāramārthikaṃ vyāpyatvam*[408]*. yatrānyagataṃ sāhacaryādidoṣāt tu <sphurati tad apāramārthikaṃ>*[409] *tac ca <vyāpyatvam asiddham>*[410] *etasmin*[411] *dharmiṇi mukhyavyāpyatvajñānavirodhisadbhāvāt. mukhyavyāpyatvasiddhivirodhijñānam api vyāpyatvāsiddhir ity abhidhīyate.*

tathāpi cānyagatavyāpyatvapratibhāso 'pi vyāpyatvāsiddhir[412] *bhavati. evaṃ sati yadi parato vyāpyatvamukhyād adhikaraṇaṃ tat svagatavyāpyatvam anyatrāvabhāsayad vyāpyatvāsiddhyāpādakam*[413] *abhidhīyate. etad eva vyāptivirodhyupādher vyāpyatvāsiddhyāpādakatvam iti gīyate. tad yathā. hiṃsātvaṃ hi vyāpyatvāsiddhihetuḥ. niṣiddhatvaṃ hi tasya vyāpyatvāsiddhyāpādaka*[414] *upādhir abhidhīyate. etadgataṃ sādhyaṃ*[415] *prati vyāpyatvaṃ mukhyam. hiṃsātvam api sāmānyavattve sati bāhyendriyagrāhyatvam ivādharmasādhanam.*

tasyaiva sādhanāya na svataḥ <samarthaṃ yāgīyahiṃsāyāṃ>[416] *niṣiddhatvena virodhāt. hiṃsātvasya*[417] *hi pakṣe niṣiddhatvasyādharmasādhanatvaprayojakatvam. nipātād*[418] *eva tatsādhanāya yatnata iti virodhaś caitadvaiparītyenāpi*[419] *virodhasya sādhāraṇyād vyāpyatvāsiddhiḥ.*

kiṃ na syād iti na vācyam. niṣiddhatvasya samāvinābhāvatayā[420] *prayojakatvena sādhakatvadārḍhyāt. tathā ca niṣiddhatvagam eva vyāpyatvaṃ <hiṃsāyāṃ sāhacaryadoṣāt>*[421] *sphurati. tad eva smaraṇaṃ hiṃsātvasya mukhyavyāpyatvajñānavirodhīti tasya vyāpyatvāsiddhir ity abhidhīyate. tad*

---

[401] Ms. *vyāthatvāvabhāsakatvam* corrected to *vyāpyatvāvabhāsakatvam* [402] Ms. *vyāptitam* [403] Ms. *nirupādhikasaṃbandhaḥ* corrected to *nirupādhikaḥ saṃbandhaḥ* [404] Ms. *dvaupa* corrected to *dvau* [405] Ms. *vyāpakau vyāpakau* [406] Ms. *vyāpakaṃ vyāp ... tvaṃ* (≈ 1 *akṣara* missing) [407] Ms. *tatha* [408] Ms. *vyāpyaṃ* [409] Ms. *sphuratidapāramārthikaṃ* corrected to *sphurati tad apāramārthikaṃ* [410] Ms. *vyāpyatvāsiddhaṃ* [411] Ms. *ceyat(tai?)tasmin* [412] Ms. *vyāpyatvasiddhir* [413] Ms. *vāpyatvāsidhyāpādaka(tva?)m* [414] Ms. *vyāpakatvāsidhyāpādaka* corrected to *vyāpakatvāsiddhyāpādaka* [415] Ms. *sādhya* [416] Ms. *samarthayāgīyahiṃsāyāṃ* [417] Ms. *hiṃsātvaṃ* [418] Ms. *nipad* corrected to *nipatad** [419] Ms. *caiva vaiparītyenāpi* [420] Ms. *samāsamāvinābhāvatayā* [421] Ms. *hiṃsāsāhacaryadoṣāt*

api <niṣiddhatvaṃ vyāpyatvasyālambanam>[422] *iti. vyāpyatvāsiddhyāpādakam*[423] *ity abhidhīyate. evaṃ sarvatra samavyāpakopādhiṣu vyāpyatvāsiddhyāpādakatvaṃ*[424] *yojyam. evaṃ ca sati nirupādhikasādhyasādhanasāmānādhikaraṇyam*[425] *iti vyāptilakṣaṇavākyasyāyam <arthaḥ svagatavyāpyatvāvabhāsakaprayojakībhūtadharmavirahānvitasāmānādhikaraṇyam>*[426] *iti. tathā ca sādhanagatāropitavyāpyatvapratibhāyāṃ tv evaṃ virodhavyāptivirodhijñānamūlam iti vyāpyatvāsiddhiḥ. tadāpādakasyopādher vyāpyatvāsiddhyāpādakatvaṃ*[427] *ceti sarvaṃ susthitam.*

yad vā sādhyasādhanasāmānādhikaraṇyasyopādhivirahā vyāptiḥ. upādhau vidyamāne vyāptiviraha eva bhaved iti sākṣād vyāptivirahabhūtatvenaivopādher dūṣaṇatvam. asmin pakṣa <upādhāv avidyamāne>[428] *tanniṣṭhavyāpyatvahetor*[429] *viruddhavyabhicārisādhāraṇabhūtasādhyābhāvasādhakatvaṃ*[430] *tadvyatirekasya paryavasyatīti sādhanasāmānādhikaraṇyasyopādhivirahānvitam āvaśyakatvam iti. tasyopādhiviraha eva sādhyasādhakatve prayojakatvenābhyupagantavyam iti rahasyam.*

pakṣadvayasya vaiṣamyapūrvoktanyā[M8a]*yena*[431] *vyāpyatvāsiddhyāpādakatvaṃ*[432] *tasyāparatra vyāptivirahātmakatvam iti tad etad dvayam*[433] *api vyāpyatvābhyupagamapakṣāvirodhatvenāsmanmatam*[434]. *tasmād upādher <vyāpyatvābhyupagame vyāpyatvāsiddhyāpādakatvena>*[435] *vyāpyatvāsiddhatvarūpatvena*[436] *vā dūṣaṇatvam. siddhavyabhicāronnāyakatvapakṣas tu jaghanyatvadoṣāt.*

pūrvam iva gamitaḥ[437] *pratipakṣaparyavasānapakṣas tu prayojake vyatireke <rūpatvād anupādhivyatirekasya>*[438] *sādhyābhāvaṃ prati prayojakatvasamarthanena bādhakatvaparyavasānād ūrīkṛtaḥ. bādhakaparyavasāna-*

---

[422]Ms. *niṣiddhatvavyāpyatvasyālambanam* [423]Ms. *vyāpyatvāsidhyāpādakam* corrected to *vyāpyatvāsiddhyāpādakam* [424]Ms. *vyāpyatvāsidhyāpādakatvaṃ* corrected to *vyāpyatvāsiddhyāpādakatvaṃ* [425]Ms. *nirupādhir asādhyasādhanasamānādhikaraṇyam* [426]Ms. *arthaḥ. na svagatavyāpyatvāvabhāsakaprayojakībhūtadharmavirahānvisāmānādhikaraṇyam* corrected to *arthaḥ. na svagatavyāpyatvāvabhāsakaprayojakībhūtadharmavirahānvitasāmānādhikaraṇyam** [427]Ms. *vyāpyatvāsidhyāpādakatvaṃ* corrected to *vyāpyatvāsiddhyāpādakatvaṃ* [428]Ms. *upādhau viyamāne* corrected to *upādhau vidyamāne** [429]Ms. *tanniṣṭavyāpta …hetor* (≈ 2 *akṣaras* missing) [430]Ms. *-sādhāraṇī-* [431]Ms. *vaiṣamyapūrvoktanyāna* [432]Ms. *vyāpyatvāsidhyāpādakatvaṃ* corrected to *vyāpyatvāsiddhyāpādakatvaṃ* [433]Ms. *vayam* [434]Ms. *vyāpyatvābhyupagamapakṣāvirodhatvenāsmanma* corrected to *vyāpyatvābhyupagamapakṣāvirodhatvenāsmanmataṃ* [435]Ms. *vyāpyatvābhyupagame pakṣāvirodhitvenaiva vyāpyatvāsiddhyāpādakatvena* corrected to *vyāpyatvābhyupagame naiva vyāpyatvāsiddhyāpādakatvena** [436]Ms. *vyāpyatvāsiddharūpatvena* [437]Ms. *gamiva gamitaḥ* [438]Ms. *rūpatvā(dva?)nupādhivyatirekasya*

pakṣas tu <tavīti sākṣād vyāpyatvāsiddhiparyavasāne tūhyānumitim api bibheti>[439]. *tasmād asmaduktapakṣa eva jyāyān iti siddham.*

nanv evaṃ sarvam upādher vyāpyatvābhyupagamena[440] *bhavati. tadabhyupagama eva kiṃ mūlam iti cet.*

maivam. prayojakatvād evopādher vyāpyatvam abhyupagantavyam ity uktam. tan na prasmartavyam. pakṣetaratvopādhinirāsaś ca vinā <vyāpyatvaṃ samavyāpakopādhinirāsaś>[441] *ca vinā vyāpyatvaṃ nāstīty uktam apy anusandheyam.*

kiṃca vyāpyatvānabhyupagame hiṃsātvāder vyāpyatvam ivopādher vyāpakatvam[442] *api pratītimātrasiddhaṃ ceti tat kathaṃ tadvyatirekāt sādhyavyatirekāvagataṃ pakṣe bhavet kathaṃ vā niścitasādhyābhāvavadvṛttitvalakṣaṇavyabhicāronnāyakatvaṃ bhavet.*

(**2.1.4**) *atha tarkasahakṛtasāhacaryapratītisiddhatve naṣṭaṃ cet tarhi kim upādhyudbhāvanena tasyaiva tarkasya hiṃsātvaprakṛtatarkatvenodbhedārhatvāt. asmanmate tu na tarkāpekṣā hiṃsātvādyapekṣayā sāmānādhikaraṇyabhāvenaiva*[443] *tasya prabalatvāt.*

nanu yatra sādhyasādhanayoḥ sādhyena saha samavyāptis[444] *tatra bhavatām apy upādhyudbhāvanaṃ*[445] *vṛtheti samānam etad iti cet.*

maivam. tatropādhiprābalyaṃ yady anukūlatarkasāhacaryād bhavati. tathāpy asmanmate[446] *tadanugṛhītasyāpy upādher udbhāvanaṃ varam upādhyudbhāvanasya*[447] *sākṣād dhetudoṣatvena paryavasitatvāt.*

tarkodbhedane tu paraṃparayā tarkaparyavasānād vyāpyatvānabhyupagamapakṣe tūpādhidoṣam api paraṃparayaiveti pratikūlatarkasādhyam eva <vyāpyatvam upādher>[448] *āvaśyakam iti mantavyam.*

(**2.1.5**) *nanv etādṛśavyāpyatvadvāram upādher dūṣaṇatvaṃ kevalavyatirekānumānopādhau na prasarati. pṛthivītarebhyo bhidyate pṛthivītvāt. anubhūtiḥ*[449] *svayaṃprakāśānubhūtitvāt. vyatireke jalādivad ghaṭavad ityādikaṃ tu kevalavyatirekyanumānam. tatra vyāpyapṛthivītvādikam. tatra svaniṣṭhavyapyatvāvabhāsakaḥ*[450] *pakṣaniṣṭhasthitimataḥ. tatsahacarito niṣiddhatvādivad upādhirūpo dharmaḥ kaścid api na pratibhāti yadi hetor vyāpyatvā-*

---

[439]Ms. *te vātisākṣād vyāpyasiddhiparyavasāne tu hy ānumapitibheti* corrected to *te vātisākṣād vyāpyatvāsiddhiparyavasāne tu hy ānumapitibheti** [440]Ms. *vyāpyatvabhyupagamena* corrected to *vyāpyatvābhyupagamena* [441]Ms. *vyāpyatvopādhinirāsaś* [442]Ms. *vyāpakatva(?)m* [443]Ms. *sāmānādhikaraṇa-* [444]Ms. *samavyāpti* corrected to *samavyāptiḥ* [445]Ms. *upyedhyudbhāvanaṃ* corrected to *upādhyudbhāvanaṃ* [446]Ms. *anmate* [447]Ms. *upādhyudbhavanasya* corrected to *upādhyudbhāvanasya* [448]Ms. *vyāpyatvasyam upādhir* [449]Ms. *anubhūti* corrected to *anubhūtiḥ* [450]Ms. *svaniṣṭhāvyāpyatvāvabhāsakaḥ*

siddhir āpādyate. yadi tādṛśo dharmaḥ[451] *pratibhāti*[452] *kevalavyatirekatvam eva bhajyeta. pakṣavyatireke*[453] *hetūpādhyoḥ sāhacaryāvaśyaṃbhāvena sādhanasādhyayor anvayavyāptyāpatteḥ.*

vyatirekiṇi[454] *vyatirekavyāptāv upādhir ucyate. nānvayavyāptau tasyā evābhāvāt. tatra hi sādhyābhāvo <vyāpyaḥ sādhanābhāvas>*[455] *tu vyāpakaḥ. tādṛśavyāpyenopādhirūpadharmasya vipakṣa eva sāhacaryaṃ yujyate.*

vyāpakatvam api tatraiva bhavet. lakṣaṇaṃ tv evaṃ paryavasyati sādhanābhāvasamavyāpakatve sati sādhyābhāvāvyāpaka[456] *iti. tatrāpi saṃbhavaty evopādhir iti cet.*

maivam. astu vyāpyatvāṃśasaṃmataṃ[457] *sādhanābhāvavyāpakatvaṃ*[458] *nāsty eva. yady upādhiṃ parityajya sādhyābhāvalakṣaṇaṃ sādhanaṃ pakṣe*[459] *bhavet tarhi sādhanābhāvas*[460] *tarhi sādhanābhāvavyāpakatvam*[461] *api bhajyeta*[462].

yady upādhisādhyābhāvayor vyabhicārasthe vyāpakavirahakevalavyatirekisādhanam[463] *api varteta tasya viruddhatvāpattau kevalavyatirekitvabhaṅgaḥ.*

upādheḥ sādhanāvyāpakatvāṃśānabhyupagame[464] *pakṣe vidyamānasyāpi dharmasyopādhitvāpattāv anityatve sādhye sāmānyavattve saty asmadādibāhyendriyagrāhyatvakṛtakatvayoḥ*[465] *parasparavirodhaṃ nibādhakatvārhatvena*[466] *dhūmavahnisāmagryor iva sapakṣaikadeśavṛttitvarūpavaiṣamyamātreṇobhayor*[467] *api vyāpyatvāpattāv ekatra <vyāpyatve 'vartamāne>*[468] *bhrāntitvāyogāvyāghātāt*[469].

svagatavyāpyatvāvabhāsakadvārā[470] *vyāpyatvāsiddhyāpādakatvaṃ*[471] *na saṃbhāvyeta. tasmāt kevalavyatirekiṇi bhavadabhimatopādher abhāvād upādhidūṣaṇakāras*[472] *tatra nāstīti siddham iti cet.*

---

[451]Ms. *dharma* corrected to *dharmaḥ* [452]Ms. *pratibhāyāt* [453]Ms. *pakṣavyatirekasyāne* [454]Ms. *nanu vyatirekiṇi* [455]Ms. *vyāpyasādhanābhāvas* [456]Ms. *sādhyābhāvavyāpakaḥ* [457]Ms. *vyāpyatvāṃśasaṃbhā* corrected to *vyāpyatvāṃśasaṃ** [458]Ms. *sādhanāvyāpakatvaṃ* [459]Ms. interpolates *yadi* after *pakṣe* [460]Ms. *sādhanābhāva* [461]Ms. *sādhanābhā ... vyāpakatvam* (≈ 1 *akṣara* missing) [462]Ms. *bhajye* corrected to *bhajyeta* [463]Ms. *vyāpakaviratmakevala-* [464]Ms. *sādhanavyāpaka-* [465]Ms. *asmadādibātvakṛtakatvayoḥ* corrected to *asmadādibādhatvakṛtakatvayoḥ** [466]Ms. *nisādhakatvarhatvena* [467]Ms. *sapakṣaikadeśavṛttitvarūpavaiṣamātreṇobhayor* corrected to *sapakṣaikadeśavṛttitvarūpavaiṣamyamātreṇobhayor* [468]Ms. *vyāpyatva 'vartāne* [469]Ms. *bhraṃtiitvāyogāvyāghātāt* corrected to *bhrāṃtitvāyogāvyāghātāt* [470]Ms. *svagatavyāpyatvāsakadvārā* [471]Ms. *vyāpyatvāsidhyāpādakatvaṃ* corrected to *vyāpyatvāsiddhyāpādakatvaṃ* [472]Ms. *upādhidūṣa ... kāraḥ* (≈ 1 *akṣara* missing)

tatra vadāmaḥ[473]*. tathā hi. yadā hi yadā. kevalavyatirekihetau*[474] *pratikūlatarkaparāhatir bhavet. tatra tasmād unnayopādheḥ sādhyābhāvarūpasādhanāvyāpakatvaṃ ca bhavaty eva pratikūlatarkaparāhatatvena kevalavyati*[M8b]*rekisādhanasya svasādhakatvasāmarthyasya kuṇṭhībhāvāt*[475]*.*

tatpakṣe <kevalavyatirekisādhyābhāvaśaṅkāyām avidyamānasyopādheḥ>[476] *sādhyābhāvarūpasādhanavyāpakatvanirṇayābhāve*[477] *sādhanāvyāpakatvopapattau tatronnīyamānasyopādheḥ prayojakatvena svagatavyāpyatvāvabhāsakatvena dūṣaṇatvaṃ nirupadravam*[478] *eva. pratikūlatarkasya vyāptivirahonnāyakatvenāhatāv upādhyunnayanasyāvaśyakatvāt. kevalavyatirekyanumānasthale 'py upādhiḥ prasaṅgaghātāt. atra yady api nirūcānaṃ*[479] *jaḍatvādikaṃ pakṣetare paryavasitaṃ tathāpi pakṣasyaiva vipakṣatvasaṃbhāvanāyāṃ*[480] *tasya pakṣamātravyāvartakaviśeṣaṇatvabhāvāt*[481]*.*

atra kaiścid uktam. etatsādhyānyad apakṣaniṣṭhānyat prameyatvāt. etatsādhyavad ity anenānumānena kutracit sādhyam[482]*. tatrānvayavyāptim āpādyopādhir vaktavya iti.*

tad anupapannam. kevalavyatirekyanumānodbhāvyopādhitvābhāvāt. na hy anvayapadena[483] *kevalavyatirekyanumānaṃ bhavati virodhāt. tasmād uktaprakāreṇopādhyudbhāvanaṃ varam. tasmād upādheḥ sarvaśaḥ*[484] *sarvatra vyāpyatvāsiddhyāpādakatvena*[485] *vyāptivirahabhūtatvena vā dūṣaṇatvaṃ siddham ity alam*[486] *atiprasaṅgenety upādhidarpaṇe dūṣaṇaviveko nāma dvitīyaḥ paricchedaḥ.+*

(**3**) *upādhibhedaprakāraś cintyate.*

(**3.1**) *tathā hi. upādhayo dvividhāḥ. niścitāḥ śaṅkitā iti. tatra sādhyavyāpakatvaṃ ca dvayam*[487] *apy upādhiniścitam. te niścitā yathā <hiṃsātve niṣiddhatvam>*[488] *upalabhyamānasparśādhiṣṭhānatve*[489] *cākṣuṣadravyatvam*[490] *ityādayo niścitopādhayaḥ.*

(**3.1.1**) *śaṅkitopādhayaś*[491] *ca dvidhā.*

---

[473]Ms. *vadoma(ḥ?)* corrected to *vadāma(ḥ?)* [474]Ms. *kevalavyatirekīhetā* ... (≈ 1 *akṣara* missing) [475]Ms. *kuṇṭhībhavet* [476]Ms. *kevalavyatirekisādhyābhāvaśaṅkāyāṃ (?) avidyamānasyopādheḥ* corrected to *kevalavyatirekisādhyābhāvaśaṅkāyāṃ avidyamānasyopādheḥ* [477]Ms. *-vyāpakatvani* ... *yābhāve* (≈ 1 *akṣara* missing) [478]Ms. *nirupadravatvam* [479]Ms. *nirūcāmānaṃ* corrected to *nirūcānaṃ* [480]Ms. *vikṣatvasaṃbhāvanāyāṃ* corrected to *vipakṣatvasaṃbhāvanāyāṃ* [481]Ms. *-viśeṣaṇatvābhāvāt* [482]Ms. *sādhyaṃ ta* corrected to *sādhyaṃ* [483]Ms. *anvaya* ... *padanena* (≈ 2 *akṣaras* missing) [484]Ms. *sarvaḥ* [485]Ms. *vyāpyatvāsidhyāpādakatvena* corrected to *vyāpyatvāsiddhyāpādakatvena* [486]Ms. *alakṣam* [487]Ms. *vayam* [488]Ms. *hiṃsātvaniṣiddhatvam* [489]Ms. *upālabhyamāna-* corrected to *upalabhyamāna-* [490]Ms. *cākṣuṣatvadravyatvam* [491]Ms. *śaṅkitopādhiś* corrected to *śaṅkitopādhayaś*

sādhyavyāpakatvasādhanāvyāpakatvaniścayabhāvapadānāṃ <tatra niścitasādhyavyāpakatvaṃ>[492] *yathā mano vibhv asparśadravyatvād ātmavad*[493] *ityāder*[494] *amūrtadravya*[495] *iti.*

sa copādhiḥ sādhanaṃ ca dvayam api sādhyena[496] *samavyāptam. tathā ca tulyabalena sādhanena pratirathatvād*[497] *upādheḥ sādhyavyāpakatvaṃ*[498] *niścitam iti.*

<aniścitasādhyavyāpako niścitasādhanāvyāpakaś>[499] *ca. mitrātanayatvādyanumāne*[500] *<śākādyāhārapariṇatipūrvakatvavad ihasthāyāḥ>*[501] *kasyāścit kāntāyā dṛṣadvatyās*[502] *tatra pañca samīpe vartante. <sarve śyāmāḥ>*[503]. *anyas tu deśāntaragataḥ. tatra <śyāmatety āpattiḥ>*[504] *sañjāyate. tathā ca pūrvādy āha. vimataḥ śyāmo bhavitum arhati. etattanayatvāt. sampratipannavad iti.*

śākādyāhārapariṇatipūrvakatvam upādhir bhavati. tasya ca sādhanāvyāpakatvaṃ na niścitam. tasyāpi śākādyāhārapariṇatipūrvakatvasaṃdehaḥ. tathā hi. tasyāḥ śākādyāhāreṣu[505] *pravṛttiḥ pañcasu*[506] *garbheṣu vartamānā dṛśyata*[507] *eva. ṣaṣṭhagarbhānuvṛttāv api tatrābhiratir asti na veti <saṃdehān nāpi>*[508] *tathā dṛśyate kutracid <artha ekadāsaktau>*[509] *satyām api kadācid*[510] *virāgadarśanāt*[511]. *<tasmāt sādhanāvyāpakasiddham>*[512] *evety ayam aniścitasādhanāvyāpaka iti nābhidhīyate.*

yad vā mitrātanayatvaśākādyāhārapariṇatipūrvakatvayoḥ[513] *saṃbandhe śyāmatvam evopādhir bhavet.*

na ca sādhanāvyāpakatvaṃ śākādyāhārapariṇatipūrvakatvasyaiva[514] *mitrātanayatvaśyāmatvayoḥ*[515] *saṃbandha upādhitvābhyupagamāt*[516]. *tathā ca śākādyāhārapariṇatipūrvakatvopādhiḥ sādhanam. saṃbandha upādhyabhāvasya niścetum aśakyatvāt sādhanāvyāpakatvaniścayābhāvād aniścitasādhanāvyāpakatvena śaṅkitasādhanāvyāpakatvam asyopādhir iti siddham.*

nanv evaṃ cet sāmānyavattve saty asmadādibāhyendriyagrāhyatvād anityatvānumāne kṛtakatvam upādhir[517] *bhavet. tatrāpi bhavaduktanyāye*

---

[492]Ms. *tatrāniścitasādhyavyāpakaṃ* [493]Ms. *ātmāvad* [494]Ms. *ityāde* corrected to *ityādeḥ* [495]Ms. *amūrtadrava* [496]Ms. *sādhanena* [497]Ms. *pratirathātvaṃtvād* [498]Ms. *sādhyavyāpakatvena* [499]Ms. *niścitasādhyavyāpakaḥ aniścitasādhanāvyāpakaś* [500]Ms. *maitratanayatvādyanumāne* [501]Ms. *-pūrvakatvādihiyasyāḥ* corrected to *-pūrvakatvādih(e?)yasyāḥ** [502]Ms. *dṛṣadvatāḥ* [503]Ms. *sarvaśyāmāḥ* [504]Ms. *śyāmatāv iti pattiḥ* [505]Ms. *sākāśādyāhāreṣu* corrected to *śākādyāhāreṣu* [506]Ms. *pañcāsu* [507]Ms. *dṛśyaṃte* [508]Ms. *saṃdehāl lāpi* [509]Ms. *padārthaikadāsaktau* [510]Ms. *gadācid* corrected to *kadācid* [511]Ms. *v(i?)rāgadarśanāt* [512]Ms. *tasmādhanāvyāpakasiddham* corrected to *tasmāt sādhanāvyāpakasiddham* [513]Ms. *maitratanayatvaśākādyāhārapariṇatipūrvatvayoḥ* [514]Ms. *śākādyāhārapariṇatapūrvakatvasyaiva* [515]Ms. *maitratanayatva-* [516]Ms. *upādhitvenābhyupagamāt* [517]Ms. *upādher*

sādhanopādhyoḥ saṃbandhe 'nityatvasyopādhitvād[518] *anityatvasādhanāvyāpakatvam iti.*

maivam. yadi śabdo nityo bhavet tarhi taratamabhāvo na syād ity etattarkānugṛhīte sādhane <śabdānityatvāvaśyaṃbhāvena vyāpyavyāpake 'py>[519] *akṛte kasya sādhanavyāpakatvaniścaye tadaniścayāyogāt. nāsty eva kṛtakatvopādheḥ. śaṅkitopādhitvasyaiva tatropādhisaktau*[520] *mitrātanayatvasya*[521] *tv anukūlatarko nāstīti. pakṣe śyāmatvaniścayāyogaḥ*[522]. *tadvyāpakasyopādhir api sādhanaṃ vyāpyam iti niścayāyogāt. upādhisaṃbhāvanāyām asādhanavyāpakatvaniścayāyogābhāve na śyāmatvasyaivopādhitvasaktau*[523] *sādhanāvyāpakatvaniścayābhāvāt tadaṃśena śaṅkitopādhitvam upapadyata iti.*

(**3.1.2**) *te copādhayaḥ ṣoḍhā dṛśyante. kevalasādhyavyāpakāḥ. yatkiṃcidviśeṣaṇāvacchinnasādhyavyāpakāḥ. sādhanābhāvavyāpakāḥ. sādhyābhāvavyāpakāḥ āpāāvyāpakā*[524] *iti.*

tatrā[M9a]*dyodāharaṇaṃ kṣityādikaṃ sakartṛkaṃ śarīryajanyatvāt. dhūmavad ity atra kāryatvādayaḥ.*

dvitīyodāharaṇaṃ tu samavāyaḥ samavetasaṃbandhāt saṃyogatvādayaḥ.

tṛtīyodāharaṇam tu mitrātanayatvādyanumāne[525] *puruṣatvāvacchinnaśyāmatvavyāpakaśākādyāhārapariṇatipūrvakatvādayaḥ.*

caturthodāharaṇaṃ tu svaprakāśatvādisādhyānubhūtitvādikevalavytirekyanumāneṣu[526] *sādhanābhāvavyāpakajaḍatvādayaḥ.*

pañcamodāharaṇaṃ tu śarīrijanyatvādisādhanavyatirekasakartṛkatvādisādhyavyatirekayoḥ saṃbandhe gaganādayaḥ.

ṣaṣṭhodāharaṇaṃ[527] *tu yadi kṣityādikaṃ sakartṛkaṃ bhavec charīrijanyaṃ*[528] *bhaved <ghaṭavad ityādau>*[529] *karacaraṇādivyāpārapūrvakatvādayaḥ*

(**3.2**) *teṣāṃ sarveṣām upādhīnāṃ lakṣaṇe sādhyapadena vyāpakatvasya vivakṣitatvāt tatra paryavasānaṃ bhaviṣyatīty uktam. sarvopādhivinirmuktānumānaṃ dhūmādikaṃ prayujyata iti cet.*

na. tatpratyayo vaidharmyasāmarthyāt[530].

pakṣadharmatvaprakāśārtham iti cet.

---

[518]Ms. *anityatvasyopādhitvāv* corrected to *anityatvasyopādhitvād* [519]Ms. *śabdānityatvātvavaśyābhāve tadvyā . . . vyāpaka py* (≈ 1 *akṣara* missing) [520]Ms. *tatropattathasaktau* [521]Ms. *maitratanayatvasya* [522]Ms. *śyāmatvaniścayāyogāḥ* corrected to *śyāmatvaniścayāyogaḥ* [523]Ms. *śyāmatvasyaivopādhitvaṣrasaktau* [524]Ms. corrupt reading, not conjecturable [525]Ms. *maitratanayatvādyanumāne* [526]Ms. *svaprakāśatvādisādha . . . nubhūti-* (≈ 1 *akṣara* missing) [527]Ms. *ṣoḍhā udāharaṇaṃ* [528]Ms. *śarīrajanyaṃ* corrected to *śarīrijanyaṃ* [529]Ms. *ghaṭavadidau* corrected to *ghaṭavad ityādau* [530]Ms. *vai . . . rthyāt* (≈ 5 *akṣaras* missing)

na. hetuvacanena pratipādanam.

kim antasyānumānāṅgatvād iti cet.

na. vyāpter apy anumānāṅgatvāt.

pratipādanaṃ vyāptadhūmavattvād iti kiṃ na kriyate na tūdāharaṇavacanāt. vyāptiḥ pratipadyate. na tena hetuvacanād[531] *iti cet.*

pakṣadharmatvam apy upanayād[532] *bhaviṣyati. kiṃ hetuvacanena. ato dhūmavad ity eva prayogaḥ.*

kiṃcākāṅkṣāgamaparyālocanāyāṃ[533] *tapovaiyarthyam*[534]. *tathā hi. vipratipannaṃ pratijñā kartavyā parvato 'gnimān iti. tadanantaraṃ kuta ity ākāṅkṣāyāṃ hetur vaktavyaḥ. dhūmād iti. katham iti*[535] *sakalāpekṣāyāṃ vyāptyā nimitteneti vyāptiṃ prakāśya*[536] *tadanantaraṃ tathā suloke prakṛte kim āyātam ity apekṣāyāṃ tādṛśahetoḥ pakṣe* <*vyāptiḥ sthāpanīyā*>[537]. *tadanantaraṃ bādhakābhāvaḥ prakāśyaḥ. yasmād bādhakaṃ nāsti tasmād agnimān ity evaṃ dhruvaparyālocanayāpi*[538] *hetuvacanena tapovaiyarthyam iti dhūmād ity eva prayoktavyam iti sthitam. tatra prayogas tu vṛddhavyavahārānusāreṇety anusaṃdheyam.*

nanv atra pakṣetaratvopādhir[539] *bhavati. katham ayaṃ nirupādhika*[540] *iti cet.*

na. pakṣetarasyānupādhitvenoktatvāt.

(**3.3**) *nanu kiyanta upādhyābhāsā*[541] *iti cet*

kevalasādhyavyāpakāḥ. kevalasādhyavyāpyāḥ[542]. *kevalasādhanāvyāpakāḥ. kevalasādhyavyāpakatve sati sādhanāvyāpakāḥ. kevalasādhyavyāpyatve sati sādhanāvyāpakā iti.*

(**3.3.1**) *tatrādyapakṣo yathā sāmānyavattve saty asmadādibāhyendriyagrāhyatvād ityādinānityatvānumāne kṛtakatvādayaḥ.*

dvitīyodāharaṇaṃ tu tasminn evānumāne sāvayavatvādayaḥ. yad vā śabdo 'bhidheyo guṇatvād ityādau sattāyogitvādayaḥ[543].

tṛtīyodāharaṇaṃ tu <*kṛtakatvād eva sāmānyavattve satītyādayaḥ*[544]>[545].

caturthodāharaṇaṃ tu kṛtakatvānumāna 'śrāvaṇatvādayaḥ.

pañcamodāharaṇaṃ tu śabdo 'bhidheyaḥ prameyatvād ity atra guṇatvādayaḥ.

---

[531] Ms. *hevacanād* corrected to *hetuvacanād* [532] Ms. *upananāt* corrected to *upanayāt* [533] Ms. *-paryālocanayām* corrected to *-paryālocanāyām* [534] Ms. *anupovaiyarthyaṃ* [535] Ms. om. *iti* [536] Ms. *prakāśyā* corrected to *prakāśya* [537] Ms. *vyāptis pāpanīyā* [538] Ms. *dhru . . . paryālocanayāpi* (≈ 1 *akṣara* missing) [539] Ms. *pakṣetaratopādhir* [540] Ms. *nipādhika* corrected to *nirupādhika* [541] Ms. *upādhyābhāvā* [542] Ms. *kevalasādhyāvyāpyāḥ* [543] Ms. *-yogitvāyaḥ* [544] Ms. *sati ityādeyaḥ* [545] Ms. probably has a lacuna in the passage marked off by angular brackets

(**3.3.2**) *pakṣetaratvam api vyarthaṃ pakṣa evāpatitaṃ naṣṭasthagābhāse*[546].

(**3.4**) *evaṃ sābhāsā*[547] *upādhibhedā nirūpitāḥ. evam uktena mārgeṇa lakṣaṇābhyām alaṃkṛtaḥ. prayojakaḥ sādhyasiddheḥ. svavirodhisamarthakaḥ.+*

nānādibhedabhinno 'yaṃ rāmacandrānupālataḥ/
jīyād[548] *upādhir jagati vidvajjanamanoharaḥ//+*

ity upādhidarpaṇe tṛtīyaḥ paricchedaḥ.+ śrī.+

[546]Ms. *naṣṭathagābhāsa* [547]Ms. *sābhāṣā* corrected to *sābhāsā* [548]Ms. *jīvād* corrected to *jīyād*

Chapter 4

Annotated English Translation

4.1 Prefatory Remarks

Rendering the terse nominalistic style of a very technical Navya-Nyāya treatise such as the UD into good English is almost impossible if one still wants to keep the translation as literal as possible instead of tampering with the original by merely paraphrasing the presumptive meaning. Our aim is to satisfy the needs of a reader who prefers a more literal translation, which reveals the exact correspondence between linguistic elements in the Sanskrit text and their English equivalents. However, since the literal translation is sometimes rather cryptic, we have added numerous explanatory notes to individual passages (cf. section 4.3). Moreover, the notes provide information concerning authors, works and philosophical doctrines which are referenced in the UD. Inquiries into the logical content from a modern perspective have been largely avoided, so that the notes are also accessible to a reader without any background in modern logic.

The following notational convention has been adopted in the translation: Square brackets indicate that the words in between have been added because of grammatical or stylistic requirements. Round brackets in the translation are used to mark off words added by the translator in order to clarify the contents. In some rare places of the translation a sentence cannot be completed due to a lacuna or a corrupt reading in the manuscript which are unconjecturable. The ellipsis is indicated by "…".

4.2 Translation of the UD

(**1**) Om, Salutation!

> Having bowed with the head to the moon Śrīrāma[1] and to our teacher Yajñeśvara,
> this deep determination of the associate condition, which has to be defined in general and in particular (i.e., in terms of a general and a particular defining characteristic), is undertaken.

(**1.1**) [Opponent:][2] Is there a general or a specific defining characteristic of the associate condition?

(**1.1.1**) [Respondent:] First of all, in that case a general defining characteristic is inappropriate. After all, it has been said that "being the counterpositive of an absolute absence" is actually a general defining characteristic. This is not [so]. Because of over-pervasion with respect to eternal substances.[3] After all, the ether etc. are only counterpositives of an absolute absence on account of a self-resident absolute absence[4], but they do not occur there[5]. Because self-dependence would be the undesirable consequence.[6] And these are not associate conditions, because there would be the undesirable consequence of a failure of all inferences.[7]

(**1.1.2**) [Opponent:] "Being a property which is a counterpositive of an absolute absence" [is a general defining characteristic].[8] These[9] are not associate conditions because of the absence of propertyness due to the fact that they have no substrate.

(**1.1.2.1**) [Respondent:] This is not [so]. The *atyantābhāvapratiyogidharmatva* itself is not an associate condition or it is an associate condition. In the first [case] there is over-pervasion of the defining characteristic there[10]. Because it is a self-resident counterpositive of an absolute absence. And because it would be a property of something which is not an associate condition.[11] And in the second case this [*atyantābhāvapratiyogidharmatva*] does not occur there[12] or it does occur there. If not, there would be non-pervasion.[13] In the second [case] it occurs itself [in the defining characteristic]. Or another one [occurs there].[14] In the first [case there would be] self-dependence. In the second [case there would be] a conflict between the defining characteristic and its [required] generality.[15] And (the second alternative is unwarranted), because there would be the undesirable consequence of a regressus ad infinitum.[16]

(**1.1.2.2**) Moreover, properties which reside only in this defining characteristic are associate conditions or they are not associate conditions. In the first [case] just this defining characteristic occurs there[17] or another one. The first [case] is not [possible], because mutual dependence would be the undesirable consequence.[18] For, there would be [the defining characteristic's] own residence in a property which resides in [the defining characteristic] itself, i.e., there would be the residence of this property[19] in its own [property][20]. If another [defining characteristic of the associate condition resides in the properties which reside in the defining characteristic, we get] the afore-mentioned mistake[21]. In the second [case][22] there is over-pervasion of the defining characteristic.[23] As a property which resides only in that [defining characteristic] is a counterpositive of an absolute absence which[24] resides in something else than that [defining characteristic], one should not say that this defining characteristic does not reside there[25], since eternal substances and knowability etc. are excluded by the words "property" and "absolute absence".[26] And so, one has to say that the defining characteristic necessarily resides there[27], since they are properties of the defining characteristic and the counterpositive of an absolute absence which[28] resides in these two[29]. Otherwise, there would be the undesirable consequence of the eternal substances, knowability etc. being among them.[30]

(**1.1.2.3**) So, the *atyantābhāvapratiyogidharmatva* residing in the defining characteristic[31] is different from this defining characteristic or not different. In the first [case] this [*atyantābhāvapratiyogidharmatva*, which resides in the defining characteristic], is also a defining characteristic of an associate condition, or not. If not, the defining characteristic of an associate condition has to be specified as "devoid of the [property of] residing in the defining characteristic", since otherwise a suspicion concerning the defining characteristic would be the undesirable conclusion.[32] If [the *atyantābhāvapratiyogidharmatva*] is a defining characteristic, it is contradictory because of the contradiction that something which resides in the defining characteristic of an associate condition excludes the associate condition.[33] In the case [that the *atyantābhāvapratiyogidharmatva*, which resides in the defining characteristic, is] not different [from the defining characteristic, we would end up with] self-dependence.

(**1.1.2.4**) [Opponent:] In the case of occurrence self-dependence is not a fault, because this [self-dependence] is [only] an obstacle to production and cognizing.[34] Otherwise, the failure of [a property's or an inference's] being universally positive/only positive would be the undesirable consequence.[35] After all, what is discussed is exemplified by the only positive [inference] "It is perceptible for somebody, because it is an object of knowledge, such as a myrobalan (or: the fruit of a myrobalan) on the palm of the hand." etc.[36] Here, the probandum occurs on the probandum or not. If not, the result would be the fallacy of inconclusiveness[37], insofar as the probans would occur on the probandum which possesses the absence of the probandum.[38] In the first case[39] [the result would be] a regressus ad infinitum, if another [probandum] occurred [on the probandum][40], and self-dependence, if [the probandum] occurred on itself. And so, if [self-dependence] should be a fault, [a property's or an inference's] being universally positive/only positive fails.

(**1.1.2.5**) [Respondent:] It is not [so that self-dependence in the case of occurrence should not be regarded as a fault]. If one does not admit that self-dependence is a fault, even a positive and negative inference etc.[41] fail. After all, in the case of the inference "The mountain possesses fire, because it possesses smoke" the fallacy of inconclusiveness would result from the possibility that smoke-possessingness, e.g., occurs in itself as something which possesses the absence of the probandum, since there would be no exclusion of the self-dependence of something which occurs in itself.[42] And so, as self-dependence in the case of occurrence is a fault, the validity of positive and negative [inferences] can be asserted.

[Opponent:] If one admits that [self-dependence in the case of occurrence] is a fault, then the only positive inference fails.

[Respondent:] It shall fail, because it is necessary to admit the validity of this [inference][43] which possesses both, positive and negative correlation.[44] Therefore, it is established that self-dependence is also a fault in the case of occurrence.

(**1.1.2.6**) Moreover:[45]

> Insofar as even on the basis of a distinction the mistake ("self-dependence") is involved in the thesis concerning [the *atyantābhāvapratiyogidharmatva*'s] being an associate condition,[46]
> how should there not be a regressus ad infinitum because of the existence of another distinction?[47]
> If this very [distinction][48] can be accomplished,[49] there is the absence [of the *atyantābhāvapratiyogidharmatva*] in one place.[50]

In the case of the other distinction, however, the previous mistake lingers.[51]

Therefore, it is established that [the definition of the associate condition] should not be undertaken, because there is no purpose for a defining characteristic of an associate condition.

(**1.1.3**) [Opponent:] First of all, the expression "associate condition" is [commonly] used in the world. This usage depends on an origin. The origin, however, does not pertain to the individuals. Because of the infinity of individuals. Therefore, first of all, one has to talk about a common cause of usage.

On account of there being also a universal of [the individuals] which possess that defining characteristic, the mistake of an overlap of universals would ensue if this (universal) were accepted (as a common cause of usage). After all, existence occurs in the eternal substances, setting aside the (putative) universal associate-conditionness. The (putative) universal associate-conditionness occurs in universals etc., setting aside existence. There is, however, an overlap of these two with regard to qualities etc., and since [the associate-conditionness] exists in universals etc., it does not have the form of a universal.[52]

[Respondent:] This is not [so], because of the use of this [expression "associate condition"] only due to an application which is established by mundane practice. *upa*, [i.e.] nearby, [the associate condition] transmits a property residing in itself to something else.[53] It is not the case that the expression "associate condition" is established as having a wider [range of] usage, since it has a verb as its part.[54] And so, it is established that the expression "associate condition" serves its purpose independently of what you have said.

[Opponent:] First of all, the association [with the meaning of the verbal root] has too far-reaching undesirable consequences on account of the similarity with a China rose etc.

[Respondent:] This is not [so], because someone who teaches that the *atyantābhāvapratiyogidharmatva* is a defining characteristic of associate conditions acknowledges that somewhere the China rose etc. are also associate conditions.

[Opponent:] If this is so, then the bringing to light of its own pervadedness might be a defining characteristic of associate conditions. For us this (i.e., the China rose) [does] not [bring to light its own pervadedness].

[Respondent:] It is not so,[55] because, since an associate condition with non-coextensive pervasion does not bring to light its own pervadedness, there is the undesirable consequence that it would not be an associate condition.[56] Therefore, it is established that (this) defining characteristic of associate conditions is of no use, because it is inapplicable to different usages.

(**1.1.4**) Moreover, [for the following reason the *atyantābhāvapratiyogidharmatva* is] not [a defining characteristic of associate conditions]: There is over-pervasion because of the occurrence of the defining characteristic in knowability etc., which are not considered as associate conditions, because of a proof that knowability etc. are counterpositives of an absolute absence due to [the inference] "Knowability is a counterpositive of an absolute absence, because it is a property" etc.

[Opponent:] The substrate of the absolute absence of knowability etc. is knowable or not. If not, the absolute absence of that (knowability) is not possible, because there is no substrate.[57] If there is a cognition of the absence due to the fact that the substrate is described in opposition [to the previous alternative], then it is excluded that it is a substrate of an absolute absence of that (i.e., knowability), because it is knowable.[58] And so, this inference is not [valid], because it is refuted due to a contradiction.

[Respondent:] No. Because [your argument] amounts to [the thesis of the afore-mentioned inference], because it rather justifies [the claim] that [knowability] is a counterpositive of an absolute absence, since [the substrate of the absolute absence of knowability] is a substrate of something which has no substrate.[59]

[Opponent:] There is the undesirable conclusion of the afore-mentioned mistake (i.e., the dilemma concerning the knowability of the substrate of the absolute absence of knowability) by establishing [something as] the substrate because of [the valid inference:] "An absolute absence is somewhere dependent on a substrate, because it is an absence."[60]

[Respondent:] No. Because, on account of that (i.e., your inference) there is an inconsistency due to an absolute absence's being known (in some cases) and its being not known (in others). After all, if [an absolute absence] is not known, then there is no evidence for a substrate. If it is known, then it is known [to be] somewhere.[61]

[Opponent:] Since the afore-mentioned mistake is obtained because of its (i.e., the substrate's of the absolute absence of knowability) being known and its being not known, and since there is no knowledge source (for a substrate of the absolute absence of knowability), we and others agree [that knowability is not a counterpositive of an absolute absence] because of the previous inference ("An absolute absence is somewhere dependent on a substrate, because it is an absence").

[Respondent:] No. Because of the undesirable conclusion that your inference has no force, because it is opposed to that which [you] depend on (in order to demonstrate that my inference is invalid).[62] The over-pervasion of the defining characteristic of associate conditions is established,[63] because our inference is not refuted by a reductio ad absurdum due to a contradiction on account of the fact that it (i.e., our inference) has an absolute absence without a substrate as its object.[64]

[Opponent:] Then, "being a property which is a counterpositive of an absolute absence which has a substrate" should be a defining characteristic of associate conditions, because [the absolute absence of knowability] is not like that, because knowability etc. are counterpositives of an absolute absence without a substrate.[65]

[Respondent:] No. Because you do not get around the previously mentioned mistake of an overlap.[66] Therefore, neither a general nor a specific defining characteristic of associate conditions has been established, because there is no specific defining characteristic, since there is not even a general defining characteristic.

(**1.1.5**) [Opponent:] Just as the qualifiers "substance" and "non-substance" etc. are used in spite of the absence of a general defining characteristic for the seven categories, in the same way should there here also be a qualifier (i.e., a specific defining characteristic of the associate condition) without a general defining characteristic.[67] In this case the specific defining characteristics do not depend on a general defining characteristic with respect to production, knowledge [or] occurrence.[68] Therefore, specific defining characteristics are possible without a general defining characteristic.

[Respondent:] In this case, however, there is, first of all, a dependence on knowledge, for, after all, if there is no general defining characteristic, there is according to your opinion not even an application of the word "associate condition".[69] Because, in the case of the undesirable conclusion that no [general defining characteristic] indicates [an associate condition] there is then not even a cognition of these (associate conditions), since there is no recognition of a specific defining characteristic which has as its object the cognition of the associate condition for that inference.

But in the case of [the word] "category" there is not this same mistake. The (specific) defining characteristic consists in "sound" etc., because the derivation (of the application) with respect to this and that is possible on account of the seven defining characteristics "substance" etc. alone.[70]

Moreover, because of the thesis that a *padārtha* belongs to ordinary life, and since there is even an explication of [the word] *pada* by means of a defining characteristic, there is a derivation (of the application) of [the word] *padārtha* with respect to that which is expressed and which is connected with that (i.e., with the word *padārtha*).[71]

In the present case, however, one does not obtain the [property of] having various meanings, as in the case of the word *akṣa* because of the infinite number of qualifiers which are defining characteristics of associate conditions, since, by contrast, the derivation (of the application of the word *upādhi*) is not even possible on account of the infinite number of individuals which are associate conditions.[72]

However, the thesis concerning the connection (of the word *upādhi* with its root) is impossible, because this property, [namely] "It transmits a property residing in it to something *upa*, [i.e.,] nearby", does not pervade the asscociate condition which you have in mind.[73]

Therefore, it is established that in the present [case] there is no specific defining characteristic in the absence of a general defining characteristic, because in the case of the associate conditions which you have in mind the specific defining characteristic can be stated for the purpose of understanding the word, only if one knows the general defining characteristic.

(**1.1.6**) [Opponent:] The general defining characteristic is the pervasion of the probandum, while there is non-pervasion of the probans.[74] And this is a specific defining characteristic on account of the qualifier "being [the probans and the probandum] under discussion etc.".

(**1.1.6.1**) [Respondent:] No. The pervasion of the probandum is not a relation without an associate condition which is endowed with a probandum (as a relatum) because of the undesirable conclusion of the group of three [defects, viz.] self-dependence, mutual dependence and circularity, because it (i.e., the relation) would depend on the cognition of an associate condition [and] this (i.e., the associate condition) would depend on the cognition of the defining characteristic. After all, there is a cognition of an associate condition by means of the defining characteristic of an associate condition. Therefore, there is self-dependence if one wants to express merely the state of being a root of itself, in the sense that the defining characteristic presupposes the knowledge of being devoid of an associate condition. There is mutual dependence if one wants to express the group of two, but there is circularity if one wants to express the group of three.[75]

Therefore, the defining characteristic is impossible, because something which contains a blocker, [viz.] self-dependence etc., would cause the [probans's] being essentially unestablished. And so [says] Varadarāja:[76]

> Self-dependence and also mutual dependence, circularity,
> the regressus ad infinitum – these instances of a reductio ad absurdum[77] are the causes of the [probans's] being essentially unestablished.[78]

(**1.1.6.2**) But insofar as there is a reference to the probandum in every [inference] by the word "probandum", just because this defining characteristic is a general defining characteristic, there is non-pervasion of the defining characteristic with respect to such an associate condition (i.e., an associate condition according to Udayana's defining characteristic) on account of there being no pervasion of that (i.e., the probandum), since somewhere the probans appears also as the probandum.[79]

(**1.1.6.3**) The defining characteristic is over-pervaded with respect to something which is different from the subject of the inference, because the [property of] being different from the mountain pervades the probandum in the form of the [property of] possessing fire and because it does not pervade the probans on account of its being excluded from the subject of the inference, which possesses the probans. If this were also an associate condition, there would be the undesirable consequence of putting an end to all inferences.[80]

[Opponent:] The pervasion of the probandum is, indeed, the possession of a positive and negative pervasion with the probandum (as a relatum). And the property of being different from the subject of the inference does not have that [positive and negative pervasion with the probandum as a relatum], because there is no determination of the absence of the probandum on the subject of the inference.[81]

[Respondent:] No. Because, insofar as the state of being the pervaded and the pervader is ascertained just by inferences[82], and insofar as an indication of a deviation is ascertained due to the necessity of the absence of the pervaded in the case of the absence of that (associate condition), there is the undesirable conclusion of the inapplicability of the defining characteristic in that part (i.e., *sādhyena sahānvayavyatirekavyāptimattvam*) on account of the absence of the necessity of a negative pervasion.[83]

[Opponent:] The [defining characteristic] which allows to infer [the absence of fire] on the mountain[84] does not have the purpose of excluding that which is different from the subject of the inference considering the thesis of the failure (of valid inferences).[85]

[Respondent:] Since the way of vitiating by means of an associate condition is the same, it is inappropriate to exclude it (i.e., the *bādhonnītopādhi*) because of the necessity of the indication of a deviation.

[Opponent:] Otherwise (i.e., if we admit the property of being different from the subject of the inference as an associate condition), all inferences would fail.

[Respondent:] If so, let the associate condition not be a fault. By all this there will be no abatement of the fear of an associate condition with respect to the probans.[86]

[Opponent:] But how is it possible for us to say that something which indicates a deviation is not a vitiator?

[Opponent (with a tentative suggestion):] In the case of a deviation which is induced (by an inference) the inference is a vitiator.[87]

[Opponent:] Then the view with respect to that which is different from the subject of the inference shall be granted to you in such a way,[88] because this also indicates a deviation in the manner described by us.[89] But in that case there is no positive correlation.[90]

[Respondent:] No. Because [one] only agrees to an associate condition and to a deviation without bringing [them] to the fore. Therefore, the defining characteristic would become a meaningless qualifier, because the [property of] being different from the subject of the inference cannot be excluded by those who teach that this[91] is an associate condition.[92]

Moreover, it is difficult to keep off the over-pervasion of the defining characteristic, even when there is such an explication of the pervasion, because that very negative correlation is also possible because of the impossibility of one's own residence in oneself due to the self-dependence of the [property of] being different from the subject of the inference.[93]

Moreover, (it is difficult to keep off the over-pervasion of the defining characteristic) because of the over-pervasion with respect to the [property of] being an agreeing instance, and because in that case the negative correlation is possible precisely in the range of disagreeing instances.[94]

[Opponent:] The over-pervasion with respect to that which is different from the subject of the inference is excluded by means of the qualifier "insofar as it is other than the [property of] being different from the subject of the inference".

[Respondent:] Be it [so]! Nevertheless, (this can also not be a general defining characteristic), because, insofar as the over-pervasion with respect to the [property of] being an agreeing instance would be present in that (defining characteristic), it is included in the [property of] being different from the subject of the inference, such as the [property of] being produced by a body etc., because they are also qualifiers which exclude only the subject of the inference.[95]

[Opponent:] The [property of] being an agreeing instance is the ascertained possession of the probandum. But what is associated with the word "ascertain" excludes only the mere subject of the inference because of the exclusion of disagreeing instances by means of the word "probandum" alone.[96] There is still no over-pervasion of the defining characteristic.[97]

[Respondent:] This is not [so], because of the pervasion of that which is different from the subject of the inference and which is induced by a patent falsehood.[98] After all, with respect to inferences which are inconsistent with perception etc., [viz.] "Fire is not hot, because it is an object, like a pot etc." etc., one should speak of the existence of a pervasion, because, otherwise [i.e.], if [the probandum] were not pervaded [by the property of being different from the subject of the inference], the universality (of the property of being not hot) would be ascertained, because [the probandum] would be a property of the subject of the inference.[99]

[Opponent:] The subject of the inference possesses the probandum which is associated with a doubt. In that case there is no inference of something which has the defining characteristic of being a property of the subject of the inference, because there is – due to the absence of a doubt concerning the probandum on account of the determination of the absence of the probandum – no such [property of] being a property of the subject of the inference.[100] Only because of a defect which amounts to being the mere appearance (of an inferential subject), not because there is a pervasion (of the property of being not hot by the property of being different from the subject of the inference). And so, the bringing to the fore (of the defect) by means of an associate condition is not necessary in that case.

[Respondent:] No. There would not be the thesis concerning the visible world etc., since with respect to the unreality of the visible world etc. there is no doubt for a philosopher etc. who boast of the infallibility of a knowledge source for (absolute) truth etc.[101] And therefore, one should call [the following] a defining characteristic (of the inferential subject): "The subject of the inference possesses a property which [will be there] at a later time, which (is presently there, but) not nearby, or which [was there] in the past."[102] And since it is so, the non-pervasion (with respect to the property of being different from the subject of the inference) is difficult to keep off, because the property of being different from the subject of the inference will be an associate condition, since it indicates a deviation, because there is another associate condition[103] due to the undesirable conclusion of the bringing to the fore (of a deviation of the probans from the probandum) by means of an associate condition which is opposed to a (purported) pervasion in the form of a relation without associate condition, insofar as the bringing to the fore of the existence of a pervasion is necessary, because it is not enough for a proof that[104] the probans "being an object" can be a property of the subject of the inference, while [fire] is ascertained as a subject of an inference, because it is appropriate not to assent to [the inference] "Fire is not hot, because it is an object" etc.[105]

(**1.1.7**) Therefore, what is stated by Udayana, [viz.] "[It] pervades the probandum coextensively, while [it] does not pervade the probans" is also not a defining characteristic of an associate condition.[106]

(**1.1.7.1**) Because there is non-pervasion with respect to the property of being different from the subject of the inference which is induced by a patent falsehood and which has no coextensive pervasion. And because it is afflicted with some afore-mentioned defects, namely [the defects of] self-dependence etc. which are connected with the pervader of the probandum,[107] the defect of non-pervasion which depends on the naming of the probandum in every [inference] by means of the word "probandum",[108] over-pervasion with regard to the property of being different from the subject of the inference etc.[109] and impossibility[110].

[Opponent:] Since a coextensive pervasion (of the probandum by the property of being different from the subject of the inference) is impossible, how can there be a pervasion of that which is different from the subject of the inference with regard to that (defining characteristic)[111]?

[Respondent:] No. Because of the inappropriateness of that which is different from the subject of the inference which has a coextensive pervasion. Because, after all, in the case [of the inferences] "Sound is nameable" etc. there is the possibility of a coextensive pervasion because of the property of not being a sound etc. and because of the possession of fire (residing in) something which is different from the mountain etc.[112]

(**1.1.7.2**) And this is not the defining characteristic, because it does not pervade the associate condition which has a non-coextensive pervasion.

After all, [consider the inference]: "The colour of earth atoms etc. are eternal, because they are specific qualities of the atoms, such as the colour of water atoms etc." In that case the absence of the [property of] being a specific quality of the earth atoms is an associate condition.[113] But this has a non-coextensive pervasion.[114] It has to be understood that this is also an associate condition like the [properties of] not being fire etc., which have a coextensive pervasion.[115]

One says that this is an associate condition, because it indicates a deviation. The [property of] indicating that (i.e., a deviation) is obtained, because the probans occurs in something which possesses the absence of the probandum, since the absence of the probandum is necessary if the associate condition, which pervades the probandum, is absent from the subject of the inference. But the general usage "This probans deviates from this probandum, because it deviates from something which pervades this probandum, such as in the case of the (given) object of cognition", this is also the same for [an associate condition] which has a non-coextensive pervasion. Therefore, the non-pervasion (of the present defining characteristic with respect to an associate condition with non-coextensive pervasion) is established in that case.

[Opponent:] There is the [property of] being an associate condition due to the superimposition of the pervadedness occurring in itself and this does not exist in the case of an associate condition which has a non-coextensive pervasion. After all, [consider the inference]: "An injury which is involved in a sacrifice causes harm, because it is an injury like an injury for the purpose of wealth." Here, the [property of] being forbidden is actually an associate condition which has a coextensive pervasion.[116] For this (property of being forbidden) there is a pervasion of the probandum and there is the [property of] being pervaded by this (probandum) and there is a coexistence of the [property of] being forbidden and the [property of] being an injury with the [property of] bringing about guilt[117] due to an example.[118] And in this way the [property of] being forbidden brings the pervadedness connected with it to light in the probans for the probandum on account of the concomitance, like the China rose [brings to light] the redness in the crystal due to its proximity. So, since [an associate condition] which has a non-coextensive pervasion does not have the [property of] bringing to light the pervadedness connected with it, the application of the word "associate condition" should be correct only with respect to an associate condition which has a coextensive pervasion and which is well known by the people, because it causes a property to appear which resides in it.

However, the associate condition should not be regarded as a vitiator on account of the [property of] indicating a deviation, because of a knowledge source which causes the deviation to appear as that which is (certainly) knowable etc.[119] Otherwise (i.e., if the associate condition is regarded as a vitiator), this knowledge source[120] would be regarded as another vitiator, insofar as it indicates a deviation. Therefore, there is no non-pervasion with respect to that (i.e., with respect to the associate condition which has a non-coextensive pervasion), because that which has a non-coextensive pervasion is not an associate condition.[121]

[Respondent:] It is not so, because (if we accept the defining characteristic which postulates a coextensive pervasion) there is not one defining characteristic which comprehends the knowledge sources (in the form of associate conditions) which indicate a deviation. If the deviation had a sudden appearance in one's presence, it would not be an object of [one's] thinking.[122] And because in the present case, however, the comprehending in the manner referred to[123] is impossible. Insofar as it is appropriate to bring to the fore an associate condition which indicates a deviation, it is proved that the associate condition is a vitiator in this case as well, because the indicator of this is also a fortifier (i.e., a means to correct an invalid inference). Moreover, because the bringing to light of the pervadedness (as a condition for the purpose of excluding the associate condition with non-coextensive pervasion) is of no purpose, insofar as it is ascertained that [an associate condition] with non-coextensive pervasion is also an associate condition due to its bringing to light the pervadedness connected with it.

(**1.1.8**) Moreover, where there is a coextensive pervasion of probans and probandum, there it is not appropriate that something which possesses a non-coextensive pervasion of that which is limited by the probans is an associate condition.[124]

And insofar as this (associate condition with non-coextensive pervasion according to the proto-version of Prabhākara Upādhyāya's defining characteristic) brings to light its own pervadedness[125] because of its coming to light in the mere probans[126], how can that which has a non-coextensive pervasion not be an associate condition? Therefore, the non-pervasion with respect to [the associate condition] with non-coextensive pervasion is established.

Moreover, the word "coextensive" in this defining characteristic is meaningless, because nothing has to be excluded (by it), since that which has a non-coextensive pervasion is also an associate condition. Since in the case of the possession of fire in another [locus] than the mountain, which has a coextensive pervasion, [that which is different from the subject of the inference] is to be found in the world too, that which is different from the subject of the inference cannot be excluded either.

(**1.1.9**) Moreover, this (i.e., Udayana's defining characteristic with coextensive pervasion) is not the defining characteristic, because it does not include the associate condition which pervades the relation between probans and probandum.[127]

After all, here, (i.e., in the inference) "Inherence is assumed (to reside in the subject of the inference), because it (i.e., the subject of the inference) is a relation, such as contact", properties which reside in contact, [viz.] contactness, effectness, beingness etc., which pervade the relation between probans and probandum, are associate conditions.[128] And it is not [correct] that these are not associate conditions, because they do not pervade the probandum,[129] since it is possible that they are associate conditions, because – as in the case of other associate conditions – there is an indication of a deviation in this case as well. After all, the associate condition which pervades the relation between probans and probandum and which is absent from the subject of the inference excludes also the relation of the probans (with the probandum), which is pervaded by it. And the absence of the relation between probans and probandum is possible in three ways,[130] [viz.] "due to the absence of the probans, due to the absence of the probandum and due to the absence in both ways". Among those, the first and the last [case] are impossible, insofar as the (presence of the) probans (on the subject of the inference) is proved for both (kinds of) theorists (i.e., those who teach a definition with non-coextensive pervasion and those who teach a definition with coextensive pervasion). In the second [case] it is proved that insofar as the subject of the inference possesses the absence of the probandum, [the associate condition] also indicates a deviation of the probans from the occurrence of the probandum. Therefore, since this is also an associate condition, the non-pervasion of the defining characteristic (with coextensive pervasion of the probandum), which does not reside in that (i.e., in an associate condition which pervades only the relation between probans and probandum), is proved.

(**1.1.10**) [Opponent:] Then that which has been stated by Śivādityamiśra, [viz.] "[The associate condition] does not pervade the probans, while it pervades the relation between probans and probandum"[131] shall be the defining characteristic, because it includes the associate condition which pervades the relation, since, as the associate condition with non-coextensive pervasion is also found to be pervading the relation, [the present defining characteristic] occurs there as well. Therefore, there is also no non-pervasion with respect to an associate condition in the case of that which is different from the subject of the inference and which is induced by a patent falsehood.[132]

After all, [consider now the inference]: "It (i.e., the subject of the inference) is eternal, because it is created."[133] In that case there is not even a relation between probans and probandum. How can there be a pervasion of that by the associate condition? It is not so, because in that case the probans is defective, because it is even incoherent (with the probandum). How can there be a bringing to the fore of an associate condition (in this case)?[134]

(**1.1.10.1**) [Respondent:] It is not so. An inference has two parts, [viz.] the pervasion and the [property of] being a property of the subject of the inference. Actually, in that case (i.e., in the case of the preceding inference) a deficiency in one of the two parts is necessary because of the fallacious appearance (of a concomitance) in every [case], for, otherwise, there would be the undesirable conclusion that [the inference] proves [that something which is created is eternal]. And so, one should say that there is no pervasion in the case of the incoherent [probans], because the [property of] being a property of the subject of the inference is there. And pervasion is a relation without associate condition. And so, there is a bringing to the fore of an associate condition which is opposed to it. The defining characteristic is necessarily over-pervaded because of the fact that there is merely that (incoherence of the probans) in the case of the audience's enquiry to the opponent due to the bringing to the fore of the fault of the incoherence [of the probans] by the opponent.[135]

(**1.1.10.2**) [Opponent:] According to whose opinion the defining characteristic of a pervasion [consists in] "Pervasion is a relation without a deviation", in the opinion of that one there is only in the case of a deviation a positive correlation (of the associate condition with the deviation). Because in that case the [property of] being an associate condition lacks the [property of] having a form which is opposed to that (kind of deviation).[136] And therefore, there is also no non-pervasion.

(**1.1.10.3**) [Respondent:] No. According to the opinion of that one [a mere deviation] (i.e., a deviation such that probans and probandum have no common loci) cannot be brought to the fore, because there is no perception etc. of a mere deviation. One necessarily has to talk about an associate condition which indicates that (i.e., a "mere" deviation), for, otherwise, there would be the undesirable consequence that a deviation (i.e., a "mere" deviation) would not be related to a knowledge source.[137] And therefore, it is established that the non-pervasion of the defining characteristic with respect to that (i.e., with respect to an associate condition which indicates a "mere" deviation) is difficult to restrain because of the bringing to the fore of an associate condition which is inseparably connected with a deviation.

(**1.1.10.4**) Moreover, there is non-pervasion if contact, inherence etc. are meant by the word "relation", because these do not apply to probans and probandum in every case.

(**1.1.10.5**) If a pervasion as a relation without associate condition is meant, the bringing to the fore of an associate condition would be futile, because an inference is flawless due to a relation without associate condition.[138]

(**1.1.10.6**) If, however, the co-occurrence of probans and probandum is meant, the mere co-occurrence would be excluded in the case of the absence of the associate condition. And there would be no absence of the probandum, because the associate condition would lack the pervasion with respect to the probandum.[139]

[Opponent:] But the absence of the co-occurrence gives a clue to the absence of either, insofar as there is a pervadedness (of the absence of the associate condition) by the absence of either of the two in the relation. Therefore, there is indirectly the absence of the probandum.[140]

(**1.1.11**) [Respondent:] It is not so. What is the use of the effort (of trying to explicate the term "relation" in the defining characteristic), since, if, anyway, the pervasion of the probandum limited by the probans is meant, there is an indistinguishable absence if there is just an absence of an associate condition?[141] Because something which indicates a deviation is established due to the fact that (an absence) related to the absence of the probandum in the form of something qualified is established.[142] Therefore, this[143] is also not the general defining characteristic.

[Opponent:] The non-pervasion of the probans, while there is a pervasion of the probandum limited by the probans, shall be the defining characteristic of an associate condition. And in this way [the defining characteristic][144] should be an explication of the afore-mentioned [defining characteristic].

[Respondent:] It is not so (i.e., this is not the defining characteristic). Because the over-pervasion with respect to the [property of] being such [a locus which is] different from the subject of the inference etc. is difficult to exclude.[145]

(**1.1.12**) And because of the non-pervasion with respect to an associate condition which pervades the probandum limited by a certain qualifier.[146] And therefore, the learned Śrīdhara [says]: "Air is tangible and directly perceptible, because it is a substrate of perceptible touch (as a quality), like the pot." Here, the tangibility of a substance is pervaded by visibility.[147] Therefore, visibility, where it is missing, excludes tangibility as well.[148]

[Opponent:] If this is so, then the non-pervasion of the probans, while there is pervasion of the probandum limited by a certain qualifier, shall be the defining characteristic, because it includes the afore-mentioned associate conditions.[149]

[Respondent:] No. Because of the non-pervasion with respect to the mode of bringing to the fore an associate condition which pervades the relation between probans and probandum.[150]

[Opponent:] In that case there is also the pervasion of the probandum limited by a certain qualifier. How can there be non-pervasion?

[Respondent:] It is not so. We do not talk about the non-pervasion with respect to the exclusion of a thing, but about the non-pervasion with respect to the mode of bringing to the fore. After all, there is necessarily something which brings to the fore or characterizes, as well as a mode of bringing to the fore. And this defining characteristic does not occur [anywhere] due to the mode of bringing to the fore an associate condition which pervades the relation between probans and probandum, but on account of the pervasion of the probandum limited by a certain [qualifier]. Insofar, the defining characteristic occurs [somewhere] on account of the mode of bringing to the fore an associate condition. And so, it has to be understood that one talked about the non-pervasion of the mode of bringing to the fore because of the inconsistency with the mode of bringing to the fore.

And moreover, there would be the undesirable consequence of a failure of all inferences. Because an associate condition which pervades the probandum limited by a certain [qualifier] can be brought to the fore everywhere. After all, [in the inference] "Sound is non-eternal, because it is produced, like the pot", here, potness would be an associate condition with respect to the probandum which is qualified by the [property of] being either pot or sound.[151] So, insofar as the probandum is qualified by the [property of] being the subject of the inference or an agreeing instance, a property residing in this and that example[152] is called "associate condition".[153] So, it would follow that somewhere a property residing in a disagreeing instance is also an associate condition.[154]

[Opponent:] Here, in this pot-example, there would be an associate condition in the case of the absence of knowability:[155] "The pot under discussion is knowable, because it is nameable, like the sky." Here, the associate condition mentioned by you[156] is impossible due to a proof for the knowability of the pot.[157]

[Respondent:] And in this inference skyness is not an associate condition with respect to the probandum which is qualified by the [property of] being either pot or sky.[158] And that (skyness), while staying away from a pot, excludes knowability if it is [knowability limited by] the [property of] being either pot or sky.[159] Since therefore, either of the two is established by that which expresses both, [either of the two] excludes knowability.[160] And so, the absence of knowability is proved for you. Insofar, a property residing in a disagreeing instance would indirectly become an associate condition.[161]

In the same way as the sound is also an example such as the sky etc., it would then be an associate condition even for a property which occurs on the subject of the inference.[162] For, sound, while staying away from the pot, excludes qualified knowability (i.e., knowability restricted to the property of being a locus of potness or sound) in that case, because a qualifier (namely "being a locus of potness or sound") is established by something which expresses both.[163] Insofar as it excludes knowability, the [property of] being an associate condition is indirectly knowable,[164] because the associate condition is a means which indicates the absence of knowability, although [knowability] is a property of the subject of the inference. Therefore, there would be a failure of all inferences.

And the word "qualifier" is pointless.[165] Because, if the mere pervasion is meant, which derives from separating *yatkiṃcidavacchinna* from *sādhya*, then [the defining characteristic] comprehends the associate conditions which are brought to the fore by propounders of both (defining characteristics).[166]

(**1.1.13**) [Opponent:] Then, the defining characteristic should be like that.[167]

[Respondent:] No. Because there is nevertheless no getting rid of the previous mistakes. And because of the non-pervasion (of the defining characteristic which contains the specification *yatkiṃcidavacchinna*) if [the associate condition] pervades the entire probandum.[168]

(**1.1.14**) [Opponent:] Then, the defining characteristic of associate conditions shall be the non-pervasion of the probans, while there is a pervasion with respect to the [property of] being either the probandum or the probandum limited by something.

[Respondent:] No.

(**1.1.15**) [Opponent:] Because of the non-pervasion with respect to the associate condition which pervades the relation (between probans and probandum) the defining characteristic shall pervade any one of those.[169]

(**1.1.15.1**) [Respondent:] No. Because there is no explication of the [property of] being any one of many.

[Opponent:] Any one of that triad is the absolute absence of the mutual absence of this triad.[170]

[Respondent:] No. Because there are many mutual absences which have this triad as a counterpositive and which reside in all things which are distinct from this triad, and because there are also many correlative absolute absences, the meaning (of "any one of many") is obtained in the sense that every single absolute absence occurs in every single one (of the triad), but not in the other two. In that case there would be the undesirable conclusion of a regressus ad infinitum if one wants to express "any one of many".[171]

[Opponent:] The [property of] being an absolute absence is one [object] which is meant.

[Respondent:] No. Because of the non-pervasion with respect to every single absence. Because in one case there is the absence of alcohol.[172]

(**1.1.15.2**) Moreover, there is the mistake in the thesis concerning the pervasion of the probandum etc.[173] And because of the incompatibility (of the three alternatives).[174]

(**1.1.16**) [Opponent:] The defining characteristic of associate conditions should obtain in the case of something which pervades only the examples. There is a restriction of the totality by means of the word "only". One obtains the coextensive pervasion of the probandum[175] and the non-pervasion of the probans if one wants to express both features[176]. Due to inserting the words "pervading the probandum" etc.[177] there is the mistake connected with that.

[Respondent:] No. [The defining characteristic] would be impossible if by the word "example" one wants to express the example "the mountain" etc., because a certain associate condition lacks the pervasion of the example in all inferences.[178] There is non-pervasion if one wants to express only some examples[179], and there is over-pervasion with respect to a certain [property of] being different from the inferential subject etc.[180] Therefore, this is not the defining characteristic.

(**1.1.17**) [Opponent:] [The following] shall be the general defining characteristic: "That is an associate condition with respect to that [probans] without which[181] there is no observation of a concomitance between the two[182] and there is a deviation of that [probans] with respect to that [probandum]." And so, there is not the afore-mentioned mistake.

[Respondent:] No. Because there is no consecutive character[183] for the meaning of the words "which" and "that". For, there is no general defining characteristic "which-ness" and "that-ness", and [what the respondent suggested cannot be the general defining characteristic], because there would be the undesirable consequence that "which-and-that-ness" would lack an application to something else than the words "which" and "that" (in the context referred to). In the case of that (defining characteristic) one would also encounter the self-dependence of the old (defining characteristics).[184] Therefore, all these are not general defining characteristics of an associate condition.

(**1.1.18**) Yet, without the qualifier "being [the probans and the probandum] referred to etc." these are not specific defining characteristics either. Because the absence of a specific defining characteristic in the absence of a general defining characteristic was mentioned (already), and because the afore-mentioned general defining characteristic amounts to this and that specific [defining characteristic] due to the difference with regard to the kind of associate condition which is brought to the fore by this and that [probans and probandum]. Therefore, these are not general defining characteristics. They are not specific defining characteristics either. It is established that there is no explication of a defining characteristic of associate conditions. This is the *pūrvapakṣa*.

> (**1.2**) Having respectfully saluted the pair of lotus feet of the one who desires to rule the world,
> the settled opinion is duly stated to the best of one's judgement and according to precept. 1

(**1.2.1**) [Proponent of the right view:] In that case, first of all, the *atyantābhāvapratiyogidharmatva* (i.e., the property of being a property which is a counterpositive of an absolute absence) is a general defining characteristic of an associate condition. Since only (the part) "something which is a counterpositive of an absence" has a similarity to knowability etc. [And] since (only the part) "being a counterpositive of an absolute absence" has a similarity to the eternal substances.[185]

And there is not the previously mentioned mistake that this defining characteristic is an associate condition or not an associate condition, because this is also an associate condition, since it is admitted that something occurs in itself. And there is not the mistake which consists in the self-dependence of the essence[186], because there would be the undesirable consequence of a blockage of a defining characteristic for a veridical awareness etc.[187]

After all, a defining characteristic for a knowledge source etc. is established because of there being a defining characteristic. Or, when something is established, a mistake concerning the defining characteristic is excluded, because there can be no veridical awareness of that[188] on account of a false defining characteristic. If something which is known were not part of the knowledge sources, there would be the undesirable consequence of a confusion of valid probantia and pseudo-probantia.[189]

And (there has to be a defining characteristic) due to the absence of the [property of] being a counterpositive (of an absolute absence) in the case of the alternative [that something is] not an associate condition.[190] Because of the contradictoriness of an ingress of the alternative [that the *atyantābhāvapratiyogidharmatva* is] a counterpositive there is an indefiniteness with respect to that [alternative that the *atyantābhāvapratiyogidharmatva* is a counterpositive]. In certain cases one allows the self-inclusion.[191]

In the case of the application of the defining characteristic of associate conditions that [alternative] itself, however, is temporarily doubted. At that time one does not yet attain the alternative of a substrate[192]. After that [the alternative] is established due to the defining characteristic. One attains the alternative that it is an associate condition, since it is a substrate of the defining characteristic. However, in the state of the doubt concerning the defining characteristic there is due to the absence of an ingress (of the alternative that the *atyantābhāvapratiyogidharmatva* is a substrate of itself) no unwarranted conclusion with respect to one part of the substrates.[193] This is the secret.

Or, in the case of the thesis concerning the defining characteristic that the subject of the inference possesses a property which is not acknowledged by someone else,[194] the [property of] being a subject of an inference is ascertained, because the absence and also the non-absence (of the probandum in the subject of the inference) are not acknowledged, and the [property of] being a probandum is ascertained, because one wants to prove [something] with respect to something at issue, since there is a common practice with respect to both (i.e., the property of being a subject of an inference and the property of being a probandum), because they are ascertained by both defining characteristics,[195] as in the case of the common practice with respect to something that needs to be measured by means of scales and weights.[196] Therefore, it is established that there is no non-pervasion (of the defining characteristic) due to the non-absence of the defining characteristic (in itself)[197] and no regressus ad infinitum.[198]

(**1.2.1.1**) It is also established that there is no uselessness. The common practice has here the defining characteristic as its object. On the other hand, the defining characteristic is the cause of the application of the word "associate condition", since it has been said before that there is no universal.

And there is no derivation due to the connection with the activity of transmitting a property occurring in [the associate condition] itself. Because the word "associate condition" is connected with the aim of refuting an inference. There is no manifestation of a refutation of an inference because of the mere transmitting of a property which is resident in [the transmitting substrate] itself, but [there is such a manifestation] because of the bringing to light of the pervadedness (of the probandum by the associate condition). However, there is no mundane derivation with respect to such a connection with an activity.[199] Because, otherwise, there would be the undesirable consequence of the [property of] being so (i.e., of being an associate condition) in the case of the China rose etc.[200]

Therefore, due to the disagreement with mundane common practice[201] the fact that the word "associate condition" has the purpose of refuting an inference is only connected with the [property of] possessing a defining characteristic as the motive for its application owing to a general [defining characteristic], which includes a specific defining characteristic.[202] Insofar, it is established that the defining characteristic has a common practice[203] as its purpose.

(**1.2.1.2**) It is possible that there is no over-pervasion with respect to knowability etc. Because there would be the undesirable consequence of a rejection of what is universally positive if knowability etc. were counterpositives of an absolute absence.

[Opponent:] The [property of] being universally positive is the residence in all things. How can there be a knowledge source for that (i.e., for the residence in all things)? There is no residence of knowability etc. in all things, because there is no perception which grasps [it]. There is also no (valid) inference "[These are] all things because of knowability etc.",[204] because it would be afflicted with the absence of similar examples. Because due to [the thesis] "The residence in all things does not reside in knowability etc." etc. [knowability etc.] are unestablished with regard to the substrate.[205] Because [the claims] "Knowability resides in all things" etc. have an unestablished qualifier (viz. the residence in all things). Testimony etc. are, however, impossible (as a knowledge source for the property of being universally positive). Hence, since there is no knowledge source for the [property of] being universally positive of knowability etc., [a universally positive property][206] is faulty due to the failure of the only positive inference.[207]

[Proponent of the right view:] If the absence of the [property of] being universally positive were present in all things, this very property (i.e., the absence of the property of being universally positive) should then be universally positive. Hence, due to the absence of the residence in all things there should be a universally positive [property] under that very [assumption] (*tatraiva*) under which (*yatra*) it itself does not exist.

Therefore, which of the blocking counterfactual (or reductio) arguments should there be for an ascertainment of the fallaciousness (of the thesis that there are universally positive properties), since there is no amounting to the contrary? [What is for you] an undesirable conclusion, [viz.] that universally positive properties exist, is necessary. Therefore, it is not established that there is the desirable conclusion[208] [that universally positive properties exist] due to the absence of a knowledge source.[209] Moreover, there is the fallacy of the inconclusive probans due to the fact that [properties] are either way (i.e., universally positive and not universally positive) if there is a universally positive property which has been accepted by you and which resides in all things on account of the probans "propertyness",[210] and due to the absence of a knowledge source for positive and negative correlation the [property of] possessing smoke etc. would be no evidence, just as in the case of an only positive inference.[211]

[Opponent:] The positive correlation of the [property of] being a locus of smoke [with the property of being a locus of fire], namely the co-occurrence [of the property of being a locus of fire] with [the property of being a locus of smoke] itself, is the occurrence [in loci], insofar as they possess the probandum.

With respect to that [co-occurrence] perception, first of all, is not a knowledge source, because perception is incapable of grasping the occurrence in the referent of the expression "something, insofar as it possesses the probandum, which is a common locus of [the probans] itself and the past, future and present [instances of the probandum]".

Inference is in that case also not a knowledge source, because there is no member (in an inference) which proves the occurrence of the [property of] being a locus of smoke in something, insofar as it possesses the probandum. And if [such a member] existed, there would be the undesirable conclusion of a regressus ad infinitum. Because a series [of members ultimately proving pervasion] would be necessary, since, as for that member[212] there would also be the undesirable conclusion of [the existence of] another member which grasps the occurrence [of the probans] in something, insofar as it possesses the probandum, it would be like that also for that one. In just the same way one should say that there is also no knowledge source for a negative correlation which has as a defining characteristic the absence of the occurrence [of the probans] on something, insofar as it is a disagreeing instance. Testimony etc. are, however, impossible [as a knowledge source].

[Counterobjection of the proponent of the right view:][213] Grasping a positive and a negative correlation for smoke etc. is possible. After all, frequent observation arises [in the case of the positive correlation:] "Where there is smoke, there is fire." And it (i.e., frequent observation) arises [in the case of the negative correlation:] "Where there is the absence of fire, there is the absence of smoke." And this frequent observation imparts a corresponding mental impression. Due to a causal efficacy which is characterized by such a mental impression the faculty of sight aided by that [mental impression] grasps the positive correlation, [i.e.] the occurrence on something, insofar as it possesses fire. In just the same way [it grasps] the possession of fire. Such a causal efficacy is acquired by the faculty of sight due to expedients. After all, the faculty of sight aided by a connection and a property[214] grasps the multitude (*jāta*) of all things in the universe of entities. In this way the faculty of sight aided by collyrium[215] etc. makes known [everything] from the ocean to the elements. And in this way the faculty of sight etc. equipped with a mental impression and the study of treatises on jewels and music etc. perceive sounds etc. like differences between classes of jewels etc., and aided by black tarnish etc. they are absorbed in the connection with the [property of] being silver etc. which occurs in another place.[216] Therefore, the faculty of sight endowed with expedients grasps the positive correlation, which has as a defining characteristic the residence [in a locus], insofar as it has a past, future or present [instance of the probandum], and in just the same way the faculty of sight grasps the negative correlation.

[Opponent:] The positive and negative inference shall fail.[217]

[Proponent of the right view:] Then, [the failure] shall be likewise accepted also with respect to a positive correlation of knowability etc., which have as a defining characteristic the occurrence [in a locus], insofar as it possesses the probandum. And, because in that case there is also an expedient, [viz.] the mental impression caused by frequent observation.[218]

[Opponent:] Someone who grasps a positive correlation of knowability etc. has omniscience.

[Proponent of the right view:] It is not so. Does someone who grasps a positive and a negative correlation of the [property of] possessing smoke etc. have [omniscience]? This might rather not be the case.[219]

[Opponent:] Such an omniscience is related to that case.

[Proponent of the right view:] What is the use of your polemics with respect to the present case?

[Opponent:] Grasping a positive correlation of knowability etc. is not possible without [omniscience]. A relation is not grasped if a property is grasped without the grasping of a substrate.[220]

[Proponent of the right view:] And we agree to that. If [someone] will not tell [me], it does not come to my mind.

[Opponent:] For, it is not so [as you say] and it is so [as I say] (i.e., a positive correlation pertaining to knowability cannot be grasped), because there is no grasping of all objects of knowledge. For knowability etc. a grasping of that (i.e., of a positive correlation) is not feasible, since there are 100000 [objects of knowledge] which are all connected with knowability.

[Proponent of the right view:] But for grasping the positive and the negative correlation of smoke etc. it is not necessary to grasp all substrates of the positive and the negative correlation. How should this ever be entirely possible?

[Opponent:] An inference with respect to every [substrate of a positive or negative correlation] shall be invalid.

[Proponent of the right view:] [Inferences which are not based on the knowledge of all substrates of a positive or negative correlation can also be valid], because [otherwise] there would be the undesirable consequence of a disturbance of everyday life. Observing day by day that for someone who seeks food eating brings about benefit, one acts [in accordance with that] immediately after having inferred that also for the future. Because, otherwise, there would be the undesirable consequence of an obstacle to active life. Who, however, does not agree to [this] inference, how should he respond?

[Opponent:] A mere sequence of words would not be conclusive.[221] Neither does someone attain to victory (in a debate), nor can someone be understood to be inferior due to someone else's proof. Insofar, the thesis would be either of the two, since there would be the undesirable consequence of a loss of what is established. Moreover, it would not be possible to bring an established qualifier to the fore.[222] There is no proof by means of [an inference] for oneself, because it does not have the [property of] confronting [an argument] as a knowledge source.[223] Because, only the proof by means of [an inference] for others is part of the knowledge sources. Moreover, how shall one obtain a formulation of [the inference] for others due to the articulation of sounds etc.? Since there is not even an [inference] for others which is an inference for oneself, there is non-pervasion with respect to that.[224] Pervasion and the [property of] being a property of the subject of the inference have been agreed to (as the essential parts of an inference).[225]

[Proponent of the right view:] In that case[226] it is admitted that an inference is valid. Therefore, it has to be admitted that there is no inequality of only positive and positive and negative inferences. And since it is therefore established that knowability etc. are universally positive, there is no conclusion which is desirable (for you).[227] Therefore, it is established that there is no failure of the only positive inference.

[Opponent:] It is proved that knowability etc. are a counterpositive of an absolute absence without a substrate. And insofar, there is not the undesirable consequence of a failure of the only positive inference. Because, although knowability etc. reside in everything, there is no conflict with an absolute absence[228]. And thus, the over-pervasion of the defining characteristic of the associate condition (with respect to knowability etc.) is also difficult to keep off.

[Proponent of the right view:] No. Because even without your probandum there is no ascertainment on account of the probans "being a property".[229] And the [property of] being a property, i.e., the [property of] having a substrate, is not ascertained without a substrate. But not the [property of] being a counterpositive of an absolute absence.[230] Moreover, the probans "being a property" is only accompanied by the [property of] being a counterpositive of an absolute absence which has a substrate.[231] While it (i.e., the probans "being a property") does not allow us to infer the [property of] being such a counterpositive of an absence (i.e., the property of being a counterpositive of an absolute absence which has a substrate), it includes it.[232] But [the probans "being a property" does not include] the property of being a counterpositive of an absolute absence without a substrate.[233]

[Opponent:] There is a proof (that the property of being a counterpositive of an absolute absence without a substrate occurs on the subject of the inference),[234] because [the probans "being a property"] is a property of the subject of the inference.[235] After all, the [property of] being an effect proves an incorporeal, indeed, an omniscient creator[236], insofar as it is also endowed with [properties] accompanying it, such as the [property of] being preceded by an omniscient creator etc. In the same way, the [property of] being a property connected with the subject of the inference which has as a defining characteristic knowability as something which pervades the whole range of true existence[237] proves – due to [their property of] having a common goal etc.[238] – the [property of] being a counterpositive of an absolute absence which has a substrate.

[Proponent of the right view:] It is not so. Because, if something sublating is established with respect to the counter-thesis[239], [this] is necessarily conclusive (as a means to prove the opponent wrong). It (i.e., the counter-thesis) amounts to [something] which is opposed to what is seen.[240] And in the case of the present thesis[241] nothing sublating is obtained.

Moreover, if an absolute absence had no substrate, how should then the essence of form be thwarted in the case of something which is not a counterpositive?[242] Or, if it is thwarted, how should there not be a fallacious reasoning, as in the case of inferring the barrenness of a mother? Therefore, the (alleged) proof that [knowability etc.] are counterpositives of an unlocatable absolute absence is not feasible. Insofar, it is established that there is no over-pervasion of the defining characteristic of associate conditions due to knowability etc.

(**1.2.1.3**) [Opponent:] The defining characteristic of an associate condition is characterized by the impossibility of an absolute absence without the counterpositiveness. After all, first of all, there is no [counterpositiveness] owing to the undesirable conclusion of an empty explanation referring to "which" etc.[243] [Counterpositiveness] is also not a relation. Because, if that [counterpositive] exists, there is an inconsistency with the [property of] being a counterpositive of an absolute absence. But if it does not exist, there should not even be a cognition [of the absolute absence of the counterpositive].

[Proponent of the right view:] [The property of being a counterpositive does exist], because there is a cognition based on an unsublated awareness.

[Opponent:] This cognition grasps only the (absolute) absence, not the [property of] being a counterpositive.

[Proponent of the right view:] How can there then possibly be a knowledge which is contained in "someone who needs to be guided as someone who needs to be guided in the future", insofar as it is an activity [dealing] with something desired?[244]

[Opponent:] But [the knowledge of a counterpositive is] the knowledge of an indicative mark.[245] [This knowledge] is also possible for someone who nonetheless does not know the property of being an indicative mark. Because, there is such a perception [of the Kurus] in the case of "the field of the Kurus which has been appropriated by the Kurus" etc.[246] And so, it is thwarted that there is no cognition of a counterpositive (without a defining characteristic).

[Proponent of the right view:] It is not so. Even if there is an indicative mark, there needs to be a cognition sometime. The Kurus etc. are cognized by means of perception or testimony etc. Afterwards one remembers that which can be marked. And so, there needs to be a cognition sometime. Because it is a rule for the totality of what is cognized.

[Opponent:] And it is established that it is excluded that something existing is a counterpositive of that (absolute absence). The defining characteristic "[Being a counterpositive] of an absolute absence as something which is separated [from the counterpositive]", that is impossible.[247]

[Proponent of the right view:] No. [The counterpositiveness] is obtained because of the [property of] being a counterpositive of an absolute absence which is united [with the absolute absence]. After all, [in the statement] "The pot is not here on the ground" an absolute absence is perceived according to an awareness, indeed, according to the configuration of the ontological categories. And, hence, Udayana [says]: "For, consciousness alone is divine." – "There is something to resort to (viz. conscious experience) with regard to the attainment of the existence of objects."[248] The pot which is characterized by a relation to an absence due to its being not established on a substrate appears here in an awareness as a counterpositive. Although neither the mere pot, nor the mere relation fits on account of there being an absolute absence only of pots etc., they nevertheless fit due to the form of being related (to an absolute absence). However, the form of that which is related is: "It is absent."

The [property of] being a counterpositiveness of an absolute absence of that (pot) fits, but it is not an indicative mark. There is the rule that [an indicative mark] is something about which a correct notion has been formed sometime, because there is a knowledge source. However, the veridical awareness of that which is indicated depends on the cognition of an indicative mark. And this cognition is only recollection with respect to something real. This (i.e., recollection) indicates only a former awareness. Not a (novel) veridical awareness, because there is no pervasion (of recollection) by veridical awareness.[249] Because in that case (i.e., in the case of recollection) there is only a recollection of something real etc. from within.[250] This very awareness (i.e., a former awareness which is remembered) is also based on erroneous wishful thoughts (*ādhī*). A thought etc. awaken the seed of recollection with respect to something which is not real and which is opposed to the absolute absence of something which is known by means of a knowledge source.[251] So, it is established that the defining characteristic of an associate condition is not impossible, since there is no absolute absence without a counterpositiveness, insofar as there is (what appears to be) an undesirable conclusion (from your point of view, viz.) that something which is united qua form[252] is a counterpositive. Therefore, it is established that a general defining characteristic of the intended associate condition has been established. Salutation!

(**1.2.2**) [Opponent:] Let there be a general defining characteristic. However, a specific defining characteristic cannot be explicated because of the afore-mentioned rationale. Insofar as it (i.e., a specific defining characteristic) is unavailable, a refutation by means of an associate condition cannot be accomplished by you. If [one] suggests that a mere property which is defined by a general defining characteristic is an associate condition, then the [property of] being an associate condition would be everywhere without exception.[253] Thus, we would be faced with the failure of all inferences. It is correct that an associate condition vitiates, insofar as an indication of a deviation is easy to be done, because [one] reveals the occurrence of the probans right there, [i.e.] on something which possesses the absence of the probandum, since [one] reveals the absence of the probandum-property by hinting at the reference to a property which is defined by means of the defining characeristic "being [a property] which pervades the probandum, while it does not pervade the probans". You cannot explicate such a defining characteristic.

[Proponent of the right view:] With regard to this it is said: "There should be no pervasion of the (assumed) probans (by the assumed probandum) if there is non-pervasion of the probans, while there is a coextensive pervasion by the probandum." This is what the learned teachers say (or: the teachers who follow [Parāśara]bhaṭṭa):

> "Coextensive or non-coextensive pervasion are always there in
> the case of one and the same [associate condition].

> If [an associate condition] which is not pervaded coextensively lacks both, then it is not a fortifier."[254]

In this sense the teachers who follow Udayana also say that something which has a coextensive pervasion is an associate condition.[255]

> "Insofar as there is (only) one inseparable connection with the probandum[256], among two, which do not have a mutual relation, that one is the associate condition whose absence is inseparably connected with the absence of the probandum."[257]

Here, the [property of] pervading is mentioned by means of the expression "one inseparable connection with the probandum". The [property of] pervading is (also) mentioned by means of this, [viz. the expression] "whose absence is inseparably connected with the absence of the probandum".

It should be understood that a coextensive pervasion is meant. One has to say that consenting to the old [property of] being pervaded by the associate condition is improper. Because, insofar as an associate condition is a fortifying property, the intended meaning of "something which effects a refutation as an associate condition" arises in such a way. After all, the [property of] being an injury which is not furnished by you (with an associate condition) is not a means [to infer the probandum] "guilt". However, the intended meaning of the theorist of the associate condition is: "The [property of] being forbidden, from which [the probandum] does not deviate, is a means [to infer the probandum] because of the [properties of] pervading and being pervaded." Because, otherwise, it would not be brought to the fore that this here is an associate condition because of the appearance of the mere pervadedness connected with that property (i.e., with the probandum) by that which brings to the fore [the deviation] (i.e., by the associate condition).[258] Because of an error [on] your [side] there is a bringing to the fore of an associate condition due to the misconception that there is a pervadedness concerning the ultimate goal (of correcting an assumed inference) which is not related to every respective means (of refutation).[259] But not because of the misconception concerning the indication (of a deviation) on account of a conflict (with my view).[260] Otherwise,[261] it would not be brought to the fore that this here is an associate condition. By contrast, one should say that this (property of being forbidden) indicates a deviation here. Therefore, something which has a coextensive pervasion is an associate condition.

(**1.2.2.1**) [Opponent:] What is to be excluded by the word "coextensive"?

[Proponent of the right view:] The [property of] being different from the subject of the inference which has a non-coextensive pervasion.

[Opponent:] That which is different from the subject of the inference does not pervade the probandum. How can it be excluded in consequence of the word "coextensive"?[262]

[Proponent of the right view:] No. Because, insofar as there is the pervasion "Where there is a probandum, there is the [property of] being different from the subject of the inference", and because of the deviation [of the probans] from the associate condition ("being different from the subject of the inference"),[263] one cannot talk about the absence of an admissible pervasion (of the property of being different from the subject of the inference by the defining characteristic without the specification "coextensive").

[Opponent:] Only the (associate condition's) pervasion of the probandum fails, because of the sublating [reductio ad absurdum]: "Since there would be the undesirable consequence of a failure of all inferences if the [property of] being different from the subject of the inference were an associate condition."

[Proponent of the right view:] No. We must not broaden [the defining characteristic] in such a way.[264] Since a pervasion of the associate condition "being different from the subject of the inference" and the failure of all inferences are not experienced anywhere, how should there be this reductio ad absurdum? Agreeing to the fact that the pervadedness constitutes the [property of] being an associate condition excludes that (property of being different from the subject of the inference). What is the use of this effort concerning the bringing to the fore of a sublating reductio ad absurdum?

[Opponent:] How is it possible that that (property of being different from the subject of the inference) is a pervader, since it lacks the negative pervasion?

[Proponent of the right view:] It is not so (that the property of being different from the subject of the inference cannot pervade anything if it lacks the negative pervasion). For, pervading is the [property of] effecting a pervasion. A positive pervasion is also a pervasion, not only the negative [pervasion]. Otherwise, there would be the undesirable conclusion of an opposition between a positive and negative [inference] and an only positive [inference].[265] And therefore, it is established that on account of a positive pervasion the [property of] being different from the subject of the inference is also pervaded (by the defining characteristic without the specification of a coextensive pervasion).

[Opponent:] But the [property of] pervading is not only based on a positive correlation. In the case of the defining characteristic of an associate condition the pair of positive and negative pervasion is meant by the word "pervading", so that the [property of] being different from the subject of the inference is excluded from being an associate condition.[266]

[Proponent of the right view:] What is the use of this (explication of the) meaning? Why is the pervadedness of the associate condition not meant, which is agreeable due to [my] argument? There is an exclusion of the [property of] being different from the subject of the inference insofar as well.

(**1.2.2.2**) [Opponent:] In such a way, however, that which is different from the subject of the inference and which possesses a coextensive pervasion is not excluded.

[Proponent of the right view:] No. In that case (i.e., in the case of the property of being different from the subject of the inference) there is no pervadedness.[267] For, pervadedness depends on a knowledge source. For, that very [cognition] "Where there is possession of fire in something different from the mountain, there is possession of fire" is not qualified and unqualified, and it is not amenable to grasping by means of one cognition, because of incompatibility.[268] After all, only one cognition surely does not grasp that which is not limited and that which is limited by blueness. Because [the cognition] which grasps that which is limited is opposed to [the cognition] which grasps that which is not limited. Therefore, it is excluded that [the cognition] which grasps that which is limited grasps that which is not limited. Therefore, there is no pervasion of the [property of] being a locus of fire other than the mountain and the [property of] being a locus of fire, because there is no (single) grasping of a pervasion which distinguishes between both objects and is intimately united with one result, [viz.]: "This is pervaded by this." Therefore, what has to be excluded by the word "coextensive", is established.[269]

[Opponent:] Since in the case of the inference of the [property of] having a causal agent [pertaining to] the earth etc. with respect to (the probans) "having parts" etc. there is due to the previous rationale no elimination of the [properties of] being produced by someone having a body etc., which have a coextensive pervasion, how can these possibly be eliminated by inserting the word "coextensive"?[270]

[Proponent of the right view:] No. Because in that case there is also no pervasion[271], because [the relation between the associate condition and the probandum] is endowed with (another) associate condition. There is a deviation of an associate condition which possesses a specification by means of an expression (for the coextensive pervasion) because of the constraint of the [property of] being endowed with an associate condition which has a special coextensive pervasion.[272] And so, here, [i.e., in the case of the pervasion] "Where there is the [property of] being produced by someone having a body, there is the [property of] having a causal agent", the [property of] being produced as something which has become a qualificand should be an associate condition.[273] And it is not the case that this is not an associate condition because of the [property of pervading] the probans, since the probandum is also an associate condition for the relation between the probans and the associate condition.[274] And so, there should be an associate condition for the relation between the probandum and the associate condition which[275] is characterized by the [property of] being produced due to the presence of the [property of] not pervading the probans, insofar as there is the [property of] being endowed with an associate condition. And so, it is established that (the property of being produced by someone having a body) can be eliminated by means of the word "coextensive", because there is no pervadedness of the associate condition "being produced by a body".

[Opponent:] How is it possible that for someone who teaches the coextensive pervasion something which has a coextensive pervasion is not an associate condition, because in the case of [the inferences] "Sound is nameable, because it is knowable" etc. one cannot talk about the absence of the [possibility of] grasping the pervasion and of the absence of the pervasion of the [property of] not being sound etc. in the afore-mentioned manner.[276]

[Proponent of the right view:] It is not so. An object's [property of] being different from sound is the [property of] possessing the mutual absence of sound.[277] And so, something which on account of a qualifying associate condition needs to be qualified is an associate condition for that (probandum) and for the probans for which it is an associate condition in relation to something which is nameable. Or, who will therefore prevent the way of elimination by means of the [property of] not being produced etc. Hence, that very [property of being different from sound] is excluded by the word "coextensive" alone.[278] And moreover, since (the property of being different from sound etc.) are useless qualifiers, they are not included [in the definition of the associate condition].[279]

[Opponent:] [They] are not useless. [Something is] a qualifier, because its purpose is to exclude the pervasion of the probans.

[Proponent of the right view:] No. For, the [property of] being a qualifier is associated with a purpose due to the [property of] avoiding a deviation. Otherwise, there would be an inconsistency with (the concept of) a specific defining characteristic. For, a qualifier is a limitor or an indicative mark. For, a qualifier or an indicative mark which have some purpose have not been conceded by anybody. And so, there is no qualifier due to there being some purpose. Hence, insofar as the [property of] avoiding a deviation is necessary, [the opponent's associate conditions] are, by contrast, useless qualifiers, because that [purpose of avoiding a deviation] is missing in the present case.

[Opponent:] The pervadedness (of the associate condition by the probandum) is not appropriate, because those who propound the associate condition with the absence of [the condition] "coextensive" do not approve of the coextensive pervadedness of the associate conditions as something which is different from the (respective) inferential subject.[280] The fact that the associate condition is a qualifier for the purpose of keeping off a deviation is no harm (for the definition without the condition "coextensive").[281]

[Proponent of the right view:] No. If it is so (i.e., if the associate condition is defined without the condition of a coextensive pervasion), the coextensive pervasion is really lacking. After all, a pervasion is grasped due to frequent observation. And [the property of not being produced etc., i.e. of being a locus of a property which is not a property of sound] is a qualifier which is an associate condition, because of the [property of] not being produced of individuals (belonging to the associate condition) [which are there] at the times of (i.e., simultaneous with) that (i.e., with the observation of the individuals of the probandum).[282]

How should [the probans] not deviate [from the probandum] on account of the deviation [of the probans from the associate condition] together with the [property of] having a causal agent etc. (as the probandum)?[283] For, the faculty of sight assisted by the impressions of frequent observation does not grasp a pervadedness (i.e., the property of being something pervaded) related to [a pervader] characterized as exceeding that [range of the pervaded].

Otherwise, one would grasp a pervadedness (i.e., the property of being something pervaded) related to [a pervader] characterized as exceeding [the range of the pervaded] in addition to the [property of] possessing smoke etc.[284] That [non-coextensive pervasion] should also be a pervadedness. And so, there is frequent observation due to deviation and concomitance,[285] because there is no grasping of the pervadedness related to [a pervader] characterized [as coextensive with or exceeding the range of the pervaded], insofar as the faculty of sight assisted by the impressions "Wherever [there is the probans], there [is the probandum]" grasps the [property of] being pervasive. There is no pervadedness (of the associate condition by the probandum in the definition of the associate condition) due to something which has a useless qualifier.[286] Hence, it is established that there is an elimination of such a [locus which is] different from the inferential subject[287] only by means of the word "coextensive".

(**1.2.2.3**) [Opponent:] How can there be an elimination of the (associate condition with) non-coextensive pervasion? Since it is similar to an effective associate condition with coextensive pervasion due to the fact that it also indicates a deviation or due to the fact that it brings to light a pervasion which occurs in itself.

Or, in what way is the associate condition which pervades the relation (between probans and probandum) comprehended in this [defining characteristic with coextensive pervasion]? Since that is lacking the coextensive pervadedness of the probandum. Since, although there is a coextensive pervasion of the relation, there is somewhere no coextensive pervadedness of the probandum.[288]

[Opponent:] A pervader is meant by the word "probandum", not, however, the mere probandum.[289]

And others [say]: "Since there would be the undesirable consequence that in the case of the inference [with] smoke [as the probans] mountainness etc. would be associate conditions, the defining characteristic of the probandum[290] is actually wrong.[291] The pervasion of such a probandum[292], [viz.] the pervasion by mountainness etc. aims at letting [someone] undertake a proof concerning the counter-thesis."[293]

And the non-pervasion of the probans, (while there is a pervasion) only with respect to the range of agreeing instances, is an ill-formed defining characteristic, because it lacks a part[294] and because of a deviation (from the defining characteristic which posits the pervasion of the relation).[295] And so, one should say that the [property of] being a pervader is meant by the word "probandum". And that [property of] being a pervader is only what is left of what is related to probandum and probans. In this way, the remainder is relevant to the case of something which pervades the probandum which is not cut off (from the probans).[296] And so, because one obtains that the non-pervasion of the pervaded, while there is a pervasion of the [property of] being a pervader, amounts to a defining characteristic, therefore the pervader of the relation (between probans and probandum), [viz.] contactness etc. will be comprehended by this defining characteristic.[297]

(**1.2.2.3.1**) [Proponent of the right view:] It is not so.

[Opponent:] Only the [property of] being a pervader shall be intended. Nevertheless, one might obain an associate condition due to the fact that a means which has a coextensive pervasion is also the meaning of this defining characteristic.[298] After all, there is, however, [the associate condition] which consists in [the property of] being non-eternal etc.[299] on account of being a non-coextensive pervader of the probandum etc.[300] because of the [property of] being a pervader [of the probandum] which is not a pervader [of the probans] and because of (the associate condition's and the probandum's) [property of] being pervader and pervaded due to the absence of the (probandum's) [property of] being a pervader of [the associate condition] itself. Since therefore [an associate condition] which pervades the relation etc. is not comprehended in the defining characteristic mentioned by you, [viz.] the [property of] pervading the probandum coextensively etc., and since it is inappropriate to eliminate the [associate condition] with non-coextensive pervasion due to the similarity with the associate condition which is intended by you, how can this[301] possibly be the defining characteristic?

[Proponent of the right view:] With regard to this it is said: Something which has a non-coextensive pervasion is not an associate condition, since it does not have the [property of] being a fortifier. The [property of] being a fortifier depends on the [property of] being pervaded. Because, otherwise, there would be an inconsistency with the [property of] being a fortifier because of the absence of the [property of] being a means.[302] The associate condition's [property of] being a vitiator, however, is appropriate only due to the [property of] bringing to light a pervadedness which occurs in [the associate condition] itself, but not because of the [property of] indicating a deviation due to the supremacy of the part "being a pervader". Or, because of the [property of] bringing to light the pervadedness by the negation of that (probandum) which occurs in [the negation of the associate condition] itself.[303] [And] because a mere refutation by way of the [property of] being a pervader (of the probandum) does not yet amount to the truth of the counter-thesis.[304] The [property of] being a refutation by way of the [property of] bringing to light a pervasion which pertains to [the associate condition] itself, however, amounts to the probans's pervadedness being unestablished, insofar as a refutation concerning the counter-thesis[305] is not settled only by means of positive and negative correlation.[306] For, the associate condition "being forbidden" etc. do not lead to the counter-thesis due to a positive pervasion of "bringing about [guilt]"[307] and also not due to a negative pervasion.[308] The negation (of the associate condition) qua its (i.e., the associate condition's) pervadedness (by the probandum) pervades the adjunct (i.e., the absence of the probandum).[309] Since there is (in the case of the non-coextensively pervading associate condition) no pervadedness of the absence of the probandum, on which [the absence of the associate condition] depends, the refutation concerning the counter-thesis is inappropriate. If (in general) the negation of the pervaded were also pervaded (by the negation of the pervader), one would obtain that the absence of smoke would be pervaded by the absence of fire.[310] Or, even though it is possible that the negation (of the associate condition) pervades (the absence of the probandum) due to the (associate condition's) [property of] being a pervader,[311] [the coextensively pervading associate condition] is nevertheless fortifying on account of the agreement to the pervadedness in the case of the absence of an amounting to the counter-thesis. Since a true associate condition is not at all opposed to the [property of] being a fortifier, it is appropriate that the associate condition with non-coextensive pervasion is not comprehended by the defining characteristic, insofar as the associate condition with non-coextensive pervasion is not an associate condition in virtue of being of such a nature, insofar as the [property of] leading to the pervadedness's being unestablished is possible for something which leads to the failure of the non-pervasion of the probans (by the probandum) due to the fact that it brings to light the pervadedness which occurs in [the associate condition] itself.[312] Moreover, the non-coextensively pervading associate condition's [property of] being a pervader, however, is not an associate condition's way to vitiate in the sense that [the property of being a pervader] proves the absence of the probandum (on the subject of the inference) dependent on the negation of that which is pervaded (by the associate condition)[313] in the form of the counter-thesis.[314]

[Opponent:] If it were like that, a pervader would be without purpose, since only the [property of] being pervaded would be useful for a refutation by means of an associate condition.[315] Why? That (property of being pervaded) is accepted for an associate condition with coextensive pervasion.

[Proponent of the right view:] It is not so. Considering the collection of properties[316] which are not without a coextensive [pervasion] and those which are not without a non-coextensive [pervasion], co-occurrence and absence of a deviation are established in both ways[317] due to the dependence on properties which are not without a coextensive [pervasion], since their [property of] being a fortifier is obvious. What has to be considered is that for the purpose of emphasizing the resemblance to the [property of] being a fortifier [the coextensive pervasion has been included in the defining characteristic]. Hence, since – either on account of the afore-mentioned argument concerning the [property of] bringing to light the pervadedness occurring in itself, or, because there is no amounting [to the property of being a fortifier] due the [property of] indicating a deviation – the non-coextensively pervading associate condition does not have the [property of] being a fortifier, it is not comprehended in the defining characteristic, since it lacks the [property of] being an associate condition. It is established that the part ["coextensive"] is necessary.

(**1.2.2.3.2**) It is not the case that the defining characteristic which pervades the relation between probans and probandum is (by mistake) not comprehended (by the defining characteristic). In that case it is appropriate that associate conditions which pervade the relation between probans and probandum, [viz.] the [property of] being a product etc., and which have a non-coextensive pervasion are not comprehended [by the defining characteristic], because they lack the [property of] being an associate condition on account of the afore-mentioned argument.[318] However, the comprehension of contact etc., which have a coextensive pervasion, is appropriate, since there is the [property of] being a coextensive pervader of the relation as a means (i.e., as a corrector), which is a pervader and a coextensive pervader.[319] The defining characteristic is also meant in this way: "There is a pervasion of that which is pervaded[320] if this (i.e., the associate condition) pervades that which is not a pervader[321] coextensively." For something pervading the probandum limited by something it is also possible that it is comprehended by this defining characteristic. Because visibility etc. also pervade the pervader, since it is actually the case that something which has pervasion of the probandum limited by substanceness is a pervader with respect to the probans.[322]

(**1.2.2.4**) [The associate condition] does not pervade that which is pervaded (i.e., the putative probans). There is no over-pervasion of the defining characteristic by the probans.[323] Because, as there would be a mistake (if the probans were an associate condition), with regard to that the part of the defining characteristic in the form of the [property of] not being a pervader of that which is pervaded is missing. Because that (i.e., the probans) also pervades itself as that what is pervaded (by it). After all, the non-pervasion of the probans is the [property of] being a counterpositive of an absolute absence which resides in something which possesses the probans.[324] For, the probans is not a counterpositive of an absolute absence which co-occurs with (the probans) itself, because there would be a contradiction. Therefore, there is no over-pervasion of the defining characteristic with respect to the probans, because [the defining characteristic] lacks the [property of] pervading that (i.e., the probans), since [the probans] pervades that (i.e., the probans). For, the pervasion of the probandum is expressed with reference to the counterpositive of an absolute absence which resides in something which possesses the probans.[325]

[Opponent:] This is not the case.

[Proponent of the right view:] And since it is so, the afore-mentioned mistake of self-dependence etc. is just a bagatelle[326] and, moreover, a defect [such as] "because somewhere the probans is the probandum" etc. is eliminated due to the specification "being referred to".[327]

And there is not the mistake of non-pervasion.[328] Since this is a specific defining characteristic, the non-pervasion with respect to the mode (of presentation) due to the difference from a defining characteristic referring to the [property of] being different from the subject of the inference with coextensive pervasion etc. is nevertheless refuted.[329]

It has been said that the non-pervasion of the associate condition which has a non-coextensive pervasion is, however, not harmful.[330] It has been properly said that where there is a (putative) coextensive pervasion of probandum and probans, there the pervasion of the associate condition with non-coextensive pervasion limited by the probans is inappropriate.[331] [Such a pervasion][332] is a pointless qualifier (for an associate condition), such as for the associate condition "being produced by an embodied [agent]" etc.[333] Because there is no pervadedness (of a non-coextensively pervading associate condition by the defining characteristic), since there would be no grasping of a (genuine) pervasion due to the associate condition inaudibility etc. with respect to that which is limited by the [property of] being produced as a pointlessly specified [probandum].[334]

[Opponent:] As a result of the thesis concerning the defining characteristic which you mentioned[335] there would be the undesirable conclusion that something which debunks all inferences would be an associate condition, due to the fact that [the properties] "potness" etc., which coextensively pervade the [properties] "being non-eternal" etc., which possess as a qualifier the [property of] being either a pot or sound etc., come up in all inferences. There would be an over-pervasion by that defining characteristic of something which is not an associate condition.

[Proponent of the right view:] No. Because, due to the qualified [property of] being non-eternal etc. there would be no cognition of the [property of] being a pervader with regard to the probans "being produced".[336] Due to the absence of that part of the defining characteristic which has the form of "being pervaded and pervader",[337] it is established that this [defining characteristic] has no over-pervasion with respect to the [property of] not being an associate condition. Therefore, it is established that a defining characteristic of an associate condition can be explicated in the manner described (above). It is well established that [there is] a general and a specific defining characteristic of an associate condition.

In what way there is no rival for the arrow Śrīrāma,
in the same way is there never any opponent to this investigation.

This is the first part in the Upādhidarpaṇa, viz. the determination of the defining characteristic.

(**2**) Now, an investigation of the associate condition is undertaken.

(**2.1**) With respect to this the theorists are debating. Some say that the associate condition is a vitiator, because it indicates a deviation. But others claim: "[It vitiates] as something which amounts to the counter-thesis." And others again say: "[It vitiates] as the cause which leads to the pervadedness's being unestablished." But the followers of Vādīndra say that there is no refutation on account of an associate condition.

(**2.1.1**) The way in which an associate condition vitiates as an indicator of a deviation is explained here. After all, there are two parts, "the pervasion of the probandum and the non-pervasion of the probans". The associate condition is not to be found on the inferential subject. Because, otherwise, there would be an inconsistency with the part "non-pervasion", insofar as it is ascertained that [the associate condition] does not pervade the probans.[338] However, if something pervading the probans were an associate condition, the [property of] being produced would be an associate condition with respect to the probandum "being non-eternal" due to [the probans] "being graspable by the external senses for us and others, insofar as it possesses a universal".[339]

The associate condition does not pervade the probans. With respect to something there is an associate condition for the probans because of a deviation.[340] There is that deviation (of the probans from the associate condition) with respect to the range of agreeing instances if that pervasion (of the probans) by the probandum should be violated on account of an associate condition. And therefore, one should say: "(A deviation) with respect to the range of agreeing instances only"

In the same way one should say that the probandum does not occur on the subject of the inference either.[341] Because, otherwise,[342] there would be the undesirable consequence of a failure of the pervasion of the probandum (by the associate condition). For, something pervading the probandum does not turn away (from the inferential subject) with the exception of the probandum, because there would be a contradiction.[343]

And the probans which turns away from the associate condition as a pervader of the probandum is not deviating due to the fact that it occurs on the inferential subject, which possesses the absence of the probandum.[344] The associate condition is called "indicating a deviation", insofar as there should be that very deviation, because the associate condition, which turns out to be a pervader of the probandum, is not present on the inferential subject.

But there is the application: "The probans under discussion, [viz.] 'being an injury' etc., deviates from the probandum 'bringing about guilt' etc., because it deviates from something pervading that (i.e., the probandum), such as in the case of the [property of] being an injury related to a sacrifice etc." All that depends on the fact that an associate condition is a pervader which is not present on the inferential subject. Hence, they do not agree to the doctrine of the pervadedness (of the associate condition by the probandum), insofar as the associate condition's pervasion (of the probandum) is necessary with regard to the thesis concerning the indication of a deviation, whereas the pervadedness is inappropriate. Somewhere, the pervadedness also exists, because it is somewhere unavoidable.[345]

[Opponent:] Are the associate condition's [function of] being a vitiator and its [function of] being a fortifier with respect to the probandum feasible due to the [property of] being pervaded and the [property of] being pervading? Neither of the two [alternatives] is approved of.[346]

[Proponent of the right view:] No. Because the inference stated by a debater needs to have a disclosure of the refutation by an opponent. One should agree that for this there is a function of that (reductive explanation of the function of an associate condition by means of the concept of pervasion). This is the opinion of those (theorists who explain the function of an associate condition reductively by means of the concept of pervasion).

(**2.1.2**) The manner of the amounting to the counter-thesis is going to be described. After all, the associate condition pervades the probandum. And the appearance of something which pervades (the probandum) has the purpose of making known the absence of the probandum by its (own) absence. But the amounting to the counter-thesis is like this: There is not the controversial "causing harm" because of the [property of] not being forbidden.

[Opponent:] How is it possible that as a result of the thesis concerning the indication of a deviation there is a production, [viz.] the arising of this thesis?[347]

[Proponent of the right view:] It is not so.[348] In the case of this thesis (concerning the residence of the probandum in a locus of the probans) it is similar, insofar as (now) [everything depends on the pervadedness] of [the associate condition] which is present [on that inferential subject].[349]

[Opponent:] Moreover, the thesis concerning the indication of a deviation is subordinate: In how far [the absence of the associate condition] allows one to infer a deviation which is characterized by the occurrence of the probans on the inferential subject which possesses the absence of the probandum because of the absence of the associate condition which appears as a pervader, insofar the absence of the associate condition pertaining to the counter-thesis amounts to a deviation for the purpose of a refutation of the probans. How, indeed, can the amounting to a deviation, which appears afterwards, be that which is desired?[350]

Moreover, without rejecting the [property of] being a fortifier, how should there be in your doctrine an associate condition's amounting to a deviation which is characterized by the occurrence (of the probans) on something possessing the absence of the probandum, since there is (according to your view) no determination of the absence of the probandum due to the mere absence of a pervader[351]? Therefore, the thesis concerning the amounting to the counter-thesis is superior. That is [our] opinion.[352]

(**2.1.3**) [Proponent of the right view:] Then, the thesis amounting to the pervadedness's being unestablished, which we agree to, is duly investigated.[353]

(**2.1.3.1**) [Opponent:] The thesis concerning a (possible) refutation by means of the associate condition is a sophistry. How is it possible that you agree to this thesis? After all, one should say that the associate condition at issue pervades the probandum at issue and it does not pervade the probans at issue. If such a property is not known in valid inferences, how is then possibly its absence granted? Since there is no denial of something which is not attached [to a valid inference]. If [an associate condition] is known, then the denial is not possible. For, in the case of the cognition of the pot on the ground its absence cannot be known. In fact, even if the counterpositive exists, this [absence] is not possible. Hence, since the absence of an associate condition cannot be determined in a valid inference, one has to admit that it does not vitiate, because (otherwise) there would be an annihilation of valid inferences.

[Proponent of the right view:] Ah, you possess an abundance of wisdom wherefore you do not even know[354] the self.[355] After all, insofar as there is a suspicion, there will be an abandoning.[356] After all, there are also [properties] which are suspected [to be associate conditions]. If it is suspected that properties which pervade the probandum are genuine associate conditions there (i.e., with respect to a certain inference), then the [property of] being an associate condition is denied to them due to the absence of the [property of] not pervading the probans. Now, it is suspected that [properties] which share the part "non-pervasion of the probans" are associate conditions. In that case the [property of] being an associate condition is denied to them due to the absence of the [property of] pervading the probandum. However, for properties beyond that[357] there is not even a suspicion, because there is no association with the [property of] being an associate condition. If someone in ordinary life should suspect a probans's being connected with an associate condition or its deviation, thereby overstepping the boundary between a doubt and the right view, then that one can, however, be warded off due to a favorable reductio ad absurdum.[358] The reductio ad absurdum exists of its own accord, insofar as [a suspicion], which is a demon to be feared and which deals with a failure concerning a pervasion, would be difficult to remove with simplicity. So, this has no dependence on a pervasion. There is no regressus ad infinitum. Because that [reductio ad absurdum] has as a root the cognition of a contradiction.

An example [of a reductio ad absurdum], however, consists in the cases "My mother would be barren", "The effect 'smoke' etc. would be without the cause 'fire' etc." etc. The fruit of a contradiction is the cessation of a suspicion concerning an associate condition or a deviation.

However, whoever is prudent, for that one [smoke] is produced from fire. He would not agree to the barrenness of a mother [and] also [not] to the production of an effect even without a cause, in order to turn the inconsistency into a seemingly plausible argument by disregarding even an obvious contradiction. And in the case of agreeing [to that], which thesis would then not obtain for that one? Or, if it should obtain, how should the ascertainment of the probandum not be possible even without the probans stated by a debater? How should a proof of the fire's [property of] being not hot etc. not possibly be conducive to a veridical awareness? For that one there is not that very contradiction.

And how should one, indeed, not be someone who oversteps the limits of propriety if one eliminates the suspicion of various blockers for all worldly affairs related to knowledge sources? How should the fruit of this not give rise to a similarity of the one who disagrees (with the suspicion) with a maniac etc.?

[Opponent:] That very contradiction appears only because of a pervasion, on account of the non-existence of the barrenness of a mother and because of the cause for an effect etc. Insofar, the suspicion of a deviation nevertheless sticks.

[Proponent of the right view:] No. In the case of a contradiction, however, a pervasion is not the root. It is rather just the denial that it is so. Nobody agrees to the barrenness of a mother and the separation of the effect from a cause in [a statement of] the right view etc. If someone ever agrees [to this], there would be a contradiction between agreement and denial.[359] Only such a contradiction is the root of an inconsistency. This is the secret of those who know the doctrinal tenets.

[Opponent:] It shall be like that. However, in the case of the agreement to the production of an effect without a cause there is no contradiction, because there is no contradiction in the case of a suspicion concerning a production from another cause. For the possession of smoke etc. the cause "fire etc." might not be fixed.

[Proponent of the right view:] No. If that other cause (of smoke) should ever be seen or heard of, then it should be suspected. If [another cause] is neither seen nor heard of in whatever way, then it should not be suspected, insofar as thereby one does not suspect the [property of] being one's own of what does not belong to oneself, or whom or what (as an effect) due to *kāśa*-grass[360] etc. as that what belongs to the preparation of a sacrificial fire[361]. There is another cause for smoke etc., co-located with (fire) and equally fit (for the production of smoke etc.) as fire[362]. It is proved that the faculty of sight etc. allow one to see due to the interaction with collyrium etc.[363]

(**2.1.3.2**) Therefore, we share the view that the associate condition brings to light the pervadedness (of the probans) as something which brings to light the pervadedness occurring in itself, insofar as it is ascertained that the associate condition vitiates in the above-mentioned manner. This is going to be explained: After all, [what is called] "being endowed with a pervasion" is a relation without associate condition. The two relata of this relation are the pervaded and the pervader. And [in this expression, viz.] "being a pervader of the pervaded", "being a pervader" means to be the agent of the pervasion. Being the pervaded, however, is the object of that. So, where that pervadedness appears in a primary sense, it is a true pervadedness.[364] However, where [a pervadedness] pertaining to another one[365] appears on account of a defect of the concomitance etc., that [pervadedness of the probans by the probandum] is not a true one and that pervadedness is not established due to the presence of a blocker[366] of the cognition of a pervadedness in a primary sense on this substrate (i.e., on the substrate of the probans which is not genuinely pervaded). The cognition which blocks the proof of the pervadedness in a primary sense is called "the failure of the pervadedness".

And the appearance of the pervadedness pertaining to the other one[367] is nevertheless a failure of the pervadedness (of the probans). Since it is like that, a locus is called "leading to the failure of the pervadedness" if it brings to light the pervadedness pertaining to itself elsewhere, due to a pervadedness in a primary sense, dependent on another one.[368] This is expressed [by means of the words]: "The associate condition which blocks the pervasion leads to the failure of the pervadedness." [In such a manner] as follows: For, the [property of] being an injury is a probans which possesses the failure of the pervadedness. For, forbiddenness is called "an associate condition which leads to the failure of the pervadedness of that (probans)". The pervadedness with respect to the probandum pertaining to this (associate condition) is [a pervadedness] in a primary sense. The [property of] being an injury, however, brings about guilt, such as the [property of] being graspable by the external senses if there is the possession of universals (as a probandum).[369]

Of its own accord that (property of being an injury) is not capable of proving that (property of bringing about guilt), because in the case of a sacrificial injury there is an incompatibility with forbiddenness. For, for the [property of] being an injury the forbiddenness fortifies the [property of] bringing about guilt in the inferential subject. There is a blocker [in the sense of the inconsistency] "on account of an effort (i.e., an injury) for bringing about that (viz. guilt) only once in a while", and on account of the sameness of the blocker with this very inconsistency there is a failure of the pervadedness.

One should not say: "Why should it not be like that?"[370] Because of the (probans's) probative force on account of forbiddenness's [property of] being a fortifier due to the fact that it has a coextensive concomitance. And so, the pervadedness which pertains only to forbiddenness occurs in the injury because of a defect of the concomitance. That remembrance [of the pervadedness pertaining to forbiddenness] blocks the cognition of the pervadedness of the [property of] being an injury in a primary sense. Insofar, it is said that there is a failure of its pervadedness. That forbiddenness is the support of the pervadedness. Therefore, it is said that it leads to the failure of the pervadedness. Thus, the [property of] leading to the failure of the pervadedness is everywhere applicable to coextensively pervading associate conditions. And since it is like that, the meaning of the expression for the defining characteristic of a pervasion, [viz.] "the co-occurrence of the probans and the probandum without an associate condition" is this, [viz.] "the co-occurrence which is attended by the absence of a property which is a fortifier which brings to light the pervadedness pertaining to itself". And so, there is a failure of the pervadedness, insofar as [this pervadedness] is in that way the root of a cognition which opposes the pervasion due to a contradiction, owing, however, to the appearance of the superimposed pervadedness pertaining to the probans. And hence, the efficacious associate condition leads to the failure of the pervadedness. Insofar, everything is well established.

Or, a pervasion is devoid of an associate condition for the co-occurrence of probans and probandum. If there is an associate condition, there should be the absence of a pervasion. Insofar, the associate condition is obviously a vitiator due to the [property of] being in effect the absence of a pervasion.[371] If an associate condition is not present on this inferential subject, then it (i.e., the property of being a vitiator) amounts to the fact that the absence of that (i.e., the absence of the associate condition) is like an incoherent or a deviating [pseudo-probans] and proves the absence of the probandum, because of the pervadedness (by the absence of the probandum) resident in that (absence of the associate condition).[372] Insofar, the invariability of the co-occurrence of the probans (with the probandum) is attended by the absence of an associate condition. Hence, one should agree (to the invariability of the co-occurrence) only in the case of the absence of an associate condition for that (co-occurrence), because [the associate condition] is a fortifier for the proof of the probandum. This is the secret.

Due to the afore-mentioned rationale concerning the inequality of the pair of theses (concerning the manner of vitiating), [viz.] "the [property of] leading to the failure of the pervadedness, in the other case of that (pair of theses) the possession of the essence of the absence of a pervasion",[373] we agree to both of these, since there is no contradiction to the thesis of an agreement to the pervadedness. Therefore, there is in the case of an agreement to the pervadedness of the associate condition the [property of] being a vitiator due to the [property of] leading to the failure of the pervadedness (of the probans) or due to the (probans's) [property of] having as a characteristic the [property of the] pervadedness's being unestablished.[374] However, there is the thesis concerning the indication of an established deviation owing to the flaw of being least important.

As explained before, the thesis concerning the amounting to the counter-thesis has been accepted, because it amounts to the [property of] being a blocker on account of the fact that in the case of a fortifying negative correlation an absence which is not the associate condition[375] is capable of being a fortifier with respect to the absence of the probandum due to its [property of] being a characteristic (of the absence of the probandum). As for the thesis concerning the amounting to a blocker, it is strong[376]. However, in the case of the amounting to the failure of the pervadedness one is obviously anxious about the inferential awareness which has to be inferred as well.[377] Therefore, it is established that the thesis stated by us is stronger.

[Opponent:] Everything is like that because of the agreement to the pervadedness of the associate condition. What is the basis in the case of the agreement to that?[378]

[Proponent of the right view:] It is not like that.[379] It has been said that one has to agree to the pervadedness of the associate condition only because of its [property of] being a fortifier. That should not be forgotten. One also has to take into account what has been said, [viz.] that there is no elimination of the associate condition "being different from the inferential subject" without the pervadedness, and that there is no elimination of the coextensively pervading [associate condition "being different from the inferential subject"] without the pervadedness.

And moreover, insofar as one does not agree to the pervadedness of (the probans) "being an injury" etc.,[380] the (associate condition's) [property of] being a pervader is established by mere cognition, as is the pervadedness of the associate condition. Then, how can there be something recognized as the absence of the probandum on the inferential subject without that (property of being a pervader),[381] or, how can there be an indication of a deviation which is characterized by the occurrence (of the absence of the associate condition) on something which possesses the ascertained absence of the probandum?[382]

(**2.1.4**) Now, if [this] failed, insofar as [a pervasion] is established by means of the cognition of a concomitance assisted by a reductio ad absurdum, what would then be the use of bringing to the fore an associate condition, since this reductio ad absurdum should appear as a reductio ad absurdum for the [property of] being an injury as [the probans] in the present case?[383] But according to our opinion there is no dependence on a reductio ad absurdum, because that [reductio ad absurdum] prevails only due to the actual presence of a co-occurrence, dependent on the [property of] being an injury etc.[384]

[Opponent:] Where there is in the case of a probans and a probandum a coextensive pervasion with the probandum, there the bringing to the fore of an associate condition is useless also for you. Insofar, this is the same.[385]

[Proponent of the right view:] It is not so. In that case[386] the associate condition prevails if it arises due to the concomitance with a favorable reductio ad absurdum.[387] Nevertheless, according to our opinion it is better to bring to the fore an associate condition, which is supported by that (reductio ad absurdum), because the bringing to the fore of an associate condition is obviously determined as a defect of the probans.

In the case of the appearance of a reductio ad absurdum, however, there is indirectly also the mistake of the associate condition, because there is indirectly an amounting to a reductio ad absurdum with respect to the thesis of the non-agreement to the pervadedness.[388] In that way, one has to agree that the associate condition's pervadedness is necessarily provable by means of an unfavorable reductio ad absurdum.

(**2.1.5**) [Opponent:] The associate condition's [function of] being a vitiator via such a pervadedness does not cover the associate condition for an only negative inference. Earth is different from other [things], because it is earth.[389] Direct experience is self-illuminating, because it is direct experience.[390] With respect to the negative correlation the only negative inference, however, possesses [the examples] "such as in the case of water etc., such as in the case of a pot" etc.[391] In that case [the only negative inference] possesses earthness etc. as that which is pervaded.[392] In that case [an associate condition] which brings to light the pervadedness occurring in itself is supposed to be [something] whose residence is confined to the inferential subject.[393] No property in the form of an associate condition such as forbiddenness etc., which is accompanied by that (i.e., by the probandum), seems fit if the failure of the pervadedness of the probans is brought about (by the associate condition). If such a property seems fit, [an inference's property of] being only negative would fail. Because of the undesirable conclusion that there would be a positive pervasion of probans and probandum due to the necessity of a joint occurrence of probans and associate condition outside the inferential subject.[394]

[Proponent of the right view:][395] In the case of an only negative inference one talks about an associate condition for the negative pervasion. Because it is not the case that that [negative pervasion] does not exist in the case of a positive pervasion. For, in that case the absence of the probandum is the pervaded, whereas the absence of the probans is the pervader.[396] The concomitance of a property in the form of an associate condition with such a pervaded [property][397] is only possible in the range of negative instances.

In that case there can also be a pervasion [of the associate condition by a defining characteristic]. The defining characteristic, however, amounts to the following: "[The associate condition] does not pervade the absence of the probandum, while it pervades the absence of the probans coextensively."[398] In that case an associate condition is also possible.

[Opponent:] It is not so. The pervadedness-part (i.e., the pervasion of the associate condition by the absence of the probans) shall be granted, [but] there is no pervasion of the absence of the probans (by the associate condition). If the probans which is defined as the absence of the probandum[399] should be present on the inferential subject in the absence of the associate condition, then the absence of the probans might fail and then also the pervasion of the absence of the probans (by the associate condition).[400]

If a probans of an only negative [inference] without the pervader should occur in the place of a deviation of associate condition and absence of the probandum, the [property of] being only negative would fail, insofar as there would be the undesirable conclusion that [the occurrence of the probans without the pervader in such a place] would be opposed to that (probans of an only negative inference).[401]

Because, if there is no agreement to the part concerning the associate condition's non-pervasion of the probans,[402] and if there were the undesirable conclusion that a property occurring on the inferential subject would be an associate condition, then there would be no obstacle to the impossibility of there being an error[403] if the pervadedness failed in one locus and if there were the undesirable conclusion of a pervadedness of both (the probans and the probandum) only due to the non-coextensiveness in the form of an occurrence of a part (of the probans) on the agreeing instances, as in the case of the totalities of smokes and fires,[404] because one needs to limit the mutual opposition between the [property of] being graspable by means of the external senses for us and for others and the [property of] being produced, insofar as there is the probandum "being non-eternal"[405] if there is the possession of universals.[406]

The [property of] leading to the failure of the pervadedness by means of something which brings to light the pervadedness pertaining to itself might not be possible.[407] Since therefore the associate condition which has been assumed by you does not exist in the case of an only negative [inference], it is established that in that case there is nothing which effects a refutation as an associate condition.

[Proponent of the right view:] In that case we say: "After all, whenever [etc.]."[408] In the case of a probans in an only negative [inference] there might be a contradiction to an unfavorable reductio ad absurdum.[409] And therefore, in that case an indicating associate condition does not pervade the probans in the form of the absence of the probandum, because the utility of the probans of an only negative [inference] in proving something by itself is impaired, since it is contradicted by an unfavorable reductio ad absurdum.[410]

Insofar as the absence of the probandum of an only negative [inference] on that inferential subject is suspected in the case of the ascertainment of a missing associate condition's non-pervasion of the probans due the absence of a determination of the pervasion of the probans in the form of the absence of the probandum, the [property of] being a vitiator is secured,[411] since an associate condition which is induced in that case is a fortifier due to the [property of] bringing to light the pervadedness pertaining to itself.[412] Because the associate condition's [function of] indicating [a deviation] is necessary, insofar as it beats an unfavorable reductio ad absurdum as something which indicates the lack of a pervasion. In the case of an only negative inference there is also an associate condition due to the falsification by means of an undesirable consequence. Since here, although the [property of] being insentient etc., which were explained, amount to that which is different from the inferential subject,[413] that [property of being insentient] has nevertheless the property of being a qualifier which (by its absence) excludes only the inferential subject (from the range of loci of the probandum), insofar as only for the inferential subject there is an expectation[414] that it is a disagreeing instance.[415]

With regard to this some have said: "'That which is other than this probandum is not other than that which occurs on the inferential subject, because it is knowable, such as this probandum.' On account of this inference there is somewhere the probandum.[416] Since one obtains a positive pervasion in that case, an associate condition should be named."[417]

This is not correct. Because there would be no [property of] being an associate condition, which is (actually) brought to the fore in the case of an only negative inference. For, due to the expression "positive correlation" there is no only negative inference (as a potential target of an associate condition), since [the assumption of a positive correlation] contradicts [the only negative character of an inference]. Therefore, it is better to bring to the fore an associate condition in the manner outlined [by us]. Hence, it is established that an associate condition is always and everywhere a vitiator due to its [property of] leading to the failure of the pervadedness or due to the (probans's) [property of] being in effect the absence of a pervasion.[418] Enough with prolixity. This is the second part in the Upādhidarpaṇa, viz. the investigation of the (associate condition as a) vitiator.

(**3**) The manner of subdividing the associate conditions is taken into account.

(**3.1**) After all, the associate conditions are twofold, [viz.] "ascertained and dubious". And with regard to that, the pervasion of the probandum which is ascertained in the associate condition is also twofold.[419] These (associate conditions) are ascertained, such as the ascertained associate conditions "forbiddenness in the case of the [property of] being an injury[420] [and] the [property of] being a visible substance in the case of the [property of] being a substrate of perceptible touch[421]" etc.

(**3.1.1**) And the dubious associate conditions are twofold.[422]

Among the expressions in the sense of a certitude of the pervasion of the probandum and the non-pervasion of the probans there is "the ascertained pervasion of the probandum", as in the case of "amorphous substance" for [the inference] "The mind is all-pervasive, because it is an intangible substance such as the soul" etc.[423]

And that associate condition and the probans are both coextensively pervaded by the probandum.[424] And so, the associate condition's pervasion of the probandum is ascertained, because it (i.e, the actual probans, viz. "being an intangible substance") clashes with a probans (i.e., the actual probans limited by the associate condition) which is equipollent[425] (with the probandum).[426]

[The associate condition] pervades the probandum, [but] without certainty, and it certainly does not pervade the probans. As in the case of the [property of] being preceded by (prenatal) digestion of food [consisting of] vegetables etc. in the inference with the [property of] being a son of Mitrā etc. (as a probans), with regard to that (i.e., as an example of a similar kind of associate condition) five [sons] of a certain dear Dṛṣadvatī standing here are near at hand. They are all dark-complexioned. Another one, however, has gone to another region. In that case the undesirable conclusion "being dark-complexioned" incurs. And so, one says [what has been said] previously etc. The [son] at issue should be dark-complexioned. Because it is a son of this [Dṛṣadvatī]. Such as in the case [of the other sons' dark complexion] which has been acknowledged.[427]

The [property of] being preceded by (prenatal) digestion of food [consisting of] vegetables etc. is an associate condition. Its non-pervasion of the probans is not ascertained. For that (coextensive pervasion of the probandum by the associate condition) there is also a doubt concerning the [property of] being preceded by (prenatal) digestion of food [consisting of] vegetables etc. After all, her predilection for food [consisting of] vegetables etc. is only seen to be ongoing in the case of five children. But, as regards a continuation in the case of the sixth child, her predilection for that (i.e. for food consisting of vegetables etc.) is not in that way seen [to be ongoing] as well, because of a doubt whether it (i.e., the predilection) is there or not, since in some cases a dissatisfaction sometimes appears, even though there is once an attachment to an object. Therefore, "this pervades the probans in an uncertain way" is not said in the sense of "established as a pervader of the probans"[428].

Or, the [property of] being dark-complexioned should be an associate condition for the relation between the [property of] being a son of Mitrā and the [property of] being preceded by (prenatal) digestion of food [consisting of] vegetables etc.[429]

And it is not the case that there is a non-pervasion of the probans because of the agreement to the fact that the [property of] being preceded by (prenatal) digestion of food [consisting of] vegetables etc. is an associate condition for the relation between the [property of] being a son of Mitrā and the [property of] being dark-complexioned.[430] And in this way the associate condition "being preceded by (prenatal) digestion of food [consisting of] vegetables etc." is a means (to vitiate the inference of "being dark-complexioned" from "being a son of Mitrā"): The dubious non-pervasion is established, [which means] "For this (relation) [there is] an associate condition", due to an uncertain non-pervasion of the probans because of the absence of an ascertainment concerning the non-pervasion of the probans due to the fact that the absence of an associate condition for the relation cannot be ascertained.

[Opponent:] If it is so, the [property of] being produced should be an associate condition for the inference of the [property of] being non-eternal from the [property of] being graspable through the external senses by us and others if there is the possession of universals.[431] In that case there is also a non-pervasion of the probans "being non-eternal", because due to the rationale mentioned by you the [property of] being non-eternal is an associate condition for the relation between the probans and the associate condition.[432]

[Proponent of the right view:] It is not so. Because in the case of a probans which is supported by a reductio ad absurdum for this (inference[433]), [viz.] "If the sound were eternal, then it would not increase and decrease in loudness", there is due to the necessity of the sound's being non-eternal no connection with the non-ascertainment of that (i.e., of the sound's property of being non-eternal), since the ascertainment of what pervades the probans is not only accomplished with regard to [something] pervaded and the pervader.[434] The associate condition "being produced" has no [connection with a non-ascertainment of the property of being an associate condition].[435] However, due to the connection of the [property of] being a dubious associate condition with the associate condition in that case (i.e., in the case of the Mitrā-example) there is no favorable reductio ad absurdum for the [property of] being a son of Mitrā. Hence, an ascertainment of the [property of] being dark-complexioned on the inferential subject is inappropriate. There is, however, an associate condition for that pervader, because there is no connection with the certitude: "The probans is pervaded." Insofar as in the case of the expectation of an associate condition there is no connection of the [property of] being an associate condition for the [property of] being dark-complexioned with the absence of the non-appropriateness of the ascertainment of the non-pervasion of the probans,[436] the [property of] being a dubious associate condition is possible due to that part (i.e., the non-pervasion of the probans by the associate condition), because there is no ascertainment of a non-pervasion of the probans.

(**3.1.2**) And these associate conditions are seen to be sixfold, [viz.] those which pervade the whole probandum, those which pervade the probandum which is limited by a certain qualifier, those which pervade the absence of the probans, those which pervade the absence of the probandum, those which pervade ... .[437]

Among those, an example for the first [type] is: "The earth etc. have a causal agent, because they are not produced by an embodied [agent], such as smoke." In this case "being produced" etc. [are associate conditions].[438]

An example for the second [type], however, is: There is inherence, because there is a relation with something inhering. Contactness etc. [are associate conditions].[439]

An example for the third [type], however, are the [property of] being preceded by (prenatal) digestion of food [consisting of] vegetables etc., which pervade the [property of] being dark-complexioned limited by humanbeingness etc. in the case of the inference with the [property of] being a son of Mitrā etc. (as the probans).[440]

An example for the fourth [type], however, are the [property of] being insentient etc., which pervade the absence of the probans in the case of the only negative inferences of (the probandum) "being self-illuminating" etc. from the [property of] being direct experience etc.[441]

An example for the fifth [type], however, are the ether etc. in the case of the relation between the negation of the probans "being produced by an embodied [agent]" etc. and the negation of the probandum "having a causal agent" etc.[442]

An example for the sixth [type], however, are the [property of] being preceded by the action of hands and feet etc. in [the cases] "If the earth etc. had a causal agent, they would be produced by someone having a body, such as the pot" etc.[443]

(**3.2**) [Opponent:] Since in the defining characteristic of all these associate conditions the [property of] being a pervader is meant by the word "probandum", it has been said that [the concept of pervasion] will be included in that.[444] An inference which is devoid of all associate conditions, [viz.] the one which has smoke etc. [as a probans], is suitable.[445]

[Proponent of the right view:] No. The cognition of that (i.e., of the validity of an inference) is owing to a dissimilarity.[446]

[Opponent:] [The second member of an inference is enunciated] for the purpose of elucidating the [property of] being a property of the inferential subject.

[Proponent of the right view:] No. Due to the mentioning of the probans it is stated (that it is devoid of an associate condition).[447]

[Opponent:] [This is not right], because [one might ask then] why the end (of the inference) is a part of the inference.[448]

[Proponent of the right view:] No. [The question is pointless], since the pervasion is also a (necessary) part of the inference.

[Opponent:] Why is the statement [that the probans is devoid of an associate condition] not formulated [by means of the words] "because it possesses a smoke which is pervaded", not, however, due to the mentioning of the example?[449] The pervasion is acknowledged [by means of the example]. Because there is no mentioning of the probans together with that (pervasion).[450]

[Proponent of the right view:] The [property of] being a property of the inferential subject will also ensue from the application. What is the use of the mentioning of the probans?[451] Therefore, there is the application: "As in the case of the smoke (in the examples)."[452]

Moreover, when one thinks about adding something (to the probans) due to an expectancy[453], heat is futile. After all, the thesis "The mountain possesses fire" has to be stated in a debatable way. Thereupon, the probans "Because of smoke" has to be stated due to the expectancy: "Why?" After the pervasion has been elucidated [by means of the words] "By means of the pervasion as an efficient cause with reference to all [individuals]" [as an answer to the question] "How is that possible?", thereupon the pervasion has to be located on the inferential subject (as a locus) of such a probans due to the expectancy: "In a favorable place it is so. What is attained in the case of the present one?" Thereupon, the absence of a blocker should be elucidated. Since there is no blocker, therefore it has fire. Insofar, heat is in this way futile due to the mentioning of the probans, at least, when one thinks deeply about it. Insofar, it is established that one should say: "Because of smoke."[454] With regard to that, however, one can check whether (our) presentation is in accordance with heirloom practice.

[Opponent:] In this case there is the associate condition "the [property of] being different from the inferential subject". How is it possible that this[455] is devoid of an associate condition?

[Proponent of the right view:] No. Because it has been said: "On account of the fact that that which is different from the inferential subject is not an associate condition"

(**3.3**) [Opponent:] How many kinds of apparent associate conditions are there?

[Proponent of the right view:] Those which only pervade the probandum, those which are only pervaded by the probandum, those which only do not pervade the probans, those which do not pervade the probans, while they only pervade the probandum, [and] those which do not pervade the probans, while they are only pervaded by the probandum.[456]

(**3.3.1**) Among those, the first case are the [property of] being produced etc. in the case of the inference of the [property of] being non-eternal by means of [the probans] "on account of the [property of] being graspable by means of the external senses for us and for others if there is the possession of universals" etc.[457]

An example for the second [type], however, are the [property of] having parts etc. in this inference.[458] Or, the [property of] being accompanied by beingness etc. in the case of the [inference] "The sound is nameable, because it is a quality" etc.[459]

An example for the third [type], however, are ... etc. [for the inference] "Because of the [property of] being produced ... if there is the possession of universals."[460]

An example for the fourth [type], however, are inaudibility etc. in the case of the inference with the [property of] being produced (as a probans).[461]

An example for the fifth [type], however, are the [property of] being a quality etc. in the case of this [inference]: "The sound is nameable, because it is knowable."[462]

(**3.3.2**) The [property of] being different from the inferential subject is, however, useless. It only falls to the share of an inferential subject which has the appearance of a past, present or future [locus of the probandum].[463]

(**3.4**) In such a way the different kinds of associate conditions together with the ones which appear to be [associate conditions] are described. Thereby, [the associate condition] has been equipped with two defining characteristics in the afore-mentioned manner. [The associate condition] is a fortifier for the proof of the probandum. It is of its own accord capable to oppose [a false thesis].

This [associate condition] is not dashed to shivers by bottomless distinctions. Under the protection of Rāma
the associate condition, which fascinates wise men, shall excel[464] in the world.

This is the third part in the Upādhidarpaṇa. Glory!

4.3 Notes: Chapter 4

1. cf. Monier-Williams 1872, s.v. *śrīrāma*: "the divine Rāma, i.e., Rāma-candra (whose name in this form is used as a salutation by those who worship Vishṇu in this Avatāra)"

2. The opponent is here an opponent in a long *pūrvapakṣa* (1.1 – 1.1.18), who argues that there is a general and a specific defining characteristic, i.e., his position is close to that of the *siddhāntin* (1.2 – 1.2.2.4). The respondent in the *pūrvapakṣa* holds the opposite view.

3. "Over-pervasion" means that the defining characteristic would be too wide. The opponent's defining characteristic resides also in eternal substances. However, according to the respondent such entities should be ruled out as loci of a putative defining characteristic of associate conditions.

4. The absolute absence of the ether is omnipresent, because the ether is unlocatable (cf. BN: 8, 13 = Guhe 2014: 60: *ākāśādikaṃ tu na kutrāpi vartata iti. ākāśaṃ na kasyāpi dharmaḥ.*). Being omnipresent, the absolute absence of the ether resides also in itself.

5. i.e., among the associate conditions

6. According to the respondent an associate condition should not be the counterpositive of an absolute absence which depends on itself as a substrate, such as the absolute absence of the ether.

7. If the ether is admitted to function as an associate condition, i.e., as a vitiator, one might say that it undermines valid inferences as well. An associate condition is supposed to be a necessary precondition for the presence of the probandum in an invalid inference, i.e., at least in the range of the probans the probandum should be absent, wherever the associate condition is absent. Since the ether is unlocatable, its absence is universally present. So, if the ether were an associate condition, its absence would entail the absence of any probandum, no matter whether it is the probandum of an invalid or a valid inference.

8. Hereafter, the term *atyantābhāvapratiyogidharmatva* ("being a property which is a counterpositive of an absolute absence") will mostly be left untranslated.

9. i.e., eternal substances like the ether

10. i.e., with respect to the *atyantābhāvapratiyogidharmatva*

11. The defining characteristic *atyantābhāvapratiyogidharmatva* is absent from the ether. So, it does not occur in certain loci and it is therefore itself a property which is a counterpositive of an absolute absence. Hence, it is self-resident. If it were itself not an associate condition, it would be a property of something which is not an associate condition (namely a property of itself). So, there would be over-pervasion.

12. i.e., in itself

13. The defining characteristic would be too narrow, because it would not reside in something which is regarded as an associate condition according to the present alternative, namely in the defining characteristic itself.

14. This other property might be a property which is related to the *atyantābhāvapratiyogidharmatva* in the same way as "being non-eternal" (*anityatva*) and "being poduced" (*kṛtakatva*) are related to each other (cf. Matilal 1990: 131). They are distinct properties, but they are "equilocatable" (*samaniyata*, cf. ibid. 166f), i.e., they occur in the same loci. In this sense they are at least extensionally identifiable.

15. Since the *atyantābhāvapratiyogidharmatva* was assumed to be an associate condition, it should itself be a property of the *atyantābhāvapratiyogidharmatva.*

16. The "other property" which is equilocatable with the *atyantābhāvapratiyogidharmatva,* in which it resides, can also be regarded as an associate condition. Being equilocatable with the *atyantābhāvapratiyogidharmatva,* it is a property which does not reside in the ether. Since it is also an associate condition, it would again require the assumption of another property which is equilocatable with it and which resides in it etc.

17. i.e., it resides in the properties referred to

18. If the properties referred to are associate conditions, then the defining characteristic should reside in them. But since the defining characteristic is also supposed to be a substrate of these properties, we run into a case of mutual dependence.

19. i.e., of the defining characteristic

20. i.e., in a property which resides in the defining characteristic

21. i.e., lack of generality of the general defining characteristic and a regressus ad infinitum

22. i.e., if the properties residing only in the defining characteristic of the associate condition are not associate conditions

23. Properties which reside *only* in the defining characteristic are not omnipresent. Hence, the *atyantābhāvapratiyogidharmatva* should reside in them. If they were not associate conditions (as presupposed in the present case), the defining characteristic would reside in something which is not an associate condition. This is explained in the next sentence.

24. i.e., the absence

25. i.e., in the properties which reside only in this defining characteristic

26. Properties like knowability are omnipresent and therefore they are not substrates of the *atyantābhāvapratiyogidharmatva.* Since a property which resides only in the defining characteristic is a property and a counterpositive of an absolute absence, it is distinct from eternal substances like the ether and also from properties like knowability. Hence, it should possess the defining characteristic of an associate condition.

27. i.e., in the properties which reside only in this defining characteristic

28. i.e., the absolute absence

29. "These two" refers to eternal substances like the ether and to properties like knowability. The absolute absence of a property which resides only in the defining characteristic resides in eternal substances like the ether and in properties like knowability, since they are distinct from the defining characteristic. Hence, a property residing only in the defining characteristic does not reside in them. Therefore, the absolute absence of such a property resides in them.

30. If a property residing only in the defining characteristic did not possess the defining characteristic, it would not be a counterpositive of an absolute absence, i.e., it would be omnipresent. So, it would also reside in unlocatable entities like the ether and in universal properties like knowability, which would be "there", i.e., among the loci of such a property. On the other hand, this is impossible, because these properties reside only in the *atyantābhāvapratiyogidharmatva.*

31. The *atyantābhāvapratiyogidharmatva* actually resides in a defining characteristic of associate conditions, because a defining characteristic of associate conditions is a property which is not omnipresent.

32. If the *atyantābhāvapratiyogidharmatva* is not a defining characteristic of associate conditions, one needs to specify an alternative defining characteristic of associate conditions in such a way that it does not reside in itself. Otherwise, there will be a suspicion that the assumption of such a defining characteristic violates commonplace ontological commitments.

33. If the *atyantābhāvapratiyogidharmatva* residing in the defining characteristic of associate conditions u were a defining characteristic different from u, then u would have to be regarded as an associate condition, which is impossible, because this would entail the residence of u in u and u would be self-dependent then. In other words: Because of the residence of the *atyantābhāvapratiyogidharmatva* in u, the latter would have to be an associate condition. On the other hand, the residence of the *atyantābhāvapratiyogidharmatva* in u excludes the possibility that the latter is an associate condition, because this would engender a case of self-dependence.

34. An effect cannot depend on itself as its cause. Moreover, a cognition cannot be grounded in itself. But it is admitted that something resides in itself.

35. *kevalānvayin* ("universally positive, only positive") refers (1) to a ("universally positive") property which has no negative range, such as, e.g., "nameability" and (2) to an ("only positive") inference whose inductive support consists only of instances of the co-presence of probans and probandum with no instances of a co-absence, such as, e.g.: "The pot is nameable, because it is knowable." (Matilal 1990: 132)

36. Since there are valid only positive inferences with omnipresent and therefore self-resident properties as probans and probandum, there should be no reason to exclude a self-resident defining characteristic of associate conditions. The myrobalan lying in the hand, which occurs in the example of the opponent's inference, is a kind of paragon of "anything quite clear to all eyes" (cf. Monier-Williams 1872, s.v. *karatalāmalaka*).

37. This is the fallacy of an inconclusive probans, i.e., a probans which is indecisive in favour of either side, the thesis or the counter-thesis.

38. Since the probans in such an inference is universally positive, it should also reside in the probandum.

39. This is the case that the probandum itself or an equilocatable equivalent occurs on the probandum.

40. This is again the idea of avoiding self-dependence by introducing a distinct equilocatable property, so that a probandum is admitted to be the substrate of a distinct equilocatable probandum.

41. "etc." refers here probably to the case of only negative (*kevalavyatirekin*) inferences, whose inductive support consists only of instances of a co-absence of probans and probandum with no instances of a co-presence. This is Bhāsarvajña's very clear albeit controversial example: "The living body has a soul, for it has life." (Matilal 1998: 10)

42. If self-dependence is admitted, one might also regard smoke-possessingness as a self-resident property. Since it possesses the absence of fire, there would be a locus (namely smoke-possessingness) of the joint occurrence of the probans (smoke-possessingness) and the absence of the probandum (fire) and this might be taken as counter-evidence to valid inferences like "The mountain possesses fire, because it possesses smoke".

43. "The mountain possesses fire, because it possesses smoke."

44. So, one might rather sacrifice the only positive inference than giving up a positive and negative inference, whose validity is well established.

45. The following verse picks up some arguments of the previous discussion.

46. There should be an equilocatable defining characteristic u residing in the *atyantābhāvapratiyogidharmatva* which is distinct from the latter. Otherwise, there would be the defect of self-dependence. However, u would also be an associate condition, because it does not occur in loci such as, e.g., the ether. So, even on the basis of this distinction we would encounter the problem of self-dependence.

47. So, we have to assume another equilocatable defining characteristic u' which is distinct from u in order to avoid self-dependence. But then we run into a regressus ad infinitum.

48. i.e., the distinction between the *atyantābhāvapratiyogidharmatva* and u

49. "Accomplishing the distinction" would mean to specify u in such a way that it is distinct from, but equilocatable with the *atyantābhāvapratiyogidharmatva.*

50. If u resides in the *atyantābhāvapratiyogidharmatva* rather than the *atyantābhāvapratiyogidharmatva* itself, the latter would be afflicted with the defect of a conflict between a defining characteristic and its required generality (i.e., with the defect of non-pervasion), as has been argued already.

51. In the case of the distinction between u and u' we would be faced with the problem that u as a defining characteristic of associate conditions loses its required generality.

52. If *upādhitva* were a universal, there would be an overlap with the universal "existence", which Navya-Naiyāyikas regard as inadmissible. Moreover, universals can be *upādhis* (cf. Fig. 1). However, if *upādhitva* were a universal, it could not inhere in a universal.

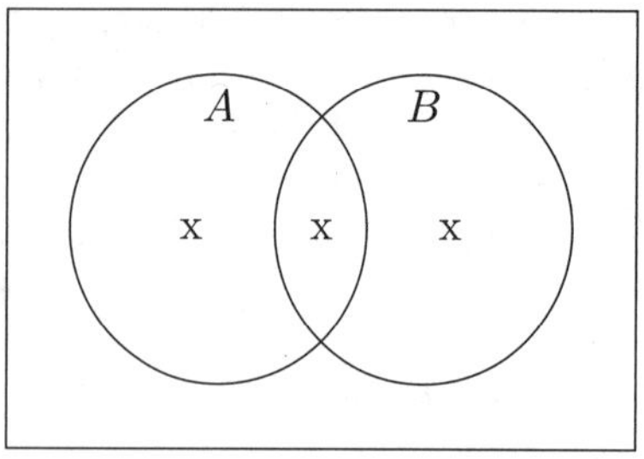

Fig. 1

A = the class of loci of *sattā*

B = the class of loci of *upādhitva*

nityadravyas $\in A \setminus B$; *guṇas* $\in A \cap B$; *sāmānyas* $\in B \setminus A$

53. Naiyāyikas often explain the functioning of an associate condition by referring to the analogy of a China rose which is put in the vicinity of a crystal. In the same way as the China rose transmits its red colour to the crystal, the associate condition transmits the pervasion by the probandum to the probans of an assumed inference, because the probans allows us to infer the probandum in the presence of the associate condition (cf. TR: 68f).

54. The expression "associate condition" does not refer to a "common cause of usage" (*anugataṃ pravṛttinimittam*), a property which all associate conditions have in common. The verb *upādhā*, from which *upādhi* derives, merely indicates a particular mode of functioning. We are not just talking about *upādhis* in a wider sense by referring to this mode of functioning.

55. The property "bringing to light one's own pervadedness" cannot be regarded as a defining characteristic of associate conditions.

56.

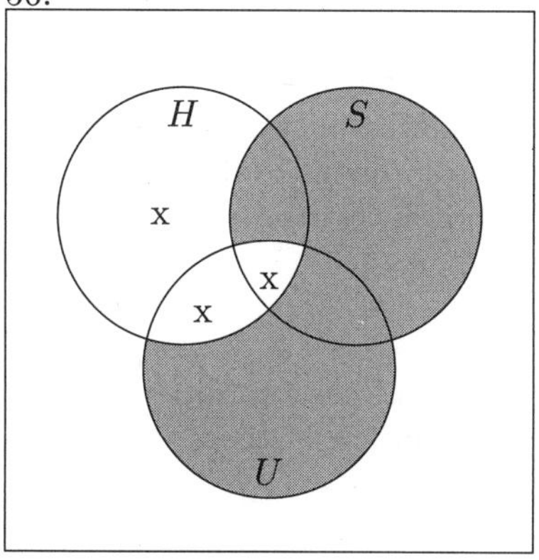

Fig. 2

H = the class of loci of the probans
S = the class of loci of the probandum
U = the class of loci of the associate condition

$S \subset U \subset H$ in Fig. 2. There is no coextensive pervasion between probandum and associate condition. Since $(H \cap U) \setminus S$ is non-empty, the probans co-occurs with the associate condition in loci of the absence of the probandum.

57. A substrate which is not knowable does not exist. However, an absence always needs a substrate.

58. The expression "knowable substrate of the absolute absence of knowability" is a contradiction in terms.

59. As the opponent has just demonstrated, the absolute absence of knowability would fail to reside in any substrate, be it knowable or unknowable, i.e., any putative substrate of the absolute absence of knowability would be a substrate of something which has no substrate. According to the respondent such a substrate which is characterized in a contradictory way cannot be knowable and it is therefore a substrate of the absolute absence of knowability. But this would mean that knowability is the counterpositive of an absolute absence. This argument is, of course, hardly convincing, because it amounts to locating the absolute absence of knowability in a substrate of something which has no substrate, i.e., in a non-existent substrate.

60. Absences always depend on a substrate. Therefore, it is legitimate to inquire after the substrate of the absolute absence of knowability. But then we are faced with the afore-mentioned dilemma.

61. So, an absolute absence does not always depend on a substrate.

62. The respondent refers again to the dilemma which the opponent derived from the two alternatives of knowability and unknowability of the substrate of the absolute absence of knowability. By taking into account both alternatives the opponent admits that an absolute absence need not always have a substrate.

63. over-pervasion with regard to knowability

64. According to the respondent an absolute absence need not have a substrate. So, no contradiction can be derived from the assumption of there being such an absence.

65. If the respondent insists that an absolute absence need not always have a substrate, one might specify the defining characteristic in such a way that absolute absences without a substrate (such as the absolute absence of knowability) are ruled out, although from the point of view of the opponent this is gratuitous, because an absolute absence always has a substrate.

66. This is, of course, only a problem if the suggested general defining characteristic is supposed to be a universal (cf. 1.1.3).

67. A general defining characteristic for the seven categories would distinguish individuals which belong to one of the categories from those which do not belong to any of them. But since every entity is an instance of one of the categories, a defining characteristic with such a demarcating function does not exist. Nevertheless, every individual can be specifically characterized as a substance or as belonging to any other category than "substance".

68. Specific defining characteristics are not produced by a general defining characteristic. The cognition of specific defining characteristics does not depend on the cognition of a general defining characteristic and a general defining characteristic is not the substrate of specific defining characteristics.

69. cf. 1.1.3

70. The respondent agrees that the use of the word "category" is entirely based on specific characteristics, i.e., on the seven categories and their sub-categories. (The category "sound", e.g., is a sub-category of the category "quality".)

71. Unlike the word *upādhi*, which is used in a technical sense in Nyāya, the word *padārtha* has basically a straightforward non-technical meaning. The only part

which might need an explanation is *pada*, but this can be accomplished: "Pāṇini (c. fourth B.C.) defined *pada* or word as that which has either a verbal or a nominal inflection, and, thus apparently used a formal criterion. Gautama, the founder of the Nyāya school of philosophy, also supported this definition and asserted that a *pada* or word is any sound-sequence which has inflection (*vibhakti*)." (Matilal 1990: 400f)

72. There are plenty of individuals which can have the function of an associate condition. (By specifying probans and probandum in a specific defining characteristic of associate conditions in different ways we can come up with infinitely many specific associate conditions.) Therefore, *upādhi* is different from words like *akṣa*. Among other things *akṣa* can mean "axis", "wheel", "cart", "cube" and "eye", but it refers only to finitely many things. The range of objects which can be associate conditions is much wider and it is impossible to derive the application of the word *upādhi* from a finite set of criteria. (A *vyutpatti* is probably always based on such a finite set of criteria. The application of the word *padārtha*, e.g., is like that of the word *akṣa* based on finitely many criteria, namely on the seven categories.)

73. In paragraph 1.1.3 the opponent had already dismissed such a property as a defining characteristic of associate conditions, because it would apply to the China rose, which he does not regard as an associate condition.

74. Now, the opponent suggests another defining characteristic, namely the one enunciated by Udayana (cf. Kir: 564, 1, ĀTV: 163, 13, NKus: 352, 1 and NVTP: 704, 6f). It is important to note that the opponent regards it as a general defining characteristic, from which a specific defining characteristic can be derived via instantiation.

75. Although the opponent admits circular residence relations, he excludes circularities with regard to cognitive and causal processes (cf. 1.1.2.4). Therefore, the respondent has a good point in criticizing the general defining characteristic suggested by the opponent. The cognition of this defining characteristic depends on itself if we assume that pervasion is a relation without an associate condition. One can also say that there is a mutual dependence between the cognition of an associate condition and the cognition of the suggested defining characteristic. Moreover, the defect of circularity is involved, because the cognition of the suggested defining characteristic depends on the cognition of the state of being devoid of an associate condition, which depends on the cognition of an associate condition, which depends on the cognition of the suggested defining characteristic.

76. The significance of the following quotation in the present context is explained in the introduction (cf. chapter 1, section 1.6.1.5).

77. I understand *tarka* here in the sense of the so-called "unfavorable" *tarka* (*pratikūlatarka*), i.e., in the sense of a reductio ad absurdum which functions as an inferential blocker (cf. Phillips 2002: 94).

78. TR: 234f (v. 90)

79. The respondent wants to show that one can easily read the defect of an undue narrowness into Udayana's definition if one understands it in the sense of a general defining characteristic. Udayana's definition is, of course, not meant in the sense that something which functions as a probandum in one invalid inference $\mathcal{I}_1$ and which is pervaded by an associate condition u_1 must also be pervaded by an associate condition u_2 vitiating an invalid inference $\mathcal{I}_2$ where it functions as a probans. If u_2 fulfills Udayana's criteria with respect to probans and probandum in $\mathcal{I}_2$, it would nevertheless be ruled out as an associate condition according to the respondent, because u_2 fails to pervade the probandum in $\mathcal{I}_1$ (which is the probans in $\mathcal{I}_2$ and which is therefore not pervaded by u_2). The respondent deliberately misunderstands Udayana's definition in the sense that a certain probandum in an invalid inference should be pervaded by an associate condition in any other invalid inference, no matter whether it might function as a probans or as a probandum in that inference.

80. The property of being different from the subject of the inference does not pervade the probans, because the subject of the inference has been established as a locus of the probans. Moreover, in the case of a positive and negative inference there is inductive support for the pervasion of the probandum by the *pakṣetaratva*, since the sample of positive examples can also be regarded as a sample exemplifying the co-occurrence of the probandum and the *pakṣetaratva.* Therefore, the respondent is somehow justified in regarding the property of being different from the subject of the inference as an associate condition according to Udayana's defining characteristic. It could, however, be used as a vitiator of any positive and negative inference. The respondent has cooked up a kind of knock-out argument on the basis of Udayana's defining charactersitic. "It is as though the problem of the fallibility of inductive generalization has been distilled as a universal *upādhi.*" (Phillips 2002: 43f) However, the respondent's claim that the *pakṣetaratva* vitiates all inferences seems to be unwarranted. Only positive inferences are immune to such a vitiator.

81. If the pervasion of the probandum by the associate condition is required to be positive and negative, the property of being different from the subject of the inference is ruled out as an associate condition, because the only potential locus of a co-absence of the probandum and the property of being different from the subject of the inference is the subject of the inference. But since the subject of

the inference is an open issue, there is no inductive support for a pervasion of the absence of the property of being different from the subject of the inference (which is identical to the property of being the subject of the inference) by the absence of the probandum.

82. The purpose of the word *mātra* is probably to point out that the pervasion of the probandum by an associate condition should be understood in accordance with the concepts of pervader and pervaded in inferences in general, not only in positive and negative inferences. A pervasion as in the case of an only positive inference should not be excluded.

83. With respect to inferences like "Fire is not hot, since it is a product, like a pot" (cf. Phillips 2002: 44) the property of being different from the subject of the inference can be said to function as a so-called "associate condition which is induced by a patent falsehood" (*bādhonnītopādhi*), which should not be ruled out as an associate condition. The absence of the negative pervasion of the probandum by the property of being different from the subject of the inference is inevitable in this case, since fire is the only entity which is hot.

84. The opponent is probably referring to the defining characteristic without the specification *sādhyena sahānvayavyatirekavyāptimattvam*. This defining characteristic would also apply to the property of being different from the subject of the inference, which could then be used to vitiate the valid inference of fire from smoke on the mountain, i.e., it could be used to demonstrate that there is no fire on the mountain.

85. Since the *pakṣetaratva* knocks out valid inferences, one should have a defining characteristic which excludes it, but Udayana's defining characteristic without the requirement of a positive and negative pervasion of the probandum by the associate condition does not serve this purpose.

86. Since the opponent is so concerned about safeguarding the defining characteristic against the applicability to a universal vitiator, one might as well stop trying to characterize the associate condition as a vitiator. However, without any identifying characterization of an associate condition it will be difficult to eliminate the doubt concerning the genuineness of a probans.

87. A blatantly invalid inference like "Fire is not hot, because it is a product" indicates that the purported pervasion does not obtain, i.e., that the assumed probans deviates from the assumed probandum. Hence, in this case the function of indicating a deviation can be attributed to to an inference rather than to an associate condition.

88. The opponent probably means this concession to the respondent in the sense that at least the property of being different from the subject of the inference and of being induced by a patent falsehood should be accepted as an associate condition.

89. The property of being different from the subject of the inference and of being induced by a patent falsehood also indicates the absence of the assumed probandum in a locus of its own absence, viz. on the subject of the inference.

90. There is no positive correlation between the defining characteristic suggested by the opponent and the associate condition which consists in the property of being different from the subject of the inference and of being induced by a patent falsehood. Such an associate condition can only be accepted as an exceptional case.

91. i.e., an object which matches the modified version of Udayana's defining characteristic

92. The respondent questions the utility of a defining characteristic of the associate condition. He maintains that one agrees to the presence of an associate condition and a deviation without "bringing them to the fore" by means of a defining characteristic. After all, the devastating property of being different from the subject of the inference in general (*pakṣetaratva*) cannot be excluded from the scope of such a defining characteristic. Even the opponent's modification of Udayana's defining characteristic does not yield the desired result, as the respondent is going to show in the next sentence.

93. The specification *sādhyena sahānvayavyatirekavyāptimattvam* is not a means to get rid of the property of being different from the subject of the inference as a potential associate condition. Since this property cannot be a locus of itself, it must be a locus of its own absence. (Otherwise, we would be faced with the defect of self-dependence.) So, the negative variant of the pervasion of the probandum by the property of being different from the subject of the inference is attested by loci of their co-absence which are different from the subject of the inference.

94. Udayana's defining characteristic (even when modified in the way suggested by the opponent) would also apply to the property of being an agreeing instance of a valid positive and negative inference, because in this case there is positive and negative inductive support for the pervasion of the probandum by the property of being an agreeing instance. Moreover, the latter does not pervade the probans, which resides in the subject of the inference, where the property of being an agreeing instance does not occur.

In contrast to the property of being different from the subject of the inference the property "being an agreeing instance" is also absent from other places than the subject of the inference if the inference is positive and negative. In this case there is also a negative pervasion of the probandum by this property in the realm of disagreeing instances.

95. Even if Udayana's defining characteristic is modified in such a way that the property of being different from the subject of the inference is excluded as a potential substrate, it would still apply to the property of being an agreeing instance, because it pervades the probandum. Only the subject of the inference is excluded by the requirement that the associate condition should not pervade the probans. So, the associate condition would be a kind of property of being different from the subject of the inference in the range of the properties of agreeing instances. An example of such an associate condition might be the property of being produced by a body (*śarīrajanyatva*) with regard to a Nyāya argument for the existence of God, which we will simply call "the design inference", although, properly speaking, it is both, a cosmological argument and an argument from design (cf. Patil 2009: 33 and 57f): *kṣityādikaṃ sakartṛkaṃ kāryatvāt.* – "The earth etc. have a creator, because they are products." (Cf. Frauwallner 1970: 15, 23f and 17, 8) *ādi* ("etc.") refers here to entities like growing grass or a big tree, which are like the earth not produced by any visible agent (cf. Potter 1977: 103f, Patil 2009: 141f, Phillips 2012: 68 and Phillips 2017b: 551). Following Gaṅgeśa, we may understand "being produced" (*kāryatva*) in the sense of a property of a positive effect, i.e., something previously non-existent which is not a posterior absence. In the technical language of the Naiyāyikas the loci of this property can be described as "counterpositives of prior absences which inhere in something" (cf. Bhattacharyya/Potter 1993: 215). The purpose of the inherence-condition is to exclude the non-inhering posterior absences. Since *kāryatva* expresses only the transient character of the positive entity in which it resides, it cannot be said to be trivially pervaded by "having a causal agent" (*sakartṛkatva*).

According to Gaṅgeśa the design inference seems to be refutable by means of a so-called "dubious associate condition" (*saṃdigdhopādhi*), namely the property of being produced by a body (cf. Frauwallner 1970: 59). Naiyāyikas hold that the earth has a creator, who may assume a body for certain purposes, but is "essentially bodiless" (Phillips 2012: 70). So, from a Nyāya perspective the non-pervasion of the probans by the associate condition is warranted in this case. However, everything which has a causal agent may or may not have an embodied agent. Both possibilities are apparently equally matched. A pot, e.g., does have an embodied causal agent, namely the potter. The earth may or may not be a counter-example. Therefore, the pervasion of the probandum seems doubtful in this case. However, according to Gaṅgeśa a dubious associate condition can function as a vitiator as well. In order to secure the design inference in Nyāya he tries to refute the purported pervasion of the probandum by the property of being produced by a body (cf. Vattanky 1984: 146f, Phillips 2012: 69 and Phillips 2017b: 551f). The UD pursues a different strategy: Since according to the UD the associate condition should also be pervaded by the probandum, the author tries to demonstrate that "being produced by a body" is in fact only an apparent associate condition, since it lacks the pervadedness-property (cf. 1.2.2.2).

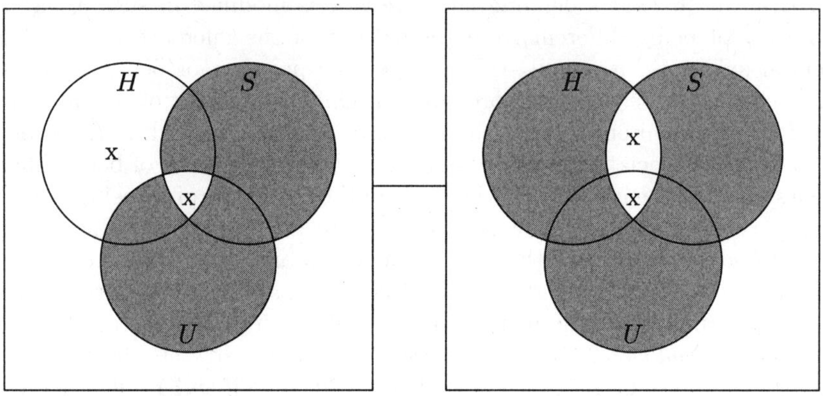

Fig. 3

H = the class of loci of the probans *kāryatva*
S = the class of loci of the probandum *sakartṛkatva*
U = the class of loci of the associate condition *śarīrajanyatva*

kṣityādi $\in H \setminus (S \cup U)$, or *kṣityādi* $\in (H \cap S) \setminus U$; *ghaṭa* $\in H \cap S \cap U$

In accordance with a convention introduced by Sun-Joo Shin the straight line between both diagrams in Fig. 3 means "or" (cf. Shin et al. 2018). If *śarīrajanyatva* is admitted as a doubtful associate condition, the earth (*kṣiti*), growing grass etc. may or may not be elements of $(H \cap S) \setminus U$. Hence, this class may or may not be empty, i.e., the probandum may or may not be pervaded by the associate condition. If the earth, growing grass etc. are products without a corporeal agent, they may well be elements of $H \setminus (S \cup U)$. In this case *kāryatva* is not pervaded by *sakartṛkatva* and *śarīrajanyatva* fulfills the criteria of an associate condition.

An opponent in Gaṅgeśa's Īśvaravāda argues that the design inference does not prove that the earth is the product of a single causal agent, i.e., a sovereign creator, since *sakartṛkatva* can also be understood in the sense of collective agency, as in the case of an anthill or a palace (cf. Bhattacharyya/Potter 1993: 223f). Ratnakīrti, e.g., is a proponent of this argument against the design inference in Nyāya (cf. Patil 2009: 168f). However, according to Gaṅgeśa's *siddhāntin* the possibility of collective agency, which is admittedly included in the probandum of the design inference, can be ruled out by taking into account the principle of parsimony (cf. ibid.).

96. The subject of the inference is excluded as a substrate of the property of possessing the probandum with certainty, but it is not excluded as a *potential* substrate of the probandum. So, it cannot be a disagreeing instance. "Being a disagreeing instance" is excluded "by means of the word 'probandum' alone", i.e., by the word "probandum" without the specification "ascertained". Therefore, one can say that whatever exhibits the probandum, exhibits the absence of the property of being a disagreeing instance. However, one cannot say that whatever exhibits the probandum, exhibits the property of being an agreeing instance.

97. The property of being an agreeing instance is not an associate condition according to Udayana's (original or modified) defining characteristic, because the pervasion of the probandum does not exclude the subject of the inference as a potential substrate of the probandum. It excludes only the disagreeing instances. According to the opponent the property of being an agreeing instance applies only to ascertained occurrences of the probandum. Therefore, it does not reside in the subject of the inference and, hence, it cannot be said to pervade the probandum.

98. The property of being different from the subject of the inference and of being induced by a patent falsehood has to be included in the definition.

99. Since everything apart from fire is not hot, the property of being not hot would be universal if fire were also a substrate of it. So, the property of being different from the subject of the inference is needed as an associate condition which vitiates such an inference, and for that purpose it has to pervade the probandum in the sense suggested by the respondent, i.e., in such a way that a pervasion is possible, even if it excludes the subject of the inference.

100. The defect of the above-mentioned invalid inference is rather a violation of the inferential-subject-proviso (*pakṣatā*), since the probandum does not have the characteristic of being a property of the subject of the inference (*pakṣadharmatvalakṣaṇa*). This characteristic consists in being a property whose residence in the subject of the inference is an open issue.

101. Adherents of Advaita have no doubts about the result of the application of a knowledge source which reveals the true nature of the phenomenal world. In inferences of this kind the residence of the probandum in the subject of the inference is supposed to be an indisputable fact. An example from Śaṅkara's Upaniṣadbhāṣya is the following *prapañcamithyātvānumāna*: *jāgraddṛśyānāṃ bhāvānāṃ vaitathyam iti pratijñā. dṛśyatvād iti hetuḥ. svapnadṛśyabhāvavad iti dṛṣṭāntaḥ. yathā tatra svapne dṛśyānāṃ bhāvānāṃ vaitathyaṃ tathā jāgarite 'pi dṛśyatvam aviśiṣṭam iti hetūpanayaḥ. tasmāj jāgarite 'pi vaitathyaṃ smṛtam iti nigamanam.* (UBh: 255, 3f) – "The thesis is: 'The entities which one sees while being awake are unreal.'

The reason is: 'Because they are visible.' The example is: 'Like an entity which is visible in one's sleep.' The application to the probans is: 'In the same way as entities which are visible in that case, [i.e.] in one's sleep, are unreal, so is the visibility not different [from that], when one is awake.' The conclusion is: 'Therefore, one remembers the unreality also when being awake.'"

102. The respondent replaces the opponent's characterization of a probandum as a property whose residence in the subject of the inference is in doubt with a characteristic which attaches potential doubts concerning the residence relation to the situation of the cognizing subject. The latter might not yet or no more perceive the probandum, or the probandum is just too far from the cognizing subject to be directly perceivable, but it is, will be, or was nevertheless definitely present on the subject of the inference.

103. i.e., an associate condition whose defining characteristic does not contain the specification *pakṣetaratvānyatve sati*

104. literally: "because there is no amounting to a proof in the sense that ..."

105. The validity of an inference depends on a pervasion. The fact that one has chosen an appropriate subject of the inference and that the probans is a property of this subject is not enough. The inference "Fire is not hot, because it is an object" fails, because there is no pervasion of the probans by the probandum and the only way to demonstrate this is by means of the associate condition "being a property which is different from the subject of the inference". Therefore, it should not be ruled out as an associate condition by inserting the specification *pakṣetaratvānyatve sati* in the defining characteristic.

106. According to Mallināthasūri there should be a passage in the Ātmatattvaviveka where Udayana refers indirectly (*bhaṅgyantareṇa*) to this definition (cf. NiṣK: 68, 13f: *atrāpi sādhanāvyāpakatve sati sādhyasamavyāpakatvam eva bhaṅgyantareṇoktaṃ tad etad ātmatattvaviveke 'py uktam ity āha. anyatrāpī-ti.*) Unfortunately, we did not find any such textual evidence. As confirmed by the above-mentioned references, it seems that Udayana rather favored the defining characteristic *sādhanāvyāpakatve sati sādhyavyāpakatvam.* The present defining characteristic was, however, definitely enunciated by Śivādityamiśra (cf. SP: 70, 22: *upādhiś ca sādhanāvyāpakatve sati sādhyasamavyāptiḥ.*).

107. cf. 1.1.6.1

108. cf. 1.1.6.2

109. Not every property of being different from the subject of the inference can be an associate condition, only the one which is induced by a patent falsehood.

110. This might refer to the impossibility of characterizing the associate condition in such a way that the property of being different from the subject of the inference is ruled out as an associate condition. Various attempts of the opponent to specify the defining characteristic in an appropriate way (by inserting such phrases as *sādhyena sahānvayavyatirekavyāptimattvam* or *pakṣetaratvānyatve sati*) have been proved to be ineffective.

111. i.e., a pervasion of that which is different from the subject of the inference by the defining characteristic

112. Valid inferences, such as the stock example of the inference of fire from smoke on a mountain, could be refuted by means of an associate condition which pervades the probandum coextensively. In the case of the fire-smoke-example the property of possessing fire residing in something which is different from the mountain might be regarded as an associate condition, because the probandum can be said to be pervaded by this property if the subject of the inference is bracketed. Another example is just indicated here, namely an inference which contains the thesis "Sound is nameable". We might think of knowability as an appropriate probans in this case. The property of being different from sound would be an associate condition which can be said to pervade the probandum coextensively if the subject of the inference is bracketed.

113. According to Vaiśeṣika ontology the specific qualities of earth atoms are non-eternal, as opposed to the specific qualities of other kinds of atoms (cf. Frauwallner 1956: 84).

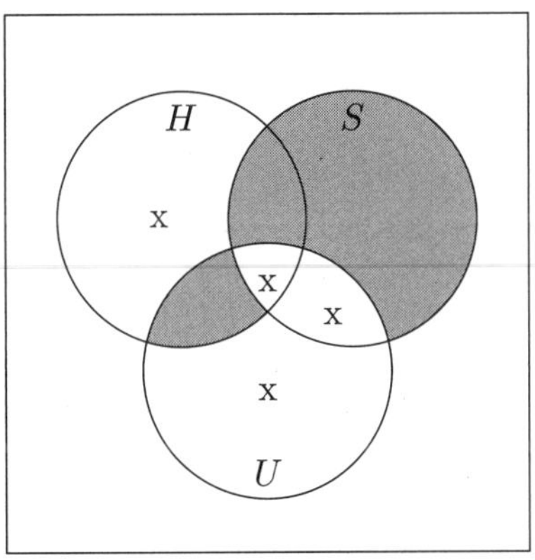

Fig. 4

H = the class of loci of the probans *paramāṇuviśeṣaguṇatva*
S = the class of loci of the probandum *nityatva*
U = the class of loci of the associate condition *pārthivaparamāṇuviśeṣaguṇatvābhāva*

pārthivaparamāṇurūpa $\in H \setminus (S \cup U)$; *āpyaparamāṇurūpa* $\in H \cap S \cap U$; *ākāśa* $\in (S \cap U) \setminus H$; *ghaṭa* $\in U \setminus (H \cup S)$

114. This associate condition resides also in non-eternal entities like a pot.

115. The property of not being fire is an associate condition with respect to the inference "Fire is not hot, because it is an object".

116.

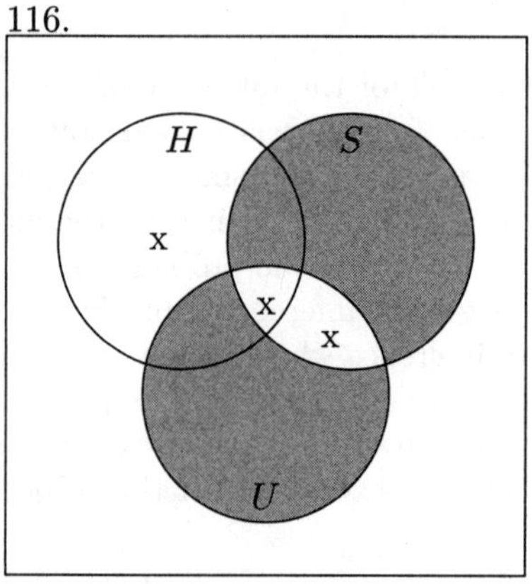

Fig. 5

H = the class of loci of the probans *hiṃsātva*
S = the class of loci of the probandum *adharmatva* or *pāpasādhanatva*
U = the class of loci of the associate condition *niṣiddhatva*

yāgīyahiṃsā $\in H \setminus (S \cup U)$; *brāhmaṇaghāta* $\in H \cap S \cap U$; forbidden offences other than *hiṃsā* $\in (S \cap U) \setminus H$

117. *adharmasādhanatva* and *pāpasādhanatva* (as in the original formulation of the inference) have roughly the same meaning.

118. Wherever the probans (viz. the property of being an injury) and the associate condition (viz. the property of being forbidden) "coexist", there is the probandum (viz. the property of causing harm or bringing about guilt). Such a locus of the coexistence of probans plus associate condition with the probandum exemplifies the transmission-function of the associate condition.

119. The respondent tried to explain what it means to indicate a deviation: *etatsādhanam etatsādhyavyabhicāry etatsādhyavyāpakavyabhicāritvāt prameyavad.* – "This probans deviates from this probandum, because it deviates from something which pervades this probandum, such as in the case of (the given) object of cognition." This is obviously an inference. Therefore, one should rather say that such a knowledge source functions as a vitiator. The word *ādi* which is here attached to *prameyatva* might refer to cases where the deviation is doubtful (*saṃdigdha*).

120. i.e., the above-mentioned inference

121. The respondent justified the assumption of an associate condition with non-coextensive pervasion on the basis that it indicates a deviation. Since this justification has been scotched by the opponent, one should rather give up the idea of an associate condition with non-coextensive pervasion.

122. A deviation is not a phenomenon which comes to one's mind spontaneously. There should be something which indicates it.

123. i.e., in the manner of a defining characteristic for associate conditions with coextensive and non-coextensive pervasion

124. If the associate condition is supposed to pervade the joint occurrence of probans and probandum coextensively, then the defining characteristic would fail to capture those legitimate cases of an associate condition where this pervasion is non-coextensive. The respondent refers here to a defining characteristic which is also mentioned by Gaṅgeśa in his Upādhivāda (cf. Frauwallner 1970: 11, [§3] 33): *sādhanāvacchinnasādhyavyāpakatve sati sādhanāvyāpaka upādhiḥ.* – "The associate condition does not pervade the probans, while it pervades the probandum limited by the probans." According to Frauwallner this defining characteristic is a precursor of the one which Gaṅgeśa cites in the Ataevacatuṣṭayaprakaraṇa of the Anumānakhaṇḍa of his Tattvacintāmaṇi and which commentators attribute to Prabhākara Upādhyāya (cf. Frauwallner 1965: 200 and 205): *sādhanatāvacchedakabhinnena yena sādhanatābhimate sādhyasaṃbandho 'vacchidyate sa eva tatra sādhane viśeṣaṇam upādhiḥ.* – "Whereby the relation with the probandum with respect to that which is assumed as the probans is limited, while it is different from a limitor of the probansness, that is in that case an associate condition, [i.e.] a qualifier with respect to the probans."

Hereafter, we will refer to the above-mentioned precursor of Prabhākara Upādhyāya's defining characteristic as the "proto-version of Prabhākara Upādhyāya's defining characteristic". According to Frauwallner (cf. 1965: 203f), it probably inspired Prabhākara Upādhyāya to design a defining characteristic based on the concept of a limitor (*avacchedaka*). As the direct source of inspiration for Prabhākara

Upādhyāya's defining characteristic, however, Frauwallner mentions another one (cf. 1965: 205), viz. the one which the UD attributes to Śivādityamiśra in section 1.1.10 and which is based on the concept of a relation (*saṃbandha*).

125. The associate condition with non-coextensive pervasion according to the proto-version of Prabhākara Upādhyāya's defining characteristic can also be pervaded by the probandum in the range of the probans. Then there would be a coextensive pervasion of the probandum by the associate condition in the range of the probans. But the joint occurrence of probans and probandum need not pervade the associate condition as a whole. The proto-version of Prabhākara Upādhyāya's defining characteristic does not exclude a non-coextensive pervasion of the joint occurrence of probans and probandum by the associate condition.

126. i.e., in the probans without the associate condition

127. This defining characteristic is mentioned and rejected by Maṇikaṇṭha (cf. NR: 73, 1f and 88, 8 – 89, 10). As noted above, the UD attributes it to Śivādityamiśra and it was probably the direct inspirational source for Prabhākara Upādhyāya's defining characteristic. Hereafter, we will refer to it as the "nutshell version of Prabhākara Upādhyāya's defining characteristic".

Pervading the "relation" (*saṃbandha*) between probans and probandum is to be understood here in the sense of a pervasion of the property of being a common locus of probans and probandum, which is tantamount to a pervasion of the probandum limited by the probans. Thus, the present defining characteristic is basically a paraphrase of the above-mentioned proto-version of Prabhākara Upādhyāya's defining characteristic (cf. Frauwallner 1965: 203).

128. The subject of the inference seems to be unspecified in this example. As far as we can determine from the probans, it should be a relation, because the subject of the inference is supposed to be a locus of the probans "relationness". The probandum is the property of being a relatum (and, hence, a locus) of inherence. The probans "relationness" is not pervaded by the probandum, because inherence is a locus of the probans, but not a locus of the probandum. Inherence does not reside in itself (cf. Fig. 6). The associate condition consists in certain properties which reside in a contact (and in some other loci as well) via inherence. The locus of the probans "relationness" and of any of these properties must be contact. Inherence is excluded, because it is not a locus of effectness, beingness and contactness. So, the associate condition pervades the realm of the joint occurrence of probans and probandum. However, the associate condition does not pervade the probandum as a whole, because inherence resides also in "beingness", which is not a locus of any of the properties which constitute the associate condition.

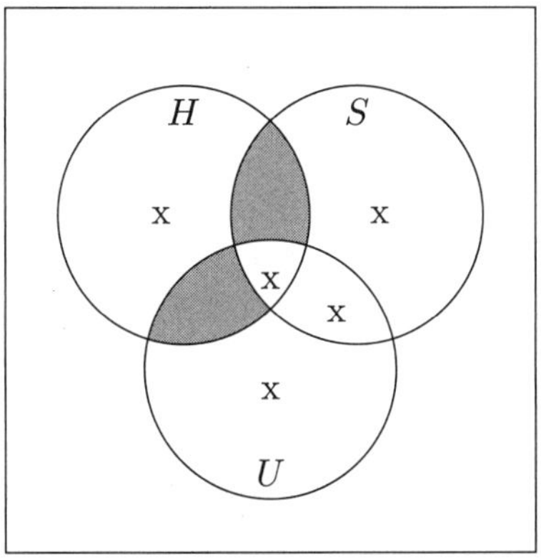

Fig. 6

H = the class of loci of the probans *saṃbandhatva*

S = the class of loci of the probandum *samavāyādhikaraṇatva*

U = the class of loci of the associate condition *saṃyoganiṣṭhadharmavattva* ("being a locus of properties which reside in contact")

samavāya $\in H \setminus (S \cup U)$; *sattā* $\in S \setminus (H \cup U)$; *saṃyoga* $\in H \cap S \cap U$; *ghaṭa* $\in (S \cap U) \setminus H$; *ghaṭābhāva* $\in U \setminus (H \cup S)$

129. According to the present defining characteristic the associate condition pervades only the realm of the joint occurrence of probans and probandum.

130. x is a locus of the absence of "the relation between probans and probandum", i.e., of the property of being a common locus of probans and probandum *iff* $\neg(Hx \wedge Sx)$, where Hx translates into "x is a locus of the probans" and Sx translates into "x is a locus of the probandum". This absence "is possible in three ways", since $\neg(Hx \wedge Sx) \leftrightarrow (\neg Hx \wedge Sx) \vee (Hx \wedge \neg Sx) \vee (\neg Hx \wedge \neg Sx)$.

131. The opponent advocates here the nutshell version of Prabhākara Upādhyāya's defining characteristic. Since the respondent had objected against Udayana's defining characteristic with coextensive pervasion that it does not cover cases which are included in the nutshell version of Prabhākara Upādhyāya's defining characteristic, the latter seems preferable.

Oddly enough, the UD attributes the nutshell version of Prabhākara Upādhyāya's defining characteristic to Śivādityamiśra, who advocates another defining characteristic in his Saptapadārthī, viz. the one mentioned in 1.1.7f: *sādhanāvyāpakatve sati sādhyasamavyāpakatvam.* (SP: 70, 22)

132. In the case of the inference "Fire is not hot, because it is produced", e.g., the property of being different from the subject of the inference pervades the realm of the joint occurrence of probans and probandum non-coextensively: Whatever

is produced and not hot, is different from the subject of the inference. The ether, which is different from the subject of the inference, is not a locus of the joint occurrence of probans and probandum, because it is not produced.

133. The subject of the inference is again unspecified in this example. As far as we can determine from the probans, it should be something which is created. Since probans and probandum exclude each other in this example, the probans is here a special type of "pseudo-probans" (*hetvābhāsa*), viz. the "incoherent" (*viruddha*) probans.

134. An associate condition is not needed for the purpose of refuting the above-mentioned inference, because its invalidity ensues from a pseudo-probans.

135. The defining characteristic which requires a pervasion of the relation between probans and probandum fails to apply to the case of an incoherent probans. According to the respondent it is too narrow, i.e., "over-pervaded" by certain cases of associate conditions, because the fallacy should be owing to an associate condition. He claims that any defect of an assumed pervasion ultimately boils down to the presence of an associate condition. The opponent's defining characteristic proves to be too narrow when in a public debate the incoherence of a probans in an inference of the proponent is pointed out by the opponent and the audience probes into the ultimate reason for the purported defect of the probans.

136. So, if there is an associate condition (according to the present defining characteristic), then there is a deviation, i.e., the probans co-occurs with both, the probandum and the absence of the probandum. In this sense there is a positive correlation between an associate condition and a deviation. However, the property of being an associate condition lacks the property of "having the form of", i.e., of being tailored to exceptional cases of a deviation in which probans and probandum are mutually exclusive properties.

137. As explained above, a mere deviation cannot be detected by means of perception. So, there would be nothing which indicates a deviation if there were no associate condition which might serve this purpose.

138. If the word "relation" in the defining characteristic of an associate condition is supposed to refer to a pervasion, then the assumed probans would be pervaded by the assumed probandum and it would not make any sense to try to vitiate an inference by means of an associate condition. Every inference would be based on a genuine pervasion, i.e., a relation without associate condition.

139.

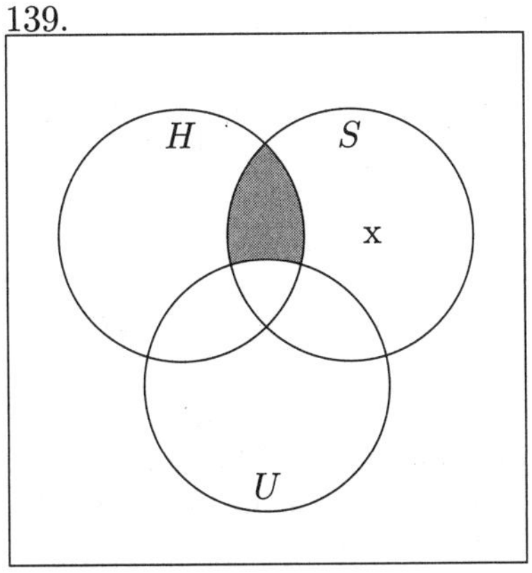

Fig. 7

H = the class of loci of the probans
S = the class of loci of the probandum
U = the class of loci of the associate condition

$H \cap S$ is the class of the loci of a mere co-occurrence (*sāmānādhikaraṇyamātra*) of probans and probandum. As indicated by the "x" here, the absence of the associate condition might co-occur with the probandum in this case.

140. According to the present defining characteristic of an associate condition the absence of the associate condition might, in fact, not entail the absence of every instance of the probandum, but it does entail the absence of every instance of the probandum which co-occurs with an instance of the probans.

141. Instead of explicating the term "relation" in the nutshell version of Prabhākara Upādhyāya's defining characteristic, one can as well endorse the proto-version of Prabhākara Upādhyāya's defining characteristic. The absence of an associate condition according to the nutshell version of Prabhākara Upādhyāya's defining characteristic entails the absence of the probandum in the range of the probans, which is "indistinguishable" from the absence engendered by the absence of an associate condition according to the proto-version of Prabhākara Upādhyāya's defining characteristic.

142. The absence of the probandum, which is related to the absence of the associate condition, is qualified as an absence in the range of the probans.

143. i.e., the nutshell version of Prabhākara Upādhyāya's defining characteristic

144. i.e., the proto-version of Prabhākara Upādhyāya's defining characteristic

145. The expression *tādṛśapakṣetaratva* might refer to a property of loci which exhibit the joint occurrence of probans and probandum in the range of loci which are different from the inferential subject. *tādṛśapakṣetaratva* would then pervade the probandum limited by the probans and might therefore be regarded as an associate condition according to the proto-version of Prabhākara Upādhyāya's defining characteristic.

146. The present defining characteristic is also mentioned by Jānakīnātha in a *pūrvapakṣa* (cf. NSM: 132, 8). A similar defining characteristic, which is discussed by Gaṅgeśa, contains the phrase "limited by the probans or by a property of the subject of the inference" (cf. Frauwallner 1970: 9 [§1b], 19, 36f and Phillips 2002: 38f, 71f). Gaṅgeśa motivates this formulation by means of an example which is similar to the one referred to by the respondent below. So, it seems that what the latter means here by "limited by a certain qualifier" can be understood in terms of Gaṅgeśa's more explicit formulation.

147. The formulation of the example is literally the same as in NK: *sparśanapratyakṣo vāyur upalabhyamānasparśādhiṣṭhānatvād ghaṭavad ity anumānaṃ śaśādiṣu paśutvena śṛṅgānumānavad anupalabdhibādhitam. dravyasya sparśanatvaṃ cākṣuṣatvena vyāptam avagataṃ ghaṭādiṣu …* (NK: 46, 7f) – "The inference 'Air is tangible and directly perceptible, because it is a substrate of perceptible touch (as a quality), like the pot' is contradicted by non-perception (i.e., by the fact that the subject of the inference is never perceived to be a locus of the probandum), like the inference of horns on a hare etc. by means of the [property of] being a domestic animal. A substance's tangibility (in the realm of the probandum) is understood to be pervaded by visibility in the case of pots etc. …" The inference is invalid, because air cannot be directly perceived according to Vaiśeṣika ontology (cf. Fig. 8). A substance needs to be tangible and visible in order to be directly perceptible (cf. Frauwallner 1958: 32, 176f). Hence, visibility (*cākṣuṣatva*) may function as an associate condition. However, it does not pervade the probandum, because touch (*sparśa*) is also an instance of the probandum, but it is not visible. Yet, within the realm of the probandum (which excludes entities like the air) visibility does pervade a substance's tangibility. So, one might restrict the realm of individuals pervaded by the associate condition to instances of substanceness. The associate condition would then pervade the probandum limited by a property of the subject of the inference, because air possesses substanceness. Visibility is here an associate condition according to the present definition (with *dravyatva* functioning as the *viśeṣaṇa*) as well as according to the proto-version of Prabhākara Upādhyāya's defining characteristic.

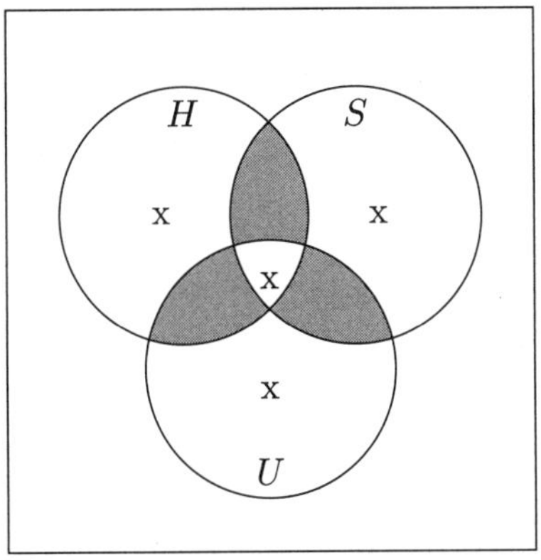

Fig. 8

H = the class of loci of the probans *upalabhyasparśādhiṣṭhanatva*
S = the class of loci of the probandum *sparśanapratyakṣatva*
U = the class of loci of the associate condition *cākṣuṣatva*
$H \cap S \cap U$ = the class of loci of *pratyakṣadravyatva*

vāyu $\in H \setminus (S \cup U)$; *sparśa* $\in S \setminus (H \cup U)$; *rūpa* $\in U \setminus (H \cup S)$; *ghaṭa* $\in H \cap S \cap U$

148. Where there is a substance's tangibility within the realm of the probandum "being directly perceptible" (which excludes air), there is visibility. In substances where there is no visibility and which are distinct from air, there is no tangibility.

In a slightly modified version of this inference cited by Frauwallner touch is an instance of both, the probans and the probandum (cf. Fig. 9): *vāyuḥ pratyakṣaḥ, tvagindriyagrāhyadharmavattvāt, sparśavat.* (Frauwallner 1970: 37) – "Air is directly perceptible, because it possesses a property which can be grasped by means of the sense organ 'skin', like touch." An appropriate associate condition is supposed to be "possession of colour in a distinct form" (*udbhūtarūpavattva*), a property which is present only in aggregates of earth-, water- and fire-atoms, whereas the colour of single atoms is regarded as imperceptible in Vaiśeṣika. Since touch possesses touchness, it possesses a property which can be grasped by means of the sense organ "skin". But then, the associate condition "possession of colour in a distinct form" fails to pervade an instance of the probandum limited by the probans, namely touch. In this case the present definition of an associate condition does apply (with *dravyatva* functioning again as the *viśeṣaṇa*), whereas the proto-version of Prabhākara Upādhyāya's defining characteristic (which posits the pervasion of the probandum limited by the probans) does not.

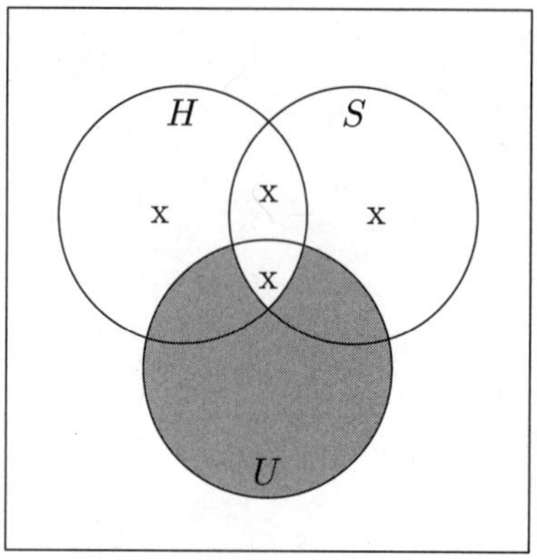

Fig. 9

H = the class of loci of the probans *tvagindriyagrāhyadharmavattva*
S = the class of loci of the probandum *pratyakṣatva*
U = the class of loci of the associate condition *udbhūtarūpavattva*
$H \cap S \cap U$ = the class of loci of *pratyakṣadravyatva*

vāyu $\in H \setminus (S \cup U)$; *sparśa* $\in (H \cap S) \setminus U$; *śabda* $\in S \setminus (H \cup U)$; *ghaṭa* $\in H \cap S \cap U$

149. This remark might refer to the defining characteristics which require the associate condition to pervade the probandum limited by the probans or the relation between probans and probandum, respectively.

150. What the respondent observes here, sounds like an anticipation of the distinction between sense and reference or intension and extension in the tradition of Western logic. From an extensional point of view, the present defining characteristic includes the two previously mentioned ones. But intensionally speaking, they are different. The expression *udbhāvanaprakāra* ("mode of bringing to the fore") is reminiscent of Frege's paraphrase of the concept of "sense" ("Art des Gegebenseins", i.e., "mode of givenness", cf. Frege 1986: 41 and Guhe 1996: 223f).

151. A correct inference like the one mentioned here could be undermined by an associate condition which pervades the probandum limited by the property of being either pot or sound as a qualifier of the subject of the inference (cf. Fig. 10). Potness can be regarded as an associate condition according to the present defining characteristic if pervasion is understood as a relation of concomitance which may exclude the subject of the inference. In all loci other than the subject of the inference the property of being either pot or sound co-occurs with potness.

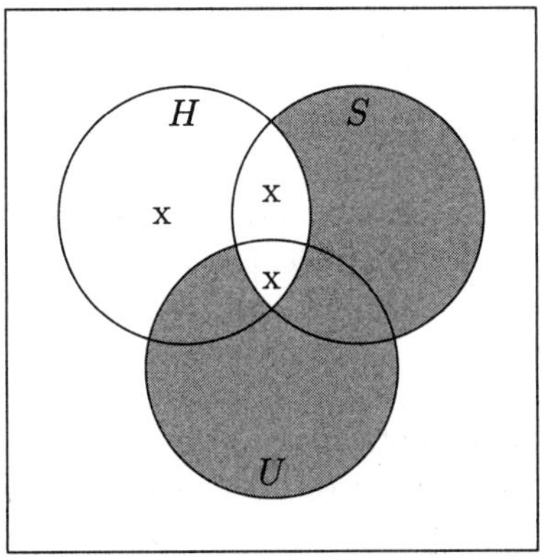

Fig. 10

H = the class of loci of the probans *kṛtakatva*
S = the class of loci of the probandum *anityatva* $\setminus$ {*śabda*}
U = the class of loci of the associate condition *ghaṭatva*
$H \cap S \cap U = U$ = the class of loci $\in S$ qualified by *ghaṭaśabdānyataratva*

śabda $\in H \setminus (S \cup U)$; *paṭa* $\in (H \cap S) \setminus U$; *ghaṭa* $\in H \cap S \cap U$

152. It should be noted that the expression *dṛṣṭānta* can refer to positive and negative examples alike.

153. One can always conceive of an associate condition (according to the present defining characteristic) which consists in a property residing in an agreeing instance (*sapakṣa*), such as potness in the case of the afore-mentioned inference.

154. Since the expression *dṛṣṭānta* can also refer to negative examples, one might as well conceive of an associate condition as a property of a negative example.

155. There would be an associate condition if the probandum "knowability" did not reside in the subject of the inference which the opponent is going to discuss now.

156. i.e., an associate condition which consists in a property residing in a negative example

157. The opponent probably tries to argue here that not all valid inferences can be undermined by an associate condition which consists in a property residing in a negative example. In the present example skyness (*gaganatva*) can be regarded as an associate condition which pervades the probandum limited by a certain qualifier, as will be explained below. The qualifier is the property of being sky or pot (*ghaṭa-gaganānyataratva*) in this case. However, this is a property of a positive example.

In this case there is no associate condition which pervades the probandum limited by a qualifier of a negative example.

158. Since the inference is valid, there should not be any associate condition as an invalidating factor involved in it. However, contrary to the allegation of the opponent, the present defining characteristic would be applicable in this case.

159. Knowability restricted to the disjunctive property "being pot or sky" is pervaded by skyness if we exclude the pot as the subject of the inference from the loci involved in the pervasion. Hence, in all loci except for the pot the absence of skyness entails the absence of knowability restricted to the disjunctive property "being pot or sky" (cf. Fig. 11).

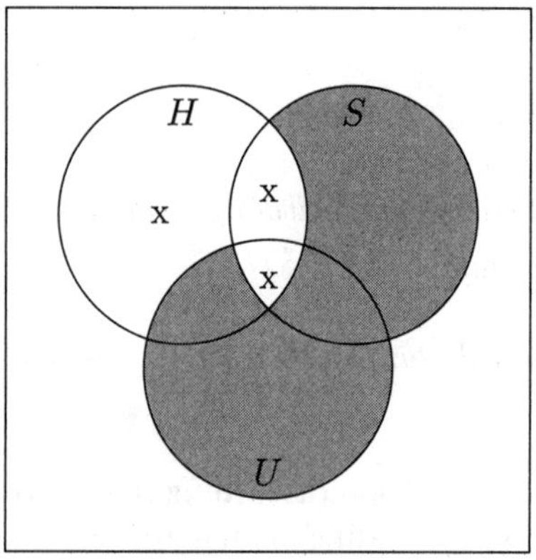

Fig. 11

H = the class of loci of the probans *abhidheyatva*
S = the class of loci of the probandum *prameyatva* $\setminus$ {*ghaṭa*}
U = the class of loci of the associate condition *gaganatva*
$H \cap S \cap U = U$ = the class of loci $\in S$ qualified by *ghaṭagaganānyataratva*

ghaṭa $\in H \setminus (S \cup U)$; *paṭa* $\in (H \cap S) \setminus U$; *gagana* $\in H \cap S \cap U$

160. Since either of the two, i.e., "potness" and "skyness", is referred to by the expression "being pot or sky", either of the two pervades knowability restricted to the disjunctive property "being pot or sky" in an inference in which the respective other one functions as a property of the subject of the inference.

161. First, we prove the absence of knowability restricted to the disjunctive property "being pot or sky" from the sky by means of an inference in which the sky functions as the subject of the inference. Potness is used as an associate condition. Then, we prove the absence of knowability restricted to the disjunctive property "being pot or sky" from the pot by means of an inference in which the pot functions

as the subject of the inference. Skyness is used as an associate condition. Since by means of the first inference we have proved that the sky possesses the absence of knowability restricted to the disjunctive property "being pot or sky", skyness, the associate condition applied to the second inference, is indirectly (i.e., by means of the first proof) established as a property of a disagreeing instance.

162. Instead of the sky one might also have chosen sound as an example in the preceding correct inference "The pot under discussion is knowable, because it is nameable, like the sky". If we agree to the present definition of an associate condition, we might regard sound as an associate condition for the property "knowability", which actually resides in the subject of the inference referred to, for sound pervades knowability restricted to the disjunctive property "being a locus of potness or sound" if we exclude the subject of the inference from the pervasion.

163. Apart from the subject of the inference every locus of knowability restricted to the disjunctive property "being a locus of potness or sound" is a locus of sound. So, in any locus apart from the pot the absence of sound indicates the absence of knowability restricted to the disjunctive property "being a locus of potness or sound".

164. The associate condition is only indirectly knowable, insofar as its absence from the inferential subject indicates the absence of the probandum "knowability".

165. The expression *viśeṣaṇa* in the part *yatkiṃcidviśeṣaṇāvacchinna* of the defining characteristic (see above) is superfluous. One can leave it out.

166. If one leaves out the whole part *yatkiṃcidavacchinna*, one ends up with a defining characteristic which requires the associate condition to pervade the probandum as a whole. This defining characteristic would include all the associate conditions ensuing from both definitions, the one with and the one without *yatkiṃcidavacchinna*.

167. Now, the opponent probably affirms the defining characteristic which requires the associate condition to pervade the probandum as a whole.

168. Although the defining characteristic without the qualifier applies also to associate conditions whose defining characteristic contains the qualifier, the defining characteristic without the qualifier fails to capture the above-mentioned "mode of bringing to the fore" (*udbhāvanaprakāra*) which is expressed by the defining characteristic with the qualifier.

169. The opponent suggests an alternative as a defining characteristic which consists in the one postulating the pervasion of the entire probandum by the as-

sociate condition, the one postulating the associate condition's pervasion of the probandum limited by something and the one postulating the associate condition's pervasion of the relation between probans and probandum.

170. This explication has been analyzed in section 1.6.1.3 of the introduction.

171. The respondent seems to understand the counterpositive *etattraya* here in the sense of any group of three kinds of individuals which are instances of properties p_1, p_2 and p_3, respectively. Specifying this counterpositive in various ways yields a plethora of mutual absences and a plethora of absolute absences of these mutual absences. Each of these absolute absences can be understood as a disjunction of three absolute absences $([\neg\exists y(y = [\neg xLp_1]_x \wedge xLy) \vee \neg\exists y(y = [\neg xLp_2]_x \wedge xLy) \vee \neg\exists y(y = [\neg xLp_3]_x \wedge xLy)]_x)$, such that the absentee of every single one (i.e., of every *ekaikātyantābhāva*) is the mutual absence of one of the three kinds of instances referred to. If the ranges of p_1, p_2 and p_3 are disjoint, the respondent can reasonably claim that any one of these absolute absences resides only in one of the three kinds of instances and not in the other two. Moreover, the meaning of "any one of many" need not be restricted to "any one of three". This is another gateway to a regressus ad infinitum, which is not explicitly mentioned here.

172. If the expression "absolute absence" did refer to a single entity, it would fail to comprehend the abundance of absolute absences which ensues from the fact that one can determine the counterpositive in different ways. Alcohol is also a possible counterpositive.

173. All the defects which were queried with respect to Udayana's defining characteristic (such as, e.g., the defect that the concept of pervasion, which is inherent in his defining characteristic, presupposes the concept of an associate condition) would apply to the present defining characteristic as well.

174. A uniform defining characteristic (instead of a rather patchy one) would probably be more appropriate from the point of view of the respondent.

175. Pervading only the examples amounts to pervading the probandum coextensively if "pervasion" is supposed to refer to a relation of concomitance which may exclude the subject of the inference.

176. i.e., the relation between probandum and associate condition and the relation between probans and associate condition

177. *sādhyavyāpakādi* might refer to the expressions "pervading the probandum", "pervading the probandum limited by the probans", "pervading the proban-

dum limited by a certain qualifier" etc. All these formulations turned out to be problematic. Therefore, the opponent suggests here another possibility.

178. An associate condition's pervasion of the examples might include the mountain in some inferences, but not in others. In the case of the inference "The mountain possesses smoke because of fire, like the kitchen" the mountain is the subject of the inference. So, it is not an example within the range of individuals pervaded by the associate condition "wet fuel". But in the case of the inference "The kitchen possesses smoke because of fire, like the mountain (on which a fire has been sighted)" the mountain is an example within the range of individuals pervaded by the same associate condition.

179. Some associate conditions pervade all examples, such as the associate condition "being forbidden" with reference to the inference "A sacrifical injury brings about guilt, because it is an injury, like an injury for one's own profit".

180. viz. the downscaled variant of the property of being anything different from the inferential subject which is equilocatable with the property of being a positive example

181. *yena* refers to *sa* (the associate condition).

182. *yayoḥ* might refer to *tasmin* (the probans) and *tatra* (the probandum).

183. According to Phillips *anugama* ("uniformity", "consecutive character") is "one of the criteria of a true universal natural kind, *jāti*. Recurrent experience of a property is taken by Naiyāyikas to be evidence that the property is universal." (Phillips 2002: 146)

184. The problem of circularity which we encountered in the case of the old defining characteristics, such as the one enunciated by Udayana, encumbers the present defining characteristic as well, since it is based on the concepts *sahabhāva* and *vyabhicāra*. In order to explicate these concepts we already need to know the defining characteristic of the associate condition.

185. Universal properties such as knowability are counterpositives of a mutual absence, but not of an absolute absence. The eternal substances are counterpositives of an absolute absence, but they are not properties.

186. The "essence" of the associate condition consists in its defining characteristic.

187. *ādi* might refer to *apramā*. The proper identification of an associate condition by means of a general defining characteristic is crucial for distinguishing between veridical and non-veridical awarenesses which have been obtained by means of inferences. Although the only plausible candidate for a defining characteristic turns out to be self-resident, it is nevertheless indispensable as a prerequisite for the identification of an associate condition.

188. *tat* refers to *kasmiṃścit.*

189. If something is identified as an associate condition, there can be no doubt about the defining characteristic whereby it is identified. There is no veridical awareness of an associate condition by means of a bogus defining characteristic. An associate condition as a knowledge source depends for its identification on a defining characteristic. A defining characteristic is similar to a probans in an inference, insofar as it functions as an indicator. If we regard it as obsolete, we might as well say that the distinction between a valid probans and a pseudo-probans is negligible.

190. Something which does not have the property of being a counterpositive of an absolute absence is not an associate condition. Therefore, this property should be part of a defining characteristic of associate conditions.

191. Regarding self-residence as counter-intuitive is a kind of cognitive default of our subjective experience. Hence, encountering such an absurdity might block the process of the identification of an associate condition from the start. Therefore, the problem of the self-residence of the *atyantābhāvapratiyogidharmatva* should be left in abeyance until the identification of the associate condition by means of this defining characteristic is accomplished. The determination of the self-residence concerns a cognizing subject only in hindsight.

192. i.e., the alternative that the *atyantābhāvapratiyogidharmatva* is a substrate of itself

193. As long as one is still in doubt whether the defining characteristic resides in itself, its residence "in one part of its own substrates" (*āśrayaikadeśa*), viz. in itself, is still an open issue.

194. In the present case the thesis features the *atyantābhāvapratiyogidharmatva* as a property of itself as the subject of an inference: The *atyantābhāvapratiyogidharmatva* possesses the *atyantābhāvapratiyogidharmatva*, because it is a property which is a counterpositive of an absolute absence.

195. The property of being a subject of an inference is ascertained by means of the defining characteristic *avyāvṛtter api vyāvṛttyanabhyupagama*, and the property of being a probandum is ascertained by means of the defining characteristic *vipratipannaṃ prati prasādhayitum abhipretatva.*

196. The relation between a defining characteristic and its substrate is similar to that of scales and weights on the one hand, and something which needs to be weighed on the other hand.

197. The defining characteristic is also an associate condition. Therefore, it has to be self-resident. Otherwise, it would be non-pervasive.

198. There is no need to assume an equilocatable property which is different from the *atyantābhāvapratiyogidharmatva* and which functions as a characteristic defining the latter as an associate condition. Since this property would also be an associate condition, we would need another equilocatable property which functions as a characteristic defining that one as an associate condition etc. If we admit the self-residence of the *atyantābhāvapratiyogidharmatva*, we can avoid such a regressus ad infinitum.

199. The application of the expression "associate condition" is not motivated by the activity of transmitting something, but by a defining characteristic which accounts for the vitiating force of an associate condition.

200. The China rose could then be said to be an associate condition in virtue of its function of transmitting its red colour to something.

201. The application of the term "associate condition" cannot be motivated by taking into account a mundane usage which derives from the literal meaning of *upādhi.* An associate condition would then be anything which transmits one of its own properties to something else.

202. The mundane common practice alone cannot account for the associate condition's function to refute an inference.

203. viz. the common practice of refuting an inference

204. If this were a valid inference, the probans "knowability" would have to reside in all things. The totality of all things constitutes the subject of the inference here. However, the opponent tries to argue that knowability is not universally present.

205. *āŕayāsiddha* is a pseudo-probans (*hetvābhāsa*). "The logical defect called *āŕayāsiddhi* (literally, 'lack of a proper substratum') arises if a property is assigned by a sentence to such a locus or substratum as is entirely unknown (to both the speaker and the hearer). The defect is connected with the problem of empty subject term in logic." (Matilal 1990: 182f) The objection refers to the above-mentioned inference "These are all things because of knowability etc.". Only an omniscient being would be able to cognize the probans in the inferential subject, the totality of all things.

206. *kevalānvayidharma*

207. This refers again to the above-mentioned inference "These are all things because of knowability etc.".

208. cf. Apte 1992, s.v. *iṣṭāpatti*: "occurrence of what is desired; a statement by the debater which is favorable to his opponent also"

209. The thesis that there are universally present properties cannot be disproved by means of a reductio argument. Their existence is a logical necessity, since the assumption of the opposite leads to a contradiction, i.e., it is rather the opponent's position which is assailable by means of a reductio argument.

210. The property of not occurring in everything, which the opponent is supposed to accept as a universally positive property, should have the capacity to function as a probandum in an inference with "propertyness" as the probans. However, the opponent claims to have demonstrated that there are no universally positive properties. So, the probans "propertyness" turns out to be a so-called "inconclusive" (*anaikāntika*) pseudo-probans (*hetvābhāsa*), i.e., it seems to admit two contradictory conclusions: Properties are universally positive and they are not.

211. If someone should object that the validity of an only positive inference is inscrutable, because one would have to be omniscient in order to verify whether the concomitance of probans and probandum is universal, a similar objection would strike in the case of a positive and negative inference such as the smoke/fire-example, since nobody has ever verified the co-occurrence of smoke with fire in all other places than the mountain.

212. i.e., for a member which putatively proves the pervasion at issue

213. If the particle *nanu* is not owing to a scribal error here, the following can only be understood as a counterobjection of the *siddhāntin*, since it contradicts the view of the opponent. According to Tubb and Boose counterobjections of the

siddhāntin can be indicated by means of the same catchwords as objections of an opponent (cf. Tubb/Boose 2007: 242).

214. The proponent of the right view is probably referring here (i) to the "sensory connection based on the general character" (*sāmānyalakṣaṇāpratyāsatti*), which admits the perception of all things of a certain kind, and (ii) to the general character of the probans (cf. Chakrabarti 2010: 149f).

215. Collyrium (*āñjana*) is a lotion or liquid wash used as a cleanser for the eyes, particularly in diseases of the eye.

216. The mental impression created by a former perception of black tarnish as a token of silver in one place enables the faculty of sight to identify the material of an object as silver in another place.

217. The opponent seems to be turning the tables here. Now, he endorses the only positive inference, while rejecting the positive and negative one.

218. There is no reason to reject the positive and negative inference, while holding onto the only positive inference, since the process of grasping a pervasion is the same in both cases.

219. If the cognition of a positive correlation pertaining to knowability requires omniscience, one might argue that the same is true of a positive correlation pertaining to the property of possessing smoke. However, grasping such a positive correlation surely does not require omniscience.

220. In order to grasp a positive correlation pertaining to knowability etc. one has to grasp the substrates of knowability etc., i.e., one has to grasp everything.

221. As "a mere sequence of words" the above-mentioned inference for oneself (cf. Potter 1977: 183f and 449) lacks the argumentative force associated with an inference for others.

222. The opponent might be referring here to the probandum as a qualifier of the subject of the inference. An inference as a mere sequence of words does no give a clue to the presence or absence of the probandum on the subject of the inference.

223. The reliability of an inference depends on its capacity to bear up against opposing arguments in a debate.

224. An inference for oneself can, of course, be formulated in the style of an inference for others. But it is still only a means to convince oneself. Hence, it might

lack the argumentative force of an inference for others, which derives from the intersubjective authentication of each member.

225. Although the proponent of the right view holds that knowing every object of a certain kind is not necessary in order to gather some inferential knowledge, he admitted that knowability can function as a probans in an inference, i.e., it should be a property of the subject of the inference and it should be pervaded by the probandum at issue. However, this assumption entails the possibility of an acquaintance with all objects of knowledge.

226. i.e., if the probans is a property of the subject of the inference and if it is also pervaded by the probandum

227. Contrary to what the opponent thinks, knowability is not a counterpositive of an absolute absence.

228. i.e., they can be a counterpositive of an absolute absence

229. Because of counter-examples such as knowability etc. the property of being a counterpositive of an absolute absence cannot be inferred from the probans "being a property". So, the inference fails even without the opponent's additional specification. Specifying the probandum as the property of being a counterpositive of an unlocatable absolute absence, i.e., of an absence without a substrate, makes things even worse, because an absolute absence is always locatable. The absentee, however, might be unlocatable. The absolute absence of the ether, e.g., is an omnilocated absence with an unlocatable absentee.

230. Since all *atyantābhāvas* have a substrate, differentiating between *āśritātyantābhāvapratiyogitva* and *anāśritātyantābhāvapratiyogitva* makes sense only if we refer the attributes *āśrita* and *anāśrita* to *pratiyogin*, not to *atyantābhāva*, as in the opponent's inference. The smoke on a mountain, e.g., is ascertained as an absolute absence's counterpositive, which has a substrate. The ether, however, is ascertained as an absolute absence's counterpositive without a substrate.

231. If something is a property, it cannot be an absolute absence's counterpositive which does not have a substrate.

232. The property of being a property pervades the property of being an absolute absence's counterpositive which has a substrate, but not vice versa, since knowability etc. are properties, but they are not counterpositives of an absolute absence which have a substrate.

233. The ether, e.g., is a counterpositive of an absolute absence without a substrate, but it is not a property. Hence, the property of being a property does not pervade the property of being an absolute absence's counterpositive which does not have a substrate.

234. The opponent is going to defend his claim that the property of being a counterpositive of an absolute absence which has no substrate can be inferred from the property of being a property. For that purpose he tries to disprove what he seems to regard as the opposite claim, viz. that the property of being a counterpositive of an absolute absence which has a substrate can be inferred from the property of being a property. In his opinion this inference is encumbered with an associate condition, viz. knowability. He is going to argue that the presence of the probandum can only be inferred from the co-presence of the probans "being a property" and the associate condition "knowability". The opponent seems to presuppose here that a property cannot be self-resident. In that case knowability, which is a property, cannot be a locus of itself, i.e., knowability does not pervade the property of being a property. In order to avoid a case of mutual dependence, other omnipresent properties such as nameability should likewise be excluded from the loci of knowability.

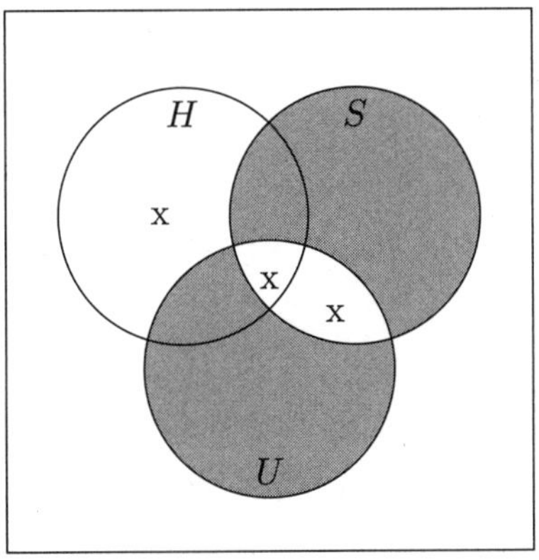

Fig. 12

H = the class of loci of the probans *dharmatva*

S = the class of loci of the probandum *āśritātyantābhāvapratiyogitva*

U = the class of loci of the associate condition *prameyatva*

prameyatva, *abhidheyatva* $\in H \setminus (S \cup U)$; *ghaṭa* $\in H \cap S \cap U$; *gagana* $\in (S \cap U) \setminus H$

235. Similarly, the inference "The earth etc. have an incorporeal causal agent, because they are produced" can be vitiated by means of the associate condition "being preceded by an omniscient creator". If we understand *kartṛ* here in a very general sense, one might be inclined to regard merit (*dharma*) and demerit (*adhar-*

ma) as bodiless non-omniscient causal agents. However, Naiyāyikas ordinarily understand "creator" in the sense of an intelligent being who is endowed with "(i) immediate awareness of the appropriate materials, (ii) desire to produce, (iii) mental eagerness (effort)." (Bhattacharyya/Potter 1993: 607) Therefore, $(H \cap S) \setminus U = \emptyset$ in Fig. 13. The probans resides also in loci such as a pot, which is created by an embodied causal agent, viz. the potter. However, omniscience is here obviously regarded as a property which excludes an embodied causal agent. Therefore, the property "being preceded by an omniscient creator" restricts the range of the probans in such a way that the probandum can be secured. The property of the subject of the inference which functions here as a corrector fits the profile of an associate condition according to a definition mentioned in 1.1.12. As explained earlier, this definition is also discussed by Gaṅgeśa in his Tattvacintāmaṇi. It characterizes an associate condition as pervading the probandum, insofar as the latter is limited by properties of the subject of the inference (cf. Frauwallner 1970: 37).

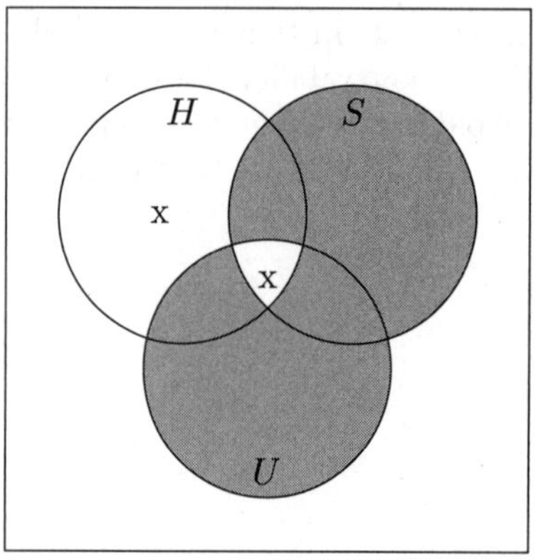

Fig. 13

H = the class of loci of the probans *kāryatva*
S = the class of loci of the probandum *aśarīrikartṛkatva*
U = the class of loci of the associate condition *sarvajñakartṛpūrvakatva*

ghaṭa $\in H \setminus (S \cup U)$; *kṣityādi* $\in H \cap S \cap U$

236. Strictly speaking, the probandum should be *aśarīrikartṛkatva.*

237. Since anything which exists can be the subject of an inference, knowability might be regarded as a defining characteristic of every subject of an inference.

238. The probans and knowability (as a property of the subject of the inference) are jointly conducive in securing the probandum.

239. i.e., the opponent's thesis that knowability etc. are counterpositives of an unlocatable absolute absence

240. An absolute absence is always seen to be locatable. Hence, the opponent's thesis is untenable.

241. i.e., in the case of the thesis that knowability etc. are not counterpositives of an absolute absence

242. The "essence of form", which the *siddhāntin* is referring to here, is probably the form of not appearing as a counterpositive of an absolute absence. How is it possible that in the case of something like knowability, which is not a counterpositive, this form is thwarted? Or, if it is thwarted, i.e., if knowability is a counterpositive of an absolute absence, then this absolute absence should be locatable, since according to the *siddhāntin* an absolute absence needs a substrate. Hence, one would be able to infer the existence of the barrenness of a mother as a substrate of the absolute absence of knowability, since the barrenness of a mother is not knowable.

243. Explicating the concept of counterpositiveness by means of pronouns would result in an empty explication according to the opponent, since a pronoun does not have any specific referent.

244. In statements referring to the future we are also talking about something which is presently non-existent. Nevertheless, such statements are meaningful and can impart knowledge.

245. There is no need to look for a defining characteristic of counterpositives. The knowledge of a counterpositive does not depend on the knowledge of a defining characteristic. Indicative marks (*upalakṣaṇa*) can also be known without knowing any defining characteristic of indicative marks. The opponent seems to regard a counterpositive as an indicative mark of an absence.

246. The Kurus are here an indicative mark of the field known as "the field of the Kurus". The field of the Kurus can be perceived without perceiving the Kurus. In the same way an absence can be preceived without perceiving the counterpositive.

247. *pratiyogitvam* has to be supplemented here as the word on which the genitive *viyogitvātyantābhāvasya* depends.

248. As realists, Navya-Naiyāyikas believe that the objects of conscious experience, such as the counterpositive of an absolute absence, are real. "The [Nyāya-

Vaiśeṣika] system represents an extreme form of realism. Originally verging on naive realism, it has gradually evolved into a highly developed form of critical realism. In thoroughness, we suppose, it is next only to Meinong's, S. Alexander's, some ancient Sāṅkhyas', Prabhākara's, and Rāmānuja's what may be termed absolute realism, which, so far as we can see, sets a limit to the length realism can ever hope to go. Its motto is: 'The goddess experience alone is our refuge.' Accordingly, it ascribes some sort of reality or isness to everything that is experienced." (Narain 1976: 88f)

However, Narain attributes the above-mentioned "motto" to Vācaspati Miśra, not to Udayana: "Śrīvallabhācārya attributes this dictum – quoted in full by Śaṅkara Miśra in *VSU* (7.2.26, p. 194) and Vācaspatimiśra II in *Khaṇḍanoddāra* (p. 103) as *saṃvid eva hi bhagavatī vastūpagame naḥ śaraṇam*, in the *Parimala* commentary on *Mahārthamañjarī* (v. 32, p. 80) as *saṃvid eva bhagavatī viṣayasattvopagame naḥ śaraṇam*, and Śālikanātha Miśra in *Prakaraṇapañcikā* (p. 77) as *saṃvid eva hi bhagavatī viṣayasattvopagame naḥ śaraṇam*, to 'Tātparyācārya.' (...) the dictum in question occurs for the first time in *NVT* (2.1.36, p. 399), verbatim, the reading being *saṃvid eva bhagavatī vastūpagame naḥ śaraṇam.* (...) In *HNNM* (p. 58) it has been well established that Śrīvallabha never refers to Udayana by the honorific title 'ācārya' (p. 533), the Tātparyācārya (p. 358), and the 'Paramanyāyācārya' (p. 762). This leaves no doubt that the dictum belongs to Vācaspati and no one else." (ibid. 89)

249. Naiyāyikas commonly distinguish between a recollection (*smṛti*) and an awareness (*anubhava*): *anubhavo nāma smṛtivyatiriktaṃ jñānam.* (TBh: 28, 4) – "'awareness' is a knowledge which excludes recollection." A recollection merely invokes former awarenesses.

250. A recollection creates a mental image of something real or unreal.

251. An absolute absence and its counterpositive are real entities, whereas the content of a recollection is a fabrication of the mind, which is merely based on a former awareness.

252. The form (*rūpa* or *ākāra*) of something which functions as a counterpositive of an absolute absence has been characterized before by means of the expression *avidyamāna* ("absent").

253. Since every property is endowed with some kind of general defining characteristic, it would qualify as an associate condition according to the present assumption.

254. Veṅkaṭanātha quotes this verse without naming the source (NP: 276, 14 – 277, 1). Apparently, Parāśarabhaṭṭa also advocated a formulation of the definition

of the associate condition which covers both types of associate conditions, the coextensively pervading one and the non-coextensively pervading one (cf. Oberhammer 1968: 267). Since he is also a Viśiṣṭādvaitin, he might have been Veṅkaṭanātha's source. It should be noted that the *siddhāntin* disagrees with the view expressed in this verse, because he insists that the associate condition should also be pervaded by the probandum.

255. When the followers of Udayana advocate the coextensively pervading associate condition, they do not mean to exclude the non-coextensively pervading variant. Varadarāja is cited below as an example of a disciple of Udayana who does not restrict the pervasion of the probandum by the associate condition to cases of a coextensive pervasion.

256. *sādhyāvinābhāva* can refer to both, the pervasion of the probandum by the associate condition as well as the pervasion of the associate condition by the probandum. According to the proponent of the present view the pervasion relation between the two may be asymmetrical in the sense that there is only one inseparable connection.

257. TR: 67, 9f

258. "mere pervadedness" (*vyāpyatvamātra*) refers to the pervadedness (of the probandum by the associate condition) without the specification "coextensive".

259. The proponent of the right view criticizes the opponent's idea that the pervadedness-condition in the definition of the associate condition can be sometimes construed in terms of a coextensive pervasion and sometimes in terms of a non-coextensive pervasion. There is only one type of pervadedness, namely the coextensive one, which should apply to every associate condition if the latter is supposed to function as a corrector.

260. The issue is not whether or not the associate condition indicates a deviation.

261. i.e., if the associate condition did not indicate a deviation

262. Since the property of being different from the subject of the inference does not pervade the probandum, it is ipso facto not a candidate for an associate condition.

263. Since the probans resides in the subject of the inference, it deviates from the property of being different from the subject of the inference.

264. The manuscript reads *vyādamaivam*, which we corrected to *vyādāma maivam* (= 1st person plural injunctive of *vi-ā-dā* + *mā* + *evam*). The manuscript reading without emendation can be parsed as *vyāda maivam*, where *vyāda* can be interpreted as a perfect parasmaipada (1st or 3rd person singular or 2nd person plural) of *vi-ad* ("to bite through"), which, however, does not make much sense here. Unlike the opponent, who suggests to broaden the defining characteristic by dropping the pervasion condition, the proponent of the right view restricts its scope by adding the requirement of a coextensive pervasion.

265. In contrast to positive and negative inferences, only positive inferences would have to be regarded as invalid if all inferences had to be based on a positive and a negative pervasion.

266. The opponent insists that even without the coextensiveness constraint the property of being different from the subject of the inference is excluded from the scope of the defining characteristic.

267. The assumed associate condition is not pervaded by the probandum.

268. The qualifier (the pervader) is here less specific than the qualificand (the pervaded) in the said cognition. However, qualified and unqualified cognition are mutually exclusive. In the case of two cognitions as successive stages of one cognitive process the unqualified cognition needs to precede the qualified one.

269. "Being a locus of fire other than the mountain" (*parvatetaravahnimattva*) has to be ruled out as an associate condition with respect to the valid inference of fire from smoke on a mountain. If the associate condition is also supposed to be pervaded by the probandum, "being a locus of fire other than the mountain" fails to qualify as an associate condition, because such a pervasion is epistemically impossible.

270. The opponent tries to argue that the design inference in Nyāya with "having parts" as the probans and "having a causal agent" as the probandum might be refuted by means of an associate condition which pervades the probandum coextensively, viz. "being produced by someone having a body". The argument trades on the assumption that the properties "having a causal agent" and "being produced by someone having a body" are equilocatable, so that the earth etc. are $\notin S$, if we assume that they are $\notin U$.

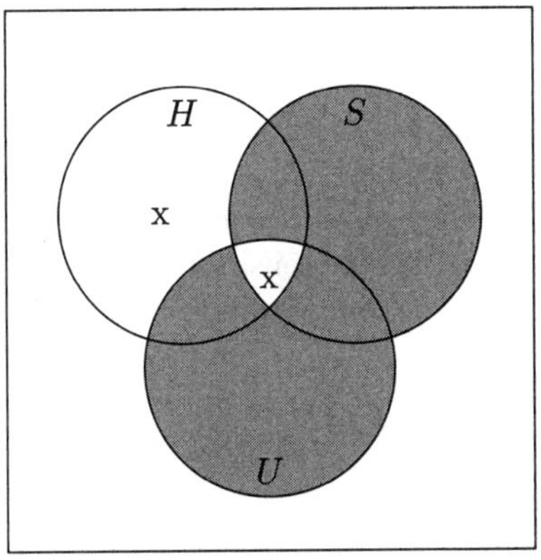

Fig. 14

H = the class of loci of the probans *sāvayavatva*
S = the class of loci of the probandum *sakartṛkatva*
U = the class of loci of the associate condition *śarīrijanyatva*

kṣityādi $\in H \setminus (S \cup U)$; *ghaṭa* $\in H \cap S \cap U$

271. i.e., no pervasion of the associate condition by the probandum

272. Since there is a deviation of the putative associate condition *śarīrijanyatva* from the probandum *sakartṛkatva*, the latter cannot be coextensively pervaded by *śarīrijanyatva*.

273. According to the requirement of a coextensive pervasion the putative associate condition which purportedly vitiates the design inference should be pervaded by the probandum in this inference. However, the pervasion at issue is apparently refutable by means of another associate condition, a vitiator of the vitiator, viz. the property "being produced as something which has become a qualificand" (*viśeṣyabhūtajanyatva*). This expression might be taken to refer to the above-mentioned three characteristics of a "creator" (awareness of the material, desire and effort), which are also referred to as "qualifiers" (*viśeṣaṇa*) by Gaṅgeśa (cf. Vattanky 1984: 188 and Bhattacharyya/Potter 1993: 217). In this sense human beings could also be regarded as creators of the world, since the three "qualifiers" are involved in the performance of rituals etc., which produce the *adṛṣṭa*. God creates the world only in accordance with the *adṛṣṭa* accumulated by human beings existing in the previous cycle of creation. In order to exclude the earth from the range of human agency, Gaṅgeśa suggests a special understanding of the probandum *sakartṛkatva* in the design inference, viz. "being *the object* of the three qualifiers." (cf. Bhattacharyya/Potter 2011: 608) Although the earth is partially caused by the *adṛṣṭa* of human beings, it is not the object of their desire and they lack the omniscience and the omnipotence which are needed to produce the effect in this case. If we

understand *viśeṣyabhūtajanyatva* here in the same sense, then the earth has to be $\in (S \cap U) \setminus H$ in Fig. 15.

In order to be able to function as a vitiator the associate condition should not pervade the probans. This is actually warranted if we understand "being produced as something which has become a qualificand" here in accordance with Gaṅgeśa's concept of an "effect" in the design inference, i.e., in the sense of the result of a creative effort, which excludes posterior absences (cf. Bhattacharyya/Potter 1993: 215). In the modified version of the design inference, which the *siddhāntin* tries to defend here, the probans "having parts" has likewise been chosen in order to restrict the range of effects involved in the pervasion at issue to positive effects.

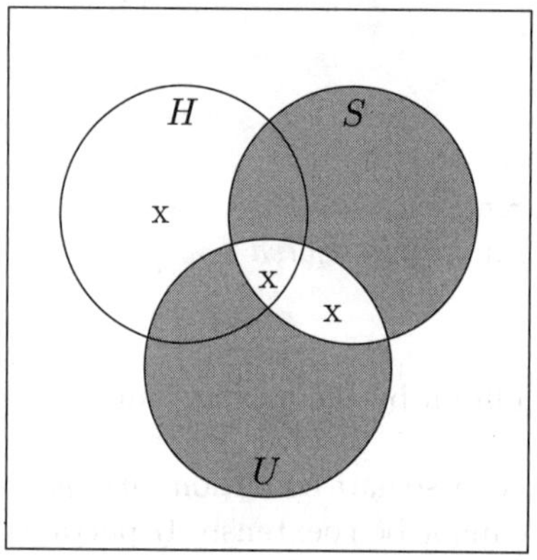

Fig. 15

H = the class of loci of the probans *śarīrijanyatva*
S = the class of loci of the probandum *sakartṛkatva*
U = the class of loci of the associate condition *viśeṣyabhūtajanyatva*

dhvaṃsābhāva $\in H \setminus (S \cup U)$; *ghaṭa* $\in H \cap S \cap U$; *kṣityādi* $\in (S \cap U) \setminus H$

274. Now, the *siddhāntin* is going to justify that "being produced as something which has become a qualificand" fulfills one of the criteria of an associate condition, viz. the non-pervasion of the probans. For that purpose he needs an associate condition which vitiates the assumption of a pervasion of the probans "being produced by someone having a body" by "being produced as something which has become a qualificand". The probandum of the design inference, i.e., "having a causal agent" turns out to be an appropriate choice.

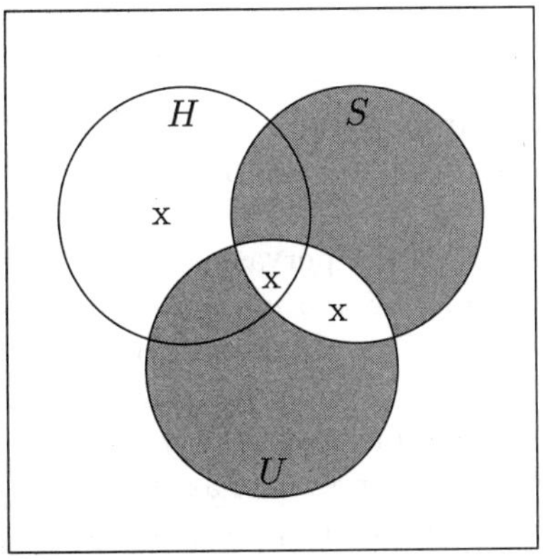

Fig. 16

H = the class of loci of the probans *śarīrijanyatva*
S = the class of loci of the probandum *viśeṣyabhūtajanyatva*
U = the class of loci of the associate condition *sakartṛkatva*

dhvaṃsābhāva $\in H \setminus (S \cup U)$; *ghaṭa* $\in H \cap S \cap U$; *kṣityādi* $\in (S \cap U) \setminus H$

275. i.e., the associate condition

276. In order to admit the property of being different from sound as an associate condition for the putative pervasion at issue, the opponent needs to bracket the subject of the inference (cf. Fig. 17). The present case is different from the case of the purported pervasion of the property *parvatetaravahnimattva* by the property *vahnimattva*, which can be refuted by the above-mentioned epistemic argument.

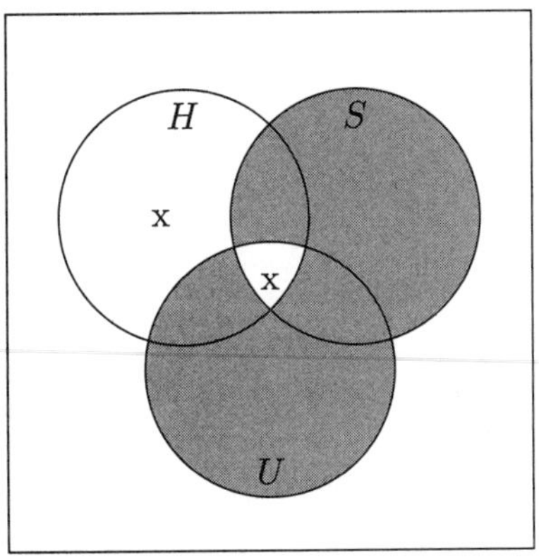

Fig. 17

H = the class of loci of the probans *prameyatva*
S = the class of loci of the probandum *abhidheyatva* $\setminus$ {*śabda*}
U = the class of loci of the associate condition *aśabdatva*

śabda $\in H \setminus (S \cup U)$; *ghaṭa* $\in H \cap S \cap U$

277. The associate condition "being different from sound" is explicated by the proponent of the right view as "possessing the mutual absence of sound".

278. If *aśabdatva* were an associate condition for the pervasion of *prameyatva* by *abhidheyatva*, *abhidheyatva* should be pervaded by *aśabdatva*. However, sound is nameable and it is not a locus of *aśabdatva*. Hence, the assumed associate condition *aśabdatva* pervades the probandum only if it is properly "qualified" or determined with regard to what it actually pervades. For that purpose another "qualifying associate condition" has to be introduced. *ajanyatvādi* serves here as an appropriate vitiator of the vitiator. Something which is nameable and not produced is a locus of *aśabdatva*. It should be noted that the associate condition is "not being produced etc.". By adding "etc." the proponent of the right view turns the associate condition into one which pervades *aśabdatva* coextensively. *ādi* seems to refer here to any other property which excludes the sound (*śabda*) such as *aguṇatva*, *ghaṭatva* etc. To be more precise, *ajanyatvādi* seems to be the property of being a locus of any property which does not reside in the sound. If we denote the sound by means of the constant s, we can render *ajanyatvādi* as the property term $[\exists y(\neg sLy \wedge xLy)]_x$. Since potness, e.g., does not reside in s, a pot is a locus of $[\exists y(\neg sLy \wedge xLy)]_x$.

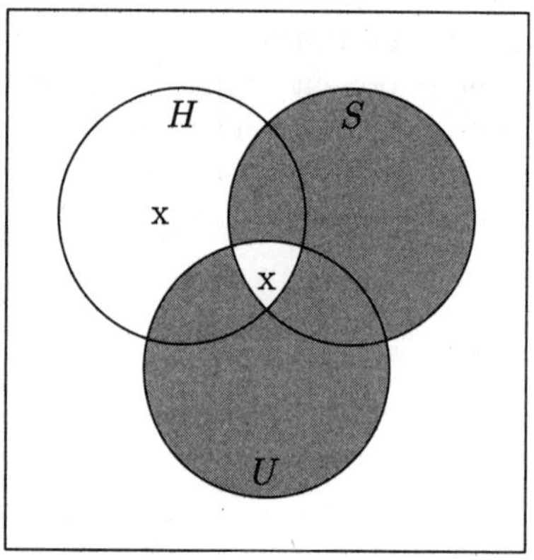

Fig. 18

H = the class of loci of the probans *abhidheyatva*
S = the class of loci of the probandum *aśabdatva*
U = the class of loci of the associate condition *ajanyatvādi*

śabda $\in H \setminus (S \cup U)$; *ghaṭa* $\in H \cap S \cap U$

279. The putative associate condition concocted by the opponent (*aśabdatva*) is coextensive with the probans, the inferential subject being bracketed. Therefore,

it does not serve the purpose of restricting the range of the probans to loci of the probandum.

280. Those who advocate the definition without the condition of a coextensive pervasion are not faced with the problem that their defining characteristic pertains to the coextensively pervading property of being different from the inferential subject.

281. The definition without the condition of a coextensive pervasion does not exclude that an associate condition pervades the probandum coextensively and, thus, serves as a corrector.

282. The proponent of the right view might be referring here to the aforementioned putative pervasion of *abidheyatva* by *aśabdatva*, which is vitiated by the associate condition *ajanyatvādi* (cf. Fig. 18 above). Since probandum and associate condition are coextensive in this example, the cognition of the pervasion of the assumed probandum by the associate condition is warranted by the frequent observation of their concomitance, i.e., of their simultaneous occurrence. However, frequent observation of the concomitance does not help to identify a pervasion as non-coextensive. The faculty of sight cannot distinguish between a pervasion which is characterized as *sama* ("coextensive") and a pervasion which is characterized as *ullaṅghya* ("non-coextensive"), i.e., if the faculty of sight grasps a pervasion, it might be non-coextensive. Identifying a pervasion as coextensive is not a spin-off of any cognition of a pervasion, so that labelling a pervasion as "coextensive" would be superfluous. In order to exclude the possibility that an associate condition pervades an assumed probandum non-coextensively, this has to be explicitly stated in the definition. The condition of a coextensive pervasion is therefore by no means useless.

283. The proponent of the right view might be referring here to the aforementioned putative pervasion of *śarīrijanyatva* by *sakartṛkatva*, which is vitiated by the associate condition *viśeṣyabhūtajanyatva* (cf. Fig. 15 above). Since the assumed probandum and the associate condition are coextensive in this example, the deviation of the assumed probans from the associate condition entails its deviation from the assumed probandum.

284. The property of possessing smoke is the property of being the pervaded in relation to fire (or the property of possessing fire) as the pervader. This is an example of a non-coextensive pervasion.

285. i.e., in the case of a non-coextensive pervasion as well as in the case of a coextensive pervasion

286. An alternative translation of this sentence would be the following: "There is no pervadedness of something which has a useless qualifier [by the defining characteristic of an associate condition]."

287. The property of being different from the inferential subject which pervades the probandum non-coextensively is excluded by integrating the condition of a coextensive pervasion in the definition.

288. An associate condition which is related to probans and probandum according to Fig. 19 (see below) pervades "the relation between probans and probandum" (represented as the class $H \cap S$) coextensively. If the class $S \setminus (H \cup U)$ were empty, the probandum would also be coextensively pervaded by the associate condition. But here it is non-empty, as indicated by the "x" in the corresponding area.

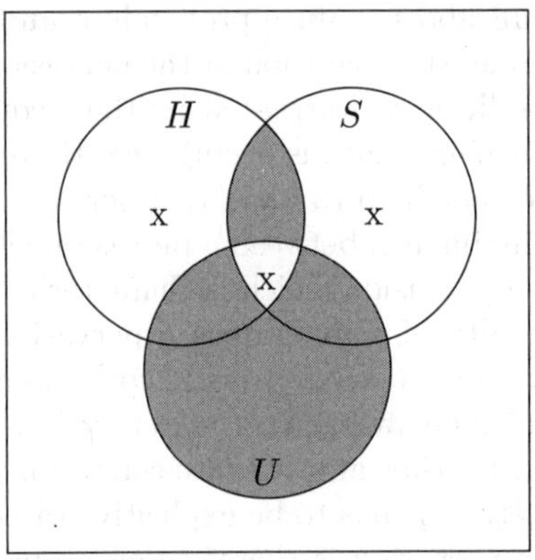

Fig. 19

H = the class of loci of the probans
S = the class of loci of the probandum
U = the class of loci of the associate condition

289. *sādhyamātra* might refer here to any instance of the probandum, whereas *vyāpaka* is to be understood as the specific individual whose presence on the inferential subject is to be inferred.

290. i.e., the defining characteristic *vyāpaka*

291. Since smoke does not only occur on mountains, mountainness does not pervade the probans of the valid inference of fire from the smoke on a mountain, but it would pervade the probandum if the latter were meant to be not any fire (*vahnimātra*), but the fire on the mountain.

292. i.e., the instance of the probandum occurring on the inferential subject

293. The explication of the pervasion of the probandum in the way suggested here gives rise to a method of refuting even valid inferences.

294. The formulation of the defining characteristic is elliptical, since only that which is pervaded by the associate condition, viz. the range of agreeing instances, is expressed, not the pervasion itself.

295. Associate conditions which pervade not *only* the range of agreeing instances, but the whole probandum, are beyond the scope of the present defining characteristic, although they might also fulfill the requirement of pervading the relation between probans and probandum.

296. The opponent suggests to explicate *sādhya* as *vyāpakatva* instead of *vyāpaka*. *vyāpakatva* is supposed to comprise only the range of instances of the probandum which co-occur with an instance of the probans. Thus, being a pervader includes only what is left of (*avaśiṣṭa*) the probandum if we subtract the surplus of individuals which are not involved in the concomitance of probans and probandum. In this way, the property of being a pervader resides only in the remaining (*śiṣṭa*) instances of the probandum which are not "cut off" from the probans.

297. The opponent replaces *sādhana* and *sādhya* in Udayana's definition with *vyāpya* and *vyāpakatva*. By appropriately defining the concept of pervaderness he tries to ensure that an associate condition which pervades only the relation between probans and probandum is included in the modified version of Udayana's definition. The example "contactness etc.", which he is referring to here, is probably the same as the one referred to as *saṃyoganiṣṭhadharmavattva* ("being a locus of properties which reside in contact") in 1.1.9 (cf. Fig. 6). Contactness is just one of the properties residing in contact which collectively constitute this associate condition.

298. Associate conditions with a coextensive pervasion of the probandum are included in the present defining characteristic.

299. *anityatva* is another one of the properties residing in contact (*saṃyoga-niṣṭhadharma*) which collectively constitute the above-mentioned example of an associate condition which pervades only the relation between probans and probandum.

300. *ādi* refers here probably to the non-pervasion of the probans, the uncontroversial property of an associate condition.

301. i.e., the defining characteristic with the condition of a coextensive pervasion

302. The associate condition would not function as a corrector without the property of being pervaded by the probandum.

303. Since the coextensively pervading associate condition and the non-coextensively pervading associate condition both pervade the probandum, the absence of the probandum pervades the absence of the associate condition in either case. Therefore, the absence of the associate condition transmits to the probans the property of co-occurring with (or being pervaded by) the absence of the probandum.

304. The thesis of an inference might be true, even though the putative pervasion is unwarranted, as in the case of the following example: *arthahiṃsādharmasādhanaṃ hiṃsātvāt.* – "An injury for the purpose of wealth brings about guilt, because it is an injury." Thus, a mere refutation due to the associate condition's property of pervading the probandum does not amount to the truth of the counter-thesis.

305. i.e., a refutation which aims at establishing the counter-thesis

306. The determination of positive and negative correlation of associate condition and probandum targets only a putative pervasion of the probans by the probandum, not the thesis of an inference.

307. *sādhana* is here probably meant in the sense of *adharmasādhana.* The proponent of the right view is apparently referring to the putative pervasion of *hiṃsātva* by *adharmasādhanatva*, which can be vitiated by means of *niṣiddhatva* as an associate condition.

308. Since the counter-thesis denies the presence of the probandum on the subject of the inference, it is rather the negative than the positive pervasion of the probandum by the associate condition which might give a clue to the truth of the counter-thesis. However, we can be sure about the truth of the counter-thesis only if we know in addition that the associate condition is absent from the inferential subject. The negative pervasion alone does not settle the issue.

309. In the counter-thesis, which denies the occurrence of the probandum on the subject of the inference, the absence of the probandum functions as an adjunct (*pratiyogin*) which is supposed to be located on the subject of the inference as the subjunct (*anuyogin*) of the occurrence relation. In the case of a coextensive perva-

sion of the probandum by the associate condition the latter's pervadedness by the probandum ensures that the absence of the probandum is pervaded by the absence of the associate condition. Hence, there is a one-to-one correspondence between the absence of a coextensively pervading associate condition and the absence of the probandum. The absence of a non-coextensively pervading associate condition may also be said to indicate the absence of the probandum. However, its presence would be consistent with the absence of the probandum as well. Therefore, the absence of the non-coextensively pervading associate condition is not an indicator in the sense of a necessary antecedent of the absence of the probandum.

310. If the probandum is pervaded by the associate condition, it is not in general true that the absence of the probandum is pervaded by the absence of the associate condition. Similarly, smoke is pervaded by fire, but the absence of smoke is not pervaded by the absence of fire. In order to ensure that the absence of the probandum is pervaded by the absence of the associate condition, we need to posit the coextensive pervasion of the probandum by the associate condition.

311. The associate condition which is a "pervader" of the probandum might be pervaded by the latter as well. Therefore, it is at least possible that the absence of such an associate condition pervades the absence of the probandum.

312. An associate condition which is merely required to pervade the probandum can function as a means to establish the non-pervasion of the probans by a putative probandum, but it might lack the property of being pervaded by the probandum, which is essential for the associate condition's role as a fortifier.

313. i.e., of the probandum

314. A non-coextensive pervasion of the probandum by the associate condition proves the absence of the probandum, wherever the associate condition is absent. However, if the counter-thesis is true, the associate condition may or may not be present on the inferential subject. In the case of a genuine associate condition the truth of the counter-thesis should entail the absence of the associate condition from the inferential subject.

315. However, from the *siddhāntin*'s point of view the condition of the pervasion of the probandum by the associate condition is by no means superfluous.

316. i.e., properties which are candidate associate conditions

317. The probandum co-occurs with the associate condition and vice versa. The probandum does not deviate from the associate condition and vice versa.

318. Otherwise, *kāryatva* could be said to function as an associate condition with respect to the following invalid inference, which is a modification of an example mentioned by Śrīdhara (cf. 1.1.12): *ayaṃ vāyur asparśanapratyakṣatvāt.* – "This is air (as an aggregate, i.e., non-atomic), because it is not (both), tangible and directly perceptible." As shown in Fig. 20, $(H \cap S) \setminus U = \emptyset$, i.e., *kāryatva* pervades "the relation between probans and probandum" (i.e., the property of being a locus of the co-occurrence of probans and probandum) and even the probandum as a whole. However, the pervasion is non-coextensive, since a pot $\in U \setminus (H \cup S)$. It is even non-coextensive in the range of the probans, since a sound $\in (H \cap U) \setminus S$.

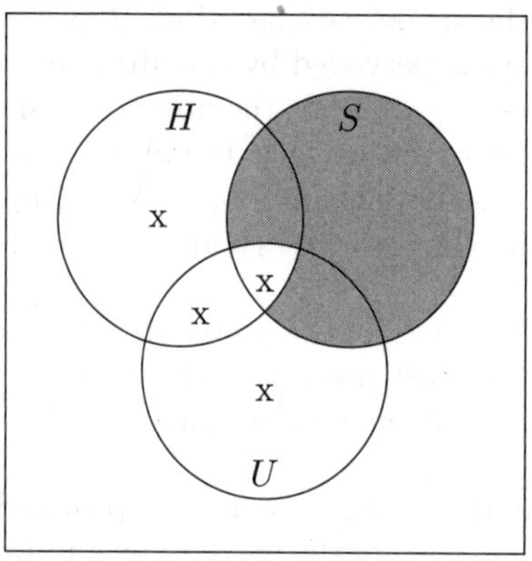

Fig. 20

H = the class of loci of the probans *asparśanapratyakṣatva*
S = the class of loci of the probandum *vāyutva* (as a property of aggregates of air atoms)
U = the class of loci of the associate condition *kāryatva*

ākāśa $\in H \setminus (S \cup U)$; *śabda* $\in (H \cap U) \setminus S$; *vāyu* $\in H \cap S \cap U$; *ghaṭa* $\in U \setminus (H \cup S)$

319. *saṃyogatva* can be said to function as an associate condition with respect to the invalid inference: *ayaṃ samavāyavyatiriktasaṃbandhaḥ kṛtakatvāt.* – "This is a relation different from inherence, because it is created." As shown in Fig. 21, *saṃyogatva* pervades the relation between probans and probandum coextensively. Moreover, it pervades the probandum coextensively.

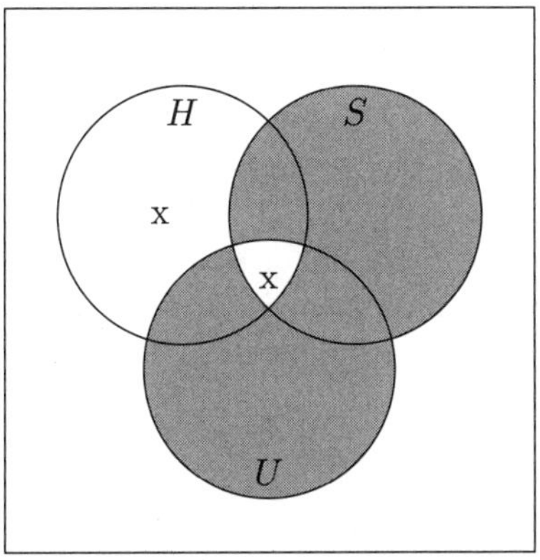

Fig. 21
H = the class of loci of the probans *kṛtatva*
S = the class of loci of the probandum *samavāyavyatiriktasaṃbandhatva*
U = the class of loci of the associate condition *saṃyogatva*

ghaṭa $\in H \setminus (S \cup U)$; *saṃyoga* $\in H \cap S \cap U$

320. A putative pervasion can be corrected, so that there is a pervasion of the probans by the probandum.

321. i.e., the putative probandum in an invalid inference

322. This is a reference to the definition according to which the associate condition pervades the probandum limited by a property of the subject of the inference (cf. 1.1.12). As shown earlier in Fig. 8, the example "visibility" pervades the probandum coextensively in the range of the probans. In this sense such an associate condition is a pervader "with respect to the probans" (*prati sādhanam*).

323. The scope of the defining characteristic is not stretched beyond the limits, since it does not include the putative probans. The latter might be said to fulfill one of the criteria of an associate condition, namely the pervasion of the probandum. In the case of a pseudo-pervasion the putative probans might pervade the putative probandum. In the case of a genuine pervasion the probans might pervade the probandum coextensively. However, the probans lacks an associate condition's property of not being a pervader of the probans.

324. The probans co-occurs with the absence of that which does not pervade the probans.

325. The specific defining characteristic characterizes the associate condition not only as a pervader of the probandum, but also as a counterpositive of an

absolute absence which resides in something which possesses the probans, since it does not pervade the probans.

326. literally: "there is insignificance of the mistake 'self-dependence' etc."

327. An *upādhi* u as a vitiator of an inference $\mathcal{I}$ cannot vitiate an inference $\mathcal{I}'$ in which the probans of $\mathcal{I}$ functions as the probandum, since in this case u cannot pervade the probandum in $\mathcal{I}'$ and fail to pervade the probans in $\mathcal{I}$.

328. i.e., the definition is not too narrow

329. In the case of the defining characteristic "having a coextensive pervasion and being different from the subject of the inference" there is no specification of the probans. The probandum is only implied by the expression "having a coextensive pervasion". Therefore, this defining characteristic is of another type than the *siddhāntin*'s specific defining characteristic. The latter is not afflicted with the defect of unduly restricting the mode of the definiendum's presentation. If one wants to define associate conditions by means of a specific defining characteristic, it has to be done in the way suggested by the *siddhāntin.*

330. It is not a mistake not to include the non-coextensively pervading associate condition in the definition.

331. If a defeasible coextensive pervasion between probans and probandum is vitiated by means of an associate condition which pervades the probandum limited by the probans, then the associate condition pervades the probandum coextensively. In this case the pervasion of the probandum by the associate condition cannot be characterized as non-coextensive.

332. The subject of this sentence is the *vyāpakatvam* of the preceding sentence.

333. The proponent of the right view is referring here to the design inference *kṣityādikaṃ sakartṛkaṃ kāryatvāt.* An opponent of this inference might accept *śarīrijanyatva* as an associate condition. As shown in 1.1.6.3 (cf. Fig. 3, the leftmost diagram), this coextensively pervading associate condition arguably vitiates a defeasible coextensive pervasion of probans and probandum.

334. This remark is probably directed against a definition according to which the associate condition pervades the probandum, insofar as the latter is limited by a property of the subject of the inference. This definition would also amount to a non-coextensive pervasion of the probandum by the associate condition. An example similar to the one which is indicated here is mentioned by Gaṅgeśa (cf. Frauwallner 1970: 38 and Phillips 2002: 72). The inference at issue, viz. *śabdo 'bhi-*

dheyaḥ prameyatvāt, is valid. Nevertheless, it could be vitiated by the associate condition *aśrāvaṇatva* if the above-mentioned definition were accepted. Gaṅgeśa chooses *guṇatva* as a property of the subject of the inference which functions as a limitor of the probandum. The author of the UD chooses *kṛtakatva* instead. Excluding the inferential subject (which is bracketed in the inferential context, not to beg the question), inaudibility pervades nameability limited by the property "being produced".

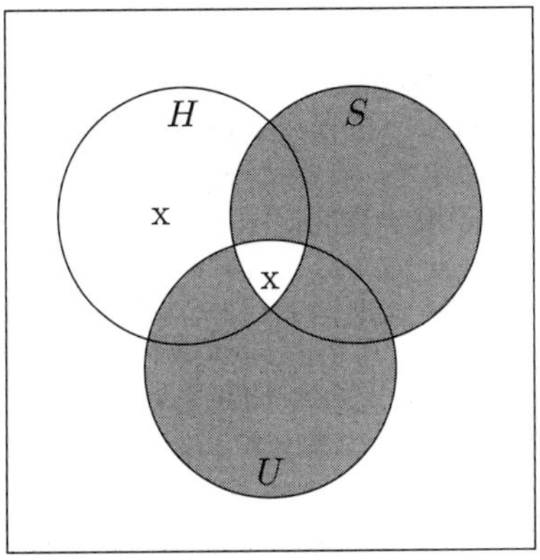

Fig. 22

H = the class of loci of the probans *prameyatva*
S = the class of loci of the probandum *abhidheyatva* $\setminus$ {*śabda*}
U = the class of loci of the associate condition *aśrāvaṇatva*
$H \setminus (S \cup U)$ = {*śabda*}

loci of *kṛtakatva* excluding *śabda* $\in H \cap S \cap U$

The proponent of the right view probably denies that there is a "grasping" of a pervasion of the probandum limited by a property of the subject of the inference in this case, because he sticks to his epistemological maxim that the pervader should not be less specific than the pervaded.

335. The opponent might be referring here to the definition according to which the associate condition pervades the probandum, insofar as the latter is limited by a property of a positive example (cf. 1.1.12). As shown in Fig. 10, the associate condition *ghaṭatva* seems to pervade the probandum *anityatva* qualified by *ghaṭaśabdānyataratva* if the inferential subject is bracketed: Whatever is non-eternal and different from the inferential subject, viz. sound, and qualified by being a pot or sound, is a pot. The putative pervasion can be said to be coextensive if the inferential subject is excluded from the loci of the probandum.

336. The proponent exposes these examples as pseudo-*upādhi*s by pointing out that in the case of a genuine pervasion the pervading property cannot be less specific than the pervaded property.

337. A defining characteristic according to which the associate condition pervades the probandum and is also pervaded by the latter is not applicable to the above-mentioned examples.

338. The probans could also deviate from the associate condition in other loci than the inferential subject. However, the purpose of the non-pervasion condition in an inferential situation is to ensure that the absence of the associate condition indicates the absence of the probandum from the inferential subject.

339. If something pervading the probans could function as an associate condition, it might vitiate a genuine pervasion. The probans in the *siddhāntin*'s example contains the specification *sāmānyavattve sati* in order to exclude the eternal universals as potential loci. The latter are graspable by the external senses, but they are not loci of universals. The specification *asmadādi* is added in order to exclude the eternal atoms as potential loci. Vaiśeṣikas hold that for Yogis the latter are graspable through the external senses (cf. Halbfass 1992: 66, fn. 51), but not for ordinary people like you and me. Hence, the probans, the probandum and the putative associate condition are coextensive in this example.

340. The probans deviates from the associate condition with respect to the realm of agreeing instances, i.e., it deviates jointly from the associate condition and the realm of agreeing instances. There should be a locus of the probans where the associate condition and the probandum are co-absent. *kvacid* is specified in the next sentence by means of *sapakṣa.*

341. The inferential subject in an inference which is vitiated by an associate condition should also be a locus where the probans deviates jointly from the associate condition and the probandum.

342. i.e., if the probandum did occur on the inferential subject in the absence of the associate condition

343. The absence of the associate condition entails the absence of the probandum because of the pervasion of the probandum by the associate condition.

344. The associate condition indicates the absence of the probandum on the inferential subject by its absence, not by its presence in that locus.

345. In some cases the associate condition just happens to be pervaded by the probandum. One cannot help coming across some examples, but for the function of an associate condition this is inessential according to the view which the proponent of the right view reports here.

346. The opponent denies the possibility of a reductive explanation of the associate condition's functions as a vitiator and as a corrector by means of the concept of pervasion.

347. The indication of a deviation seems to be an entirely negative result. How can it generate any positive result, such as the thesis that the probandum can be secured in certain loci of the probans?

348. It is not true that the indication of a deviation does not give any clue to a possible correction of an assumed inference.

349. *vidyamānasya* might be taken to be a correlate of *avidyamānasya* in: *tad eva tat sarvam upādheḥ pakṣe 'vidyamānasya vyāpakatvāyattam.* (UD: 7a, 2) – "All that depends on the fact that an associate condition is a pervader which is not present on the inferential subject." Mutatis mutandis, the statement of the associate condition's function as a corrector is the same as that for its function as a vitiator: *tad eva tat sarvam upādheḥ pakṣe vidyamānasya vyāpyatvāyattam.*

350. The indication of a deviation is not the primary function of an associate condition. According to the opponent its primary function consists in establishing the counter-thesis.

351. i.e., the absence of any pervading associate condition, not only a coextensively pervading one

352. The opponent seems to be assuming that the function of a fortifier and the function of an indicator of a deviation do not fit together. If the latter is endorsed, the former has to be rejected.

353. *vyāpyatvāsiddhi* refers here to the fallacy of the conditional probans (*vyāpyatvāsiddha*), a certain type of "pseudo-probans" (*hetvābhāsa*). According to NKoś (cf. 844) this is "a probans which is related to the probandum in connection with an associate condition" (*sopādhikasādhyasaṃbaddho hetuḥ*). By determining the function of an associate condition in this way the proponent of the right view endorses its function as a fortifier.

354. The plural of *jānate* accords with the plural of *bhavatām*.

355. Since *prajñā* is used to designate transcendental wisdom in Buddhism, the Buddhists are probably targeted here as the ones who are ignorant of the *ātman*.

356. As long as a property is only suspected to be an associate condition, because it fulfills one of the two criteria of an associate condition, it might still fail to fulfill the other one. In that case it does not qualify as an associate condition. Hence, contrary to the argument of the opponent, it can be reasonable to deny that something is an associate condition.

357. i.e., for properties which are sure to lack both, the property of pervading the probandum and the property of not pervading the probans

358. Naiyāyikas distinguish between a favorable and an unfavorable reductio ad absurdum: "There can be favorable and unfavorable *tarka*. Counterfactual reasoning in support of a good inference, i.e., *anukūla-tarka*, 'favorable *tarka*,' is not a substitute for an original prover, Gaṅgeśa has argued. Rather, it helps someone to realize that an inference is sound because an underlying pervasion holds. Counterfactual reasoning against an apparent (false but credible) inference, i.e., *pratikūla-tarka*, 'unfavorable *tarka*,' is an inferential blocker, showing that its target is wrong." (Phillips 2002: 93f)

359. One would not let an agreement to the above-mentioned absurdities pass unchallenged. The contradiction derives from the inescapability of an objection.

360. i.e., grass used for manufacturing mats

361. The presence of something else than that which is the cause of a certain effect does not raise any expectations about the production of the effect. An effect which can be obtained by sacrificing with the proper utensils for a sacrifice is not expected to be obtained by means of *kāśa*-grass "as that what belongs to the preparation of a sacrificial fire" (*āgnika*).

362. such as wet fuel, a certain temperature etc.

363. The proponent of the right view does not deny that the production of an effect might depend on a cause in combination with subsidiary conditions.

364. The pervadedness "in a primary sense" or the "true" pervadedness is probably a pervadedness which does not depend on an associate condition.

365. i.e., a pervadedness which depends on an associate condition as a corrector

366. i.e., of an associate condition

367. i.e., a pervadedness which depends on an associate condition as a corrector

368. The "locus" of the pervadedness in a primary sense is the associate condition, since it is genuinely pervaded by the probandum.

369. The inference of the possession of universals from the property of being graspable by the external senses depends on the difference from universals as an associate condition. Apart from universals everything which can be perceived through the external sense organs possesses universals. Universals can be perceived through the external sense organs, but they are not loci of universals.

370. The question seems to imply that being acquainted with instances of a deviation of the probans from the probandum need not be an inferential blocker.

371. Gaṅgeśa reports the view of a *pūrvapakṣin* (cf. Frauwallner 1970: 16, 9f = Phillips 2002: 122f) who rejects what is probably only a terminological variant of the same kind of characterization of the associate condition's function of vitiating, viz. *vyāptivirahar̄upatā* ("being involved in the absence of a pervasion").

372. This specification of an *upādhi*'s vitiating function is discussed in section 1.4 of the introduction (cf. (E3)).

373. *vyāptivirahātmakatva* ("the possession of the essence of the absence of a pervasion") is used here as a terminological variant of the above-mentioned *vyāptivirahabhūtatva* ("being in effect the absence of a pervasion").

374. As mentioned above, in the present context the failure of the pervadedness is the fallacy of the conditional probans, a special kind of "pseudo-probans" (*hetvābhāsa*). The associate condition's function as a vitiator is to expose the probans in an assumed inference as an instance of this type of pseudo-probans.

375. i.e., the absence of the associate condition

376. *tavīti* = 3rd person sg. present parasmaipada of the root *tu*.

377. A blocker in the form of evidence for the counter-thesis amounts to the fallacy of the conditional probans, which also affects the credibility of the inferential awareness.

378. The opponent questions the justification for the pervadedness of the associate condition by the probandum.

379. The pervadedness-condition is well justified.

380. i.e., insofar as there is no pervasion of "being an injury" by the probandum "bringing about guilt" (*adharmasādhanatva*)

381. The pronoun *tad* in *tadvyatirekāt* is taken here to be referring to *vyāpakatva* in the beginning.

382. On the inferential subject as well as elsewhere the absence of the associate condition is accompanied by the absence of the probandum due to the associate condition's pervasion of the probandum. All loci of the absence of the associate condition where the absence of the probandum has been ascertained provide inductive support for the pervasion of the probandum by the associate condition.

383. The proponent of the right view considers here the possibility to trace the failure of an assumed pervasion to a reductio ad absurdum, thereby rendering the associate condition superfluous. He will later on admit that wherever an associate condition is at stake, there is an indirect dependence of the failure of an assumed pervasion on a reductio ad absurdum. But he denies the possibility of a direct refutation of the putative pervasion of the property of being an injury by the property "bringing about guilt" by means of an unfavorable reductio ad absurdum. If such a refutation were possible, the pertinent reductio ad absurdum would be one referring to "being an injury" as "the probans in the present case".

384. The failure of the putative pervasion at issue cannot be demonstrated by means of an unfavorable reductio ad absurdum. However, a favorable reductio ad absurdum can help to demonstrate that properties like "being an injury" are pervaded by something else.

385. The associate condition can as well be rendered superfluous by taking into account that the probandum may fulfill the same function, because according to the proponent of the right view it is supposed to be coextensive with the associate condition.

386. i.e., in the case of a coextensive pervasion of the associate condition by the probandum

387. The favorable reductio ad absurdum serves to secure the mutual pervasion of probandum and associate condition.

388. The pervasion of the associate condition by the probandum can be proved indirectly by means an unfavorable reductio ad absurdum, which serves to attack the thesis that such a pervasion does not exist.

389. The inference is only negative, because the only instance of a co-occurrence of probans and probandum is the inferential subject. However, the probandum alone can be instantiated by other loci as well.

390. Advaitins hold that only direct experience (*anubhūti*) is self-illuminating (*svayaṃprakāśa*). Hence, the probandum resides only in the inferential subject and there is no agreeing instance. This is elaborated by Vimuktātman as follows: *yeti svataḥ siddhatāṃ dyotati, anubhūter anubhāvyatve ghaṭādivad ananubhūtitvaprasaṅgāt.* (IS: 1, 6f) – "He explains the [property of] being established by itself [by means of the word] 'which', because there would be the undesirable consequence that it would not be direct experience if direct experience were an object of direct experience, as in the case of a pot etc."

391. "Water" is a disagreeing instance with regard to the first one of the above-mentioned inferences. "A pot" is a disagreeing instance with regard to the second one.

392. In the case of the valid only negative inference "Earth differs from other things, because it is earth" the probans is actually pervaded by the probandum.

393. The corrector-function of the associate condition presupposes that probans, associate condition and probandum are instantiated in one locus. But this is not possible in the case of an only negative inference based on a pseudo-pervasion, because outside the inferential subject of such an inference the probandum can only co-occur with the absence of the probans. The inferential subject is the only locus of the probans and therefore it is also the only locus where the probandum might be secured by conjoining the probans with the associate condition. However, if the probans is not pervaded by the probandum in such an inference, the probandum has to be absent from the inferential subject.

394. Since the proponent of the right view defined the associate condition in such a way that it can function as a corrector, the probans should co-occur with the probandum, wherever it meets the associate condition. However, if the latter is absent from the inferential subject, the co-occurrence of probans, probandum and associate condition would be restricted to loci other than the inferential subject, which is impossible in the case of an only negative inference.

395. The proponent of the right view is going to claim that his defining characteristic meets the requirements of a vitiator of only negative inferences.

396. This is the contraposed form of the pervasion of the probans by the probandum: The absence of the probandum is pervaded by the absence of the probans.

397. i.e., with the absence of the probandum

398. According to this definition, $(H \cup U)^c = \emptyset$ (cf. Fig. 23), because the associate condition pervades the absence of the probans, i.e., $\forall x(x \notin H \rightarrow x \in U) \wedge \exists x(x \notin H \wedge x \in U)$ (where the second conjunct expresses the condition of existential import associated with a pervasion). Since the pervasion is supposed to be coextensive, $\forall x(x \in U \rightarrow x \notin H)$, i.e., $H \cap U = \emptyset$. Moreover, the associate condition does not pervade the absence of the probandum, i.e., $\exists x(x \notin S \wedge x \notin U)$. Hence, $\exists x(x \in H \setminus (S \cup U))$, i.e., the assumed pervasion of the absence of the probandum by the absence of the probans fails. In this sense the *siddhāntin*'s *upādhi* actually functions as a vitiator. However, the corrector-function seems problematic. One might be inclined to argue that wherever such an *upādhi* co-occurs with the absence of the probandum, it indicates the absence of the probans, i.e., $U \cap S^c \subseteq H^c$. However, if $U \setminus (H \cup S) = \emptyset$, there is no inductive support for the co-absence of probans and probandum in the presence of the *upādhi*.

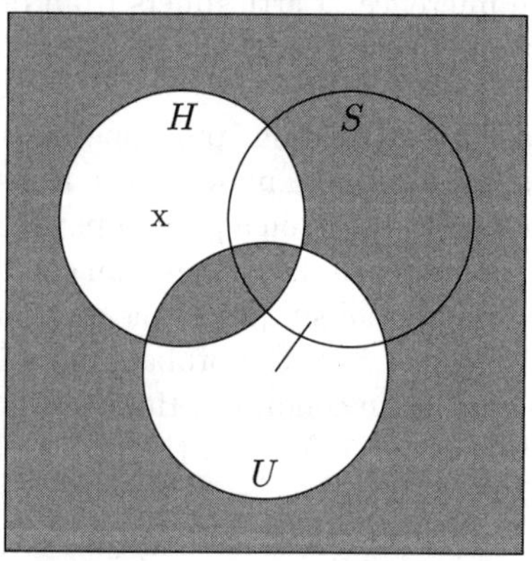

Fig. 23

H = the class of loci of the probans
S = the class of loci of the probandum
U = the class of loci of the associate condition

399. If the pervasion is cast into the corresponding contraposed form, then the absence of the probandum becomes the pervaded, i.e., it is assigned the role of the probans.

400. In the case of a defeasible positive pervasion the co-occurrence of the probans with the absence of the associate condition should entail the absence of the probandum. In the case of a defeasible negative pervasion the co-occurrence of the absence of the probandum with the absence of the associate condition should entail the presence of the probans. According to Fig. 23, $S^c \cap U^c = (S \cup U)^c \subseteq H$. Hence, in the case of a defeasible only negative inference the inferential subject exhibits the probans if it is a locus of the co-absence of the probandum and the associate condition. As opposed to what the opponent is claiming here, the absence of the probans does not fail to be instantiated and it is pervaded by the *upādhi*.

401. According to Fig. 23, $H \setminus (S \cup U) \neq \emptyset$, i.e., the absence of the probandum deviates from the associate condition in the realm of the probans. Hence, the absence of the probandum co-occurs with the probans. If there are loci of their co-occurrence other than the inferential subject, this would contradict the character of the probans in an only negative inference, which should be confined to the inferential subject, no matter whether the inference is valid or not. Outside the inferential subject the absence of the probandum should only co-occur with the absence of the probans. However, as opposed to what the opponent is claiming here, in the case of an invalid only negative inference there can be a locus of the co-occurrence of the probans with the absence of the probandum, viz. the inferential subject.

402. The *siddhāntin* had suggested to adapt the defining characteristic to the case of an only negative inference by replacing the requirement of the non-pervasion of the probans with the requirement of the non-pervasion of the absence of the probandum. The opponent tries to demonstrate here what will happen if we drop the requirement of the non-pervasion of the probans.

403. An associate condition which does not meet the non-pervasion requirement might pervade both, probans and probandum, and it would then occur on the inferential subject and fail to vitiate an inference by indicating the absence of the probandum via its own absence on the inferential subject.

404. If fire is chosen as the probans and smoke as the probandum, only some loci of the probans are agreeing instances.

405. The probandum "being produced" is here substituted by an equilocatable property, viz. "being non-eternal".

406. If the associate condition pervades both, the probans and the probandum, thus violating a part of the defining characteristic suggested by the proponent of the right view, its utility as a corrector would no longer be warranted, i.e., it would fail to limit the range of the probans to that of the probandum. If the

associate condition pervades both, the probans and the probandum, and the range of the probandum is properly contained in that of the probans (cf. Fig. 24), then $H \setminus (S \cup U) = \emptyset$. Hence, the inferential subject, which is a locus of the probans, has to be an element of $H \cap U$, i.e., the associate condition has to be a property of the inferential subject. The converse of a genuine non-coextensive pervasion such as the converse of the pervasion of smoke by fire cannot be corrected by means of such an associate condition. Even though the converted probans "fire" occurs in some loci of the converted probandum "smoke", there is no pervasion in at least one locus (*ekatra*), such as, e.g., molten metal. If the associate condition pervades both, it does not help to secure the converted probandum. The latter may or may not occur in a common locus of the converted probans and the associate condition.

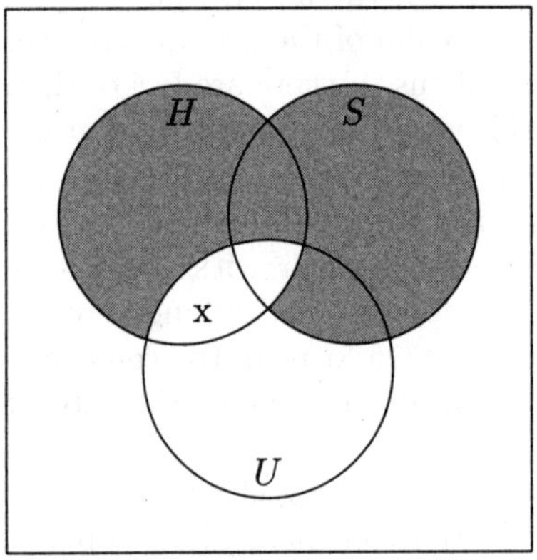

Fig. 24
H = the class of loci of the probans
S = the class of loci of the probandum
U = the class of loci of the associate condition

In order to demonstrate the indispensability of the associate condition's capacity to limit the range of an assumed probans to that of the probandum, the opponent refers to the invalid inference of the property of being produced (or non-eternal) from the property of being graspable by means of the external senses for us and for others. In this case the possession of universals serves to limit the range of the probans in an appropriate way (cf. Fig. 25).

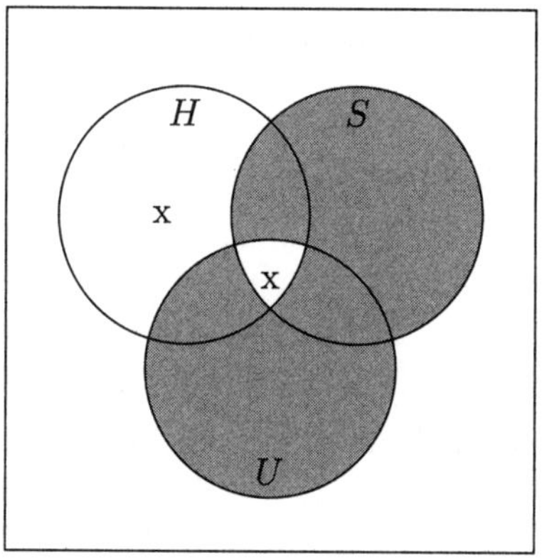

Fig. 25

H = the class of loci of the probans *asmadādibāhyendriyagrāhyatva*
S = the class of loci of the probandum *kṛtakatva* (or: *anityatva*)
U = the class of loci of the associate condition *sāmānyavattva*

sāmānyas $\in H \setminus (S \cup U)$; *ghaṭa* $\in H \cap S \cap U$

407. The opponent probably refers to the case of an only negative inference, which he regards as irrefutable by means of an associate condition according to the definition of the proponent of the right view.

408. Whenever the probans of an inference is an instance of the fallacy of the conditional probans, it can be vitiated by means of an associate condition. This includes the only negative inferences.

409. In the case of an only negative inference the probandum is known to be co-absent with the probans in any other locus than the inferential subject. Hence, a putative probans in an only negative inference might be refuted by means of an unfavorable reductio ad absurdum positing: "If the probandum did occur on the inferential subject, then it should co-occur with the probans outside the inferential subject."

410. In the case of an invalid only negative inference it is the absence of the probandum which should be regarded as the probans targeted by an associate condition. Since the actual probans in an only negative inference is co-absent with the probandum in any other locus than the inferential subject, its probative force is weak.

411. Note that $x \in S^c \cap U^c \to x \in H$ according to Fig. 23, i.e., if x is a locus of "the probans in the form of the absence of the probandum" and the absence of

the associate condition, then x is not a locus of "the probandum in the form of the absence of the probans".

412. However, as noted above, the fortifier-aspect seems to be unwarranted in this case (cf. Fig. 23).

413. *jaḍatva* is here a kind of *pakṣetaratva*-style *upādhi.*

414. *saṃbhāvanā* is a kind of biassed doubt (*saṃśaya*), i.e., an uncertainty concerning two opposing alternatives where one of them is more credible than the other (cf. Chakrabarti 2010: 3).

415. Advaitins regard the inference "Direct experience is an object of direct experience, because it is direct experience" (*anubhūtir anubhavyānubhūtitvāt*) as refutable by means of the associate condition "being insentient" (*jaḍatva*). In this case the ranges of probans and probandum are disjoint and the subject of the inference is the only instance which does not exhibit the probandum (cf. Fig. 26). Strictly speaking, the inference is devoid of disagreeing instances (something which is different from direct experience and which has been ascertained to be different from an object of direct experience) and it is therefore not only negative. However, the inferential subject comes close to a disagreeing instance, since from an Advaita perspective the inferential subject is at least more likely to be excluded from the range of loci of the probandum due to the fact that the associate condition "being insentient", which Advaitins regard as equilocatable with the probandum, is definitely not a property of the inferential subject.

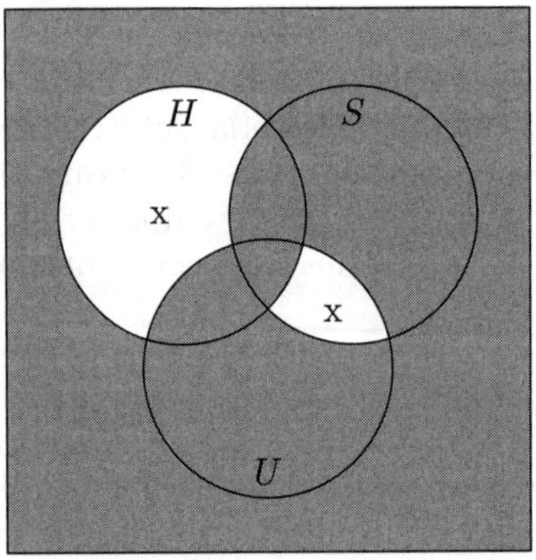

Fig. 26

H = the class of loci of the probans *anubhūtitva*
S = the class of loci of the probandum *anubhavyatva*
U = the class of loci of the associate condition *jaḍatva*

anubhūti $\in H \setminus (S \cup U)$; *ghaṭa* $\in (S \cap U) \setminus H$

416. i.e., the probandum of this inference can be secured by means of an associate condition

417. The theorists referred to as *kaiścid* seem to underscore the associate condition's function as a corrector. This function presupposes the existence of a positive correlation outside the inferential subject, which helps to secure the probandum wherever the probans co-occurs with the associate condition. Thus, the adherents of this position probably also insist that an inference targeted by an associate condition cannot be only negative. The present example of an inference which can be targeted by an associate condition is an invalid meta-inference based on a presumably valid object-level inference. The inferential subject of the former consists of every individual which is not an instance of the object-level probandum. The meta-inference probandum is the property of being identical to (i.e., "not other than") something resident in the inferential subject of the object-level inference. The meta-inference example is the object-level probandum, which occurs on the object-level inferential subject, since the object-level inference is supposed to be valid. The meta-inference probans, viz. knowability, is too wide. It is not pervaded by the meta-inference probandum: If something is knowable, it need not be identical to ("not other than") something resident in the inferential subject of the object-level inference. Since everything is knowable, everything would otherwise be a property of the object-level inference. If, e.g., the mountain is the inferential subject of the object-level inference, potness, which is knowable, would be a property of the mountain. Yet, there is a positive example of the concomitance of the meta-inference probans and the meta-inference probandum, viz. the probans of the object-level inference. Since there are agreeing instances, the meta-inference can be corrected by means of an associate condition.

418. In 2.1.3.2 *vyāptivirahabhūtatva* was introduced as a viable alternative characterization of the associate condition's function of vitiating.

419. This twofold classification cannot refer to the dubious/ascertained-distinction, since the type of pervasion which the proponent of the right view mentions here is supposed to be ascertained. Considering the examples which he is going to furnish, he seems to be referring here to the coextensive pervasion of the probandum by the *upādhi* and to the coextensive pervasion of the probandum by the *upādhi* in the range of the probans.

420. cf. 1.1.7.2

421. cf. 1.1.12

422. By contrast, Gaṅgeśa distinguishes three types of dubious associate conditions. He defines the associate condition as a property which does not pervade the probans, while it pervades the probandum in the range of the probans (cf. Phillips 2002: 21). Hence, he distinguishes three types of dubious associate conditions, since the pervasion- and the non-pervasion-condition can be both dubious, or the first one can be dubious, while the second one is ascertained, or vice versa (cf. Frauwallner 1970: 59). Since the UD includes the pervasion of the associate condition by the probandum in the definition as an additional requirement, there are three criteria, which may be dubious or ascertained. Therefore, it would have been appropriate to distinguish seven ($= 2^3 - 1$) types of dubious associate conditions. Later (cf. 3.1.2) the UD will refer to a sixfold classification schema, which is apparently based on the different ranges of loci involved in the pervasion of the probandum by the associate condition. However, the corresponding passage in the manuscript is afflicted with corrupt readings.

423. This is again an example of an associate condition where both, the pervasion- and the non-pervasion-condition, are ascertained.

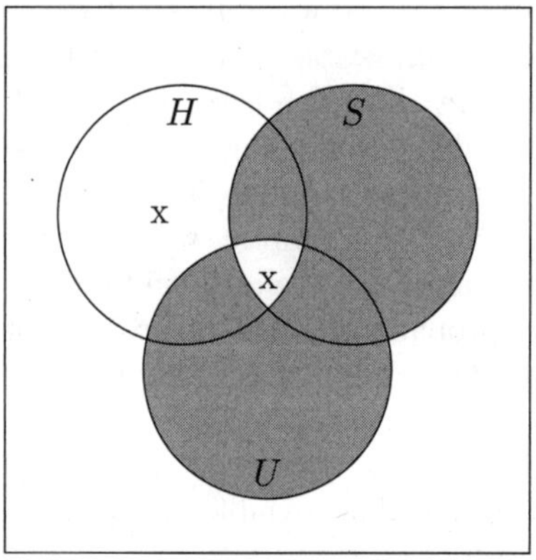

Fig. 27

H = the class of loci of the probans *asparśadravyatva*
S = the class of loci of the probandum *vibhutva*
U = the class of loci of the associate condition *amūrtadravyatva*

manas $\in H \setminus (S \cup U)$; *diś*, *kāla*, *ākāśa*, *ātman* $\in H \cap S \cap U$

424. The range of the joint occurrence of probans and associate condition is coextensively pervaded by the probandum (cf. Fig. 27).

425. i.e., equilocatable

426. Since only amorphous substances are all-pervasive, the associate condition certainly pervades the probandum. The non-pervasion of the probans by the associate condition is also warranted, because the mind is intangible, but not amorphous.

427. The Mitrā-example is understood by Gaṅgeśa in such a way that both, the non-pervasion of the probans by the probandum and the pervasion of the probandum by the associate condition, are dubious (cf. Frauwallner 1970: 59 and Phillips 2002: 19f and 111f). It is assumed that eating vegetables during pregnancy is a sufficient cause for the baby's dark complexion. Hence, $(H \cap U) \setminus S = \emptyset$ in both diagrams in Fig. 28, i.e., the pervasion of the associate condition by the probandum in the range of the probans is warranted. However, the vegetable diet is not a necessary condition for the baby's dark complexion. The dark complexion may as well be genetically determined by the father's dark complexion. Moreover, Mitrā may or may not have eaten vegetables while she was pregnant with her first five sons. Therefore, her first five sons, who are dark-complexioned, are $\in (H \cap S) \setminus U$ or $\in H \cap S \cap U$ (cf. the bar across the boundary between the corresponding areas in Fig. 28, which indicates that we are faced with an alternative here). We are also not sure about Mitrā's diet during her current pregnancy. Mitrā might not have eaten vegetables during her current pregnancy, or she has so far eaten vegetables, but will not stick to her diet, until she gives birth to her sixth son. Thus, the unborn sixth son may turn out to be fair-complexioned (cf. the leftmost diagram in Fig. 28). If he turns out to be dark-complexioned (cf. the rightmost diagram in Fig. 28), he is like the other sons $\in H \cap S$.

In the case of the Dṛṣadvatī-example the pervasion of the associate condition by the probandum in the range of the probans and the non-pervasion of the probans by the associate condition are both warranted. If someone is a son of Dṛṣadvatī who is near at hand, then he is dark-complexioned. Hence, $(H \cap U) \setminus S = \emptyset$ in both diagrams in Fig. 29. The reverse does not hold, since the sixth son of Dṛṣadvatī may be dark-complexioned, but he "has gone to another region", and it is assumed that we do not have any account of his complexion. The pervasion of the probandum by the associate condition is dubious, as in the case of the Mitrā-example.

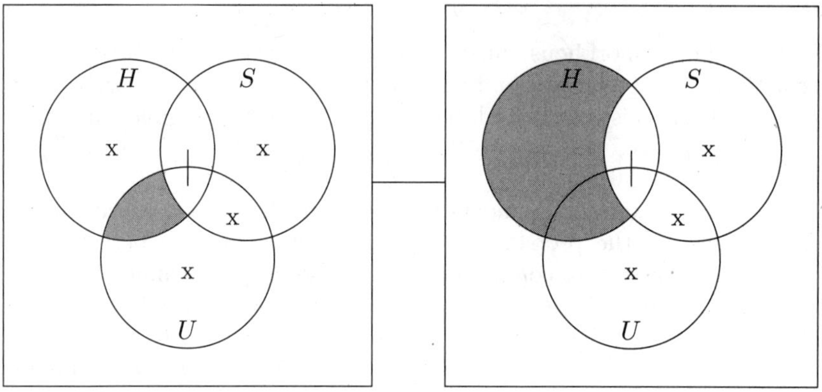

Fig. 28

H = the class of loci of the probans *mitrātanayatva*
S = the class of loci of the probandum *śyāmatva*
U = the class of loci of the associate condition *śākādyāhārapariṇatipūrvakatva*

Mitrā's 6th son is fair-complexioned and $\in H \setminus (S \cup U)$, or he is dark-complexioned and $\in H \cap S$; Mitrā's first 5 sons $\in H \cap S$; *kāka* $\in S \setminus (H \cup U)$; someone else's dark-complexioned son nourished on vegetables $\in (S \cap U) \setminus H$; *śvetaśaśa* $\in U \setminus (H \cup S)$

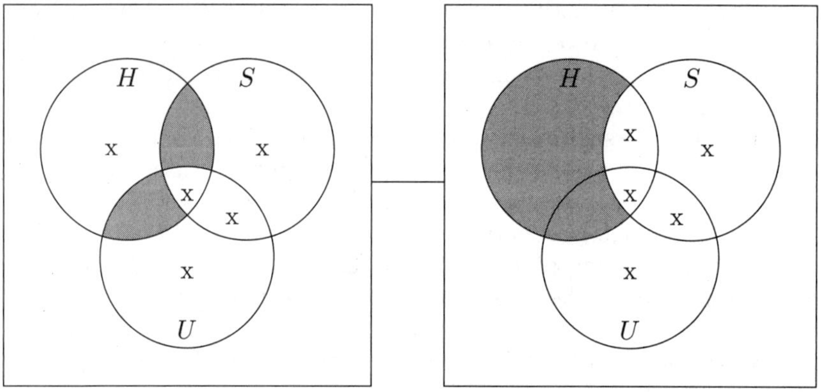

Fig. 29

H = the class of loci of the probans *dṛṣadvatītanayatva*
S = the class of loci of the probandum *śyāmatva*
U = the class of loci of the associate condition *saṃnihitatva*

Dṛṣadvatī's 6th son is fair-complexioned and $\in H \setminus (S \cup U)$, or he is dark-complexioned and $\in (H \cap S) \setminus U$; Dṛṣadvatī's other 5 sons $\in H \cap S \cap U$; *kāka* $\in S \setminus (H \cup U)$; someone else's dark-complexioned son being near at hand $\in (S \cap U) \setminus H$; *saṃnihitaśvetaśaśa* $\in U \setminus (H \cup S)$

428. The neuter ending of *sādhanāvyāpakasiddham* is owing to the fact that this compound is a Tatpuruṣa used as an adverb.

429. As noted by Gaṅgeśa as well, the inference of the property of being preceded by (prenatal) digestion of food consisting of vegetables etc. from the property of being a son of Mitrā can be vitiated by means of the property of being dark-complexioned as an associate condition (cf. Frauwallner 1970: 58).

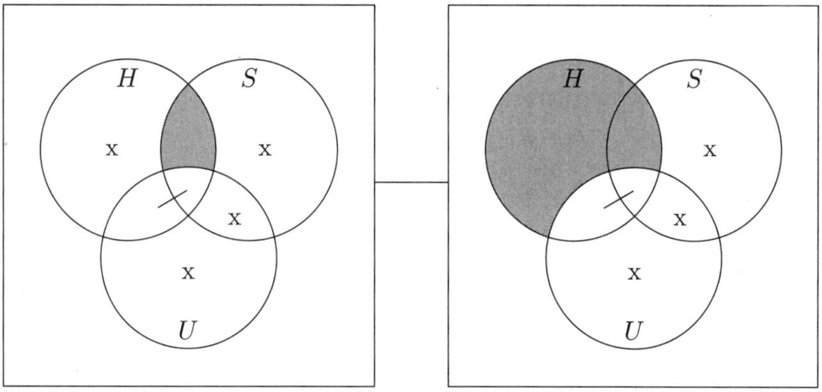

Fig. 30

H = the class of loci of the probans *mitrātanayatva*
S = the class of loci of the probandum *śākādyāhārapariṇatipūrvakatva*
U = the class of loci of the associate condition *śyāmatva*

Mitrā's 6th son is fair-complexioned and $\in H \setminus (S \cup U)$, or he is dark-complexioned and $\in H \cap U$; Mitrā's first 5 sons $\in H \cap U$; *kāka* $\in U \setminus (H \cup S)$; someone else's dark-complexioned son nourished on vegetables $\in (S \cap U) \setminus H$; *śvetaśaśa* $\in S \setminus (H \cup U)$

430. It has to be noted that the non-pervasion of the probans is dubious in this case.

431. This observation refers to the above-mentioned possibility to replace an element in an ensemble of probans, probandum and associate condition with a functional equivalent. In the case of the Mitrā-example the proponent of the right view concocted another combination of the same constituents of a defeasible inference by exchanging the roles of probandum and associate condition. The opponent argues that a similar procedure should be applicable to the inference of the property of being non-eternal from the property of being graspable through the external senses by us and others, which can be vitiated by means of the associate condition "pos-

session of universals" (cf. 2.1.5, Fig. 25). For that purpose he suggests to replace the associate condition with something else, viz. the property of being produced.

432. Since the property of being produced is now assumed as an associate condition for the original counterfeit pervasion, it should not pervade the probans "being graspable through the external senses by us and others" and there has to be an associate condition for the non-pervasion. The property of being non-eternal seems to be an appropriate candidate. As an associate condition it should not pervade the probans. But then the refutation of the original pervasion begs the question, because in order to demonstrate the non-pervasion of the property "being graspable through the external senses by us and others" by the property "being non-eternal", that very non-pervasion is presupposed.

433. i.e., the inference: "Sound is non-eternal, because it is graspable through the external senses by us and others."

434. In the case of the Mitrā-example it is uncertain whether the sixth unborn son is an instance of the concomitance of probans and probandum. In the case of the sound it is certain that it is an instance of the concomitance of the property of being graspable through the external senses by us and others and the property of being non-eternal. A supporting reductio ad absurdum can serve to settle the issue.

435. In accordance with the previous sentence *aniścayayoga* might be added here as the subject of the sentence. The property "being produced" is evidently an ascertained associate condition for the inference of the property "possession of universals" from the property "being graspable through the external senses by us and others".

436. If there is "no connection of the property of being an associate condition with the absence of the non-appropriateness of the ascertainment" of the non-pervasion condition, this means that the ascertainment of the non-pervasion condition is inappropriate in the case of the associate condition for the Mitrā-example.

437. The corresponding passage in the manuscript is afflicted with corrupt readings. The first two types of associate conditions in the present classification seem to suggest that the way in which the associate condition pervades the probandum serves here as a criterion to classify associate conditions. The examples are all dubious associate conditions. In the case of the first two examples the pervasion of the probandum by the associate condition is, however, ascertained. The third and the fourth type seem to suggest a different classification schema, since they are concerned with the associate condition's relation to the absence of the probans and the probandum, respectively. There is obviously a mismatching between the number-

ings of the types of associate conditions and the corresponding examples, because it is rather the fourth example than the third one (the Mitrā-example) which matches the specification of the third type of associate conditions. The manuscript seems to skip one of the last two types. The specification of the remaining one is afflicted with a corrupt reading, viz. *āpāāvyāpakā*. This tangle of syllables is like the other four characterizations of types of associate conditions enclosed in semi-*daṇḍas*. If it refers to merely one type, the present taxonomy falls short of one item. The scribe might also have conflated two items here. The initial *āpāā-* in *āpāāvyāpakā* possibly derives from an original *-vyāpakā*. Hence, the last two types of associate conditions might both be pervaders of something which is unnamed in the manuscript. The rather unsystematic nature of the classification does not give any clue to an appropriate emendation. It is not unlikely that the first four specifications (or some of them) are already owing to corrupt readings.

438. Smoke might be the effect of fire ignited by a human being, but it might also be the effect of a lightning stroke or a heatwave (as in the case of a forest fire). According to Gaṅgeśa such natural phenomena are the only effects in the world which are caused by God alone, i.e., without the help of merit and demerit as additional causal factors (Bhattacharyya/Potter 1993: 607). Therefore, smoke can be regarded as an agreeing instance. The assumption that "being produced" is actually an associate condition in this case is justified from the perspective of an opponent of the design inference, who doubts that $(H \cap U) \setminus S = \emptyset$ (cf. Fig. 31), i.e., although the associate condition pervades the probandum, there may or may not be a coextensive pervasion of the probandum by the associate condition. The pervasion of the whole probandum by the associate condition as a characteristic of the present type of associate conditions is warranted, since $S \setminus U = \emptyset$ in both diagrams in Fig. 31.

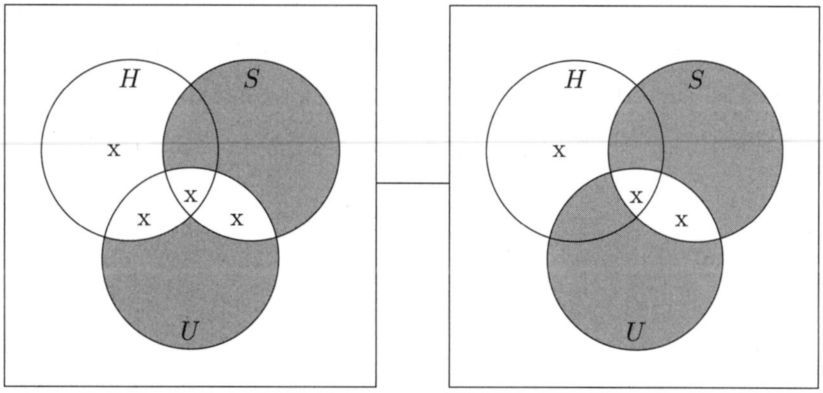

Fig. 31

H = the class of loci of the probans *śarīryajanyatva*

S = the class of loci of the probandum *sakartṛkatva*
U = the class of loci of the associate condition *kāryatva*

kṣityādi $\in (H \cap U) \setminus S$, or *kṣityādi* $\in H \cap S \cap U$; *gaganādi* $\in H \setminus (S \cup U)$; smoke which has an incorporeal causal agent $\in H \cap S \cap U$; *ghaṭa* $\in (S \cap U) \setminus H$

439. The associate condition can be regarded as dubious in this case, because the inferential subject is left unspecified. According to the system of classical Vaiśeṣika ontology, which has been adopted by conservative Navya-Naiyāyikas (cf. Ingalls 1951: 37f), there are only two primitive relations with an ontological footing, viz. contact and inherence. Navya-Naiyāyikas often take into account two additional types of relation (cf. Matilal 1968: 37), viz. "self-linking relation" (*svarūpasaṃbandha*), the relation which integrates, e.g., imposed properties (*upādhi*) or absences and their substrates, and "identity" (*tādātmya*), i.e., "non-difference" (*abheda*). However, in contrast to contact and inherence a self-linking relation or an identity is a merely "'supposed' relation" (Matilal 1968: 44), not a separate entity over and above the relata (cf. Bhattacharya/Potter 2011: 16).

Hence, from the perspective of classical Vaiśeṣika or conservative Navya-Nyāya ontology there are in the present case only two possibilities if the inferential subject is considered as a locus of the probans: Either it is contact or inherence. If we exclude the inferential subject from the range of the probandum in order to avoid begging the question, it would be $\in (H \cap U) \setminus S$ if it is contact, for contact possesses contactness and it can be a relation with something inhering like, e.g., a piece of cloth. A piece of cloth inheres in the threads, but it can also be related to the ground via contact. If the inferential subject is inherence, contact would be $\in H \cap S \cap U$ and $(H \cap U) \setminus S = \emptyset$. Hence, the pervasion of the associate condition by the probandum is again dubious. The associate condition pervades the probandum, only insofar as it is limited by the probans, i.e., the pervasion of the probandum, insofar as it is limited by a certain qualifier (viz. the probans), is warranted in this case. Inherence is $\notin (H \cap S) \setminus U$, because inherence does not inhere and is therefore not a locus of itself.

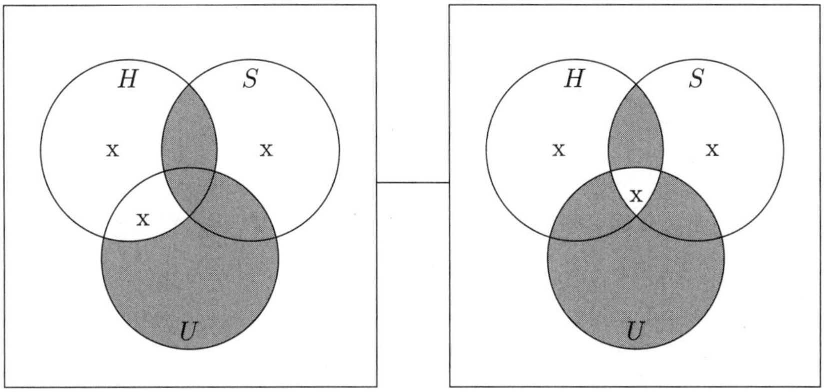

Fig. 32

H = the class of loci of the probans *samavetasaṃbandhatva*
S = the class of loci of the probandum *samavāyādhikaraṇatva* $\setminus \{$*pakṣa*$\}$
U = the class of loci of the associate condition *saṃyogatva*

saṃyoga $\in (H \cap U) \setminus S$, or *saṃyoga* $\in H \cap S \cap U$; *samavāya* $\in H \setminus (S \cup U)$; *sāmānyas* like *sattā* and a piece of cloth (which inheres in the threads) $\in S \setminus (H \cup U)$

440. There seems to be a blunder here, because the Mitrā-example with the modified probandum rather matches a type of associate condition which is like the second type a pervader of the probandum limited by a certain qualifier, save that the pervasion is now dubious (cf. the straight line across the areas for $(H \cap S) \setminus U$ and $H \cap S \cap U$ in Fig. 33, which indicates that $(H \cap S) \setminus U$ may or may not be empty).

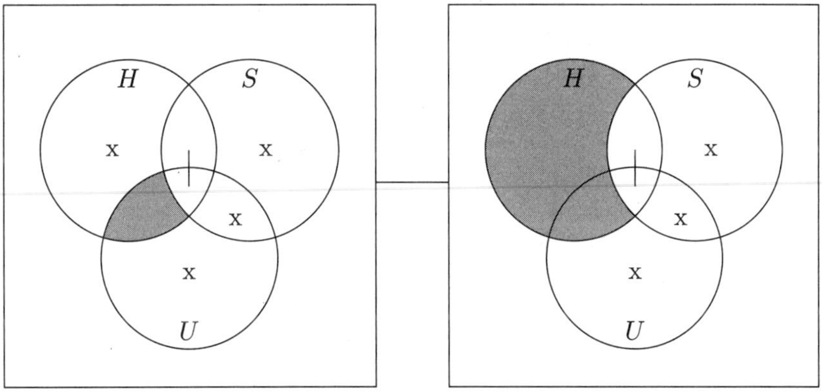

Fig. 33

H = the class of loci of the probans *mitrātanayatva*
S = the class of loci of the probandum *śyāmatva* limited by *puruṣatva*
U = the class of loci of the associate condition *śākādyāhārapariṇatipūrvakatva*

Mitrā's 6th son is fair-complexioned and $\in H \setminus (S \cup U)$, or he is dark-complexioned and $\in H \cap S$; Mitrā's first 5 sons $\in H \cap S$; someone else's dark-complexioned son not nourished on vegetables $\in S \setminus (H \cup U)$; someone else's dark-complexioned son nourished on vegetables $\in (S \cap U) \setminus H$; *śvetaśaśa* $\in U \setminus (H \cup S)$

441. The present example rather matches the third type. As explained in 2.1.5, Advaitins regard direct experience as self-illuminating. Vimuktātman identifies it with the *ātman* (cf. Bartley 2001: 13 and Potter 2006: 163). Everything else than direct experience is insentient matter, which is devoid of the property of self-illumination. The present attempt to prove that direct experience is self-illuminating can be refuted by means of a dubious associate condition: Since the occurrence of the probandum on the inferential subject is an open issue, direct experience, which is not insentient, may be $\in H \setminus (S \cup U)$, or it may be $\in (H \cap S) \setminus U$ (cf. Fig. 34). If nothing else than direct experience can be self-illuminating, then $S \setminus H = \emptyset$, i.e., the associate condition's pervasion of the absence of the probans is warranted. Its non-pervasion of the absence of the probandum is dubious. Therefore, the present example matches the third type, but not the fourth one.

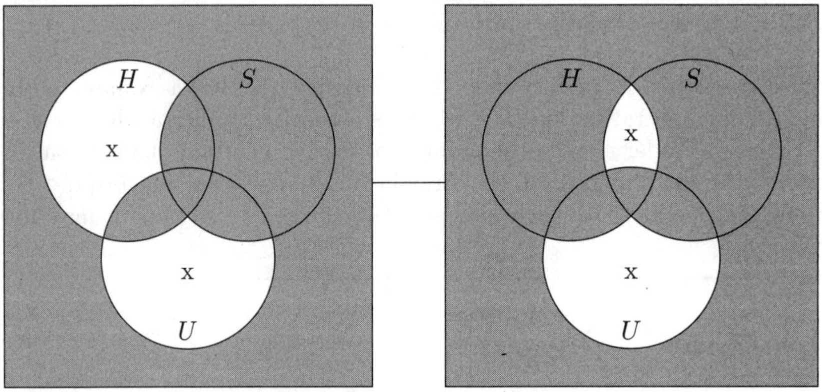

Fig. 34

H = the class of loci of the probans *anubhūtitva*
S = the class of loci of the probandum *svayaṃprakāśatva*
U = the class of loci of the associate condition *jaḍatva*

anubhūti $\in H \setminus (S \cup U)$, or *anubhūti* $\in (H \cap S) \setminus U$; *ghaṭa* $\in U \setminus (H \cup S)$

442. Since the fourth example matches the third type, one might be inclined to anticipate that the fifth example matches the fourth type. But in the case of the present example the associate condition does not pervade the absence of the probandum. As explained above, the manuscript reading for the specification of the fifth and the sixth type is corrupt.

Probans and probandum in the present example are the negations of properties which function as probans and probandum in the putative pervasion of "being produced by an embodied agent" by "having a causal agent (in the sense of: being a positive effect)". In order to demonstrate that the negated probans (i.e., *śarīryajanyatva*) is not pervaded by the negated probandum (i.e., *asakartṛkatva*), the proponent of the right view refers to the property of being ether etc. as a dubious associate condition. Ether functions here probably as an exemplary case, i.e., it is probably taken to represent the whole range of loci of eternal entities, so that the only individuals which might be $\in (H \cap S) \setminus U$ are non-eternal individuals like the earth or growing grass (cf. the rightmost diagram in Fig. 35).

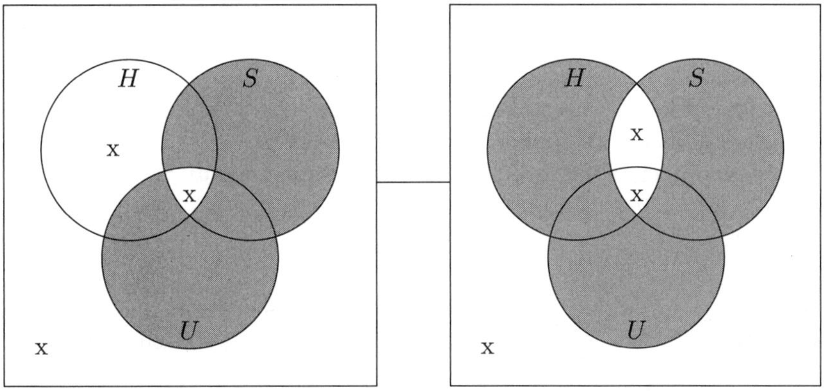

Fig. 35

H = the class of loci of *śarīryajanyatva* (= the negated probans)
S = the class of loci of *asakartṛkatva* (= the negated probandum)
U = the class of loci of the associate condition *gaganatvādi*

kṣityādi $\in H \setminus (S \cup U)$, or *kṣityādi* $\in (H \cap S) \setminus U$; *gagana* $\in H \cap S \cap U$; *ghaṭa* $\in (H \cup S \cup U)^c$

443. The context of the present example of an associate condition is a defeasible reductio ad absurdum. An inference would have been inappropriate in this case, since what purportedly functions here as a pervaded property, viz. "having a causal agent", is unlike a probans in an inference not established as a property of the putative locus, viz. the earth etc. $(S \cap U) \setminus H$ can be regarded as non-empty if *sakartṛkatva* is understood in the sense of "being a positive effect". In this case a man-made posterior absence due to a destruction by means of hands and feet is $\in (S \cap U) \setminus H$.

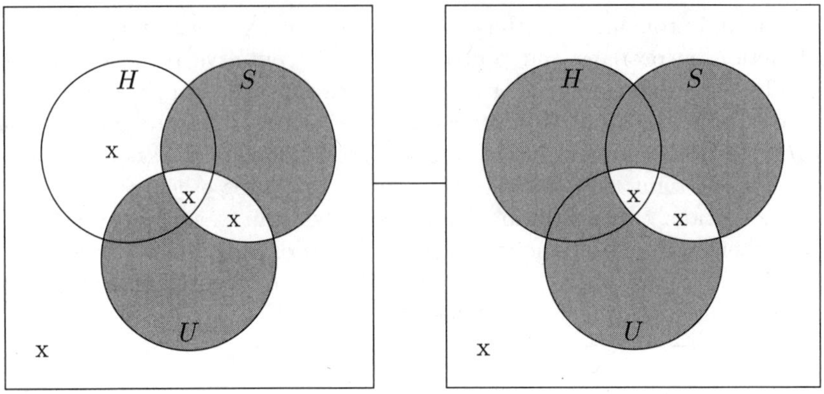

Fig. 36

H = the class of loci of the probans *sakartṛkatva*
S = the class of loci of the probandum *śarīrijanyatva*
U = the class of loci of the associate condition *karacaraṇādivyāpārapūrvakatva*

kṣityādi $\in H \setminus (S \cup U)$, or *kṣityādi* $\in (H \cup S \cup U)^c$; *ghaṭa* $\in H \cap S \cap U$; *dhvaṃsābhāva* $\in (S \cap U) \setminus H$

444. The concept of pervasion is included in the concept of an associate condition. Thus, the definition of the associate condition becomes circular, since pervasion is a relation without associate condition.

445. The opponent relates the validity of an inference to the absence of an associate condition, but he seems to be reluctant to explicate this absence by means of a defining characteristic for associate conditions. The latter are rather regarded as singular entities which defy any attempt to characterize them by means of some unifying criteria.

446. The proponent of the right view seems to be referring here to the dissimilarity between a probans in a valid inference and a probans which only in combination with an associate condition serves to secure the probandum.

447. This observation dovetails with the UD's specification of the function of an associate condition in the second *pariccheda*. According to the UD an associate condition is a means to demonstrate that the putative probans in an inference is actually a pseudo-probans, viz. the so-called "conditional probans" (*vyāpyatvāsiddha*). Hence, the second member of an inference can be understood in the sense of the implicit claim that the probans is a genuine prover, i.e., it implies the denial that the utility of the probans as a prover is refutable by means of an associate condition.

448. What the opponent refers to here as the "end" of the inference, is probably the part consisting of the last three members of a five-membered inference. This part includes the pervasion stated in the third member. The third member would be redundant if the fact that the probans is devoid of an associate condition were already implied by the second member.

449. The opponent raises the question why the pervasion which indicates the probans's independence from an associate condition is not explicitly stated in the second member rather than in the third one. If the second member had the function to state the probans's independence from an associate condition, a formulation like "because it possesses a smoke which is pervaded" would have been more appropriate.

450. The probans's independence from an associate condition is not inherent in the second member, because the latter does not include any reference to the pervasion.

451. Avoiding redundancy at all costs would have the effect of an undue truncation of an inference, which may well affect other members of an inference too. The fact that the probans is a property of the inferential subject is also stated twice in an inference, viz. in the second and in the fourth member. So, one might as well skip the second member.

452. In the case of the smoke/fire-example the fourth member expresses that the mountain possesses a smoke which is similar to the smoke in the examples, insofar as the smoke on the mountain also co-occurs with fire. In this way the fourth member contains a restatement of the probans's property of being a property of the inferential subject.

453. i.e., due to the fact that some additional information in the form of an associate condition is known to be required to secure the probandum and is therefore expected to be part of an inferential situation

454. The second member involves a careful consideration of the possibility that the probans's utility as a prover might be vitiated by means of a blocker in the form of an associate condition.

455. i.e., the smoke in the case of the correct inference of fire from smoke

456. Since the UD's definition of an associate condition comprises three criteria, which may or may not be fulfilled, there should be 6 (= $2^3 - 2$) apparent associate conditions. Hence, one case is missing in the present taxonomy, viz. the apparent

type which pervades both, probans and probandum, and is also pervaded by the latter.

457. The locative absolute *sāmānyavattve saty* is here part of the probans. The example rather illustrates that type which is missing in the UD's taxonomy. (Only the criterion "non-pervasion of the probans" is unfulfilled.)

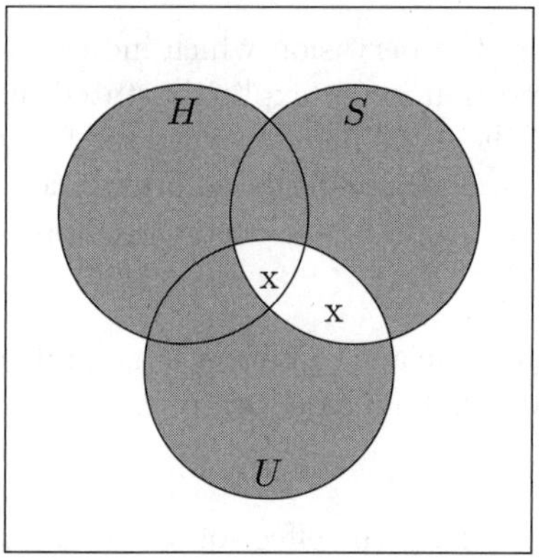

Fig. 37

H = the class of loci of the probans *sāmānyavattve saty asmadādibāhyendriyag-rāhyatva*
S = the class of loci of the probandum *anityatva*
U = the class of loci of the associate condition *kāryatva*

ghaṭa $\in H \cap S \cap U$; aggregates of *vāyu* $\in (S \cap U) \setminus H$

458. The result of replacing the associate condition in the afore-mentioned example with *sāvayavatva* is rather another example of the preceding type.

459. This is actually an example of the second type. Only the criterion "pervadedness by the probandum" is fulfilled.

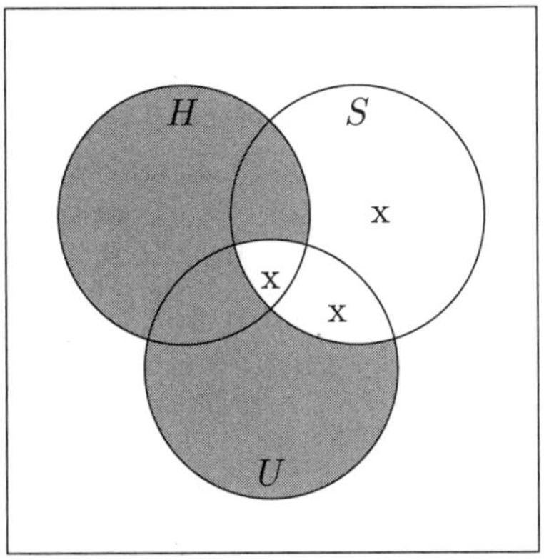

Fig. 38

H = the class of loci of the probans *guṇatva*
S = the class of loci of the probandum *abhidheyatva*
U = the class of loci of the associate condition *sattāyogitva*

rūpa $\in H \cap S \cap U$; *ghaṭa* $\in (S \cap U) \setminus H$; *sāmānyas* $\in S \setminus (H \cup U)$

460. The manuscript probably has a lacuna here, which is not indicated by the scribe. The associate condition seems to be missing and only a fragment of the inference associated with it is still extant, viz. the probans (*kṛtakatva*) and something which might be part of the probandum (*sāmānyavattve saty*). It is not obvious how to reconstruct the intended example from these remnants. The following is at least an appropriate example based on the same probans:

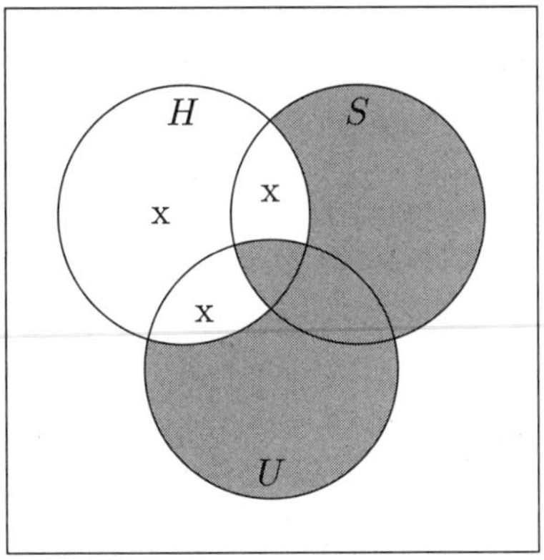

Fig. 39

H = the class of loci of the probans *kṛtakatva*
S = the class of loci of the probandum *ghaṭatva*
U = the class of loci of the associate condition *paṭatva*

ratha $\in H \setminus (S \cup U)$; *paṭa* $\in (H \cap U) \setminus S$; *ghaṭa* $\in (H \cap S) \setminus U$

461. The probandum is not mentioned here, but *ghaṭatva* would be an appropriate choice, because it is pervaded by *aśrāvaṇatva* in the range of the probans. It should be noted that for Gaṅgeśa this would be an example of a genuine associate condition. The author of the UD classifies it as an example of one of the apparent types, because he insists on the coextensive pervasion of the probandum by the associate condition.

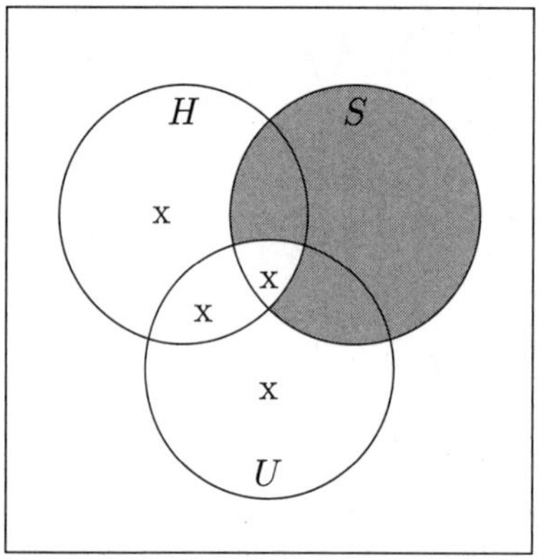

Fig. 40

H = the class of loci of the probans *kṛtakatva*
S = the class of loci of the probandum *ghaṭatva*
U = the class of loci of the associate condition *aśrāvaṇatva*.

śabda $\in H \setminus (S \cup U)$; *paṭa* $\in (H \cap U) \setminus S$; *ghaṭa* $\in H \cap S \cap U$; *ātman* $\in U \setminus (H \cup S)$

462. This example actually matches the fifth type.

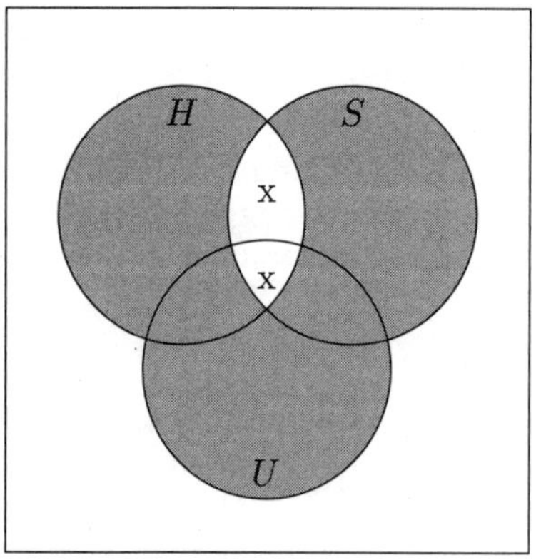

Fig. 41

H = the class of loci of the probans *jñeyatva*
S = the class of loci of the probandum *abhidheyatva*

U = the class of loci of the associate condition *guṇatva*

ghaṭa $\in (H \cap S) \setminus U$; *śabda* $\in H \cap S \cap U$

463. The property of being different from the inferential subject is not needed as a vitiator of a patent falsehood. Since in this case there is no doubt that the probandum is, has been, or ever will be locatable on the inferential subject, the latter fails to fulfill the inferential-subject-proviso (*pakṣatā*), which requires an inference to start with a doubt concerning the occurrence of the probandum on the inferential subject (cf. 1.1.6.3 and 1.2.1).

464. *jīyāt* = 3rd person sg. precative parasmaipada of the root *ji*.

Chapter 5

Glossary

ativyāpti	over-pervasion
atyantābhāva	absolute absence
adhikaraṇa	locus
anavasthā	regressus ad infinitum
anukūlatarka	favorable reductio ad absurdum
anugama	consecutive character
anubhava	awareness
anubhūti	direct experience (in the UD used in the context of an inference referring to Advaita philosophy)
anumāna	inference
anumiti	inferential awareness
anaikāntika	inconclusive (referring to a type of *hetvābhāsa*), fallacy of an inconclusive probans
anyonyasaṃśraya	mutual dependence
anyonyābhāva	mutual absence
anyonyāśraya	mutual dependence
anvaya	positive correlation
anvayavyatirekin	positive and negative (referring to a type of inference)
anvayavyāpti	positive pervasion
abhāva	absence

alaukikapratyakṣa	extraordinary perception
avacchinna	limited
avacchedaka	limitor
avyabhicāra	non-deviation
avyāpti	non-pervasion
ātmāśraya	self-dependence
āpatti	undesirable conclusion
āśraya	substrate
āśrayāsiddha	unestablished with regard to the substrate (referring to a type of *hetvābhāsa*)
itaretarāśraya	mutual dependence
udāharaṇa	example (also used in the sense of the third member of a five-membered inference)
udbhāvanaprakāra	mode of bringing to the fore (a precursor of the concept of intension in Western logic)
upanaya	application (the fourth member of a five-membered inference)
upalakṣaṇa	indicative mark
upādhi	associate condition; imposed property
upādhyābhāsa	apparent associate condition
kevalavyatirekin	only negative (referring to a type of inference)
kevalānvayin	universally positive (referring to a type of property); only positive (referring to a type of inference)
cakraka/ *cakrakāśraya*	circularity
jāti	universal; sophistry
jñāna	knowledge, cognition (in the sense of a cognitive event)
jñānavyāpti	epistemic pervasion
tarka	reductio ad absurdum, hypothetical reasoning
tādātmya	identity

dūṣaṇa	vitiating, vitiator, refuting, refutation, fault, mistake, defect
dṛṣṭānta	example (an agreeing or a disagreeing instance)
dharma	property
dhvaṃsābhāva	posterior absence
nigamana	conclusion (the fifth member of a five-membered inference)
niścaya	certitude, ascertainment, determination
niścitopādhi	ascertained associate condition
pakṣa	inferential subject; thesis
pakṣatā	inferential-subject-proviso
pakṣetaratva	the property of being different from the subject of the inference
padārtha	category
parāmarśa	reflective grasping
parārthānumāna	inference for others
pūrvapakṣa	view of an opponent
pūrvapakṣin	opponent
pratikūlatarka	unfavorable reductio ad absurdum
pratijñā	thesis (the first member in a five-membered inference)
pratipakṣa	counter-thesis
pratiyogin	counterpositive (referring to the absentee of an absence); relational adjunct
pratīti	knowledge, cognition (in the sense of a veridical awareness), understanding
pramā	veridical awareness
pramāṇa	knowledge source
prameya	knowable, an object of a veridical awareness
prayojaka	fortifying, fortifier
prasaṅga	undesirable consequence
prāgabhāva	prior absence

prāmāṇya	validity
bādha	patent falsehood, contradiction
bādhaka	sublating, blocker
bhūyodarśana	multiple observation
bheda	difference
lakṣaṇa	defining characteristic
vastuvyāpti	factual pervasion
vipakṣa	disagreeing instance, range of disagreeing instances
vibhu	all-pervasive
viruddha	incoherent (referring to a type of *hetvābhāsa*)
viśeṣaṇa	qualifier
viśeṣalakṣaṇa	specific defining characteristic
viśeṣavyāpti	particularized pervasion
viśeṣya	qualificand
viṣamavyāpti	non-coextensive pervasion
vyatireka	negative correlation
vyatirekavyāpti	negative pervasion
vyabhicāra	deviation
vyabhicārin	deviating (referring to a type of *hetvābhāsa*)
vyāpaka	pervading, pervader
vyāpti	pervasion
vyāpya	pervaded
vyāpyatvāsiddha	unestablished with respect to pervadedness (referring to a type of *hetvābhāsa*; in the UD more specifically used to designate one of its varieties, viz. the conditional probans)
saṃkara	overlap (referring to one of the *jātibādhakas*)
saṃdigdhopādhi	dubious asociate condition
saṃbandha	relation
saṃbhāvanā	expectation
saṃyoga	contact

saṃvid	conscious experience
saṃśaya	doubt
saṃsargābhāva	relational absence
saṃskāra	mental impression
sapakṣa	agreeing instance, range of agreeing instances
samaniyata	equilocatable
samavāya	inherence
samavyāpti	coextensive pervasion
sādhana	probans; proof; means
sādhya	probandum
sāmayikābhava	temporary absence
sāmānādhikaraṇya	co-occurrence
sāmānya	universal; general character; universality
sāmānyalakṣaṇa	general defining characteristic
sāmānyalakṣaṇapratyakṣa	perception that grasps the general character
sāmānyalakṣaṇāpratyāsatti	sense-object-contact which is characterized by the general character
sāhacarya	concomitance
siddhānta	right view, settled opinion
siddhāntin	proponent of the right view
sopādhikahetu	conditional probans (a type of *hetvābhāsa*)
smṛti	recollection
svarūpasaṃbandha	self-linking relation
svarūpāsiddha	essentially unestablished (referring to a type of *hetvābhāsa*)
svārthānumāna	inference for oneself
hetu	probans; the second member of a five-membered inference
hetvābhāsa	apparent probans, pseudo-probans

Bibliography

1. Primary Sources

ĀTV Ātmatattvaviveka: *Udayanācārya's Ātmatattvaviveka with the Commentaries of Śaṅkara Miśra, Bhagīratha Ṭhakkura and Tārkikaśiromaṇi.* Ed. Vindhyesvariprasada Dvivedin and Lakshmana Sastri Dravida. BI 170. Calcutta 1939: Baptist Mission Press.

BN Brief Notes: *Brief Notes on the Modern Nyāya System of Philosophy and its Technical Terms by Maheśa Chandra Nyāyaratna.* Calcutta 1891: Hare Press.

IS Iṣṭasiddhi: *Iṣṭasiddhi of Vimuktātman with extracts from the Vivaraṇa of Jñānottama.* Ed. M. Hiriyanna. GOS 65. Baroda 1933: Baptist Mission Press.

Kir Kiraṇāvalī: *Kiraṇāvalī of Udayanācārya.* Fasc. 4: Ed. Narendra Chandra Vedantatirtha. BI 200. Calcutta 1956: Asiatic Society.

MVV Mahāvidyāvidambana: *Mahāvidyā-Vidambana of Bhatta Vādīndra with the Commentaries of Ānandapūrṇa and Bhuvanasundara Sūri and the Daśa-Sloki of Kulārka Pandita with Vivarana and Vivarana Tippana.* Ed. Mangesh Ramakrishna Telang. GOS 12. Baroda 1920: The Gujarati Printing Press.

Niṣk Niṣkaṇṭaka, in: TR

NK Nyāyakandalī, in: *The Bhāshya of Praśastapāda together with the Nyāyakandalī of Śrīdhara.* Vol. IV. *Sanskrit Text.* Ed. Vindhyeśvarīprasāda Dvivedin. VSS 6. Varanasi 1895 (2nd edition: Delhi 1984: Sri Satguru Publications).

NKoś Nyāyakośa: *Nyāyakośa or Dictionary of Technical Terms of Indian Philosophy by Bhīmācārya Jhalakīkar, Revised by Vasudev Shastri Abhyankar.* Poona 1928: Chaukhamba Surbharati Prakashan.

NKus Nyāyakusumāñjali: *Nyāyakusumāñjali of Nyāyāchārya Sri Udayanāchārya, With the Commentary of Mahāmahopādhyāya Varddhamānopādhyāya, And the Gloss of Mahāmahopādhyāya Ruchi datta.* Ed. Laxman Shastri Dravid. Varanasi 1912: Vidya Vilas Press.

NM Nyāyamañjarī: *The Nyāyamañjarī of Jayanta Bhaṭṭa.* Ed. Sūrya Nārāyana Śukla. KSS 106. Varanasi 1936: Vidya Vilas Press.

NP Nyāyapariśuddhi: *Nyāyapariśuddhi, By Sri Venkatnath Sri Vedāntāchārya With a Commentary Called Nyayasar. By Sri Niwāsachārya.* Fasc. 1 – 5. Ed. Vidyābhūshan Lakshmanāchārya. CSS 249 (= Fasc. 1), CSS 250 (= Fasc. 2), CSS 262 (= Fasc. 4), CSS 299 (= Fasc. 5). Varanasi 1918 – 1923: Vidya Vilas Press.

NR Nyāyaratna: *Nyāyaratna by Maṇikaṇṭha Miśra with the Commentary Dyutimālikā of Nṛsiṃhayajvan.* Ed. V. Subrahmanya Sastri and V. Krishnamacharya. MGOS 104. Madras 1953: Rathnam Press.

NSM Nyāyasiddhāntamañjarī: *Nyāyasiddhāntamañjarī Edited with Nilakantha Diksita's Dipikatarkaprakasa.* Ed. Gauri Nath Sastri. SGDOS 95. Delhi ^{2}1990: Sri Satguru Publications.

NVTP Nyāyavārttikatātparyapariśuddhi: *Nyāyavārttikatātparyapariśuddhi by Udayanāchārya With a gloss called Nyāyanibandhaprakāśa by Varddhamānopādhyāya.* Fasc. 1. Ed. Vindhyeśvari Prasad Dvivedin and Lakshmana Sastri Dravida. BI 1302. Calcutta 1911: Asiatic Society.

SM Nyāyasiddhāntamuktāvalī: *Kārikāvalī of Mahāmahopādhyāya Viśwanātha Panchānana. With the Commentaries Muktāvalī, Dinakarī, Rāmarudrī.* Ed. Ananta Śāstry. Published by Tukārām Jāvajī. Bombay 1916: Nirnaya-Sagar Press.

SP Saptapadārthī: *Śivāditya's Saptapadārthī with a Commentary by Jinavardhana Sūri.* Ed. J. S. Jetley. LDS 1. Ahmedabad 1963: L. D. Institute of Indology.

TBh Tarkabhāṣā: *Tarka-Bhāṣā of Keśava Miŕa with the Commentary Tarkabhāṣāprakāśikā of Cinnaṃbhaṭṭa.* Ed. Devadatta Ramkrishna Bhandarkar and Kedarnath Sāhityabhūṣaṇa. BSPS 84. Bombay 1937: Aryabhushan Press.

TR Tārkikarakṣā: *tārkikarakṣā. śrīmadācāryavaradarājaviracitā. tatkṛtasārasaṅgrahābhidhavyākhyāsahitā. mahopādhyāyakolācaśrīmallināthasūriviracitayā niṣkaṇṭakākhyayā vyākhyayā jñānapūrṇanirmitayā laghudīpikākhyayā ṭīkayā ca samanvitā.* Varaṇasi 1903: Pandit Reprint.

TS Tarkasaṃgraha: *Tarkasaṃgraha of Annambhaṭṭa with the Autor's Own Dīpikā and Govardhana's Nyāyabodhini. Edited with Critical and Explanatory Notes by the Late Yashwant Vasudev Athalye, Together with Introduction and English Translation of the Text by Mahadev Rajaram Bodas.* Revised and Enlarged Second Edition. BSS 55. Poona 1930: Bhandarkar Institute Press.

UBh Upaniṣadbhāṣyam: *Shri Shankarabhagavatpada's Upanisadbhasyam.* Vol. I. *(For the first 8 Upanisads). With the commentaries of Shri Anandagiriacharya for all, and in addition commentaries for Katha, Mandukya and Taittiriya by great acharyas and Taittiriyavartika of Shri Sureshvaracharya with Commentary.* Ed. S. Subrahmanyashastri. Advaitagrantharatnamañjushā 21. Varanasi 1979: Mahesh Research Institute.

UD Upādhidarpaṇa: BORI-Ms. No. 6. 1898–99.

2. Secondary Sources

Ackermann, Wilhelm 1956. Zur Axiomatik der Mengenlehre. Mathematische Annalen 131: 336 – 345.

Aczel, Peter 1988. *Non-Well-Founded Sets.* CSLI Lecture Notes 14. Stanford: CSLI Publications.

Alama, Jesse 2018. The Lambda Calculus, in: *The Stanford Encyclopedia of Philosophy*, ed. E. Zalta. URL: `https://plato.stanford.edu/entries/lambda-calculus/`.

Apte, Vaman Shivaram 1992. *The Practical Sanskrit-English Dictionary.* Revised and Enlarged Edition. Kyoto: Rinsen Book Company.

Aufrecht, Theodor 1962. *Catalogus Catalogorum.* An Alphabetical Register of Sanskrit Works and Authors. Part 1. Wiesbaden: Franz Steiner Verlag (reprint of the 1891 edition published by Brockhaus in Leipzig).

Bartley, Chris 2001. Advaita (non-dualist) Vedanta, post-Shankara, in: *Encyclopedia of Asian Philosophy*, ed. O. Leaman. 12 – 14. London/New York: Routledge.

Barwise, Jon, and Lawrence Moss 1996. *Vicious Circles. On the Mathematics of Non-Wellfounded Phenomena.* CSLI Lecture Notes 60. Stanford: CSLI Publications.

Bealer, George 1982. *Quality and Concept.* Oxford: Clarendon Press.

Bhattacharya, Dineshchandra 1958. *History of Navya-Nyāya in Mithilā.* MIS Studies 2. Darbhanga: Mithilā Institute of Post-Graduate Studies and Research in Sanskrit Learning.

Bhattacharyya, Sibajiban, and Karl H. Potter (ed.) 1993. *Encyclopedia of Indian Philosophies.* Vol. 4. *Indian Philosophical Analysis. Nyāya-Vaiśeṣika from Gaṅgeśa to Raghunātha Śiromaṇi.* Delhi: Motilal Banarsidass.

Bhattacharyya, Sibajiban, and Karl H. Potter (ed.) 2011. *Encyclopedia of Indian Philosophies.* Vol. 13. *Nyāya-Vaiśeṣika Philosophy from 1515 – 1660.* Delhi: Motilal Banarsidass.

Chakrabarti, Kisor Kumar 2010. *Classical Indian Philosophy of Induction.* Lanham/Boulder/New York/Toronto/Plymouth: Lexington Books.

Fraenkel, Abraham, Yehoshua Bar-Hillel, and Azriel Levy 1973. *Foundations of Set Theory.* Studies in Logic and Foundations of Mathematics 67. Amsterdam/London/New York/Oxford/Paris/Shannon/Tokyo: North Holland.

Frauwallner, Erich 1956. *Geschichte der indischen Philosophie.* Vol. 2. *Die naturphilosophischen Schulen und das Vaiśeṣika-System. Das System der Jaina und der Materialismus.* Reihe Wort und Antwort 6/2. Salzburg: Otto Müller Verlag.

Frauwallner, Erich 1965. Prabhākara Upādhyāya. Wiener Zeitschrift für die Kunde Süd- und Ostasiens 9: 198 – 226.

Frauwallner, Erich 1970. *Die Lehre von der zusätzlichen Bestimmung (upādhiḥ) in Gaṅgeśas Tattvacintāmaṇiḥ.* SBph 266, 2 (= VKSKS 9). Wien/Köln/Graz: Böhlau.

Frege, Gottlob 1986. Über Sinn und Bedeutung, in: *Funktion, Begriff, Bedeutung*, ed. G. Patzig. 40 – 65. Göttingen: Vandenhoeck und Ruprecht.

Gärdenfors, Peter 1988. *Kowledge in Flux. Modeling the Dynamics of Epistemic States.* Cambridge, Massachusetts/London: MIT Press.

Ganeri, Jonardon (ed.) 2001. *Indian Logic. A Reader.* Richmond/Surrey: Curzon Press.

Ganeri, Jonardon 2004. Indian Logic, in: *Handbook of the History of Logic.* Vol. 1. *Greek, Indian and Arabic Logic*, ed. D. M. Gabbay and J. Woods. 309 – 395. Amsterdam/Boston/Heidelberg/London/New York/Oxford/Paris/San Diego/San Francisco/Singapore/Sydney/Tokyo: Elsevier North Holland.

Garson, James W. 2013. *Modal Logic for Philosophers.* New York: Cambridge University Press.

Goekoop, Cornelius 1967. *The Logic of Invariable Concomitance in the Tattvacintāmaṇi.* Dordrecht: Reidel.

Goodman, Nelson 1983. *Fact, Fiction, and Forecast.* Cambridge, Massachusetts and London, England: Harvard University Press.

Guhe, Eberhard 1996. Ansätze zur Fregeschen Semantik im Upādhidarpaṇa. Wiener Zeitschrift für die Kunde Südasiens 40: 223 – 224.

Guhe, Eberhard 1999. *Die Lehre von der zusätzlichen Bestimmung (upādhi) im Upādhidarpaṇa.* Unpublished Dissertation. Vienna.

Guhe, Eberhard 2014. *Maheśa Chandra Nyāyaratna's "Brief Notes on the Modern Nyāya System of Philosophy and its Technical Terms".* Shanghai: Fudan University Press.

Guhe, Eberhard 2015. The Problem of Foundation in Early Nyāya and in Navya-Nyāya. History and Philosophy of Logic 36/2: 97 – 113.

Guhe, Eberhard 2016. "The absence of the difference from a pot is potness" – Axiomatic Proofs of Theorems Concerning Negative Properties in Navya-Nyāya. Computer Science Journal of Moldova 24/3 (72): 312 – 334.

Guhe, Eberhard 2017. The Logic of Late Nyāya: Problems and Issues, in: *Handbook of Logical Thought in India*, ed. S. Sarukkai. URL: https://doi.org/10.1007/978-81-322-1812-8_33-1.

Guhe, Eberhard 2018. The Logic of Late Nyāya: A Property-Theoretic Framework for a Formal Reconstruction, in: *Handbook of Logical Thought in India*, ed. S. Sarukkai. URL: https://doi.org/10.1007/978-81-322-1812-8_11-2.

Guhe, Eberhard 2019. An Indian Quasi-Fregean Theory of Number. Fudan Journal of the Humanities and Social Sciences 12/3: 329 – 351.

Halbfass, Wilhelm 1992. *On Being and What There Is. Classical Vaiśeṣika and the History of Indian Ontology.* New York: State of New York Press.

Hasurkar, Shrinath S. 1969. The Scheme of Finite Universe – As Evolved in Vedāntasarvasaṃgraha, in: *Proceedings of the Twenty-Sixth International Congress of Orientalists.* New Delhi, January 4 – 10, 1964. Vol. 3. Part 1. 375 – 378. Poona: Bhandarkar Oriental Research Institute.

Hughes, George Edward, and Maxwell John Cresswell 2005. *A New Introduction to Modal Logic.* London/New York: Routledge.

Ingalls, Daniel Henry Holmes 1951. *Materials for the Study of Navya-Nyāya Logic.* HOS 40. Cambridge, Massachusetts: Harvard University Press.

Iyer, S. R. (ed.) 1979. *Tarkabhāṣā of Keśava Miśra. Edited with Translation, Notes and an Introduction in English.* GSS 36. Varanasi: Chaukhambha Orientalia.

James, William 1907. *Pragmatism. A New Name for Some Old Ways of Thinking.* New York/London/Bombay/Calcutta: Longmans, Green and Co.

Kanamori, Akihiro 2006. Levy and Set Theory. Annals of Pure and Applied Logic 140: 233 – 252.

Levy, Azriel, and Robert Vaught 1961. Principles of Partial Reflection in the Set Theories of Zermelo and Ackermann. Pacific Journal of Mathematics 11: 1045 – 1062.

Lewis, David 1973. *Counterfactuals.* Malden, Massachusetts/Oxford: Blackwell.

Mādhavānanda 1954: *Bhāṣā-Pariccheda with Siddhānta-Muktāvalī by Viśvanātha Nyāya-Pañcānana. Translated by Swāmī Mādhavānanda. With an Introduction by Satkari Mookerjee.* Calcutta: Advaita Ashrama.

Matilal, Bimal Krishna 1968. *The Navya-Nyāya Doctrine of Negation. The Semantics and Ontology of Negative Statements in Navya-nyāya Philosophy.* HOS 46. Cambridge, Massachusetts: Harvard University Press.

Matilal, Bimal Krishna 1990. *Logic, Language and Reality. Indian Philosophy and Contemporary Issues.* Delhi: Motilal Banarsidass.

Matilal, Bimal Krishna 1998. *The Character of Logic in India*, ed. J. Ganeri and H. Tiwari. Albany, NY: State University of New York Press.

Mendelson, Elliott 1997. *Introduction to Mathematical Logic.* London: Chapman & Hall.

Mill, John Stuart 1851. *A System of Logic, Ratiocinative and Inductive, Being a Connected View of the Principles of Evidence, and the Methods of Scientific Investigation. In Two Volumes.* Vol. 1. London: John W. Parker, West Strand.

Modgil, Sanjay, and Henry Prakken 2018. Abstract Rule-Based Argumentation, in: *Handbook of Formal Argumentation.* Vol. 1, ed. P. Baroni, D. Gabbay, M. Giacomin and L. van der Torre. 286 – 361. London: College Publications.

Monier-Williams, Monier 1872. *A Sanskrit-English Dictionary Etymologically and Philologically Arranged with Special Reference to Greek,*

Latin, Gothic, German, Anglo-Saxon, and Other Cognate Indo-European Languages. Oxford: The Clarendon Press.

Narain, Harsh 1976. *Evolution of the Nyāya-Vaiśeṣika Categoriology.* Vol. 1. *Early Nyāya-Vaiśeṣika Categoriology.* Varanasi: Bharati Prakashan.

Oberhammer, Gerhard 1968. Die Theorie der Schlußfolgerung bei Parāśarabhaṭṭa. Wiener Zeitschrift für die Kunde Süd- und Ostasiens 12 – 13: 253 – 273

Oetke, Claus 1994. *Vier Studien zum altindischen Syllogismus.* Philosophia Indica. Einsichten und Ansichten 2. Reinbek: Dr. Inge Wezler Verlag für Orientalistische Fachpublikationen.

Pandeya, Raghavendra 1984. *Major Hetvābhāsas. A Formal Analysis (With Reference to Nyāya and Buddhism).* Delhi: Eastern Book Linkers.

Patil, Parimal 2009. *Against a Hindu God.* Buddhist Philosophy of Religion in India. New York: Columbia University Press.

Phillips, Stephen H. 2002. *Gaṅgeśa on the Upādhi, the "Inferential Undercutting Condition". Introduction, Translation and Explanation (with N. S. Ramanuja Tatacharya).* Delhi: Indian Council of Philosophical Research.

Phillips, Stephen H. 2012. *Epistemology in Classical India. The Knowledge Sources of the Nyāya School.* New York: Routledge.

Phillips, Stephen H. 2017a. Fallacies and Defeaters in Early Nyāya, in: *Indian Epistemology and Metaphysics*, ed. J. Tuske. 82 – 124. London/Oxford/New York/New Delhi/Sydney: Bloomsbury Academic (eBook).

Phillips, Stephen H. 2017b. A Defeasibility Theory of Knowledge in Gaṅgeśa, in: *The Oxford Handbook of Indian Philosophy*, ed. J. Ganeri. 541 – 558. New York: Oxford University Press.

Pollock, John L. 1984. *The Foundations of Philosophical Semantics.* New Jersey: Princeton University Press.

Pollock, John L. 1987. Defeasible Reasoning. Cognitive Science 11: 481 – 518.

Pollock, John L. 1990. *Nomic Probability and the Foundations of Induction.* New York/Oxford: Oxford University Press.

Pollock, John L. 1992. How to reason defeasibly. Artificial Intelligence 57: 1 – 47.

Pollock, John L. 1995. *Cognitive Carpentry: A Blueprint for How to Build a Person.* Cambridge (Massachusetts)/London: MIT Press.

Potter, Karl H. (ed.) 1977. *Encyclopedia of Indian Philosophies.* Vol. 2. *Indian Metaphysics and Epistemology: The Tradition of Nyāya-Vaiśeṣika up to Gaṅgeśa.* Delhi: Motilal Banarsidass.

Potter, Karl H. (ed.) 1995. *Encyclopedia of Indian Philosophies. Bibliography.* Section I. Delhi: Motilal Banarsidass.

Potter, Karl H. (ed.) 2006. *Encyclopedia of Indian Philosophies.* Vol. 11. *Advaita Vedānta from 800 to 1200.* Delhi: Motilal Banarsidass.

Potter, Michael 2004. *Set Theory and its Philosophy.* Oxford: Oxford University Press.

Putnam, Hilary 2013. Comments on Russell Goodman's "Some Sources of Putnam's Pluralism", in: *Reading Putnam*, ed. M. Baghramian. 219 – 224. London/New York: Routledge.

Quine, Willard van Orman 1966. *Methods of Logic.* New York/Chicago/San Francisco/Toronto: Holt, Rinehart and Winston.

Quine, Willard van Orman 1973. *Mengenlehre und ihre Logik.* Transl. by Anneliese Oberschelp of *Set Theory and its Logic.* Braunschweig: Friedr. Vieweg + Sohn.

Raghavan, Venkataraman 1969. *New Catalogus Catalogorum.* An Alphabetical Register of Sanskrit and Allied Works and Authors. Vol. 5. MUSS 30. Madras: University of Madras.

Randle, Herbert Niel 1930. *Indian Logic in the Early Schools.* Oxford: Oxford University Press.

Satyanārāyaṇa, T. V. 1980. Alaṃkārarāghavam. The Mysore Orientalist 13: 71 – 75.

Schayer, Stanislaw 2001. Studies in Indian Logic (1932 – 33), in: *Indian Logic: A Reader*, ed. J. Ganeri. 93 – 101. Richmond/Surrey: Curzon Press.

Shin, Sun-Joo, Oliver Lemon, and John Mumma 2018. Diagrams, in: *The Stanford Encyclopedia of Philosophy*, ed. E. Zalta. URL: <https://plato.stanford.edu/archives/win2018/entries/diagrams/>.

Solomon, Esther A. 1976. *Indian Dialectics – Methods of Philosophical Discussion.* Vol. 1. Ahmedabad: B. J. Institute of Learning and Research.

Tubb, Gary and Emery R. Boose 2007. *Scholastic Sanskrit.* A Handbook for Students. TIS series. New York: The American Institute of Buddhist Studies at Columbia University in the City of New York and Columbia University's Center for Buddhist Studies and Tibet House US.

van Benthem, Johan 2010. *Modal Logic for Open Minds.* CSLI Lecture Notes 199. Stanford: CSLI Publications.

Vattanky, John 1984. *Gaṅgeśa's Philosophy of God.* Madras: The Adyar Library and Research Centre.

Wada, Toshihiro 2007. *The Analytical Method of Navya-Nyāya.* GIS 14. Groningen: Egbert Forsten.

3. Abbreviations

BI	Bibliotheca Indica
BORI	Bhandarkar Oriental Research Institute
BSPS	Bombay Sanskrit and Prakrit Series
BSS	Bombay Sanskrit Series
CSLI	Center for the Study of Language and Information, Stanford

CSS	Chowkhamba Sanskrit Series
GIS	Gonda Indological Studies
GOS	Gaekwad's Oriental Series
GSS	Gokuldas Sanskrit Series
HOS	Harvard Oriental Series
KSS	Kashi Sanskrit Series
LDS	Lalbhai Dalpatbhai Series
MGOS	Madras Government Oriental Series
MIS	Mithila Institute Series
MUSS	Madras University Sanskrit Series
SBph	Sitzungsberichte der Österreichischen Akademie der Wissenschaften, philosophisch-historische Klasse
SGDOS	Sri Garib Das Oriental Series
TIS	Treasury of the Indic Sciences
VKSKS	Veröffentlichungen der Kommission für Sprachen und Kulturen Südasiens
VSS	Vizianagram Sanskrit Series